A
LESS THAN PERFECT
UNION

A
LESS THAN PERFECT
UNION

Alternative Perspectives
on the
U.S. Constitution

edited by Jules Lobel

MONTHLY REVIEW PRESS
NEW YORK

Library of Congress Cataloging in Publication Data

A Less than perfect union.

    1. United States—Constitutional Law. 2. Civil
rights—United States. I. Lobel, Jules.
KF4550.A2L47   1987   342.73'029   87-28325
ISBN 0-85345-738-7
ISBN 0-85345-739-5 (pbk.)

Monthly Review Press
122 West 27th Street
New York, N.Y. 10001

10 9 8 7 6 5 4 3 2 1

Contents

Part 3: Separation of Powers
and the Structure of the Constitution

Part 4: Race, Sex, and Class:
Tensions and Dilemmas in Individual Rights

Part 5: The Constitution in an International Context

Acknowledgments

This book would not have happened without the help of Michael Ratner. When Monthly Review Press asked him to suggest an editor for what was then a very vague project, he put them in touch with me, helped develop the idea further, suggested contributors, and was a constant source of encouragement and support.

Many other people also made important contributions and suggestions, but I would particularly like to thank Rhonda Copelon, Carlin Meyer, David Cole, and Barbara Wolvovitz. The efforts of Monthly Review Press, and especially Susan Lowes, were critical to the final product. Susan's editing, work with the contributors, and overall comments and suggestions were invaluable.

The volume is about, and is dedicated to, all the struggles, at home and abroad, to achieve liberty, freedom, and justice. Two organizations that have helped lead the struggle for constitutional rights and have served as inspiration are the National Lawyers Guild and the Center for Constitutional Rights. Their work in defending, preserving, and furthering constitutional rights gives meaning and life to the ideas developed in this book.

Finally, I would like to dedicate the book to my parents, Paul and Lena Lobel, and to the memory of my grandmother, Mary Feldman.

INTRODUCTION:
Constitution Mythology and Progressive Responses

Jules Lobel

The Bicentennial of the U.S. Constitution is being conducted with all the pomp and ceremony befitting a document that Americans revere as scripture. It is an appropriate irony that Pope John Paul II's majestic tour of the United States coincided with the Bicentennial celebrations, for in the absence of an official state religion Constitution-worship has become our civic religion. President Reagan's address commemorating the Bicentennial invoked this religious symbolism: "The Constitution has endured not simply as a plan of government" but as "something more." It evokes not merely "simple admiration," but "a feeling more of reverence." Citing Presidents Madison and Washington, President Reagan described the Constitution "as a miracle; and miracles, of course have only one origin." It is "a covenant with the Supreme Being to whom our founding fathers did constantly appeal for assistance."[1]

The progressive response to this mythology should not be to celebrate the "miracle" of 1787, a miracle flawed in its compromise with slavery and its nonrecognition of women. Instead, in the recent words of Justice Thurgood Marshall, we should "commemorate the suffering, struggle and sacrifice that has triumphed over much of what was wrong with the original document, and observe the anniversary with hopes not realized and promises not fulfilled."[2] Such commemoration requires both a critique and recognition of the Constitution's positive aspects. It means demystifying the "miracle" and analyzing the contradictory nature of our constitutional structures and rights, both from a historical perspective and in relation to the economic, social, and political foundations of our society. It means using constitutional symbols to construct a radical vision of the future. This volume is a contribution to that task.

The Constitution as Civic Religion

Although the Constitution's ratification was bitterly contested, the final document nevertheless quickly became an object of worship. As early as 1791 William Maclay wrote that many talk "as if neither wood grew nor water ran in America before the happy adoption of the new Constitution."[3] In 1811 Senator W.H. Crawford observed that "it has become so extremely fashionable to eulogize the Constitution."[4] A century later, Woodrow Wilson noted that "hostile criticism of its provisions . . . not only ceased, but gave place to an undiscriminating and almost blind worship of its principles. . . . The divine right of kings never ran a more prosperous course than did the unquestioned prerogative of the Constitution to receive universal homage."[5]

In part this universal homage has been based on the belief that the Constitution has brought us unparalleled prosperity. More significantly, the Constitution—and the Supreme Court which interprets it—have become symbols of national unity in a country where the more typical symbols, God and monarchy, are absent. And probably most important of all, the Constitution is viewed as the United States' unique contribution to humankind. As a member of the U.S. Bicentennial Commission noted, "The constitution reinforces the Americans' sense that they are a people specially blessed by God and a role model for the world."[6] Other nations may have developed a more refined culture, have a grander history, governed empires even more extensive than ours, but our Constitution is the first and oldest *written* charter. It has been called our most important export. President Reagan proudly proclaimed that the work of the Philadelphia Convention had "profoundly and forever altered, not just these United States, but the world."[7]

It is no accident, therefore, that a mythology has developed around the Constitution. It is seen as virtually perfect. As Supreme Court Justice William Johnson put it in 1823, it is the "most wonderful instrument ever drawn by the hand of man."[8] The myth envelops reality: the Constitution is sanitized, its blemishes obscured. For example, President Reagan proudly proclaimed that "it was with the writing of our Constitution . . . that the noble statements and brave rhetoric of 1776 [that all men are created equal] took on substance," conveniently forgetting that the original Constitution never mentioned equality and actually sanctioned slavery. Thus the Constitution is seen to include all that is good—motherhood, apple pie, and justice—irrespective of the historical record.

Constitution-worship has had a strong hold on the working and poor people of this country. In part, the Constitution's great flexibility has allowed people to read into it what they chose. As one Abolitionist noted in 1869, the Constitution "might be whichever the people pleased to make it."[9] Moreover, as the Constitution became a symbol, Americans, ignorant of its actual provisions, began to believe that it contained a broad mandate for liberty and justice. Workers who came to my former law office after having suffered from some injustice on the job invariable claimed that "their constitutional rights had been denied," although rarely was the Constitution itself actually involved. A recent poll indicates that 45 percent of the population believe that the Constitution embodies the Marxist principle of "from each according to his ability, to each according to his need."[10] Moreover, 46 percent of the 1,000 adults interviewed did not know the purpose of the Constitution, 59 percent did not know what the Bill of Rights is, and 64 percent thought the Constitution established English as the national language. It is clear that reverence for the Constitution is based not on its provisions, but on the symbol of nationalism and ideal of justice it has come to represent.

The Constitution has thus been described as both a symbol and an instrument of government.[11] As an instrument it defines governmental powers and private rights. As a symbol it encompasses our broad sense of justice and fairness, irrespective of the specific language and content of the instrument itself.

Themes of This Volume

The underlying theme of this volume is how radicals and progressives have addressed the mythology and symbolism that surround the Constitution. Should progressives use the Constitution to argue for radical changes, such as the recognition of economic and social rights? Or should they demystify and criticize a Constitution that, despite popular belief, does not guarantee such rights? What, in other words, is the relationship between the struggle for constitutional rights and the long-range movement for a just, democratic, and egalitarian society? To return to the religious analogy, should radical lawyers follow the path of the Latin American liberation theologians, working within the church structure to achieve an alternative vision, or should they reject our civic church because of its elitist and classist nature?

Part 1 presents this debate. Arthur Kinoy argues that the Constitution is not simply a bulwark against fascism and reaction, but that the rights and frameworks it provides can be used to achieve *fundamental* social and political change. Victor Rabinowitz, on the other hand, argues that the Constitution cannot be a mechanism for radical change. Pat Williams points out that constitutional symbols can be powerful sources of inspiration to the oppressed. Mark Tushnet focuses on the Constitution's contradictory nature.

Part 2 traces this debate historically. Articles look at the different views of the formation of the Constitution that have been put forward by progressive historians, conflicting Abolitionist perspectives on the place of slavery within the Constitution, the struggles of the early women's movement for equal rights, the changing views held by the Communist Party from 1920 to 1950, and use of the Constitution by the civil rights movement of the 1950s and 1960s. Each era has witnessed similar tensions over how to view—and use—the Constitution: as an inherently conservative document or as one that can be used by popular movements to attain radical change.

Critical to developing a progressive response to the constitutional mythology is understanding the material relationship between structure and reality. Mythology feeds on philosophical idealism. The U.S. Constitution loses its mystical quality when its real functions in our economic and political system are understood. Part 3 therefore focuses on materialist and historical analyses of the structure of U.S. government, while Part 4 locates our constitutional rights in their historical and social context.

The final section looks at our rights and constitutional structures from an international perspective. One aspect of our constitutional mythology is that the Constitution is considered both universal and the best in the world. But when we look to see how universal some of our constitutional assumptions really are, when we look at human rights in the socialist world and Europe, when we examine the issue of participatory democracy in Nicaragua—then we gain a valuable perspective on our own Constitution. We must realize that we can learn from other nations' constitutional experiences and not merely trumpet our own.

Several themes run through the various sections in this volume. One is that the Constitution is a historically contested arena, its meaning determined not so much by the words (or intent) of the framers as by the content provided by the ebb and flow of the various popular movements. This theme cuts across several sections, and is raised in one form or another by Tushnet, Williams, Kinoy, Deloria, DuBois, Mishler, Braden, LaFeber, Kennedy, Copelon, Lynd, and Burnham. It is the popular movements that have put life into the Constitution, that have made it a document that inspires reverence. Yet we live in a decade where reaction seeks to deny this reality in favor of a static conception of original intent as the basis for constitutional analysis. These essays provide a critical break with this static perspective. Moreover, they illustrate the use that constitutional symbols (such as rights) can play in the struggle for social, economic, and political equality.

Another pervasive theme of the sections is the recognition that idealist perspectives must be eschewed, replaced by an analysis of constitutional rights and structures as related to economic, political, and social structures. Virtually all of the contributors seek to accomplish that task. In short, one theme of the volume is that a more historical, materialist analysis must be substituted for the doctrinal and philosophical idealism of much current discussion.

There is one final theme that underlies this volume and is the focus of the remainder of this introduction. The dilemma that radicals have faced in developing a position on the Constitution are rooted in fundamental contradictions in our constitutional structure and in our view of rights. The early sections point to the historical and contemporary dilemmas that have faced progressive movements, while the later ones analyze the positive and negative aspects of our constitutional structures and rights. The unifying focus is on the contradictions inherent in the Constitution, as opposed to the linear view put forward by mainstream celebrations.

The Ambiguity of Progressive Views of the Constitution

The progressive movement in the United States has always been divided over how to view the Constitution. The early Abolitionists viewed it, in the words of William Lloyd Garrison, as "a covenant with death and an agreement with hell." That the proslavery character of the Constitution had to be exposed was symbolized in the famous incident of 1854, when Garrison publicly burned a copy of the document.[12] The only way to achieve radical change was to expose the evils of the Constitution. The Abolitionists therefore refused to participate in the constitutional process, urging radical judges to resign and themselves refusing to run for election.[13] According to Wendell Phillips, "National evils are only cured by holding men's eyes open and forcing them to gaze on the hideous reality."

Those Abolitionists who were opposed to Garrison and favored political action were reluctant to condemn the Constitution completely. Some of them stressed a natural-law theory of the Constitution, emphasizing the Preamble, which promised "to establish Justice . . . , promote the general Welfare and secure the Blessings of liberty to ourselves and our Posterity." The purpose of these interpretations was to justify participation in the political process and to allow radical judges and lawyers to argue against slavery in the courts.

The political abolitionists were also responding to the reverence the population had for the Constitution. Jonathan Bingham, a drafter of the Fourteenth Amendment, recalled that in the decades before the Civil War "everything was reduced to a constitutional question."[14] Northerners had to be convinced that the Constitution supported black *freedom* before they would support the antislavery cause.[15] It was in response to these sentiments that Salmon Chase (and other political abolitionists) sought to develop an antislavery view of the Constitution, at the core of which was the position that the Founding Fathers deplored slavery and desired its early abolition. Chase's efforts led several newspapers, including the *Cincinnati Gazette,* to proclaim that the political abolitionists were not "radical." "Mr. Chase has selected for his exemplar upon the slavery question such men as Washington, Jefferson, Henry and Pinckney."[16]

The early women's movement also confronted the question of how to view the Constitution.[17] The women's links with the Garrisonian

Abolitionists led many of them to reject a demand for political rights, including the right to vote. At the first women's rights convention, held at Seneca Falls, New York, in 1848, the participants hesitated and debated, but eventually resolved to struggle for the elective franchise.

After the Civil War, however, the women's movement made universal suffrage a primary demand. With the passage of the Fifteenth Amendment (which prohibited voting discrimination based on race but did not grant universal suffrage), many feminists returned to the view of the Constitution urged by the political abolitionist, but in a new context. Instead of attacking the Constitution for its refusal to grant women the right to vote, they argued that the whole spirit of the document, as well as the underlying logic of the Fifteenth Amendment, meant that women *already* had the franchise.

These feminists argued for judicial and political action to enforce their "natural-law" constitutional right to vote, and they developed militant tactics to enforce their claims. Susan B. Anthony, for example, was arrested for "criminal voting" as a result of her effort to cast a ballot in Rochester, New York. By the 1880s, the feminist movement's position had been consistently rejected by Congress and in the courts. Only then did the movement give up the attempt to force a radical reinterpretation of political equality within the existing constitutional system and focus instead on a new amendment that would enfranchise women.

The post-Civil War trade union movement also developed a radical interpretation of the Constitution. In the latter part of the nineteenth century, the Supreme Court held that laborers and employers must be free to bargain without restraint from the state; therefore minimum-hour laws and laws requiring fair labor standards were unconstitutional. As William Forbath has argued, many in the labor movement, particularly the Knights of Labor, responded to this setback with a radical theory of the Constitution that rejected the liberal-capitalist notion that individuals were equal in the marketplace. For them, the republican tradition was interpreted to mean economic independence and the ownership of productive property. In the rapidly industrializing postwar United States, preserving the republican form of government required the "republicanization" of industry based on cooperative ownership. Only then could workers have the means to actually participate in government. Labor leaders repeatedly asserted that the "wage-labor system fell afoul of the republican *constitution*."[18] To them, the liberal doctrine of "free labor" was a constitutional distortion. A radical republican vision of the Constitution required not "freeing" labor, but ending "wage slavery" itself.

The Socialist and Communist parties changed their view of the Constitution several times over the years in response to their desire to develop a mass movement. Socialist theorists of the early twentieth century attacked the Constitution as a conservative document written by the wealthy elite. Socialist theorist and lawyer Louis Boudin, for instance, lambasted the theory of judicial review as tantamount to government by a few conservative men. Yet in practice the Socialist Party used the Constitution as the basis for its arguments for social reform.

In the 1920s and the early 1930s, the Communist Party criticized the Constitution, and U.S. law in general, as mere instruments of capitalist rule. By the 1930s, however, under the leadership of Earl Browder, the party stated that Communism was twentieth-century Americanism, and appealed to constitutional tradition as a springboard for socialism. The change to a popular front strategy, designed to broaden the party's mass base, led it to a new view of the Constitution. By 1938 the party was proclaiming that it "defends the United States Constitution against its reactionary enemies who would destroy democracy."[19] And in 1937, on the 150th anniversary of the Constitution, the party resurrected the old Knights of Labor vision of radical republicanism. It argued that the Jeffersonian theory of political democracy recognized the necessity of economic democracy.[20] The Smith Act trials saw the party leadership divided over strategy—whether to base its case on an inherent right to revolution or to rely on the First Amendment right to freedom of speech.

The civil rights and antiwar struggles of the 1960s and 1970s had to deal with the same issues. While the very notion of constitutional rights at first gave blacks in the South the inspiration to demonstrate for equality and freedom, by the 1970s many radical blacks were increasingly dissatisfied with reliance on the Constitution. Other civil rights activists, such as Arthur Kinoy, used radical interpretations of the Thirteenth and Fourteenth amendments to argue that the Constitution not only guaranteed equal opportunity and legal equality but mandated affirmative action to achieve these ends.

Similarly, antiwar activists argued that it was because the framers of the Constitution wanted to "curb the dogs of war" that they had given Congress the power to declare war, a power now being usurped by an imperial presidency. In the 1960s, and again in the 1980s, many of those opposed to U.S. intervention abroad argued that after the Nuremberg trials and the adoption of the U.N. Charter, the constitutional powers of the Executive and Congress were limited by international law. CIA and U.S. military adventures abroad were therefore in violation of international law; civil resistance to U.S. foreign policy was legally justified. Despite arguments by historian William Appleman Williams and others that the Constitution had always been an imperialist document, the anti-intervention movement was searching for an interpretation that would offer a radical vision.[21]

The Conflicts Among Progressives Reflect Contradictions in the Constitution

The fundamental tension in these movements' approach to the Constitution reflects a basic contradiction within the document itself. The Constitution has maintained its aura of legitimacy, and its hold on all classes of society, through its phrases—such as "equal protection" and "due process"—which are broad enough to accommodate the popular movements' demands. But the Constitution contains limitations that arise out of the nature of capitalism itself. These are not merely aberrations that can be cured by the actions of a popular movement, but are *essential* limitations of a constitution premised on a capitalist economy. The Constitution not only gives rise to demands; it makes their achievement difficult.

Consider many of the basic rights and principles upon which the Constitution is based: separation of powers, freedom of speech, equality before the law. All reflect the same tension. On the one hand, these principles embody tremendous gains, often won after bitter struggle. They have helped protect against dictatorship, given the progressive movement a certain political space in which to operate, and provided a constitutional basis for the struggles of blacks, Latinos, and women to achieve equality. Yet at the very moment when radical change is on the agenda, when black demands go beyond legal equality to social and economic integration, when the politically disenfranchised seek access to a means of communicating their views—at this point these very same principles are used to preclude such a fundamental transformation.

For example, the Fourteenth Amendment's promise of equal protection before the law provided a crucial constitutional tool in the struggle against the southern ruling elite, both in the Reconstruction era and in the 1950s and 1960s. This broad constitutional guarantee inspired the black movement and its white supporters to demand that the legal barriers to equal treatment be discarded, that blacks be allowed to share in the American dream. Yet at the very moment when victory seemed in sight, when the Supreme Court, in case after case, struck down the underpinnings of the Jim Crow system, many in the movement recognized that they had taken only a first step. Legal equality, equal opportunity, were insufficient; it was necessary to push equality into the social and economic sphere. In the 1860s this recognition led to demands for land and education: how could the newly freed slaves achieve equality if they were reduced to sharecropper status, lacking economic independence or educational opportunity. In the 1970s the same realization led to a struggle for affirmative action.

To both black movements, a century apart, the constitutional system had the same response. The equal protection clause's guarantees of individual rights, procedural equality, and equality of opportunity were read as precluding redistributive substantive justice, such as land reform or quota systems, which would accomplish economic integration. The Supreme Court developed two doctrines to accomplish this task: the state action doctrine, which provides that only government action can violate the Fourteenth Amendment;[22] and the intent doctrine, which holds that only *intentional* state discrimination violates the Constitution and that government action which merely has the *effect* of perpetuating inequality does not.[23] Together, these two doctrines have meant that the *Constitution* does not require the integration of private schools, firms, or housing (although Congress enacted statutes so providing). It has meant that the state cannot be held responsible for private discrimination and does not have to provide the financial resources to ensure that education is really equal.[24] Finally, the Court has held that in many situations government agencies are actually *barred* from providing affirmative action to cure discrimination because this would violate the individual rights of white applicants or employees.[25]

The interpretations that read the Constitution to bar group remedies to cure societal discrimination are not aberrations, as can be seen from the fact that they have endured through over one hundred years of political struggle. Even the most liberal judges have refused to discard the state action or intent standards. At root, these are based on the belief that state and civil society must be separated, a belief upon which the capitalist state is premised. This dichotomy requires that the state treat everyone as equal—at the same time that civil society constantly reproduces existing inequalities. Thus the inequalities of civil society are rendered immune from constitutional challenge.

The "American assumption," as W.E.B. Du Bois called it, holds that legal equality will lead to social and economic equality. If an individual has equal opportunity, wealth and power will result from hard work and thrift. But, as the last century demonstrated so clearly, equality under the law not only fails to provide economic equality, but by precluding state affirmative action often conflicts with the very leveling goal that it is supposed to assure.

A similar tension can be seen in the First Amendment. The battles waged by trade unions and other progressives led to the twentieth-century development of what has been called the "Free Speech Tradition."[26] That tradition, based on the premise of individual autonomy, permits every individual to speak as he or she wishes, unless such speech incites to imminent riot. The focus of the tradition is the streets, roads, parks—the places where demonstrators may assemble, leafletters ply their trade, and soapbox orators work the crowd.

Just as the "American assumption" posits economic independence stemming from equal opportunity, the Free Speech Tradition presumes that a rich diverse public debate will follow if individual actors assert their right to speak. However, as Owen Fiss has shown, diverse public debate is often precluded by the very First Amendment that proclaims such debate as its goal.[27]

In the 1970s, various movements arose seeking access to the means of communication in order to deliver their views to a mass audience. Labor unions and antiwar demonstrators sought the right to leaflet and picket at shopping centers; others sought access to the mass media—television, radio, newspapers. In a series of cases, however, the Supreme Court severely limited such access, even sometimes prohibiting the government from requiring the media to open its airwaves and pages to opposing viewpoints. The Court's explicit or implicit rationale was the Free Speech Tradition: newspaper publishers, TV networks, radio stations, and shopping-center owners all had the right to say whatever they pleased free from government interference. The government would not force them to air or accommodate diverse views. Doing so would violate the First Amendment. In a society where the main form of communication is streetcorner banter, such a position might allow the presentation of diverse views; but in a society in which a handful of owners control most of the information received by the majority of people, these rulings inhibit political pluralism. As with the equal protection decisions, these First Amendment cases, while not mechanistically determined by the requirements of capitalism, are consistent with the basic framework of a capitalist state.

Similarly, our structure of government is fraught with contradictions. Representative elections and separation of powers provide for a valuable mechanism of popular input into government and important limits on the arbitrary use of government power. But, as various essays in this book point out (Rabinowitz, Tushnet, Mullin, and myself, among others), those same principles limit radical change and maintain capitalist rule. Indeed, they were designed by the framers to do just that. For example, the system of checks and balances makes radical change unlikely by requiring the agreement of three branches of government, elected or selected at different times, before such change can be implemented.

The dilemma faced by progressive movements is thus embedded in the Constitution itself. Working people, blacks, Latinos, women, and gays have relied on the ringing phrases of the Constitution to achieve the goals that lie behind the words of the document. Inspired by the concept of legal equality, they have sought economic justice. Having struggled to open up the streets, they have sought to open up the media. Progressives, sensing the urge among the population to realize the Constitution's guarantees, have repeatedly developed a radical vision of its meaning. Yet important as this is, it is also important to recognize that the goals that lie behind the words are ultimately beyond reach. We must recognize not only the possibilities but the fundamental limitations of our constitutional system. The task for the coming decades is to find a way to combine what are in essence two contradictory perspectives: critique and radical vision.[28]

Any radical political movement must to be rooted in the accomplishments of our society, of which the Constitution is an important part. The constitutional discourse is an arena of struggle from which progressives ought not withdraw. "We live by symbols," wrote Oliver Wendal Holmes.[29] The power of our constitutional symbols is too enormous to be ignored.

Moreover, people often act out of a belief in their entitlement. Martin Luther King, Jr., used the analogy of a check returned for insufficient funds to describe the black experience with the Constitution.[30] Paradoxically, revolutionary action often develops out of a call for the enforcement of traditional constitutional guarantees.

But the development of a socialist movement in the United States will also require a critique of the mythology of our constitutional system. To return to Martin Luther King's analogy, it is not merely that a bad check has been written; it is the banking system that is seriously flawed.

Presenting the critique and arguing for a radical vision can be contradictory tasks. Yet it is precisely the recognition of this that will prevent the descent into reformism on the one hand and dogmatism on the other. The answer to this dilemma begins with its recognition.

One solution lies in history—in understanding that to develop a political movement, critique and vision must be balanced, and in recognizing the historical moment at which each task is paramount. A movement requires a vision that will motivate struggle, yet it is in the course of the struggle to realize the vision that the Constitution's limitations become clear. Once that occurs, the balance will once again shift to critique.

The Bicentennial therefore presents us with an opportunity—an opportunity to discuss the progressive tradition and the Constitution. We need to use that tradition (as well as the liberal tradition) to defend against the Reagan administration's efforts to undermine many of the important constitutional reforms of the last three decades. It is also an opportunity to develop an alternative vision and a critique of our Constitution. Both tasks are essential if we are to further a movement that seeks not merely to maintain the rights we now have, but to create a truly democratic, just, and nonimperial United States.

Notes

1. *New York Times,* 18 September 1987, p. 19.
2. Speech of 6 May 1987.
3. Cited in E. Corwin, "The Constitution as Instrument and as Symbol," reprinted in *Corwin on the Constitution,* ed. R. Loss, vol. 1 (Ithaca, N.Y., 1986), p. 171.
4. M. Lerner, "The Constitution and Court as Symbols," 46 *Yale L.J.* 1290, 1296 (1937).
5. Corwin, "The Worship of the Constitution," in *Corwin on the Constitution,* p. 47.
6. Cited in R. Higgins, "Motherhood, Apple Pie, and the Constitution," *Boston Globe Magazine,* 13 September 1987, p. 16.
7. *New York Times,* 18 September 1987, p. 19.
8. Elkisin v. Deliesseline, 8 Fed. Cas. 493 (1823).
9. M. Kammen, *A Machine That Would Go of Itself: The Constitution in American Culture* (New York, 1986), p. 6.
10. *Boston Globe Magazine,* 13 September 1987, p. 9.
11. See Corwin, "The Constitution as Instrument."
12. E. Hyman and W. Wiecek, *Equal Justice Under Law: Constitutional Development 1835–1875* (New York, 1982), p. 93.
13. R. Cover, *Justice Accused: Antislavery and the Judicial Process* (New Haven, 1975), pp. 149–58.
14. E. Foner, *Free Soil, Free Labor, Free Men: The Ideology of the Republican Party Before the Civil War* (New York, 1970), p. 85.
15. Ibid.
16. *Cincinnati Gazette,* 7 August 1855, cited in ibid., p. 86.
17. This section is largely based on Ellen Carol DuBois' article in this volume.
18. W. Forbath, "The Ambiguities of Free Labor: Labor and the Law in the Gilded Age," 1986 *Wis. L. Rev.* 767, 813.
19. Kammen, *A Machine That Would Go of Itself,* pp. 279–80.
20. E. Browder, "Democracy and the Constitution," reprinted in Browder, *The People's Front* (New York, 1938), pp. 235, 241–42.
21. Mitchell v. United States, 386 U.S. 972, 973–4 (1987) (Douglas J., dissenting); Lobel, "The Limits of Constitutional Power: Conflicts Between Foreign Policy and International Law," 71 *Va L. Rev.* 1071 (1985).
22. Civil Rights Cases, 109 U.S. 3 (1883); Moose Lodge No. 107 v. Irvis, 407 U.S. 163 (1972).
23. Washington v. Devis, 426 U.S. 229 (1976).
24. San Antonio Ind. School Dist. v. Rodriguez, 411 U.S. 1 (1973).
25. University of California v. Bakke, 438 U.S. 265 (1978).
26. D. Kairys, "Freedom of Speech," in *The Politics of Law,* ed. D. Kairys (New York, 1982), p. 140.
27. O. Fiss, "Free Speech and Social Structure," 71 *Iowa L. Rev.* 1405 (1986), and abridged in this volume.

28. For a similar position see E. Schneider, "The Dialectic of Rights and Politics: Perspectives from the Women's Movement," 61 *N.Y.U. L. Rev.* 589 (1986).
29. Oliver Wendell Holmes, *Collected Legal Papers* (1920), p. 270.
30. I am indebted to Anne Braden for directing my attention to the Martin Luther King, Jr. analogy. See also V. Rabinowitz, "The Radical Tradition in the Law," in *The Politics of Law,* p. 313.

PART 1

Contemporary Perspectives on the Constitution and Individual Rights

In recent years, a long-standing debate among radicals over the nature of the Constitution and of individual rights has resurfaced. A group, known as the Critical Legal Studies movement (CLS), has in the last five to ten years gained support among progressives in law schools across the country. CLS is dedicated to demystifying and "deconstructing," or challenging, the basic assumptions of U.S. law. A significant strand of CLS thought has been a critique of the rights that are the basis for much constitutional law. For example, Mark Tushnet, one of the movement's leading scholars, recently wrote that the "liberal theory of rights forms a major part of the cultural capital that capitalism's culture has given us. The radical critique of rights is an . . . act of creative destruction that may help us build societies that transcend the failures of capitalism."[1] He argued that the use of rights "impedes advances by progressive social forces."

This view sparked a debate that is continued in this volume.[2] Pat Williams argues that, contrary to Tushnet, rights play a vital role in black people's struggle against oppression in this country. Her view is that rights give voice to people who have historically had no voice or power. For her, the task is not to discard rights or merely to "unmask the sorcerer," but to put the mask to "good ends"—to use rights to empower and to expand their definition. Tushnet, while recognizing the positive role that constitutional rights can play, continues to point to the "systemic problem associated with aspirational appeals" to rights. Arthur Kinoy, taking Williams argument a step

17

further, argues that appeals to the idea that the Constitution protects a right to a decent home and job, as well as basic civil rights and liberties, "can be a central catalyst" in a powerful progressive alliance. He argues that the current task is not to "delegitimize" or "demystify" constitutional rights, but to defend and protect them, "to legitimize them against the effort to delegitimize them."

This debate over the nature of constitutional rights is related to differing perspectives about whether radical changes in our political and economic system are possible within the framework of the Constitution. Victor Rabinowitz argues that such radical changes—defined as the alteration "of existing relationships between those who own substantial property and those who do not"—are only possible "through the destruction of the central structure of our constitutional government." While recognizing that the Constitution is a great institution and has given us much, Rabinowitz argues that it actually protects existing property relations. Kinoy, on the other hand, sees the Constitution necessary if we are to move toward a society in which "the original constitutional commitments to freedom, justice, and equality become realities." He suggests that the struggle to protect the "elementary democratic forms" provided for in the Constitution set the stage for fundamental change. Tushnet is more cautious, claiming that "the Constitution usually stabilizes the existing order, but sometimes it can be put to progressive ends."

The debate set forth in this section is basic to many of the issues that are raised in the rest of the book. Part 2 traces this debate as it has developed historically, while Part 4 provides a more detailed look at the issue of rights. The last section puts the debate in an international context. Many articles link back to the first section in other ways. For example, Staughton Lynd's work on freedom of speech is in certain respects a response to Tushnet's view of rights. And while Kinoy argues for a constitutional right to a job or decent home, Debra Evenson's essay in the last section demonstrates that the prevailing constitutional interpretation, which negates those rights, is deeply rooted in capitalist ideology. Again: Rabinowitz's article can be read in light of Communist Party debates over the Popular Front and their constitutional implications, which are discussed by Mishler in the next section. Thus the contemporary debate is one that has recurred throughout U.S. history.

Notes

1. Tushnet, "An Essay on Rights," 62 *Tex. L. Rev.* 1363 (1984).
2. See, for example, E. Schneider, "The Dialectic of Rights and Politics: Perspectives from the Women's Movement," 61 *N.Y.U. L. Rev.* 589 (1986).

IS STABILITY AN UNMITIGATED GOOD?
The Constitution and Radical Change

Victor Rabinowitz

The Bicentennial celebration of the Constitution is taking on the appearance of a year long Fourth of July speech, with only a few voices raised to point out the racial and elitist overtones to that great document. For it was and is a great document, of surprising durability given the vast changes in our industrial, cultural, and demographic character over the past two centuries. It is the oldest written constitution on earth, and there is no threat on the immediate horizon that would prevent its continued long life.

Patriotic sentiments aside, however, the Bicentennial has provided an opportunity—indeed a challenge—to examine our Constitution and its history more closely and to attempt to evaluate and appraise its faults and virtues. Hence this volume of essays.

But the subject of this particular essay is not as broad as our constitutional history. Rather, the question I wish to address is whether a radical change in our political and economic system is possible within the framework of the Constitution. A lawyer will want, first off, a definition of "radical change," and for present purposes I will define the term as any change which, from the right, destroys our representative democracy or, from the left, changes the existing relationships between those who own substantial property and those who do not—or, to put it in classical Marxist terms, a change that alters class relationships.

A movement to the right may be defined as the repression of freedom of speech and press, a conservative *laissez-faire* economic

21

policy, and the elevation of the rights of property over the human needs of the population. Conversely, a movement to the left may be defined as an expansion of freedom of speech and press, more governmental concern over the needs of our people, and a recognition of the priority of human rights over property rights.

It is my conclusion that the basic question posed by this essay must be answered in the negative—there is no possibility of radical change by methods which are consonant with the Constitution. Radical change, of course, may come about, but only through the destruction of the central structure of our constitutional government. Neither the question of whether such radical change is desirable nor the nature of such change are within the scope of this essay, but, as we shall see, after two hundred years of constitutional government, we have not produced an economic and political society that delivers, to all its people, a living wage, adequate housing, and the other elements of a decent and productive life.

It might be helpful in analyzing the Constitution to distinguish the fundamental structure of the government it created from the ways in which that structure has been used. The framers of the Constitution had no views, so far as we know, on subjects such as child labor or abortion or trade unions, and it is a futile and foolish occupation to debate what the attitude of Washington, Franklin, or Madison would have been on such matters. But the framers had clear views on the desirability of a republican form of government, on the doctrine of the separation of powers, and on the concept of a government based on a design of checks and balances. Perhaps the Constitution might be analogized to a well-built mansion erected in 1787. The walls, roof, and cellar still exist—well, maybe a few additions have had to be built, for example, to accommodate the servants who once lived in an out-building but who now live under the master's roof. And a few other small structural changes have been necessary, as in 1800, when one of the wings of the house almost collapsed. But it was propped up three years later and has seemed quite firm ever since. The main structure even survived a dreadful fire in 1860 necessitating some rebuilding, but not very much considering the extent of the catastrophe. Most of the timbers of the 1787 house are still intact.

But inside the house everything has changed. Indoor plumbing, electricity, and central heating have been installed; walls have been moved about; the furniture is Swedish modern and the kitchen,

General Electric; there is a computer in the study and TV sets in the bedrooms. And further changes are being made inside the house every day—it might well be called a flexible institution. Inside, but not outside. There is nothing flexible about the outside. It may be altered and has been a few times, usually with difficulty and, except in the first few years, never quickly. But it cannot be changed in any fundamental way without tearing it down. We could not, for example, turn it into a collective farm or a concentration camp by making a few changes in the outer walls or by rearranging the furniture inside.

Every schoolchild knows about the structure of the Constitution. It provides for the separation of powers among the executive, the legislature, and the judiciary. It provides for an elaborate system of checks and balances. Equally important, it provides for periodic elections, so that no more than two years can pass without an election affecting the makeup of the legislature. Congress must convene at least once each year, and every four years—never more and never less, whatever the emergency—a President is elected. These features of the Constitution, as we all know, were not accidental but were very carefully worked out at the Constitutional Convention. They were intended to prevent the federal government from moving too far in any direction and to provide the electorate with a chance to correct things should such a movement threaten. Given the nature of the electorate in 1787, this meant that white male property owners would have the opportunity to prevent anything that might upset their interests.

Not that the Constitution was written by the representatives of all such property holders. It was in fact written by an agrarian and mercantile aristocracy, but the writers understood well that the government they were creating needed the support of the electorate which was, in 1787, the equivalent of our middle class.

The linchpins of the constitutional scheme are the First Amendment and the due process and just compensation clauses of the Fifth Amendment. When the Civil War was over and additional support was needed to protect the structure, the due process clause of the Fourteenth Amendment was added, to tie the states more closely to the federal government and to make sure that they did not once again try to destroy the 1787 mansion.

These linchpins were and are critical. Aside from the freedoms guaranteed to the people of the United States by the First Amendment (as supplemented by the Fourteenth), the due process clauses of the Fifth and Fourteenth provided still greater structural strength. Together, these constitutional provisions directed, first, that "no person . . . shall be deprived of life, [or] liberty . . . without due process of law"; they also provided that "no person . . . shall be deprived of . . . property without due process of law." When the "just compensation" clause is added, a full panoply of rights is provided for life and liberty, and also for property. What more could a middle class with a democratic political philosophy want? These constitutional rights are an essential part of the outer structure of the Constitution; no amount of furniture moving can destroy them without destroying the entire building.

This, then, was the building created in 1787. There have been a few changes in form over the centuries, but none have been extensive. The framework of the Constitution, created in 1787 and amended in only a few respects, still stands.

But the laws made within that framework—the inside of our 1787 mansion—have changed our nation almost beyond recognition. In this respect, the Constitution has indeed proved flexible—so long as the framework is not threatened or, to formulate it somewhat tendentiously, so long as the changes do not threaten the middle class that constitutes the effective electorate. Our government's policies and laws have moved from right of center to left of center and back again. Sometimes those policies have threatened to move beyond permissible limits, but the system of checks and balances, working with the First Amendment rights and the due process clause, has in each case "corrected" the deviation. Instances of such swings are not difficult to find in any sphere of our political life. In the area of race relations, for example, we started with a Constitution which sanctioned chattel slavery, culminating in the *Dred Scott* decision. This was followed by the three post-Civil War Reconstruction amendments. That reform movement lasted only for a few years; a strong rightward movement was started by the withdrawal of Federal troops from the South in 1876, followed by the Supreme Court's decision in *Plessy* v. *Ferguson,* and by eighty years of intense repression of blacks, not only in the South but throughout the nation. Slowly the pendulum swung back, with *Brown* v. *Topeka* and the civil rights and free speech movements of the 1960s. The consequent occasional affirmative action programs are running into difficulty with an increasingly conservative Supreme Court, while the economic conditions of blacks and other minorities in both urban and rural settings are getting worse, possibly cancelling out many of the gains of the last thirty years.

Similar instances of change in the direction of governmental policy can easily be found in considering freedom of speech and the press, separation of church and state, the rights of workers to organize into trade unions, and almost every other aspect of our political life.

The Constitution is a centrist document designed to protect private property under a republican form of government and to allow certain democratic freedoms not inconsistent with such protection. Subversion of this design, either by the far right or by the far left, cannot be accomplished without destroying the building.

For example, the periods between 1798 and 1800 and between 1947 and 1960 were clearly times of the repression of civil rights and liberties and would be considered a movement to the right. So, too, the era of the populist and progressive movement of the early part of this century and the prewar years of the Franklin D. Roosevelt administration were times of an expansion of freedom and of a recognition of the primacy of human needs. *Plessy* v. *Ferguson* may be contrasted with *Brown* v. *Topeka* and with the Civil Rights Acts of 1957, 1960, and 1964; *American Communications Association* v. *Douds* may be contrasted with *Brown* v. *United States; Hammer* v. *Dagenhart* was overruled by *United States* v. *Darby;* the Communist Control Act of 1954 has never been enforced. In each instance the pendulum swung widely, but not widely enough to break through the wall of the structure.

Or at least so our two-hundred-year history seems to teach. The republican nature of the government was made clear from the very beginning. Article IV, Section 4, of the Constitution provides that every state must have "a Republican Form of Government." Article I, Section 9, further emphasizes the framers' republican point of view: it provides that "no title of nobility shall be granted."

An incident during the first session of Congress now seems amusing but was taken very seriously at the time. There was intense debate as to the proper way to refer to the President. A Senate "Committee on Titles" recommended that the President be called "His Highness, the President of the United States of America and

Protector of the Rights of the Same." Some Senators thought "His Excellency" would be better; "Elective Highness" was suggested. Someone even suggested "His Majesty." The matter was not settled until Washington was about to enter the chamber of the House to address the first joint session of the Congress and Madison stated that, constitutionally, Washington's title was merely "Mr. President."

No more serious challenge to the concept of the republican nature of the United States has ever been made.

And the checks and balances have worked too. The first swing to the right took place at the very beginning with the Alien and Sedition laws. In 1788 a congressman was tried and imprisoned for sedition in violation of those laws and several editors were also prosecuted. The election of Jefferson put an end to those prosecutions, but only after a serious crisis that almost tore the nation apart. A faulty electoral system put the infant nation in serious danger during the presidential electoral contest between Jefferson and Burr. There was talk of civil war and a coup was threatened by the extremist wing of the Federalist Party, many of whom preferred the dissolution of the union to the election of the Jacobin atheist Jefferson. In fact, his election was in doubt until a mere three weeks before Adams' term of office expired. But the structure stood firm. There was no civil war, no coup. A President was elected in accordance with the literal terms of the Constitution, unworkable as they then seemed.

The next and by far the greatest constitutional crisis in our history came sixty years later. In the interim, much of the internal furniture of our building had been rearranged. The territory under the jurisdiction of the United States was extended to the Pacific Coast; two wars were fought; two Presidents died in office; more than twenty new states were admitted to the Union; the population increased from 5.3 million to 31 million and the total revenues of the federal government increased twelve-fold. Native Americans standing in the path of the expanding white culture were moved out of the way. The federal government was strengthened; the scope of the commerce clause was greatly expanded and various experiments to control the monetary system were tried. There were rebellions in Pennsylvania, New York, and Rhode Island, and a mini-civil war in Kansas. In 1814 there was a strong secessionist movement in New England. In 1832 South Carolina passed a nullification resolution declaring revenue acts passed by Congress to be void, but that crisis too passed. In that same year President Jackson, in vetoing a bill reestablishing the Bank of the United States, declared that the Supreme Court had no right to hold an act of Congress unconstitutional; Senator Charles Sumner repeated those sentiments in an important speech in the Senate twenty years later. Neither challenge resulted in any substantive change in the course of our history.

Other examples could easily be cited. Throughout it all the framework of the nation remained firm and constant even though the pendulum still swung from left of center to right of center and back. Presidents were elected every four years; Senators every six years, and members of the House every two. A session of Congress was convened every year, and Congress passed laws as provided in the Constitution. Such laws were vetoed now and then by the President, also as provided in the Constitution. Flexibility and imagination in passing laws was evident but no flexibility, no change, appeared in the structure.

The year 1860 saw the greatest constitutional crisis in our history. It almost destroyed the nation and the Constitution we are memorializing this year. The antislavery forces threatened to deprive the southern landowners of their property interest in about 5 million blacks whose market value has been variously estimated at figures between $2.8 billion and half that amount. In that year even the lower sum would have been beyond the imagination of the nation, when the entire revenue of the federal government was only $56 million. The southern plantation owners responded to the threat with force, starting with the firing on Fort Sumpter by the armed forces of the newly formed Confederacy.

The foregoing is a gross oversimplification of the origins of the Civil War—an event that has been analyzed, researched, and written about more than any other part of our history—but if we paint with a very broad brush the war may be seen as an attack by an extreme right, violent force against a movement that was, in the framework of 1860, seeking radical change. It can hardly be said that such radical change was brought about by constitutional means. It was effected by armed force and by the passage of amendments to the Constitution that were enacted only because the South was occupied by the northern forces.

But the framework was restored after about ten years and even before that, during the very time of war, the government continued to function after a fashion. In 1862 and 1864 elections for Congress were held and in 1864 a President was reelected. The judicial power of the United States was still effective. True, the writ of the United States did not run to the states that were attempting secession, and even in the North, conditions of warfare resulted in the suspension of the writ of habeas corpus—a most grievous blow to the structure. Had it not been repaired as soon as the war was over, it might have truly changed the nature of our political system.

But it was repaired and so, miraculously enough, was the other damage done by the war, not in a year and perhaps not in a decade, but eventually. The scars left by the war have long since disappeared. The three postwar amendments to the Constitution certainly strengthened the building. Slavery was made illegal. The due process clause was made applicable to the states. The power of the federal government was greatly increased.

Further, the electorate was greatly expanded by the Fifteenth Amendment, and again by the Nineteenth. Granting that a century passed before the Fifteenth was enforced in the South, it is by no means clear that the enfranchisement of either blacks or women has had a significant effect on our form of government. As blacks and women began to assert their independence and economic progress, so they too seemed to promote the interests of the middle class. Economic restrictions on the right to vote have been largely removed, but many of the propertyless do not vote and when they do they find only white male property owners as candidates for office, with a sprinkling of their female and/or black counterparts. And so over the years the changes in the fundamental structure of the building served only to strengthen it and its original purpose.

Of course, on the legislative (as distinguished from the constitutional) front the changes were so enormous as to defy even an attempt to make a complete list. Again, swings to the right have been balanced by swings to the left. Some of the inevitable crises may have seemed at the time to threaten the continuance of constitutional government, but in the end none of them actually posed a serious threat.

Some of the major relevant events in the period since the Civil War should nevertheless be mentioned. Depressions severely threatened the economic basis of our country in 1873, 1897, 1920, and 1929. Every bank in the country was closed in 1933. The organization of militant workers resulted in major strikes in 1877, 1919, and the 1930s, and sometimes legislation intended to be remedial was enacted.

On the other hand, reaction won a smashing victory in the long period of repression of blacks after 1876. Less dramatic but perhaps even more important was the growth of our industrial structure in the last quarter of the nineteenth century and again in the period after World War II, accompanied by an increase in the wealth of the nation and of the propertied classes. Strong antidemocratic drives were mounted in 1900, 1918, and especially in 1947, but each time the country recovered and resumed its centrist course. Given this tumultuous history, it is astonishing that not once was an election postponed, not once was a congressional session missed, not once was there a break in the constitutionally prescribed succession of presidents, congressmen, and judges. Not once was there a real breakdown in authority, save for the Civil War period.

This is not to say that every problem was easily solved by quick reference to the scripture of the Constitution. Indeed, there were instances in our history in which congressional elections were stolen and at least one instance, perhaps two, in which a man elected to be President of the United States was probably cheated out of office. Several Presidents were assassinated; one was impeached and one resigned to avoid impeachment. But even here the Constitution prevailed. There was no coup, there was no attempt to enforce the view of the electorate by extra-constitutional means. The supporters of Samuel J. Tilden did not riot in the streets or throw up barricades to enforce the election of their candidate. The normal continuity of our government was not disturbed.

This apparent stability, however, has not resulted in a marked improvement in the economic welfare of our population. There were reforms, of course. During the last half century we have seen legislation limiting child labor, providing unemployment insurance, etc., etc. But it is a commonplace that these reforms were intended to—and indeed did—reinforce the middle class whose interests the framers had in mind at the very beginning; these reforms may have thus prevented a strong attack on the edifice of 1787 by those without property.

Our 1787 mansion houses not one but two nations. As Benjamin Disraeli said of Victorian England almost one hundred and fifty years ago, we are two nations between whom there is no intercourse and no sympathy; who are as ignorant of each other's habits, thoughts, and feelings, as if they were dwellers in different zones or inhabitants of different planets; who are formed by a different breeding, are fed by a different food, are ordered by different manners, and are not governed by the same laws. [I speak of] THE RICH AND THE POOR.

After these two hundred years of relative stability the wealthiest country on earth still has millions of people unemployed, millions of homeless, millions who are functionally illiterate, millions who do not have adequate healthcare or decent housing. There are also men, and perhaps a few women, who earn millions of dollars a year and whose total assets amount to a hundred times that sum. We speak of spending billions or perhaps trillions of dollars on a space station or a trip to Mars and an equivalent amount on the "Star Wars" program, while there are men and women sleeping in the streets, in the subways, and in railroad and bus terminals across the country.

Other developments in the past few decades are not easily quantified. Perhaps they can be classified as a deterioration in the quality of life of most of our people. While the conquest of most contagious diseases and the discovery of antibiotics has lengthened our lifespan, the result—an ever increasing number of the aged—has raised problems that were not anticipated and are not being addressed seriously. Most of our large cities are disintegrating and the use of drugs is out of control. We are smothered by garbage, and we swim in and drink polluted water and breathe polluted air. The catalogue of social failures could be extended well past the point of boredom. And operating within our mansion, with its checks and balances and tripartite division of powers and regular democratic elections, we seem to be unable to cure those failures; for each problem we solve, ten more arise.

I do not by such lugubrious rhetoric intend to denigrate our Constitution. What it was intended to do it has done well and it should not be held responsible for its failure to do more. The freedoms guaranteed by the First Amendment have been of great value in developing our political institutions and our culture. The rights we describe collectively as our First Amendment freedoms have been more expansively enjoyed in this country over the past two hundred years than in any other country, and that is no small achievement. We may advocate major changes in our form of government (but watch out for the traps set by the Smith Act and the

McCarran-Walter Act and by congressional committees). We may associate with whom we please (with the same traps for the unwary). We may talk about, create, or destroy all sorts of new furniture within our house and much of it is of very great importance. Debates are now raging over such vital issues as abortion, pornography, equal rights for women, capital punishment, and a host of other issues, all of which are vital to the way we live, but none of which have anything to do with radical change as we have defined it.

It is the very system of checks and balances, periodic elections, and tripartite separation of powers that makes a change in the principles of liberal capitalism so unlikely. The chances of finding an extended period of time when the electorate, Congress, the President, and the Supreme Court will all agree on a constitutional change in those principles is so remote as to be not worthy of consideration. Indeed, with the ever present exception of the Civil War and Reconstruction, we are not sure that there was ever, even for a single year, majority support for radical change in any one of the three branches of the government.

But viewed as a whole, there can be no doubt that all three of the branches of our government have been much more protective of property rights than of human freedom. Not only would a detailed, year-by-year examination of our history show that, but, more conclusively, the results show it. The development of the most highly industrialized and developed society on earth has resulted in extraordinary wealth for a handful of our people and equally extraordinary poverty for tens of millions of others. Such a situation could not be the result of a two-hundred-year-old government with an egalitarian outlook. We need only recall that even when most of the country was in sore economic distress, the owners of significant property were only slightly or temporarily inconvenienced. A bank failure often destroyed its depositors and a factory failure often destroyed its workers, but the bank owner and the factory owner have, with rare exceptions, survived. All of our population enjoys the protection given to free speech, but the protection given to property is enjoyed only by those who have property.

The Constitution is indeed a great institution and it has given us much. We may perhaps describe its most basic premise with a paraphrase of I Corinthians 13:13: "And now abideth life, liberty, property these three; but the greatest of these is property."

THE PRESENT CONSTITUTIONAL CRISIS:
Tasks for Progressives

Arthur Kinoy

During this period of the Bicentennial of the U.S. Constitution, in the midst of national and local commemorative events organized primarily by the conservative institutions of the establishment, there is a serious need for progressive people across the country to examine carefully their own view of the Constitution—historically, at the present time, and in the immediate and more long-range future. But to do this we cannot rely on oversimplified generalizations out of the Left lexicon of the past: to say that the Constitution, and the "rights" it sets out, have been and remain products of the establishment, that they were designed to mask the oppressive control of the ruling classes and must therefore be exposed and "demystified" by the Left, is a one-sided analysis that is unrelated to the concrete realities of the present historical moment. What is urgently needed is a careful analysis of the concrete conditions that will shape the path toward a new society. Such an analysis will then determine the view of the Constitution, and rights it sets forth, that must be taken by progressives at this moment in history.

We are in the midst of an intense political crisis, one whose dimensions have not yet fully emerged. For reasons that must be carefully analyzed, the most reactionary sections of the ruling establishment, led by the present administration, have been engaged in a conscious, well-thought-through plan to experiment with the weakening, undermining, and eventual abandonment of the most elementary limitations and mandates of the written Constitution, including the Bill of Rights and the post-Civil War amendments. The Reagan administration's moves to challenge institutions and concepts that have formed an integral part of our constitutional framework began with Attorney General William French Smith's carefully formulated attack on the federal courts in 1982. The federal courts—and in particular the Supreme Court—have been, he announced, "too active" in the areas of civil rights, desegregation, affirmative action, environmental law, women's rights, the rights of labor, and the individual rights of people in criminal proceedings. The courts, and in particular the Supreme Court, must therefore be "forced back"; they must learn to leave the protection of constitutional rights to the executive branch of government. This open attack on the federal judiciary was coupled with the admonition that the people of this country must have confidence in the integrity of the executive branch of the government in the protection of any of their fundamental rights.

In July 1985, Attorney General Edwin Meese escalated this assault with his public announcement that the Reagan administration believed that the entire Bill of Rights was not applicable to state governments. This was not simply reactionary rhetoric: in every area of constitutional law enforcement that affects the immediate needs and interests of the majority of the people, the administration has moved to drastically undermine those rights, protections, and concepts that have historically been a critical part of the establishment's own governing institutions.

For example, in the area of equality and freedom for black people, and for all people of color, the administration has set in motion a carefully constructed plan to sidestep, undermine, and finally bury every legislative act and judicial decision that was produced over the past thirty years as the result of the struggles of black people and their allies, and which today offer any assistance in the continued battles against all the remaining institutions of discrimination. The Supreme Court decisions in the area of segregation in education, discrimination with respect to the right to vote, equality of participation in the political process, discrimination in housing, community services, and employment, and affirmative action have been challenged as "infamous," as not being the "law of the land," and therefore as not binding upon the executive branch of the government, on state and local governments, or on private organizations. Similarly, the Reagan administration has refused to enforce in any effective manner the basic mandates of congressional legislation in the arena of civil rights, such as the Civil Rights Act of 1964 and the Voting Rights Act of 1965 (as amended in recent years).

This well-constructed plan to experiment with the abandonment of the promises of the post-Civil War amendments is in effect a reenactment of the Hayes-Tilden betrayal of 1877, but with far more ominous implications. It is a critical aspect of an overall plan to undermine and then abandon every significant area of the written constitution that the most reactionary sections of finance capital see as present or potential obstacles to their continued existence. In every single area of constitutional law in which elementary democratic rights have been momentarily enforced as a result of long, intense struggles on the part of the people involved—such as the arena of the constitutional right of women to equality and to free control over their own lives and bodies and the arena of the constitutional right of working people to organize into trade unions and bargain collectively with their employers—the administration has launched a carefully orchestrated campaign to turn the clock back.

The move to undermine constitutional restraints on an uncontrolled repressive police power, nationally and locally are daily occurrences. The federal preventive detention statute, the all-out attack on the *Miranda* right-to-counsel requirements, the full-scale rejection of the most elementary restrictions of the Fourth Amendment with respect to wiretapping and intrusive searches and seizures are sharp indications of this well-orchestrated plan to unleash a massive oppressive police power, unrestrained by the limitations of constitutional law.

In the area of the First Amendment, the dominant sections of the power structure are moving to resurrect the lawlessness of the Cold War of the 1950s and the Nixon years with respect to political repression. In its first days, the Reagan administration began to recreate the machinery for undermining the First Amendment through massive domestic CIA and FBI operations—the sort of activity that had, apparently all too briefly, been discredited by the exposures of Watergate.

In Executive Order No. 12333, signed on December 4, 1981, the CIA was given full authority to operate within the United States (rather than solely in foreign countries). It was allowed to infiltrate domestic political organizations and to conduct "covert" actions designed to "influence" the activities of an organization in whatever direction the attorney general set forth—including, if so desired, actions that would frustrate and paralyze these organizations. The order further permitted, without consent, physical searches of personal property, physical surveillance of U.S. citizens, and wholesale electronic surveillance of any nature without a warrant or any form of judicial authorization. On March 7, 1983, the Justice Department issued guidelines for the FBI that allowed similar full-scale infiltration of domestic political organizations, as well as any coercive actions necessary to protect the "domestic security" of the nation.

The wholesale break-ins of churches and community organizations that are involved in sanctuary activities or participate in any organized opposition to the administration's policies in Central America have accelerated at a frightening rate in the last two years. The administration has turned to the resurrection of the federal criminal conspiracy charge, as in the trial of such black radical activists as the "New York Eight" in 1984 and in the on-going conspiracy trial (in Hartford, Connecticut) of supporters of Puerto Rican independence who are charged with participation in a conspiracy to commit bank robbery. These tactics are central aspects of a well-planned effort to paralyze the growing opposition to the administration's domestic and foreign policies, opposition that should be protected by the sweep of the First Amendment.

Underlying all these moves is the conscious formulation of a theory that justifies the abandonment of the protection, or affirmative enforcement, of fundamental constitutional rights. This is the theory of the "new federalism," which explicitly restates the basic concepts of the Southern Confederacy with respect to "states' rights" and thus rejects the underlying principles of the federal union. Any federal protection for the constitutional rights of individual citizens is rejected in favor of relegating that role to the states, as is any federal responsibility for meeting such elementary needs as housing, education, health care, or a decent job.

In evoking the fear of the "centralizing tendencies of the national Leviathan," Attorney General Meese makes the administration's objective the elimination of any national power or responsibility to meet the growing needs of large sections of the population. For example, the concept of a "new federalism" and a return to states' rights was the administration's response in rejecting the demands of family farmers for emergency national federal aid to meet the looming threat of farm foreclosures, which would certainly destroy their fundamental constitutional right to "life, liberty, and the pursuit of happiness."

Similarly, following massive plant closings throughout the country, the administration's response to the request for national federal assistance, coming from working people and local communities devastated by the closings, has been to assert that under the concept of a "new federalism" the national government has no responsibility in this arena.

At the heart of the plan to experiment with abandoning the central concepts of the Constitution is the open effort of the Reagan administration, intensified by the Iran-Contragate crisis, to resurrect the thesis that the President has the "inherent power" to suspend or ignore the provisions of the written Constitution, or other laws of the land, if he determines that this is in the "national interest." This ominous approach, openly advanced by the Nixon administration to justify its national program of warrantless wiretapping (in total disregard of the Fourth Amendment), emerged during an intense judicial conflict that erupted around the prosecution of antiwar activists in Detroit in 1970. The government's position, orchestrated by William Rehnquist, then an assistant attorney general, was that the President had the "inherent power" to suspend the provisions of the Fourth Amendment whenever he decided it was in the national interest to do so. In a sweeping opinion written by the conservative Justice Lewis Powell in 1972, the Supreme Court (without dissent) rejected this approach, reaffirming the underlying constitutional premise, which had emerged from the Revolution, that the President remains bound by the restrictions and mandates of the written Constitution and the laws of the land.

Yet once again, faced with the exposures of the Iran-Contragate upheavals, the most reactionary section of the ruling establishment is openly advancing this thesis. In essence the original structure of government, with the powers of each branch limited by a written constitution, has become an obstacle to their continued rule. This could become an ominous movement for the people of this country and the entire world. We may well be entering a period in which certain of the most reactionary sections of the ruling class are edging toward a substitution of the present form of rule by the capitalist class (classically known as bourgeois democracy) with another form of rule, the open terrorist dictatorship classically known as fascism. It is essential for progressives to consider very carefully what is driving the most reactionary forces in this country in this direction. Underneath the move lies the enormous pressure that flows from the growing fear on the part of sections of the power structure, governmental and corporate, that because of their inability to develop solutions for the economic crisis, millions of Americans will use the political and democratic rights provided by the Constitution to move toward a solution to these pressing problems by changing fundamental power relations. This fear is intensified by the solutions that the power structure itself puts forward—the attempt to shift the economic burden of the crisis onto the backs of the people through massive budget cuts, coupled with the overt moves toward new military adventures and the planning and preparation for a "limited nuclear war."

There is, therefore, at the highest levels of government a deep fear that the majority of the people in this country may unite and use their political rights, as set forth in the Constitution, to fight for what they believe is promised them in that same Constitution: the right to a job with a decent wage, the right to a farm, the right to full political, social, and political equality, the right to medical care—the list could go on and on. As different groups organize and use their constitutional rights to demand their most basic rights to "life, liberty, and the pursuit of happiness," they will realize that they are not "minorities" or "special interest groups." United, they can use the political system to demand solutions to their immediate needs, even if this means a sweeping change in the existing power structure.

The present rulers understand the potential of such a united movement more clearly than most progressives do. It is what they fear most. And as this fear grows, the pressure to experiment with abandoning the Constitution will intensify. The ultimate sovereignty of the people, now protected by the Bill of Rights and the post-Civil War amendments, as well as a national government committed to meeting the needs of the people, *must* be undermined if the present power structure is to maintain its control.

This view of the "concrete conditions" that are shaping the emerging political crisis puts into sharp perspective the responsibilities that progressives have to formulate an analysis of the Constitution and the rights it projects. As the most reactionary sections of the ruling class begin to turn against their own institutions, the defense of these elementary rights will become a central task and responsibility for progressives. As millions of people begin to sense that their constitutional protections are being undermined, the struggle will no longer be to "delegitimize" or "demystify" these forms, but to *defend* and *protect* them—in fact, to *legitimize* them against the effort to *delegitimize* them.

It is essential that progressives understand that participation in the struggle to defeat the plans of the reactionary establishment is not simply a defensive strategy. At the very center of this forward-moving battle is the strength of the concept that reactionary spokespeople such as Attorney General Meese most oppose: that the Constitution is a "living document for all ages" and that it must therefore be used to meet the *current* problems and needs of the people, not be restricted by the "original intent" of the white men (including southern slaveholders) who drafted it. This approach, boldly restated by Justices William Brennan and Thurgood Marshall in public opposition to the Reagan-Meese rationale, opens up a powerful means for developing broad support for mass struggles.

For example, the idea that there is a fundamental *constitutional* right to a decent home for every American can become a powerful weapon in support of the growing demand that the federal government take responsibility for massive housing programs throughout the country. Similarly, family farmers and their organizations are raising the question of their *constitutional* right to live on their farms—contrary to the attempts by major banks to use farm foreclosures to establish corporate farms. In the same spirit, millions of working people, devastated by plant closings and unemployment, will respond positively to the proposition that there is a fundamental *constitutional* right to a job if the concepts of life, liberty, and the pursuit of happiness are to have any meaning.

The struggle to defend the essence of the Constitution provides a focus for the organization of united action in the political, economic, and legal arenas on the part of millions of Americans. It permits the development, even if temporary, of alliances with middle-of-the-road and conservative forces that are not prepared to abandon the Constitution. And, most important, it puts the political questions essential to the forging of a massive strategic alliance on the agenda: Who is conspiring against the liberties of the people? Who is undermining and subverting the original promise of life, liberty, and the pursuit of happiness? The answer to these questions—that it is the ruling class itself that is doing this—can be a central catalyst in the emergence of the powerful alliance that will be necessary to frustrate the ruling-class strategy and to move toward a society in which the original constitutional commitments to freedom, justice, and equality become realities.

In the most profound sense, then, the responsibility of progressive people in this country is to participate in the struggles to reject the move on the part of the ruling class to abandon its own institutions of bourgeois democracy. This is an essential step in creating what the rulers fear most—alliance of the majority of the people, using the elementary democratic forms provided for in the Constitution, to demand solutions to the overwhelming economic and social problems that have been generated by the crisis of the present system, even if such solutions require a fundamental change in the present power structure and the transition to a new society.

THE CONSTITUTION FROM A PROGRESSIVE POINT OF VIEW

Mark Tushnet

Progressive political movements see the Constitution in three ways. First, the cultural system of the United States has made the Constitution into an icon that is taken to embody the best aspirations toward justice, fairness, and the like, that are part of the heritage of our society. Second, the Constitution has enough ambiguous terms in it to allow progressive movements to make credible legal arguments that, were they accepted, would advance the movements' political goals; sometimes, when governing elites are divided over the wisdom of accommodating a progressive movement, these arguments may be accepted by the courts and other influential agencies like the press. Finally, the Constitution serves to protect established institutions against disruption by progressive and other movements.

From a progressive point of view, these three aspects of the Constitution present opportunities and pose problems. Obviously, a progressive political movement can sometimes use constitutional arguments. Indeed, there may be only two situations in which it makes sense *not* to use such arguments: when attention to legalistic efforts will divert the movement from more productive political tactics, and—more important—when the appeal to the aspirations of the Constitution reinforces *some* existing institutions even as it serves to change others. These difficulties mean that progressives who think about the Constitution must carefully consider whether the third, establishment-protecting aspect of the Constitution is more likely to be important, in the circumstances they face, than the other aspects.

This essay examines the foregoing propositions. It begins with a broad overview of the general theory of the Constitution held by most of the framers. Then, using illustrations from U.S. history, some of which are developed in more detail in subsequent essays, it argues that most of the time the establishment-protecting aspect of the Constitution is likely to prevail. That yields the conclusion that, though progressive movements need not abandon the idea of using the Constitution to advance their political goals, we should be alert to the costs of doing so, which will always be present but which may be overlooked in the heat of the struggle.

The War of Independence mobilized large portions of the largely agrarian population of the American colonies. As the war came to a close, the citizens of the independent states began to experiment with new forms of democratic government. The depth of their democratic commitments varied from state to state, and was strikingly shallow in today's terms, for exclusion of women and blacks from democratic politics was almost universal. Yet in the world of the 1780s these experiments in democracy were quite bold. Jealous of their local governments, the citizens of the states were initially reluctant to create a powerful centralized national government that could displace whatever they chose to do in the states. Thus the first "national" government, created by the Articles of Confederation, was little more than an alliance of independent nations. The Confederation government had no power to collect taxes; it had to request state governments to collect them and send them on to the Confederation. Even when the Articles granted the government certain narrow powers, the Confederation's ability to exercise those powers was sharply limited by a requirement that the states unanimously agree to Confederation enactments.

The combination of relatively robust democratic politics in some states with a weak national government led important political elites to become deeply dissatisfied with the Confederation. Shays's Rebellion occurred in western Massachusetts in the winter of 1786–1787. Armed farmers, objecting to stringent enforcement efforts to collect debts they owed, forcibly closed several courts, impeding the ability to collect debts. Elsewhere state legislatures enacted statutes that suspended the collection of debts, or even relieved debtors entirely of any duty to repay their creditors. These actions, important in themselves, also symbolized the problems the creditors saw in the Confederation. They believed that state governments were too democratic, and that the Confederation was too weak to suppress rebellion.

In addition, important sectors of the national economy believed that economic growth would occur only if the states were united under a strong national government. Some, associated with commercial centers, were concerned that Europeans, seeing democratic "excesses" in the states, would refuse to lend money to support expansion into other states. Instability in the credit market would impair the ability to borrow money. Others believed that only a strong government could raise enough money through a tax system to finance the development of an economic infrastructure large enough to support an expanded economy. Large farmers, especially in the South, wanted to participate in the world market for agricultural goods, and effective participation required, again, a stable credit system so that they could finance present operations by borrowing against their expected sales—which would occur only when the goods reached European markets months later. Some smaller farmers, who were usually among the major supporters of democratic state governments, wanted the establishment of a regular credit system, though not one as oppressive as their creditors wished.

The Constitution was designed to satisfy the desires of these groups. It created a national government with substantial power. Under the Constitution, Congress was given the power to regulate interstate commerce. To many, this meant that state laws impairing the flow of goods across state lines were automatically invalid.[1] It certainly meant that Congress could remove such impediments if it wanted to. Indeed, the grants of power were broad enough to authorize substantial efforts to build a credit system and to create an economic infrastructure. In addition, Congress had the power to raise taxes on its own. To combat "excesses" of local democracy, Article I, Section 10, barred the states from enacting laws "impairing the obligation of contracts."

On the face of it, the Constitution seems to have served the interests of those desiring a strong and centralized government quite well. But the creation of such a government could not be sufficient. The Constitution was predicated on the assumption that the national government would be a relatively democratic one—less democratic than some state governments to be sure, but more democratic than most previous forms of government. For example, members of the House of Representatives were to be chosen in the same manner as members of state legislatures. The democratic assumption was both a matter of principle—the Revolution had been fought to increase democratic rule—and a matter of practical politics—some of the Constitution's supporters had a deep commitment to democracy, and some of its opponents might accept centralization of power but only if the government was relatively democratic.

The democratic assumption presented a problem for those who wanted centralization to combat democratic excesses. How could they be sure that the powerful national government would not fall under the control of exactly those democratic forces they feared at the local level? Without that assurance they might be worse off with the Constitution than without it. Yet they could not limit the power of the national government directly, for that would have defeated the purpose of the enterprise.

The framers devised a brilliant solution to this problem—the separation of powers. They drew upon, but transformed, existing political theories that distinguished among legislative, executive, and judicial powers. Instead of sharply defining three branches of government with different social bases, the framers created what we now call a system of checks and balances. Effective government action requires the concurrence of all three branches. Further, each branch is selected in a different way, but each ultimately rests on a process of democratic participation. Some examples of the system of checks and balances are formal parts of the Constitution. If the House and Senate agree on some proposal, the President still has the opportunity to veto it. Then Congress can override the veto, but only if two-thirds of the members of each house agree. The Supreme Court can declare unconstitutional legislation adopted by Congress and signed by the President.[2]

Other examples of the system are less formal and are part of the ordinary operation of politics. Today the President proposes a budget that embodies his priorities for military spending, taxes, and domestic programs. Congress counters with its own budget, embodying different priorities. Negotiations then occur, face-to-face and through declarations to the press. In the end some sort of deal is struck in which neither side gets all it wants. A similar political check is placed on the execution of the laws by the President's appointees. Congressional committees hold "oversight" hearings to examine what the administration is actually doing. Supporters and opponents of the administration testify, and the committees can communicate to the administration their view, which may be that the administration will suffer political damage unless it changes its enforcement policies.

The system of separated powers balancing each other does indeed substantially reduce the risk of democratic excesses, by placing a series of obstacles in the way of such programs (although, as we shall see, there are ways that these can be overcome). But it does so at a cost: the apparently powerful national government could become paralyzed, unable to do anything. A populist President could obstruct nationalist legislation that passes Congress; or a localistic Congress could refuse to enact nationalist proposals put forward by the President.

The framers had a number of solutions to the problem of paralysis, including the assumption that most of those elected would be public-spirited, but the most important in the long run has been the way in which the three branches are ultimately selected by the people. The process of selection involves staggered terms. Members of the House of Representatives are elected for two-year terms; Senators serve for six years, with one-third elected every two years; the President serves for four years and is now eligible to be reelected once. In addition, federal judges are appointed by the President and hold office for life. The overall effect of this system is straightforward. A political coalition that holds together for a period of about ten years can gain control of all three branches, and then implement its program in a coordinated way. A sustained coalition, then, can overcome the obstacles that the separation of powers creates, and therefore can use the authority that the powerful national government has.

Once again, though, this is not a complete solution to the framers' problem of creating a powerful national government that is not excessively democratic. For, after all, there is no obvious reason why the sustained political coalition could not be a democratic coalition of the sort the framers feared. The framers had two responses to this concern. First, they thought that democratic coalitions would be difficult to sustain; rival demagogues would arise and, through their quest for personal power, would quickly divide the coalition. Second, the framers tended to believe, probably correctly, that most of the time politics would be dominated by the well-to-do. Democratic forces would be weak because their supporters would be unable to divert their energies from the struggle to make a living to the political struggle—at least for long enough to create the sustained coalition that they would need.

The structure of the Constitution thus has two main dimensions. It requires a sustained political coalition if national power is to be mobilized, and it assumes that such a coalition will ordinarily consist of the relatively well-to-do. When we examine some important periods of U.S. history, we see that the framers' system has worked pretty much as they expected it to, although there have been more infusions from democratic social movements than they anticipated.

Before 1860 southern slaveowner dominance of the national political system meant that the national government did very little, for that was what slaveowners wanted. The *Dred Scott* decision, declaring unconstitutional any congressional attempts to restrict the expansion of slavery, was merely the judicial expression of a national policy that had been adopted by Congress and the President by the time the case was decided.[3] A competing vision of government as an agency that could promote economic expansion by means of a policy that the historian Willard Hurst has called "release of energy" was widely shared and was in not too great tension with southern interests. "Release of energy" policies were therefore adopted, because, once again, they were supported by a sustained political coalition.

Later in the nineteenth century, that coalition began to fall apart, resulting in some halting efforts to regulate the power of organized and increasingly monopolistic capitalism. Because the coalition supporting such efforts did not hold power for a long enough period, the constitutional system, in this case through the courts, rejected many of its programs. Notably, organized capital engaged in a continual and often successful litigation campaign aimed at getting the courts to declare these regulatory efforts, such as child labor laws, unconstitutional. This period thus illustrates the proposition that, when there is no dominant political coalition, people can use the courts to advance their political program—though of course in this period the program was not a progressive one.

The early years of the New Deal saw the Supreme Court resisting the government's attempts to respond to the economic crisis of the

Depression. Yet even that resistance is not inconsistent with the general structure of the Constitution. The crisis arose so quickly that a new coalition took over the Presidency and the Congress within an unusually short time. The courts join dominant coalitions gradually, as new judges are appointed to replace those who resign or die. The rapid change in the Presidency and Congress simply outpaced the rate of change in the court system. Still, by 1938, less than a decade after the New Deal coalition took charge, the composition of the Supreme Court had changed enough to produce general support on the Court for the Roosevelt administration's programs. The structure of the Constitution means that change cannot be instantaneous, but as the New Deal experience indicates, all parts of the system will respond to a shift in political power that lasts long enough.

More recent experience confirms the proposition that sustained coalitions have their way. Consider the Supreme Court in the 1960s and 1970s. Probably the best interpretation of its actions is that given by the political scientist Martin Shapiro, who argues that the Court was engaged in completing the program of the New Deal, satisfying demands from elements in the New Deal coalition, such as blacks, that had not yet been fulfilled by the other branches.[4] Shapiro also notes that the Court was simultaneously developing its own constituency, including women's groups. That is important because the more conservative mood of the country has not been translated into a sustained political coalition. For example, Congress and the Presidency have frequently been controlled by different parties. When such divisions persist, it is possible for the Court to be an independent political actor, pursuing the goals associated with the coalition (if there was one) that was dominant when most of the Justices were appointed.

So far I have discussed two of the three aspects of the Constitution described at the beginning of this essay. It protects established institutions, in the sense that it protects the interests of political coalitions that hold together for a long enough period. When there is no dominant coalition, segments of the society, including progressive movements, can make constitutional arguments that serve their own political goals and that the courts may accept. Both of these aspects offer some opportunities to progressive movements. Sometimes such movements become part of a dominant coalition, though the framers correctly perceived the difficulties associated with that possibility. Sometimes progressive movements, like any other, can extract victories from the courts. Before examining this latter possibility in more detail, we should introduce the third aspect of the Constitution: it embodies important progressive aspirations.

Democratic forces in the 1780s were uncomfortable with the centralization of power sought by most of the Constitution's most active supporters. They insisted on some important concessions. To combat excessive centralization, they sought to guarantee that state governments would retain substantial authority over major areas of social life. Federalism, as this allocation of authority to the states is called, promotes democracy to the extent that it allows like-minded people to reside together and resist the power of organized capital and a centralized government that is too often controlled, as the framers expected, by nationally oriented interests. The other concession to the democratic forces of the 1780s was the Bill of Rights. Initially the supporters of the Constitution contended that a bill of rights was unnecessary because the national government would only have a few powers. Their opponents understood that those powers could easily be used expansively, and knew that the proponents of the Constitution wanted a powerful national government. To guarantee that the Constitution would be adopted, its supporters promised to add a bill of rights as soon as possible. The Bill of Rights identified some major rights—free speech, religious liberty, procedural protections in criminal cases—and specified that the national government would be unable to infringe upon them.

The protections provided by the Bill of Rights at the outset were, in a sense, rather limited. The rights were guaranteed only against infringement by the national government, and the content of these rights was, from today's vantage point, not very great. For example, the prevailing theory of free speech appears to have been that government could not censor speech in advance, but could use a variety of devices, such as libel law and criminal prosecutions, to punish speech after it occurred. Similarly, religious liberty seems to have meant freedom to believe and worship as one chose, but not freedom to act, outside the church, in line with religious conviction.

Nonetheless, the very idea that governmental power could be limited by laws protecting rights had important aspirational elements to it. The drafters of the Constitution, and of the amendments added after the Civil War, responded to democratic pressure and to their own principled commitments by including provisions speaking to fundamental issues of democracy and equality. These provisions, such as the requirement that states not deny the "equal protection of the laws," do not in themselves resolve any of these fundamental issues but they do allow progressives to base their arguments for progressive change on provisions already found in the Constitution. People could appeal to the Constitution, by which they did not mean its official interpretations or even the meaning it had for the framers, but rather the values of liberty and justice it embodied. Some abolitionists, for example, developed innovative and at times rather eccentric theories about the Constitution, which led them to conclude even before the Civil War that slavery was unconstitutional.

Those theories came into their own after the Civil War, when the Constitution was amended to abolish slavery and, as important in the long run, to extend some degree of constitutional protection against overreaching by state governments. The Thirteenth Amendment, abolishing slavery, and the Fourteenth, guaranteeing equal protection of the laws and due process of law, dramatically expressed aspirations for racial justice, though once again we should keep in mind the difference between aspirations that progressives can quite properly locate in the Constitution and the actual hopes, fears, and intentions of the people who wrote and adopted these amendments. Still, the Civil War and its constitutional aftermath produced an important permanent transformation in the American understanding of the Constitution. Prior to the Civil War the general view was that centralized power posed a threat to liberty; after the Civil War, Americans saw that national power could, at least occasionally, be used to advance the cause of liberty.

Yet all three of these aspirational elements of the Constitution—federalism, the Bill of Rights, and the Fourteenth Amendment—are also problematic from a progressive point of view. Each can be used to impede progressive change, because none has a meaning precise enough to guarantee that its progressive aspirational side will be presented in practice. One of the slogans of federalism, for example, is "states' rights," a term that has been interpreted to mean that states that discriminate should be left alone. More generally, by providing local groups with the opportunity to exercise power, federalism allows self-interested groups to enact local legislation that ignores the interests of local minorities. From the 1870s to the 1930s the Fourteenth Amendment's guarantee that property cannot be taken without due process of law was interpreted by the courts in ways that erected substantial barriers to the implementation of progressive labor laws.[5] More recently, the Supreme Court has held that efforts by progressives to limit the impact of wealth on the political process by regulating campaign financing violate the free speech guarantees of the Constitution.[6]

All the provisions of the Constitution that, according to progressives, embody aspirations toward justice can therefore be turned against progressive reforms. Progressives of course disagree with the interpretations that allow such outcomes, but we have already seen that the courts in times of political change have the opportunity to enforce their own interpretations. It should also be noted that the terms of the Constitution are imprecise enough that an unbiased judge could possibly adopt an antiprogressive interpretation. Indeed, as we have seen, it is precisely this ambiguity that allows progressives to locate aspirations in the Constitution that its drafters may not have had, at least in as forceful a way.

The picture of the Constitution that I have developed so far is one in which progressive reforms are possible but difficult to accomplish and sustain. It is also one in which the provisions of the Constitution that progressives admire can be used to thwart progressive reforms. Finally, it is one in which, given the difficulty of sustaining a progressive political coalition, we can expect the courts, most of the time, to stand in the way of such reforms. Because the last of these descriptions seems to be at odds with recent progressive experiences with the courts, the next section of this essay examines in more detail the opportunities and problems associated with progressive efforts to use the Constitution as a tool for reform.

How can progressives use the Constitution as part of a political strategy? The preceding analysis suggests three possibilities. When governing elites are divided, progressives can use the Constitution to widen existing divisions and create opportunities for progressive change to occur. Even in the worst of times, progressives can appeal to the aspirations of the Constitution as a means of mobilizing support and strengthening the progressive movement from within, without being too concerned about the acceptance of their appeals by the courts. Finally, progressives can invoke those aspirations as part of a strategy to build a broader coalition that can eventually become a governing coalition.

We can see in the history of the movement for black civil rights how all three of these courses have been pursued. The challenge to segregation in the 1940s and 1950s illustrates the use of the Constitution when governing elites are divided. By the end of World War II blacks had become an important element in the New Deal coalition. Their votes played a key role in the election of Harry Truman in 1948, which occurred after southern racists led by Strom Thurmond had walked out of the Democratic Party's convention to protest its adoption of a strong civil rights platform. Segregation also became an issue in international affairs. The Soviet Union gained support in the then-existing colonies in the third world by attacking the United States for condoning racism. This produced a split in the nation's governing elites. Politicians in the North, supported by internationalist business people, came to believe that the country would be better off without segregation; politicians in the South insisted on preserving it. Under these circumstances, lawyers associated with the National Association for the Advancement of Colored People were able to get the courts to invalidate segregation.[7]

After these initial successes, the black movement turned to other strategies to challenge racism.[8] The Montgomery bus boycott was followed by Freedom Rides, sit ins, and street demonstrations. The courts were not actively hostile to these efforts, and occasionally protected black activists against certain forms of harassment, but after the late 1950s the courts played a significantly smaller role in the black struggle. That is not to say, however, that the Constitution played a smaller role. Black activists repeatedly claimed that their political efforts were aimed at securing for blacks the values of racial justice that were embodied in the Constitution. These were claims invoking the aspirational aspect of the Constitution, and they were effective in building support for the black movement, both within the black community, as black churchgoers came to connect their religion to their commitment as Americans to the Constitution, and in a broader political coalition.

A more striking illustration of how appeals to the Constitution's aspirations can help build a political coalition comes from the movement to abolish slavery. Some Abolitionists, notably William Lloyd

Garrison, argued that the Constitution affirmatively protected slavery and therefore should be repudiated. Others developed an aspirational theory of the Constitution, according to which it should be read against the background of the statement in the Declaration of Independence that all men are created equal. The antislavery constitutionalists became important supporters of the Republican Party in the late 1850s. That party was a coalition whose adherents were not all fervent abolitionists; indeed, many were racists who wanted to prevent the extension of slavery so that blacks would be kept in the South. Abolitionists could join these voters in a political party because all the of the adherents could agree on immediate political goals such as opposition to the extension of slavery.

These same examples allow us to turn to an examination of the limits on progressive uses of the Constitution. The attack on segregation succeeded in part because the country's white elites were sharply divided. Such divisions are not ordinarily available for progressive movements to exploit. Consider, for example, the difficulties faced by progressive attempts to use the Constitution to combat the poverty and racism associated with the present system of the distribution of wealth. The Supreme Court decisively rejected attempts to declare unconstitutional discrimination based on wealth, and it equally decisively refused to hold that it was unconstitutional for governments to implement programs that reinforced racial disparities in the distribution of wealth.[9] Nor should those results have been surprising, because these are issues on which governing elites are not divided enough.

A less important problem with progressive uses of the Constitution deserves brief mention. Legal strategies can sometimes divert progressive efforts from more productive political strategies. Activists can become caught up in litigation, and may come to believe that the movement's success depends on success in the courts. When defeats occur, as they will, the activists may become discouraged. Further, their commitment to the litigation may take time away from other efforts, such as community organizing. Finally, lawsuits are shaped by lawyers, who not surprisingly like to win cases. Even lawyers who are sensitive to political considerations may unconsciously shape the litigation in ways that seem more likely to produce victories, but the victories they produce may be unimportant ones in terms of the movement's overall goals.

The aspirational uses of constitutional arguments also have their limits. When they are used to build coalitions, the coalition itself may limit the effectiveness of the aspirational appeals. After the Civil War, for example, the Republican Party coalition was firmly committed to a program aimed at achieving racial equality. However, different elements in the coalition understood "equality" differently. To some it meant equality before the law: the elimination of the legal disabilities, such as a ban on black testimony, associated with slavery. To others it meant political equality: the right to vote. A third, much smaller group sought what was called social equality: integration of all the major institutions of the society. Antislavery activists had been able to assemble and strengthen the Republican coalition by focusing attention on the commitment to equality while postponing contentious discussions of what exactly they meant by it. Once the coalition attained political power, those discussions could not be deferred any longer. Republicans had to propose specific programs, and any program had to adopt one or another of the controversial definitions of equality. A coalition can hold together and accomplish something under these circumstances, but fulfilling the broad aspirations to which its most progressive elements appeal is unlikely.

Finally, and in some ways related to the problem created by the coalition-building uses of aspirational appeals, such appeals even when successful in one area may reinforce antiprogressive views in other areas. For example, during the arguments before the Supreme Court on desegregation, one of the Justices asked Thurgood Marshall how the Court should respond to southern claims that desegregation would damage the educational system in the South. Marshall deprecated that concern by saying that no educational harm would occur if schools "put the dumb colored children in with the dumb white children, and put the smart colored children with the smart white children." Note that this response accepts notions of intellectual hierarchy that have impeded attempts to achieve more substantial equality in the allocation of educational resources.

It is important to stress that I am concerned here with a systemic problem associated with aspirational appeals. Marshall was responding to a question that, were it answered badly, would have made it much more difficult to alleviate the most pressing problem facing the black movement at the time. His answer was the right one, and was what had to be said then. It is just that, in providing the right answer—that is, the answer that allayed the concerns of the white Justice who asked the question—Marshall reinforced a set of beliefs that impeded progressive reforms of a different sort later on.

Marshall's problem illustrates a final difficulty with progressive uses of the Constitution. They necessarily occur within a political context dominated by nonprogressives. Progressive lawyers make arguments to judges who are fundamentally unsympathetic to the broadest aims of the lawyers; progressive organizers who invoke the Constitution's aspirations appeal to an audience that hears many other descriptions of the Constitution. What progressives say about the Constitution will be set within a broader matrix of thought, most of which is not progressive. Thus despite their intentions, progressives who use the Constitution will frequently have their arguments distorted to fit into this broader matrix. That is how Marshall's claim for racial equality was transformed into a defense of meritocracy.

The most important example of this sort of transformation occurs in connection with the concept of rights itself. As we have seen, at the time of the framing the concept of rights served an important democratic value, protecting people against an overreaching government. Subsequent essays in this book describe the continuing use of the language of rights on behalf of the liberation of oppressed people. For example, as Patricia Williams emphasizes in her contribution to this volume, the language of rights has provided an important resource to black and other progressive movements in their continuing political struggles. In particular, the very ability to claim rights establishes that the person or group making the claim is entitled to be taken into account. And a group that can make claims of legal right, after having been denied that ability by the legal system, has already accomplished something valuable, without regard to what happens after those claims are made.

At the same time, however, being able to claim rights, while important, is not all that oppressed groups want. They want to secure the rights they claim. Thus the contemporary legacy of the concept of rights is more complex than the establishment of the ability of oppressed groups to claim rights. It also includes the availability of claims of rights-violations to people who on no account could be considered oppressed or progressive. One of the most important dimensions of this somewhat less attractive aspect of the language of rights involves the common use of governmental oppression as the central example of rights violation: legally enforced segregation, the criminalization of abortion, prosecutions for opposing government policies. These examples have generated a way of thinking about rights in which rights are seen primarily as a defense against the government. According to this way of thinking, people have rights in order to define a zone of privacy around themselves into which the government may not enter.

Progressives have historically understood that oppression occurs in other forms. One can frame the idea of wage slavery as an example of government oppression, but it is easier to see it as oppression by the capitalist class in the first instance. Similarly, the physical abuse of women can be seen as the result of government's failure to act, but it is easier to see it as aggression by men per se. In addition, the progressive tradition has opposed capitalist accumulation of private wealth and power. Under contemporary circumstances the progressive program of human liberation may require substantial affirmative efforts by government to overcome the concentrated power of capital. The "zone of privacy" image of rights does not aid that program. Progressive intellectuals have attempted to reformulate the idea of rights so that it does not have these anti-statist overtones.[10] When progressives use the language of rights, then, they need not intend—and may even reject—the definition of rights as protection against the state. But that language is not entirely under the control of progressives, and it may be understood as reinforcing an image of government that progressives ultimately wish to undermine.

The Constitution's meaning for progressive social movements has many dimensions. The Constitution usually stabilizes the existing order, but sometimes it can be put to progressive ends. When progressives use the Constitution, they must consider the ways in which the Constitution can assist *and* impede progressive change, often at the same time. The Constitution is not inherently progressive *or* antiprogressive. What it "is" depends on what people make it, and progressives who seek to use the Constitution must always be sensitive to the complex questions of political strategy that their plans raise. In the end there can be no crisp conclusion to our analysis of the Constitution from a progressive point of view; too much depends on exactly what political problems face us in each distinctive era.

Notes

1. See Gibbons v. Ogden, 22 U.S. (9 Wheat.) 1, 225–26 (1824) (Johnson, J., concurring).
2. Marbury v. Madison, 5 U.S. (1 Cranch) 137 (1803).
3. Dred Scott v. Sandford, 60 U.S. (19 How.) 393 (1857).
4. Martin Shapiro, "Fathers and Sons: The Court, the Commentators, and the Search for Values," in *The Burger Court: The Counterrevolution That Wasn't*, ed. Vincent Blasi (New Haven, 1983).
5. Lochner v. New York, 198 U.S. 45 (1905) (holding unconstitutional a state statute limiting the hours of work for bakers); Coppage v. Kansas, 236 U.S. 1 (1915) (holding unconstitutional a state statute prohibiting employers from refusing to hire union members.).
6. Buckley v. Valeo, 424 U.S. 1 (1976).
7. To some extent this describes some of the accomplishments of opponents of the Vietnam war, although there the successes in the courtroom were more equivocal.
8. One reason for the alteration in tactics was that the southern states engaged in a sustained legal assault on the NAACP, which therefore had to divert its attention to issues of self-preservation. See essays by Margaret Burnham and Anne Braden in this volume.
9. Dandridge v. Williams, 397 U.S. 471 (1970); Washington v. Davis, 426 U.S. 229 (1976).
10. See, for example, Staughton Lynd, "Communal Rights," 62 *Texas Law Review* 1417 (1984).

ALCHEMICAL NOTES:
Reconstructing Ideals from Deconstructed Rights

Patricia J. Williams

One summer about twenty years ago I went to Georgia for a family funeral. In the heat of summer and the small church, fans were passed out. On one side of each fan was printed the Lord's Prayer; on the other was a picture of Martin Luther King, Jr. I was only about twelve or thirteen at the time, but the symbolism of those fans was not lost on me: I knew that that particular juxtaposition of God and Dr. King represented the fusion of generations of black prayer and a powerful social movement. I knew that the then-recently-enacted Civil Rights Act was not only a political achievement with reference to a secular Constitution, but the cornerstone of a profoundly transformative liberation theology. And I knew that the meaning of "rights" for blacks had as much to do with self-esteem and the bonds of community as it did with the practicalities of who sat where on the bus.

Such fans are still a popular item in many black churches around the country. To this day, Dr. King's picture is not only the image of a religious leader; it remains testament to the almost sacred attachment to the transformative promise of a black-conceived notion of rights which King embodied. It is an attachment that exists somewhat apart from the reality of the legal enforcement of these rights; it nevertheless gives rise to their power as a politically animating force.

Recently, there has grown up a school of thought among legal scholars—particularly on the political left—which rejects the utility of a reliance on rights. The weight of such an argument is best

56

understood as a strategic response to those on the far right who insist on limiting the meaning of rights to the "original intent" of constitutional drafters, who were white male slaveholders. Given such a political climate, there indeed appear many good reasons for abandoning a system of rights that is based on a premise of inequality and helplessness; yet despite the acknowledged and compelling force of such reasons, most blacks[1] have not turned away from the pursuit of civil rights, even if what white Left scholars say about such rights is so: that they are contradictory, indeterminate, reified, and marginally decisive in social behavior.[2] I think this is because the metalanguage, or so-called governing narrative,[3] about the significance of rights seems to be quite different for whites and blacks. For most whites, I think, achievement is perceived as a function of self-control, of self-possession. For blacks, including black lawyers, academics, and clients, on the other hand, relationships are frequently dominated by historical patterns of physical and psychic *dis*possession. In a semantic as well as a substantive sense, then, I think that those who argue abandonment of rights-assertion have ignored the degree to which the benefits of rights have helped blacks, as well as other minorities and the poor.

For blacks in this country, politically effective action has occurred mainly in connection with asserting or extending rights. While rights may not be ends in themselves, rights rhetoric has been and continues to be an effective form of discourse for blacks—in housing, in employment, in the criminal courts. The vocabulary of rights speaks to an establishment that values certain formal manifestations of stability; change dressed, therefore, in the sheep's clothing of stability (i.e., "rights") can be extremely effective on its own terms, even as it *de*stabilizes certain other establishment values (e.g., segregation).

I by no means want to idealize the importance of rights in a legal system where rights are so often selectively invoked to draw boundaries, to isolate, to limit.[4] At the same time, it is very hard to watch their idealistic or symbolic importance diminished with reference to those disenfranchised who experience and express their disempowerment as nothing more or less than the denial of rights.[5]

It is my belief that, in general, blacks and whites differ in the degree to which rights-assertion is experienced as empowering or disempowering. The expression of these differing experiences creates a discourse boundary, reflecting complex and often contradictory societal understandings. The remainder of this article attempts to show how that opposition arises. What I propose, moreover, is not the abandonment of rights language for all purposes, but an attempt to become bilingual in the semantics of each others' rights-valuation. It is my hope that in redescribing the historical alchemy of rights in black lives, the reader will experience some reconnection with that part of the self and of society whose story unfolds beyond the neatly staked bounds of theoretical legal understanding.

The individual unifying cultural memory of black people is the helplessness, the uncontrollability, of living under slavery. I grew up living in the past: the future, some versions of which had only the sheerest possibility of happening, was treated with the respect of the already-happened, seen through the expansively prismatic lenses of past oppression.[6] Thus when I decided to go to law school, my mother told me that the "Millers were lawyers so you have it in your blood." Now, the Millers were the slaveholders of my maternal grandmother's clan. The Millers were also my great-great-grandparents and great-aunts and who knows what else. My great-great-grandfather Austin Miller, a lawyer, bought my eleven-year-old great-great-grandmother, Sophie, and her parents when he was thirty-five years old. By the time she was twelve, Austin Miller had made Sophie the mother of a child, my great-grandmother Mary.

Austin purchased Sophie, according to family lore, out of his desire to have a family. Not, of course, a family with my great-great-grandmother, but with a wealthy white widow whom he in fact married shortly thereafter. He wanted to *practice* his sexual talents on my great-great-grandmother. In the bargain, Sophie bore Mary, my great-grandmother, who was taken away from her and raised in the Big House as a house servant, an attendant to his wife Mary (after whom Sophie's Mary had been named) and to his legitimated white children.[7]

Of course, when my mother said that I had "lawyers in my blood," she did not mean that law was literally part of my genetic makeup; she meant that law was an intimate part of the socially constructed reality into which I had been born. She meant that dealing with law and lawyers was something with which my ancestors were all too familiar. In ironic, perverse obeisance to the rationalizations of this bitter ancestral mix, I took her words to heart; and the image of Austin, the self-centered child molester and maker-of-laws, became the fuel for my survival in the dispossessed limbo of my years at Harvard. Those were the Bakke years, the years when white people were running around telling black people that they were very happy to have us there, *but* after all they did have to lower the standards and readjust the grading system, *but* Harvard could *afford* to do that because Harvard was Harvard. (I do not mean this as a criticism of affirmative action, but of those who tried to devalue the presence and contributions of us, the affirmatively active.) And it worked. I got through law school, quietly driven by the false idol of white man-within-me, and I absorbed a whole lot of the knowledge and the values that had enslaved me and my foremothers.

I learned about images of power in the strong, sure-footed impersonality of the arm's-length transactor. I learned about unique power-enhancing lands called Whiteacre and Blackacre, and the mystical fairy rings which encircled—and separated—them called restrictive covenants. I learned that excessive power overlaps generously with what is seen as successful, good, efficient, and desirable in our society.

I learned that in exceptional circumstances such images of power might be undone with images of powerlessness, and the magic of inversion: I learned to clothe the victims of excessive power in utter, bereft naiveté; to cast them, in defending them, as defenseless, supplicatory, *pleading.* (A quick review of almost any contracts text will show that most successful defenses feature women, particularly if they are old and widowed; illiterates; blacks and other minorities; the abjectly poor; and the old and infirm. A white male student of mine once remarked that he could not imagine "reconfiguring his manhood" to live up to the "publicly craven defenselessness" of defenses like duress, undue influence, and fraud.)[8] I learned that the best way to give voice to those whose voice had been suppressed was to argue that they had no voice.

Some time ago, my sister went to the National Archives and found what may have been the contract of sale of my great-great-grand-mother (whether hers[9] or not, it was *someone's*), as well as a census report that does list her, along with other inanimate evidence of wealth, as the "personal property" of Austin Miller.[10]

In reviewing those powerfully impersonal documents, I realized that it was her lot always to be either owned or unowned, but never the owner. And whether owned or unowned, rights over her never filtered down *to* her; rights to her person never vested *in* her. When owned, issues of physical, mental, and emotional abuse or cruelty were assigned by the law to the private tolerance, whimsy, or insanity of an external master. And when unowned—i.e., free, freed, or escaped—again her situation was uncontrollably precarious, for as an object *to be owned,* she and the game of her conquest were seen only as potential enhancement to some other self. She was fair game from the perspective of those who had rights; but from her own point of view, she was the object of a murderous hunt.[11]

Finding what could have been the contract of sale of my great-great-grandmother irretrievably personalized my analysis of the law of her exchange. Repeatedly since then, I have tried to analyze, rationalize, and rescue her fate, employing the tools of the contract law which enslaved her—the same contract law which I mastered, at such high price, in law school: offer; acceptance; adequacy of value exchanged (How *much* was she exchanged for, I wonder. Just how did the value break down? Did they haggle? Was it a poker game, a trade, a promissory note? How much was she *worth?* With what literalism must my philosophizing be alloyed: "There's something in me which might have been great, but due to the unfavorable market, I'm only worth a little.");[12] defenses to formation; grounds for discharge; and remedies (for whom?).

That this was a dead-end undertaking is probably obvious, but it was interesting to see how the other part of my heritage, Austin Miller, the lawyer, and his confreres, had constructed their world so as to nip quests like mine in the bud. The very best I could do for my great-great-grandmother Sophie was to throw myself, in whimpering supplication, upon the mercy of an imaginary, patriarchal court and appeal for an exercise of its extraordinary powers of conscionability and "humanitarianism."[13] I found that it helped to appeal to the court's humanity, and not to stress the fullness of hers. I found that the best way to get anything for her, whose needs for rights were so compellingly, overwhelmingly manifest, was to argue that she, poor thing, had no rights.[14] It is this experience of having, for the sake of survival, to argue our own invisibility in the passive unthreatening rhetoric of "no-rights" which, juxtaposed with recent attempts to abandon rights theory, is both paradoxical and difficult for minorities to accept.

The discussion thus far may prompt the argument that this

paradox is the direct product of rights discourse itself. But, in addition, I tried arguing my great-great-grandmother's fate in terms more direct, more informal, more descriptive, and more substantive. I begged, pleaded, "acted out" (the New Age way of describing the New Black Activism), and cried. I prayed loudly enough for all the hear, and became superstitious. But I didn't get any relief for my grandmother's condition; my most silver-tongued informality got her nothing at all.

The problem, as I have come to see it, is not really one of choice of rhetoric, of formal over informal, of structure and certainty over context, of right over need. Rather, it is a problem of appropriately choosing signs within any system of rhetoric. From the object-property's point of view (e.g., that of my great-great-grandmother), rhetoric of certainty (of rights, formal rules, and fixed entitlements) has been enforced at best as though it were the rhetoric of context (of fluidity, informal rules, and unpredictability). Yet the fullness of context, the trust that enhances the use of more fluid systems, is lost in the lawless influence of cultural insensitivity and taboo. So while it appears to jurisdictionally recognized and invested parties as though rights designate outcomes with a clarity akin to wisdom, for the object-property the effect is one of existing in a morass of unbounded irresponsibility.

But this failure of rights discourse does not logically mean that informal systems will lead to better outcomes. Some structures are the direct products of people and social forces that wanted them that way. If one assumes, as blacks must, not that the many in the larger world want to overcome alienation but that they in fact heartily embrace it, driven not just by fear but by hatred and taboo (by this I do not mean to suggest a Hobbesian state of nature, but a crust of cultural habit and perception whose power shelters as it blinds), then informal systems, as well as formal ones, will be run principally by unconscious and/or irrational forces. "Human nature has an invincible dread of becoming more conscious of itself."[15]

This underscores my sense of the importance of rights: rights are to law what conscious commitments are to the psyche. This country's worst historical moments have not been attributable to rights-*assertion*, but to a failure of rights-*commitment*. From this perspective, the problem with rights discourse is not that it is constricting, but that it exists in a constricted referential universe. The body of private law epitomized by contracts, including slave contracts, is problematic not only because it endows certain parties with rights, but because it denies the object of contract any rights at all.

The quintessential rule of contract interpretation, the parole evidence rule, illustrates the mechanics by which such constriction is achieved. It says, in its relevant part, that "terms with respect to which the confirmatory memoranda of the parties agree . . . may not be contradicted [by extrinsic evidence] . . . but may be explained or supplemented . . . by evidence of consistent additional terms."[16] It is a rule, in other words, which drastically constricts the range of evidence which may be utilized in interpreting a written contract: once the parties to a contract have inscribed their intentions as private law between them—or as contract—then courts will permit very little in the way of inconsistent evidence to contradict that writing. If, however, this rule is understood as a form of social construction, the words could as well read: "Terms with respect to which the constructed reality (or governing narrative) of a given power structure agree may not be contradicted but only supplemented or explained."

Such a social construction applied to rights mythology suggests the way in which rights-assertion has been limited by delimiting undesirable others as "extrinsic" to rights-entitlement: "Europe during the Discovery era refused to recognize legal status or rights for indigenous tribal peoples because 'heathens' and 'infidels' were legally presumed to lack the rational capacity necessary to assume an equal status or exercise equal rights under the European's medievally derived legal world-view."[17] The possibility of a broader range of types of rights may be found by adding to, even contradicting, traditional categories of public and private rights-recipients.[18]

One consequence of this broader reconfiguration of rights is to give voice to those people or things that by virtue of their object relation to a contract, or to the Constitution, have historically had no voice. Allowing this sort of empowering goes beyond the narrow boundaries of linear, bipolar rights and relations, to a fuller, or circular, frame of reference.

This sort of expanded frame of rights-reference is part of a philosophy of more generously extending rights to all one's fellow creatures, whether human[19] or beast.[20] It is the basis of those theories of constantly returning cycles that are at the root of environmental reform,[21] and that give "utility" to maintaining the earth in an unexploited form.[22]

One lesson I never learned in law school, the one lesson I had to learn all by myself, was the degree to which black history in this nation is that of fiercely interwoven patterns of family, as conceived by white men. Folklore not withstanding, slaves were not treated "as though" they were part of the family (for that implies a drawing near, an overcoming of market-placed distance); too often the unspoken power of white masters over slaves was the covert cohesion *of* family.[23] Those who were, in fact or for all purposes, family were held at a distance as strangers and commodities: strangers in the sense that they were excluded from the family circle at the hearth and in the heart, and commodities in the sense that they could be sold down the river with no more consideration than the bales of cotton they accompanied.

In the thicket of those relations, the insignificance of family connection was consistently achieved through the suppression of any image of blacks as *capable* either of being part of the family of (white) man[24] or of having family of their own.[25] The recognition of such a threshold is the key to understanding slavery as a structure of denial—a denial of the generative independence of black people. Instead, a substitution occurred: instead of black motherhood being the generative source for black people, master-cloaked white manhood became the generative source for black people. Although the "bad black mother" is even today an archetypal way of describing what ails the black race, the historical reality is that of careless white fatherhood. Blacks are thus, in full culturally imagistic terms, not merely an unmothered race, but badly fathered, abused and disowned by whites.[26]

I am therefore not one who believes that the future and well-being of blacks lies solely with ourselves; although I don't always yet trust this imagery of interdependence, I think it is the reality, and necessity, if balanced coexistence is to occur. Blacks cannot be alone in this recognition, however. Whites, too, must learn to appreciate the communion of blacks in more than body, as more than the perpetually neotenized, mothering non-mother;[27] they must recognize us as kin; they must want to confer upon us the property of larger community, the integrated selfhood of owning up to family (as opposed to having, using, and disowning). They must learn to listen and speak to the grieving, *enraged* black-people-within-themselves and within our society: "Conscious realization or the bringing together of the scattered parts is in one sense an act of the ego's will, but in another sense it is a spontaneous manifestation of the self, which was always there. Individuation appears, on the one hand, as the synthesis of a new unity which previously consisted of scattered particles, and on the other hand, as the revelation of something which existed before the ego and is in fact its father or creator and is also its totality."[28]

Whites must confer upon blacks their recognition of black need and black identity, for is not "what we have in common precisely what is given to each of us as something exclusively his?"[29]

It is probably true, as maintained by much of the jurisprudence produced by the white Left in recent years, that rights are by their constitution so indeterminate and therefore marginally utile that the paper-promises of enforcement packages like the Civil Rights Act can be said to have held out as many illusions as gains. In that sense, it is probably also true that blacks have never fully believed in constitutional rights as literal mandate.

Yet it is also true that blacks always believed in rights in some larger, mythologic sense—as a pantheon of possibility. It is in this sense that blacks believed in rights so much and so hard that we gave them life where there was none before; held onto them, put the hope of them into our wombs, mothered them, not the notion of them; we nurtured rights and gave rights life. And this was not the dry process of reification, from which life is drained and reality fades as the cement of conceptual determinism hardens round, but its opposite. This was the story of the Phoenix; the parthenogenesis of unfertilized hope.

The making of something out of nothing took immense alchemical fire: the fusion of a whole nation and the kindling of several generations. The illusion became real for only a very few of us; it is still elusive and illusory for most. But if it took this long to breathe life into a form whose shape had already been forged by society and which is therefore idealistically if not ideologically accessible, imagine how long would be the struggle without even that sense of definition, without the power of that familiar vision; what hope would there be if the task were to pour hope into a timeless, formless futurism? The desperate psychological and physical oppression suffered by black people in this society makes such a prospect either unrealistic (i.e., experienced as unattainable) or other-worldly (as in the false hopes held out by many religions of the oppressed).

It is true that the constitutional foreground of "rights" was shaped by whites, parcelled out to blacks in pieces, ordained from on high in small favors, as random insulting gratuities. Perhaps the predominance of that imbalance obscures the fact that the recursive insistence of those rights is also defined by black desire for them—desire fueled not by the sop of minor enforcement of major statutory schemes like the Civil Rights Act, but by knowledge of, and generations of existing in, a world without any meaningful boundaries— and "without boundary" for blacks has meant not untrammeled vistas of possibility, but the crushing weight of totalistic—bodily and spiritual—*intrusion*. "Rights" feels so new in the mouths of most black people. It is still so deliciously empowering to say. It is a sign for, and a gift of, selfhood that is very hard to contemplate reconstructing (deconstruction is too awful to think about!) at this point in history. It is the magic wand of visibility and invisibility, of inclusion and exclusion, of power and no power. The concept of rights, both positive and negative, is the marker of our citizenship, our participatoriness, our relation to others.

In many mythologies, the mask of the sorcerer is also the source of power. To unmask the sorcerer is to depower.[30] So the white Left's unmasking rights mythology in liberal America is to reveal the source of much powerlessness masquerading as strength; it reveals a universalism of need and oppression among whites as well as blacks.

In those ancient mythologies, however, unmasking the sorcerer was only part of the job. It was impossible to destroy the mask without destroying the balance of things, without destroying empowerment itself. Therefore, the mask had to be donned by the acquiring shaman and put to good ends. As rulers range from despotic to benign, as anarchy can become syndicalism—so the power mask in the right hands can transform itself from burden into blessing.

The task for progressive legal reformers, therefore, is not to discard rights but to see through or past them so that they reflect a larger definition of privacy, and of property: so that privacy is turned from exclusion based on *self*-regard into regard for another's fragile, mysterious autonomy;[31] and so that property regains its ancient connotation of being a reflection of that part of the self which by virtue of its very externalization is universal. The task is to expand private property rights into a conception of civil rights, into the right to expect civility from others. In discarding rights altogether, one discards a symbol too deeply enmeshed in the psyche of the oppressed to bear losing without trauma and much resistance. Instead society must *give* them away. Unlock them from reification by giving them to slaves. Give them to trees. Give them to cows. Give them to history. Give them to rivers and rocks. Give to all of society's objects and untouchables the rights of privacy, integrity, and self-assertion; give them distance and respect. Flood them with the animating spirit which rights mythology fires in this country's most oppressed psyches, and wash away the shrouds of inanimate-object status, so that we may say not that we own gold, but that a luminous golden spirit owns us.

Notes

I am deeply indebted to the following people: my sister Carol Williams, whose research into our family's history gave me the idea for this piece; Richard Delgado, whose enthusiasm kept me going; the uniquely wonderful community of CUNY, past and present, faculty, students, and staff; and, of course, Derrick and Jewell Bell, teachers, friends, and inspiration to the many of us who are their students.

1. I recognize that the categories of "black" and "white" do not begin to capture the richness of ethnic and political diversity that the debate actually contains; I do believe, however, that the simple matter of the color of one's skin so profoundly affects the way one is treated, so radically shapes what one is allowed to think and feel about this society, that the decision to generalize from this division is valid. Furthermore, I am at a loss as how to describe succinctly the specifically racial perspectives and history that are my subject. "Disenfranchised" will not do, because part of my point is that a purely class-based analysis does not comprehend the whole problem. I do not like the word "minority" (although I use it) because it implies a certain delegitimacy in a majoritarian system; and if one adds up all the shades of yellow, red, and brown that the term sweeps over, we are in fact not. "Oppressed persons" is rather more inclusive than I really mean; it would have to include all victims of religious, ethnic, and sexual discrimination. I prefer, and use most frequently, the term "black" in order to accentuate the unshaded monolithism of color itself as a social force.
2. Trubek, "Where the Action Is: Critical Legal Studies and Empiricism," 36 *Stan. L. Rev.* 575, 578 (1984).
3. Governing narratives are "presiding fictions that allow us to behold ourselves and make sense of the historical world, and by them the status of knowledge is affected in intimate ways." Des Pres, "On Governing Narratives: The Turkish-Armenian Case," 75 *The Yale Review* 517 (1986).
4. Reconstruction cured most blacks of any idealization of property, authority, and

diligence: "The Reverend Henry Highland Garnet, a veteran black abolitionist, assured a gathering of freedmen, 'The more money you make, the lighter your skin will be. The more land and houses you get, the straighter your hair will be.' " Even as they found their economic opportunities sharply curtailed, even as the deepening agricultural depression of the post-Reconstruction years drove thousands off the land, southern blacks were asked to pay obeisance to the same materialist deities, values, and goals that motivated the larger society. Success came ultimately to the hardworking, the sober, the honest, and the educated, to those who served their employers faithfully, who respected property and the sanctity of contracts, who cultivated habits of thrift, cleanliness, and temperance, who led moral, virtuous, Christian lives.

"In the experience of black southerners, such advice was as naive and mistaken in its assumptions as it was persistent." Leon Litwack, " 'Blues Falling Down Like Rain': The Ordeal of Black Freedom," in *New Perspectives on Race and Slavery in America,* ed. R. Abzug and S. Maizlish (New York, 1986), p. 116.

5. D. A. Bell, "Bakke, Minority Admissions, and the Usual Price of Racial Remedies" 67 *Calif. L. Rev.* 3 (1979); Bell, *Race, Racism and American Law* (2nd ed., Boston, 1980); Bell, "The Supreme Court, 1984 Term—Foreword: The Civil Rights Chronicles," 99 *Harv. L. Rev.* 4 (1985); C. Edley, Jr., *The Moral Foundations of Civil Rights Policy* (New York, 1986).

6. "It is by now a trite observation that oppressed peoples have an acute sense of their past. Well they must: it is the crucible of their identity and their cohesion. Without it their present oppression becomes either meaningless or natural" Wiecek, "Preface to the Historical Race Relations Symposium," 17 *Rutgers L. Rev.* 412 (1986).

7. This information comes from my mother, who says that her grandmother told it to her. It was confirmed to me separately by my mother's cousin, whose own mother, my great-aunt (another Mary), was taken, from the ages of five to thirteen, into the Miller household to be the (unpaid) servant and companion to the Miller children.

8. See Frug, "Rereading Contracts: A Feminist Analysis of a Contracts Casebook," 34 *Am. L. Rev.* 1065 (1985); Klare, "Contracts, Jurisprudence, and the First-Year Casebook," 54 *N.Y.U. L. Rev.* 876 (1979).

9. I use the term "hers" intentionally, although her object-relation to such a contract technically would make it other than hers; a record *of* her, the possessory interest *in* others.

10. Census of Hardeman County, Tennessee, Roll No. 881, Schedule 2 (Slave Inhabitants of Bolivar), 29 August 1850.

11. See United States v. The Amistad, 40 U.S. 518 (1841), a suit for, among other things, the "salvage value" of a shipload of Africans who revolted during their passage to America. See also W. Breyfogle, *Make Free: The Story of the Underground Railroad* (New York, 1958), for descriptions of elaborate rituals of slave-hunting, of the history of the Fugitive Slave Act, and of the Underground Railroad.

12. S. Kierkegaard, cited in K. Jaspers, "On My Philosophy," in *Existentialism from Dostoevsky to Sartre,* ed. W. Kaufmann (New York, 1975).

13. See S. Elkins, *Slavery* (Chicago, 1963), p. 237, in which the "conduct and character" of slave traders is described as follows: "Between these two extremes [from "unscrupulous" to "guilt-ridden"] must be postulated a wide variety of acceptable, genteel, semi-personalized, and doubtless relatively *humane* commercial transactions whereby slaves in large numbers could be transferred in exchange for money" (emphasis added).

14. See Bell, "Social Limits on Basic Protections for Blacks," in *Race, Racism and American Law,* p. 280.
15. C. Jung, *Psyche and Symbol* (New York, 1958), p. 214.
16. Sec. 2–202, Uniform Commercial Code.
17. R. Williams, "The Algebra of Federal Indian Law: The Hard Trail of Decolonizing and Americanizing the White Man's Indian Jurisprudence," 1986 *Wisc. L. Rev.* 290.
18. Imagine, for example, a world in which a broader range of inanimate objects (i.e., other than corporations) were given rights—as in cases of the looting of American Indian religious objects: spurred by a booming international art market and virtually no fear of prosecution, raiders have taken "ceremonial objects and ancient tools . . . [as well as] the mummified remains of Anasazi children. . . . [T]he asking price for quality specimens starts at $5000. The best of these are said to have been preserved by casting them into acrylic blocks, an expensive, high-tech procedure. . . . The looting has struck a painful nerve for Native Americans. 'To us,' says Marcus Sekayouma, a Hopi employee of the Bureau of Indian Affairs, 'the removal of any old object from the ground is the equivalent of a sacrilege.' " Goodwin, "Raiders of the Sacred Sites," *New York Times Magazine,* 7 December 1986, p. 65.
19. Think, for example, how differently might have been the outcome in the Tuskegee syphillis experiment, in which illiterate black men were deliberately allowed to go untreated and uninformed of the nature of their disease from 1932 until 1972, observed by doctors from the U.S. Public Health Service. Approximately 400 diseased men, with 200 more as controls, were allowed to degenerate and die; doctors told them only that they had "bad blood." See J. H. Jones, *Bad Blood* (New York, 1981).
20. Every year one reads in the newspapers about millions of cattle that are periodically destroyed for no other purpose than to drive up the price of either milk or beef. One also reads about the few "bleeding hearts" who wage a mostly losing war to save the lives of the hapless animals. Yet prior to the Reformation, the bleeding heart was the Christian symbol for one who could "feel the spirit move inside all property. Everything on earth is a gift and God is the vessel. Our small bodies may be expanded; we need not confine the blood." L. Hyde, *The Gift: Imagination and the Erotic Life of Property* (New York, 1983), p. 139. Today, on the other hand, the "'bleeding heart' is . . . the man of dubious mettle with an embarrassing inability to limit his compassion" (ibid.).
21. "Increasingly, the death that occupies each human's imagination is not his own, but that of the entire life cycle of the planet earth, to which each of us is as but a cell to a body." C. Stone, "Should Trees Have Standing?—Toward Legal Rights for Natural Objects," 45 *S. Cal. L. R.* 450, 500.
22. As ought to have been done in Peevyhouse v. Garland Coal Mining Co., 382 P.2d 109 (1962). There the Oklahoma Supreme Court refused to enforce a contract provision requiring the Garland Coal Company to rehabilitate leased farm and grazing land destroyed by the process of strip-mining. The court's rationale was that "where the contract provision breached was merely incidental to the main purpose in view, and where the economic benefit which would result to lessor by full performance, the damages which lessor may recover are limited to the dimunition in value resulting to the premises because of the non-performance."
23. K. Stampp, *The Peculiar Institution* (New York, 1956), pp. 250–61.
24. See Dred Scott vs. Sandford, 60 U.S. 383, 407 (1857), in which blacks were ajudged "altogether unfit to associate with the white race, either in social or political relations; and so far inferior, that they had no rights which the white man

was bound to respect; and that the negro might justly and lawfully be reduced to slavery for his benefit." See also S. A. Cartwright, *The Dred Scott Decision: An Essay on the Natural History of the Prognathous Race of Mankind* (1859), a pamphlet in which blacks were likened to "ourang outangs" and determined to be the descendants of Canaan. ("Noah, a tiller of the soil, was the first to plant the vine. He drank some of the wine, and while he was drunk he uncovered himself inside his tent. Ham, Canaan's ancestor, saw his father's nakedness, and told his two brothers outside. Shem and Japheth took a cloak and they both put it over their father's nakedness. When Noah awoke from his stupor he learned what his youngest son had done to him. And he said:

'Accursed be Canaan.

He shall be his brothers'

meanest slave.' " [Genesis 9:20].)

25. "Since slaves, as chattels, could not make contracts, marriages between them were not legally binding. . . . Their condition was compatible only with a form of concubinage, 'voluntary' on the part of the slaves, and permissive on that of the master. In law there was no such thing as fornication or adultery between slave; nor was there bastardy, for, as a Kentucky judge noted, the father of a slave was 'unknown' to the law. No state legislature ever seriously entertained the thought of encroaching upon the master's rights by legalizing slave marriages." Stampp, *Peculiar Institution*, p. 198. Antimiscegenation laws also kept blacks outside the family of those favored with rights; and laws restricting the ability of slaveholders to will property or freedom to blacks suspended them in eternal illegitimacy. See generally, M. Tushnet, *The American Law of Slavery, 1810–1860* (Princeton, N.J., 1981).

26. Certainly, the companion myths to this woeful epic are to be found in the brutalization of the archetypes of black male (as so indiscriminately generative as to require repression by castration) and of white female (as so discriminatingly virginal as to wither in idealized asexuality). See generally, W. Jordan, *White over Black* (Chapel Hill, N.C., 1971), pp. 136–78 (" . . .castration [for blacks] was dignified by specific legislative sanction as a lawful punishment in Antigua, the Carolinas, Bermuda, Virginia, Pennsylvania, and New Jersey" [ibid., p. 154]); see also J. Dollard, *Caste and Class in a Southern Town* (New York, 1957), p. 172 (published originally in 1937, the author ominously and ambiguously reports that the mythology of exaggerated black potency is "further suspect because the same point seems to be coming up with respect to the Jews in Germany" (ibid., p. 161); see also, J. Mitchell, *Woman's Estate* (New York, 1973); E. Wolgast, *Equality and the Rights of Women* (Ithaca, N.Y., 1980).

27. E.g., the Mammy whom "W.E.B. DuBois . . . described . . . as 'one of the most pitiful of the world's Christs. . . . She was an embodied Sorrow, and anomaly crucified on the cross of her own neglected children for the sake of the children of masters who bought and sold her as they bought and sold cattle' " (Genovese, "Don't Mess With Mammy," *Washington Post,* 27 October 1974, p. C5). Mammy-exploitation persists—abounds—to this day in the too-familiar image of grossly underpaid but-ever-so-*loved* black female "help." The going rate for black female full-time live-in babysitter/maids in New York City is as low as $150 a week. "Haitians come cheaper. Their starting salary ranges form $100 to $125 a week. . . . A Hispanic woman . . . is likely to start at $200 a week, since she's white." Laurino, "I'm Nobody's Girl," *Village Voice,* 14 October 1986, p. 18.

28. Jung, *Psyche and Symbol,* p. 214.

29. I. Calvino, *Mr. Palomar* (New York, 1983), p. 14.

30. Almost every culture in the world has its share of such tales: Plains Indian,

Eskimo, Celtic, Siberian, Turkish, Nigerian, Cameroonian, Brazilian, Australian, and Malaysian stories—to name a few—describe the phenomenon of the power mask or power object. Moreover, the "unmasking" can occur in a number of less-than-literal ways: killing the totemic animal from whom the sorcerer derives power; devaluing the magician as merely the village psychotic; and, perhaps most familiarly in our culture, incanting sacred spells backward.

31. " . . . in exactly the same way that the South imagines that it 'knows' the Negro, the North imagines that it has set him free. Both camps are deluded. Human freedom is a complex, difficult—and private—thing. If we liken life, for a moment, to a furnace, then freedom is the fire which burns away illusion." J. Baldwin, *Nobody Knows My Name* (New York, 1970), p. 99.

PART 2

The Constitutional Debate
from a Historical Perspective

Because the Constitution is seen as our civic religion, it is often presented ahistorically. Mainstream ideology thus portrays our rights as "self-evident," inherent in U.S. society, failing to recognize that the First Amendment, the equal protection clause of the Fourteenth Amendment, and other important rights did not become meaningful until the twentieth century—in many cases not until the last forty years. These rights were not given but were won through struggle, beginning with the Constitutional Convention of 1787. If the Constitution is to be understood, it must therefore be viewed historically.

The tension over how to view the Constitution that was discussed in Part 1 is therefore not a recent phenomenon. The essays in this section address the question of how progressives should view the Constitution by looking at how they have dealt with such constitutional issues in the past.

It is appropriate to begin with the most influential radical critique of the Constitution, that of Charles Beard. Beard, a historian of the Progressive era of the early twentieth century, an era in which muckraking and questioning U.S. capitalism were prominent, sharply attacked those who viewed the Constitutional Convention as a democratic event. He viewed it as a conspiracy of the rich elite to protect property, and his critique has since become a central part of radical views of the Constitution: from its founding convention, our constitutional government has been flawed, not merely by racism, but by class bias. But Larry Kaplan, in the opening essay of this section, challenges Beard's critique, arguing that a more balanced view of the constitution's adoption is necessary.

We then turn to the early struggles over the Constitution's meaning. Robert Cover discusses the divisions among Abolitionists as to how to view the Constitution. The arguments of some Abolitionists that the Constitution outlawed slavery, while failing miserably in the 1850s, were resurrected in other forms by the post-Civil War and twentieth-century women's and civil rights movements. Those movements are discussed by Ellen DuBois and Anne Braden in this section and Rhonda Copelon, Randall Kennedy, and Margaret Burnham in the next.

Ellen DuBois then looks at the radical women's movement of the mid-nineteenth century. These women, like some of the Abolitionists, sought to develop a vision of equality based not on explicit constitutional phrases, but on the broad concepts of liberty and privilege, and on immunities that are contained within the Constitution. Although unsuccessful, their struggle was again taken up by the women's movement of the 1960s, as Rhonda Copelon describes in Part 4.

The divergent views of the Constitution described by Cover and Kaplan were also present in the Communist Party. Paul Mishler analyzes the party's changing views from the 1920s, to the Popular Front period of the 1930s, to the Cold War struggles of the 1950s. In each period, there was a tension between the need to use constitutional symbols and rights and the belief that the Constitution was a bulwark of private property. By the 1950s, however, that tension seems to have been resolved in favor of the former.

Finally, Anne Braden looks at the use that the civil rights movement made of the Constitution as a symbol. The movement recognized that, as Braden puts it, the "words of the Constitution don't really guarantee human rights"; yet it "continued to inspire action" and was used as "an organizing tool." Once again, her essay shows the contradictions involved in the progressive use of the Constitution: while in the 1950s the First Amendment was viewed as the key instrument for the movement, in the 1980s it is being used to protect the Ku Klux Klan's right to march, a development Braden finds distressing. Braden's article should be read in conjunction with Burnham's essay in Part 4 and Williams' theoretical essay in Part 1.

THE ORIGINS OF THE CONSTITUTION:
Thoughts on a Marxist Paradigm

Lawrence Kaplan

Because they believed that history tended to repeat itself, the Founding Fathers might not have been surprised by the way in which historical assessments of their efforts have passed through predictable cycles. With the notable exception of the pre-Civil War abolitionists, most nineteenth-century commentators imagined the Constitution to have been divinely inspired or, at the least, to have been the logical outcome of Nordic superiority. The prevailing view was best summed up by William Gladstone: "The most wonderful work ever struck off at a given time by the hand and purpose of man." Because mainstream commentators had placed the Constitution so high on a pedestal, the reform mentality of the Progressive era had little difficulty bringing it back to earth.

The first, and to this day the most prominent, critique of the framing of the Constitution was undertaken during the first two decades of the twentieth century. The best-known historian of this period, Charles A. Beard, not only impugned the motives of Washington, Hamilton, Madison, and others, but his economic interpretation of the Constitution presented it as an antidemocratic document. So persuasive was this debunking that, despite the outrage of genteel opinion, it became pervasive. By 1936, thirty-seven out of forty-two college textbooks had accepted Beard's economic interpretation.[1]

With the advent of the Cold War and McCarthyism, however, consensus historiography took over the groves of academe, swinging the pendulum back again. From the 1950s up until today, an idealistic treatment has returned with a force that even goes beyond the hagiolatry of the nineteenth century. The latest rendering, still virtually unchallenged, sees the Founders as self-sacrificing civic humanists whose commitment to the public good places them on a higher pedestal than ever before. No wonder the Reagan administration's official ideology demands adherence to a mythological vision of the unchanging perfect creation of 1787.

Clearly what is needed is a return to a more realistic reading of the Constitution's origins, as a counterbalance to the patriotic fervor generated for the use of conservative politics in the present. While an effective socioeconomic interpretation would certainly be desirable, the low esteem with which the historical establishment now holds the Progressive school renders the task that much more difficult. And while we have, from time to time, had variations on the theme first developed by Beard in his *Economic Interpretation of the Constitution of the United States* (1913) we have never had a detailed class analysis. In other words, what is badly needed is an independent Marxist treatment of these important historical events which goes beyond the limitations of the Progressive view.

The United States is unique as a capitalist country in that it has a rather weak Marxist historical tradition. A chief reason for this exceptionalism is the lack of a strong socialist or left-wing labor movement to give institutional encouragement to such an undertaking, although the role of the reoccurring rampages of political repression which regularly depopulate the universities of their leftist faculties must also be considered. But this is not the whole story. For the most part, U.S. radicals in this century have allowed themselves to be absorbed by Progressive historiography, thereby adhering to a version of the past not truly Marxist. In the process they have compromised themselves and lost their independent identity. Thus when, in the 1950s, a new generation of conservative scholars began finding glaring loopholes in Beard's methodology, leftists shared in the discredit. Now quite outside the consensus, Marxists have yet to make a significant contribution to this generation's understanding of the Constitution's origins.

To remedy this situation it would help to understand what it was that attracted people on the left to the Progressive approach. Beginning around the turn of the century and lasting until the onset of

World War I, the Progressive movement sought to place certain restrictions on the unbridled corporate capitalism unleashed after the Civil War. Along with upper-middle-class reformers, a new group of intellectuals emerged that was willing to confront the changing realities of U.S. political and economic life.[2] Although believing in the viability of representative government and private enterprise, they recognized that reforms were necessary if "the promise of American life" was to be realized once again. Abhorring revolution more than any other development, these bourgeois reformers had no identification with the working classes; nor did they advocate a socialist solution for the ills of society. Their utopia, for the most part, was to be found in the past: they offered a solution to the evils of modern capitalism that was both naive and outside the Marxist tradition.

Although the Progressive outlook took various forms, some of them contradictory, an important common ingredient was the development of a critical intelligence, one that rejected formalistic eternal truths. For example, legal realists attacked the notion that law evolved in accordance with a formal logical pattern and was therefore essentially an abstract discipline. A new school of sociological jurisprudence developed whose purpose was to demonstrate how laws were interrelated with social and economic experience, and how legal change had to be explained historically. Law, according to a moderate reformer like Oliver Wendell Holmes, was produced as part of the history of a nation and reflected the biases of each succeeding generation.

The Progressive historians were impressed by the new approach to law and tried to incorporate some of its concepts into their own work. Thus Charles Beard embodied these principles of sociological jurisprudence when he came to write his great work on the Constitution. He too rejected the conservative belief that laws could be abstractly understood apart from the social process. For him, the Constitution was a social document reflecting the realities of the postrevolutionary war era. In a manner characteristic of the muckraking style of his day, Beard destroyed the hallowed view put forth by defenders of the status quo that the Constitution emanated from the whole people.

What particularly endeared Beard to the radicals was his discrediting of the timeless, idealized version of laws and the flawless Constitution that had been used by the courts to cripple labor unions and to prevent the enactment of even minimal social welfare legislation.

Rarely has such an irreverant critique of "established truths" received such wide circulation. For this achievement alone the left should be eternally grateful to Beard.

Beard, along with Frederick Jackson Turner, was one of the first major U.S. historians to use a materialist interpretation. While he disassociated himself from any affinity with the subversive Marx (claiming somewhat disingenuously that the Founding Fathers were his inspiration—a great sacrilege), few were deceived. And to the extent that he used an economic framework, Beard was of course influenced by Marxian thought. For example, in his presentation the significant property holders—i.e., the rich—seized the initiative at the expense of their less well endowed fellow countrymen. In reshaping laws and institutions to their own advantage, they brought U.S. politics into line with the realities of economic life. With the new Constitution, the upper classes possessed a government that served their special interests. Aggressively protecting private property from the potential leveling propensities of the poor, the document was designed to ensure that the rich and well born could continue to augment their fortunes without having to worry about the threat to wealth which the eighteenth century associated with majority rule. Beard correctly saw how the Founders opposed democracy on the ground that it interfered with their privileged position in society. The Constitution was therefore an economic document, bringing distinct economic advantages to those who called the Philadelphia Convention and who then ensured the passage of the finished product.

By challenging the conservative version of the past, Beard struck a blow for radicalism in his own day. His picture of the 1780s resembled the reformers' version of their present, whether they were Populist or Progressive. For was the United States at the turn of the twentieth century not dominated by an exploiting plutocracy, similar in form to the privileged elements of the postrevolutionary era? No wonder the establishment found Beard's theories particularly threatening. And no wonder the left welcomed him as one of their own.

Unfortunately, however, there were serious limitations to the Progressives' world view, and these hindered Beard's perceptions and caused problems with his methodology. Reformers at the start of this century, whether Populist farmers or middle-class Progressives, recognized that an idealized democracy was being destroyed by the machinations of monopoly capitalism. Pernicious trusts were eliminating family farmers and small businessmen through unfair competition. At the same time, the monopolists were using their great wealth to manipulate the political system, corrupting it and thereby eliminating the noble goals of U.S. life. Reform-minded historians tended to project this contemporary scene onto the past, believing that the story of rich capitalists exploiting the poor and defiling democracy had been repeated over and over throughout much of U.S. history. From their perspective, the small farmers, who were in the majority, furthered democratic rule, while the rich preferred elite governments providing special advantages for the few. Thus, the past was a battleground of agrarians against capitalists, with the good democratic farmers continually being thwarted.[3]

Though one can almost always find a trace of the present in the past—which accounts in part for our fascination with previous eras—anachronistic history is, by definition, bad history. To take one example: the Progressive historians have viewed the Federalists (supporters of the Constitution) as the bad elitists and the Anti-federalists (opponents of the Constitution) as the good democrats. But this is clearly an oversimplification, for most of the opposition to the Constitution in 1787 and 1788 took the form of doubts, derived from Montesquieu, as to whether democracy would ever be viable in an area as large as the thirteen states. As a result, one of the main criticisms made by those who opposed ratification was that the new government would not have sufficient checks and balances—the same device decried by Progressive critiques of the Constitution because it hindered direct democracy.[4] Furthermore, many of the Anti-federalist spokesmen, like George Clinton, Melancton Smith, James Winthrop, and numerous others, had strong fears concerning government by majorities. The Anti-federalists never called for an extension of the suffrage; nor did they criticize the lack of direct election for Senators and Presidents, two of the most undemocratic features of the new government.

One variation on the Progressive theme was the view that the framing of the Constitution served as a counterrevolution, a conservative *coup d'état* that significantly reduced the level of democracy in the United States. From this perspective, following the idea of Carl Becker that the Revolution had to do with increasing self-rule at home while at the same time achieving independence, the high point of democratic government was said to have occurred under the

Articles of Confederation.[5] This first national constitution gave ultimate power to the individual states and kept the central government weak. Since the Progressives tended to believe that local control, with direct citizen participation, entailed a greater measure of democracy, any movement to a more centralized structure was viewed as reactionary. It is interesting once again to observe how twentieth-century Populist and Progressive political views resonated with those of the Anti-federalists during the late eighteenth century, a further example of how these historians fell into anachronistic traps.

Even in recent years historians influenced by the Progressive school have continued to idealize the period of the Articles of Confederation. Merrill Jensen, writing in the Progressive tradition, has produced numerous tomes praising the democratic nature of politics during the 1780s. In *The New Nation* (1950), he also tried to prove that the economy and the government at this time functioned reasonably well, making unnecessary any such drastic change as a new constitution. While Jensen did force the revision of the old image of "the critical period," the notion of a superior form of democracy during this time remains highly questionable.

Assuming that an early and pure form of bourgeois democracy did in fact exist, what great advantages accrued to the masses? Given the general ineffectiveness of the electoral process for serving majoritarian needs, we should be a bit skeptical when historians sing the praises of such developments as the final goal of mass politics. As proof for their thesis, Progressive historians pointed to the various "stay laws" helping debtors, as well as the printing of paper money, i.e., inflation. The latter happened to be one of the main Populist solutions to the farmers' plight in the 1890s, as naive an expedient then as it was in the 1780s. Moreover, it is well known that the biggest debtors were the large plantation owners in the South, many of whom favored a federal constitution. It is incorrect to assume that only the poor farmers clamored for inflation, because it has been established that there were numerous upper-class advocates of paper money who also supported the new Constitution.[6] Once again, the orientation of the modern reformers did not apply in the 1780s.

What democratic changes were enacted during the aftermath of the Revolution? Merrill Jensen would have stressed the advantages of decentralized government. This is a questionable theoretical assumption that can be debated in an abstract fashion. But if we look at the realities of elite rule in the thirteen states, it is hard to find many instances in which the old ruling groups had actually lost control. In those cases where they did, the loss was only temporary. Separation of powers, denounced as undemocratic, existed in all but two of the states under the Articles. Executive independence may have been diminished, but eleven states continued the practice of two-house legislatures.

Only five of the states instituted any kind of suffrage reform, with one—Massachusetts—actually becoming more restrictive in this regard. In those states, such as Pennsylvania, where tax-paying qualifications were exchanged for property requirements, a larger number of voters obtained the right to vote. Yet no state at this time divorced property from voting. In New York there was little change in the percentage of adult white males who could vote for assembly-men, while only about 33 percent could vote for senators and governor. In many of the states, close to one-half of the adult white male population could not even vote for the members of the lower house. Property tests for office-holding continued throughout the entire period during which the Articles remained in effect. Moreover, one must take into consideration the difficulties involved in trying to vote, such as having to travel huge distances, or the open ballot, which served to limit a poor voter's autonomy.

Even if the ballot had been widespread during the Confederation period, we cannot assume that the lower classes automatically cast their votes for candidates from their own background. To do so ignores the deferential character of eighteenth-century society, and the tendency to elect one's betters persisted throughout the period. A strong and pervasive tradition of deference, existing so overtly in Virginia, had its counterpart in many of the thirteen states and remained the rule, especially in agrarian communities. Thus we cannot expect completely independent behavior from the small farmers, at least not before the reforms of the Jackson period half a century later.

Another assumption that the Progressive school tended to make is that the period of the Revolution witnessed expanding lower class consciousness. But we know that this was not true, because the artisans in the towns and cities had little in common with farmers from the interior. It is quite clear that townspeople, both rich and not so rich, supported the federal constitution, while the small farmers were divided in their views. This is hardly strong evidence of class solidarity.

Another historian working in the Progressive tradition, Jackson Taylor Main, has argued that the Revolution democratized the state legislatures.[7] This point must be qualified, however, because it cannot always be assumed that inexperienced representatives necessarily followed their class interests, especially at an early stage of bourgeois democracy. Whether as a result of individual ambition, considerations of status, or deference to their betters, lower class assemblymen might very well have followed the lead of long-established leaders. The disappointing performance of social democratic parliamentarians in the twentieth century provides a sobering caveat against placing too strong a reliance on the personal integrity of individual representatives.

Shays' Rebellion of late 1786 is an instructive case in point regarding the limitations of viewing the period of the Articles as one in which the lower class majority possessed significant political power. In this protest movement, the small farmers in western Massachusetts, never very formidable or radical despite the great fears of the Federalists, employed illegal action to redress their grievances. These steps were directed against the state courts, which threatened to take away their farms for nonpayment of debts. In other words, the rebels wished to protect their small private holdings from the measures taken by the Massachusetts legislature, whose policies affected them detrimentally. The severity with which the state put down the rebellion revealed its lack of sympathy for the plight of these people. In addition, the Anti-federalist governor of New York, George Clinton, personally traveled with the three state militia companies he had summoned to help contain the uprising, providing concrete proof that Anti-federalists opposed the rebellion as well.[8]

The fact that the rebellion occurred at all, and the hostility it called forth from both state government officials and from respectable circles, Anti-federalists as well as Federalists, calls into question the view that the period of the Articles was one in which the small farmers controlled the legislatures. Whatever strengths it may have had, it is hard to argue that government in this country under the Articles was ideally democratic, i.e., that it truly represented the mass of Americans, who were the small farmers.

Moreover, the nature of the central government under the Articles was no more democratic than under the new constitution. The Constitution at least had direct elections for the lower house, whose members thus represented the population rather than the states. The single legislative body under the Articles had one voting delegate from each state, generally chosen indirectly by the legislature. Nine states out of thirteen had to approve matters of importance, rather than a simple majority. And it took the entire thirteen states to ratify amendments, a much more difficult process than the admittedly cumbersome arrangement created in 1787. Aside from Jefferson's Northwest Ordinance of 1784, it is difficult to point to any democratically inspired piece of legislation that came out of the national Congress under the Articles. The Congress never came close to emancipating the slaves or even placing a limit on the slave trade; nor was anything ever done about the plight of the most exploited whites, the indentured servants. In fact, if we look at key government officials, it is hard to find their points of contact with the majority of the population. When Robert Morris, the arch-conservative director of finances, was finally replaced in the mid-1780s, his successors tended to be financial speculators, including William Duer of New York. Both Foreign Affairs Secretary John Jay and Secretary of War Henry Knox were conservatives who were suspicious of democracy.

It should now be evident that the Progressive construction of a democratic United States under the Articles of Confederation was greatly exaggerated. If this is the case, then the movement toward a more centralized government, even if the discussion is confined to the political sphere, cannot be considered reactionary. For while the federal Constitution, with its elaborate system of checks and balances, served to curtail majority rule, its difference from its predecessor in this regard was only one of degree. This is not to suggest that the Founding Fathers became great friends of the masses—quite the opposite. But they were hardly worse than the Anti-federalist elite in their disdain for majority government, state or federal. It is also of note that two of the best-known democratic theorists of the day, Thomas Paine and Thomas Jefferson, both gave the Constitution their qualified support.

Because it seemed to threaten the security of property and contracts, Shays' Rebellion did affect conservative opinion, serving as the major impetus for a growing willingness to strengthen the central government. Many historians point to this event as a major catalyst in bringing about the success of the Philadelphia convention. Although the state of Massachusetts crushed the rebellion without difficulty, the Founders feared that similar types of upheavals would occur with increasing frequency in the future, not simply because democratic state legislatures would encourage them but because weak governments would be unable to put them down. From their perspective, the hapless central authority under the Articles could not be depended upon to perform this essential task. When the Federalists criticized the status quo prior to the Constitution for being too democratic, they meant that not enough restraint was brought to bear upon the masses, whom they greatly distrusted. As elitists, they worried that democratically elected legislators might be unwilling to act firmly against their volatile social equals. Following this line of reasoning, an effective central government, with ample resources at its disposal, would be better equipped to handle social unrest, in this manner providing the security required by substantial holders of property.

Beard recognized that the Founders dreaded all kinds of rebellion, including those emanating from the slave population in the South. But he believed that they had an even more compelling motive for establishing a strong government. According to Beard, the Framers harbored a deep dark secret which placed them in a special category, separating them from their Anti-federalist counterparts. For after making a careful study of Treasury Department records, he reached the conclusion that the members of the Convention stood to gain monetarily immediately after the new Constitution came into being. Here was his most shocking revelation, because it exposed these men as cynical manipulators of the national trust. In chapter 5, "The Economic Interests of the Members of the Convention," Beard used an innovative biographical approach to conclude that "the overwhelming majority of members, at least five-sixths, were immediately, directly, and personally interested in the outcome of their labors at Philadelphia, and were to a greater or less extent economic beneficiaries from the adoption of the Constitution." Specifically, these Founders held public securities, which stood to appreciate in value as soon as the new government came into being. In other words, many of them would very shortly make a fortune from their supposedly noble efforts.

Providing detailed information about individual members of the Convention proved to be a brilliant conceptual breakthrough, anticipating the much-praised work of Sir Lewis Namier by about a decade. Here was Beard at his most iconoclastic. For radicals, the enormous pleasure derived from watching the sacrosanct Framers being discredited cannot be minimized in explaining the appeal of the argument. However, Beard's use of data was based upon a presumption that had been encouraged by the Progressives' obsession with discovering underlying realities, especially regarding government and laws. Furthermore, his basic interpretation relied exclusively upon economic factors. He argued that people were motivated by economic self-interest, which overrode any other consideration. As numerous critics have pointed out, in many of his formulations Beard was an economic determinist.

This fundamental assumption regarding human behavior, while it was a useful tool for making sense of U.S. political life around the turn of the twentieth century, proved to be the weakest feature of Beard's work. Not only did exclusive causality lead to a philosophical fallacy exposed centuries ago by David Hume, but it assumed that we can achieve certainty when trying to understand people's "true" motivations. Modern-day social scientists, one would think, would be somewhat more modest in issuing claims of certainty in this regard.

The predictable attempts to disprove Beard began immediately after the publication of his book. Nevertheless, Progressive historical interpretations remained widely held until the 1950s. It was then, in the Eisenhower years, that the age of consensus history set in, ruling out conflict from the U.S. saga and replacing it with middle-class homogenization. The formulation that most Americans have always been property holders imbued with a liberal capitalistic ethic, maintaining a sincere belief in the dream of economic success, characterized the dominant school of U.S. historical writing during this time.[9] Obviously, there was little room in such an ahistorical interpretation for a Beard, let alone for the Marxists, many of whom were finding academic employment scarce during these years.

In the past three decades, however, most of the former consensus shibboleths about a middle-class, property-holding majority ruling the United States in the postrevolutionary period have been relegated to the dustbin. If anything, Beard's picture of a class society has held up much better, even by those mainstream scholars who still do social history. But his view that specific economic interests divided over the Constitution has been seriously challenged, while his notion of the decisive role played by public securities has been totally demolished.

Despite some methodological shortcomings, the most devastating criticism of Beard was made by Forest McDonald in *We the People,* published in 1958. McDonald, with access to considerably more documentation than Beard had had, actually tried to use an alternative economic approach. Yet by the time he completed his study, he decided that it was impossible to understand the framing of the Constitution as the result of any single factor, including an economic one. And after a careful survey of the ratification process in all thirteen states, he also concluded that there was so much diversity on the local level that it was impossible to explain all the separate ingredients connected with ratification using a monocausal theory.

By examining Beard's major findings at great length, in a book longer than the original, McDonald significantly challenged many of his predecessor's most important conclusions. Whereas Beard had seen the members of the Constitutional Convention as coming from the same economic group—merchants, creditors, holders of public securities—McDonald found diversity. A sizable number had supported debt-relief legislation in their states, while many of the delegates who "were among the largest holders of securities" actually opposed the new constitution. In the process of evaluating the ratification process, McDonald demonstrated that there was no significant difference between large property holders and poor farmers in terms of how they voted. According to him, "men holding the same kinds of property were equally divided on the matter of adoption or rejection." Robert Thomas had previously demonstrated that Virginia slaveowners could be found on both sides of the debate over the Constitution,[10] and McDonald arrived at the same conclusion. All these points scored against Beard undermined any thesis that saw the Constitution as a struggle between diverse interest groups or classes.

It did not take consensus historians long to delight in McDonald's demolition job. The distinctly cynical rendering of the Framers, so dear to the heart of the Progressives, was quickly put to rest, as was the simplistic, singleminded economic interpretation of events and motivation. *We the People* seemed to cry out for constitutional studies that would focus on noneconomic phenomena, and the scholars of the day rushed to take up the banner. Before long they began producing studies that emphasized the ideological predispositions of the *dramatis personae*. Intellectual approaches became the rule. And if, occasionally, one of these practitioners slipped into a simplistic, monocausal explanation for key events of the period—in this case singling out ideas—this did not prevent him from winning the highest scholarly prizes for his efforts.[11]

Thus for almost thirty years intellectual history, with different emphases, has dominated the field of constitutional studies.[12] Many of these works stress the autonomous role of ideas, removing them totally from the society producing them. Very little attention has been devoted to the social and economic context which encouraged certain political formulations. Nor have most of the scholars associated with this approach asked themselves how different classes responded to particular ideologies. For example, those who see James Madison as a dedicated public servant who wished to help create a nation of like-minded citizens never ask what groups in society found his formulations congenial. Perhaps it would be salutory for these historians to examine Marx's concept of the autonomous state, which satisfies class needs in periods of transition. For a Marxist, this approach seems especially applicable to the problematic and insecure decade of the 1780s, a time when class relationships were remarkably fluid. Indeed, it is fascinating to view Madison's Federalist writings with such a hypothesis in mind. Yet this is just one of a number of possible approaches using a Marxist perspective, any one of which would lead to a more balanced, multileveled picture of the Revolutionary era than is currently being produced by the intellectual school.

In retrospect, it is clear that the greatest lacuna in the research of the Progressive historians when considering the origins of the Constitution was the failure to recognize the significance of the slave question. In this regard, they were consistent with most of the other reformers of the Progressive era, who either ignored the civil rights issue or, worse, shared the racist attitudes of the general population. This bias led them to neglect slavery, one of the key issues of the Convention. Indeed, if we can believe the authoritative testimony of James Madison, it was the central area of discord.[13] Playing down the disagreements pertaining to the size of the states, Madison argued that "the great danger to our general government is the great southern and northern interest of the continent, being opposed to each other. Look to the votes in congress, and most of them stand divided by the geography of the country, not according to the size of the states."

The Progressives, as well as most historians of the Convention, have nevertheless stressed the compromise made between large and small states. In doing so they have overlooked what the participants themselves recognized. Rufus King of Massachusetts later wrote how the three-fifths clause regarding the computation of the number of slaves "was, at the time, believed to be a great [concession] and has proved to have been the greatest which was made to secure the adoption of the constitution."[14] Despite their keen desire to reveal special interest behavior on the part of the Framers, the Progressives ignored what turned out to be the most cynical of arrangements: southern representatives agreed to support a commerce clause if northern delegates would protect the continuation, for twenty years, of the slave trade. Thrown into the bargain was a prohibition on an export tax, which the commodity-producing South strongly opposed. South Carolina, which at first called for a two-thirds majority for any legislation of a commercial nature, led the way in voting for a simple majority. It did so because those states dependent upon servile labor had gained enormously in other areas. As delegate Charles Cotesworth Pinckney assured the South Carolina House of Representatives, "We have made the best terms for the security of this species of property it was in our power to make."

In his important article on the centrality of the slave issue, Paul Finkelman summed up just how much the slave states had benefited:

> Through the three-fifths clause they gained extra representation in Congress. Through the electoral college their votes for president were far more potent than the votes of northerners. The prohibition on export taxes favored the products of slave labor. The slave trade clause guaranteed them federal aid if they should need it to suppress a slave rebellion. The limited nature of federal power and the cumbersome amendment process guaranteed that, as long as they remained in the Union, their system of labor and race relations would remain free from national interference.[15]

If we add the Constitution's fugitive slave clause, it is clear that northern interests were willing to carry out the dirtiest of deals to accomplish their goal of a national union. Obviously their southern white counterparts did rather well in the bargaining, much of which took place behind closed doors, off the convention floor.

We can only conjecture about why Progressive historians disregarded these examples of opportunism among the Founding Fathers. Surely an awareness of such cynical dealings lowers them in our estimation. But that may be the point. The "educated" population of the Progressive era lacked real compassion for the plight of blacks, and the entire issue of the North-South compromises which perpetuated and even strengthened slavery failed to capture their interest.

Historians of the 1950s also omitted the slavery issue from their treatment of the Constitution, in part because they wished to show how harmony reigned supreme throughout our past.[16] It was not until the civil rights movement of the 1960s and the advent of the New Left, with its emphasis on history from the bottom up, that radical scholars began to move beyond the Progressive interpretation. The outstanding contribution to our appreciation of slavery's relevance to the Constitution was made by Staughton Lynd. A man of great social conscience, he reminded us of the abolitionists' justifiable scorn for this "covenant with death and an agreement with hell," as Garrison phrased it. Lynd shared the fate of his Progressive forebear, Beard, in having to leave the academic world. Nevertheless, by putting the slave compromises onto center stage, he made it impossible for any Left treatment of the subject to ignore this issue.

The now dominant intellectual school, however, continues to pretend that slavery did not exist. The social amnesia that permitted the well-intended Founding Fathers to believe they were creating a republic of virtue, where individual interests would be sacrificed for the greater good, is being repeated by a host of our most prestigious academics. How, we may inquire, can the maintenance of public and private virtue remain consistent with sordid compromises designed to perpetuate "the peculiar institution"? The current crop of historians, who emphasize the self-sacrifice of the Founders, represent the polar opposite of the Progressives. In certain ways they have overcompensated for the one-sidedness of the Beardian focus. What is needed is a more balanced approach. Many flexible Marxists, especially those influenced by Antonio Gramsci, are now willing to attribute an independent role to the superstructure. Gramsci's concept of hegemony, which assigns considerable importance to cultural phenomena, has proven to be a valuable tool in understanding twentieth-century societies. It has also been a boon to Marxist historians, who have been able to treat ideas and culture as independent variables.

In 1890, Frederick Engels dissociated both himself and Marx from simplistic economic determinism, but the allegation, repeated often enough, permitted bourgeois critics to dismiss Marxism as a single-cause philosophy. The association of U.S. Marxists with Beard and his economic determinism proved to be unfortunate indeed, for it gave credence to the charge that they were unimaginative materialists whose thoughts on historical topics need not be taken seriously.

Those Marxists who are not rigid determinists can use the concept of hegemony as a tool to integrate intellectual history into an appropriate social and economic framework. To do this we must go beyond a narrow analysis of interest-group politics. Relying too heavily on the scrutiny of individual professions or of the types of property held by individual members of a convention may actually obfuscate the larger significance of events. Beard believed that by producing the economic biographies of the participants at the Convention he could grasp the ultimate implication of their finished product. But this perception, like so much else in his work, was based upon the faulty assumption of simple economic causality and was therefore of limited application. The occupations and holdings of particular individuals at Philadelphia and at the state ratifying conventions does not explain the lasting effect their actions had on U.S. society and on the developing economy. The Founding Fathers, by creating the Constitution, served to render property secure, thereby providing free rein for the expansion of capitalist production. But while their debates and writings may have concentrated on the need to eliminate the pernicious influence of powerful interest groups and sought to imbue the people with the spirit of civic humanism, their political actions provided the prerequisites for the rapid expansion of capitalism and the social relationships that tend to go along with it. The new Constitution helped bourgeois property to flourish as never before. From an economic viewpoint, this represents the Founding Fathers' most important contribution.

Recent heirs of the Progressive tradition have begun to present the struggle over ratifying the Constitution in terms of "a contest between the commercial and the non-commercial elements in the population." Their work has directed our attention to the mercantile character of the Federalist world view. Certain contemporaries acknowledged this to be the case. At Philadelphia a delegate from Massachusetts, Nathaniel Gorham, informed his colleagues that "the Eastern States had no motive to Union but a commercial one."[17] It has been well established that the one group that unanimously supported the Constitution was the merchants. James Madison, commenting on those sectors that favored ratification, wrote, "The Sea Coast seems everywhere fond of it." But inland traders, especially those operating in river valleys, also favored the new government. Furthermore, recent studies by Joyce Appleby and Drew McCoy have demonstrated that both Jefferson and Madison appreciated the ways in which a unified country would maximize the profits of commercial agriculture. Southern elites encouraged westward expansion and were particularly sensitive to measures limiting navigation on the Mississippi. It is quite clear that enterprising agrarians shared the sentiments of urban capitalists, both groups recognizing the benefits that would accrue from a national state.

Despite their fascination with economic causality, the Progressives retained a firm interest in the political history of the Revolutionary era. Holding up for praise a paradigm of bourgeois democracy, they believed that majority rule was both the goal and the consequence of the Revolution. And in their minds, democracy was undermined mainly by the actions of Founding Fathers. This was to a certain extent true, but the Progressives made the mistake of confusing means and ends. The extension of self-rule as a consequence of the break with England obviously did occur, but within clearly circumscribed limits. While giving sections of the population a greater sense of participation, the ruling class favored a republicanism that entailed government by property holders, with established elites in most instances still wielding effective political power. A democratic rhetoric, plus a sense that they were involved, however indirectly, in the governing process, gained mass support so that the war could be won.

Yet in reality all the discussion of liberty prior to the Revolution reflected the main concern of ruling groups. The struggle that took place with England reflected their obsession with making property secure. Historically, whenever possible the bourgeoisie prefers maximum freedom of operation, and does its best to avoid restraint and arbitrary control. In this regard, the federal Constitution fulfilled the aims of the War for Independence and gave the commercial classes, urban and rural, what they wanted most.

The new government also completed the transition toward a national union, a passage that had begun with the confrontation with England. Commercial capitalism functions best with a national market and under the auspices and protection of a centralized government. The institutions established under the Articles of Confederation must be considered temporary in nature, brought about by the exigencies of a war and highlighting the inexperience and jealousies of the various local elites. But the makeshift compromises that brought about the Articles could not provide the cohesion necessary for a developing capitalist country. Its government had no means of paying its debts; nor could it successfully raise taxes. There was no authority granted to a central body that would allow it to regulate commerce or deal effectively with foreign nations. Responsible leaders were all but unanimous in accepting the necessity for drastic reform. Nevertheless, it took the commercially oriented to recognize that if the United States were to develop and maximize its potential, a total revamping of the government was essential. Resisted by local elites, who were in many instances equally undemocratic, the Federalists seized the initiative, establishing the prerequisites for a U.S. empire.

Using this framework, the outlines of a new paradigm emerge. It was the Anti-federalists who were reactionary, for their policies would have retarded economic growth and might have kept the thirteen states as a kind of backwater, easily exploited by the great powers of the world. The Federalists, at least in regard to the future economic growth of the United States, had the broader vision. In the Marxist sense, the Founding Fathers, by intelligently furthering the interests of their class, can be seen as having played a progressive role in history. They were the modernizers. It would remain for subsequent generations to repair the tragic damage done by their opportunistic compromise with slavery.

Notes

1. Richard Hofstadter, "Beard and the Constitution: The History of an Idea," in *Charles Beard: An Appraisal,* ed. Howard Beale (rept. ed., New York, 1976).
2. Morton White, *Social Thought in America* (Boston, 1947).
3. See in this regard, Charles A. Beard and Mary R. Beard, *The Rise of American Civilization* (New York, 1927).
4. Cecelia M. Kenyon, ed., *The Antifederalists* (New York, 1966), especially the Introduction.
5. Carl Becker, *History of Political Parties in the Province of New York* (New York, 1909); Merrill Jensen, *The Articles of Confederation* (Madison, 1940).
6. Forest McDonald, *We the People* (Chicago, 1958).
7. Jackson Taylor Main, "Government by the People," *William and Mary Quarterly* (1966).
8. David P. Szatmary, *Shays' Rebellion* (Amherst, 1980).
9. See especially Louis Hartz, *The Liberal Tradition in America* (New York, 1955).
10. Robert E. Thomas, "The Virginia Convention of 1788," *Journal of Southern History* (1953).
11. Bernard Bailyn, *The Ideological Origins of the American Revolution* (Cambridge, Mass., 1967).
12. The best of this genre is Gordon S. Wood, *The Creation of the American Republic* (Williamsburg, Va., 1969).
13. See Ralph Ketcham, *James Madison: A Biography* (New York, 1971).
14. Cited in Staughton Lynd, *Class Conflict, Slavery, and the Constitution* (New York, 1967), chapter 7.
15. Paul Finkelman, "Slavery and the Constitutional Convention," in Richard Beeman et al., *Beyond Confederation* (Williamsburg, Va., 1987). I have relied on this valuable article for much of my formulation on slavery.
16. To be sure, Herbert Aptheker has long tried to call our attention to the crucial role played by slavery in various aspects of U.S. life; see especially his *American Negro Slave Revolts* (New York, 1943).
17. Cited in Robert Allen Rutland, *The Ordeal of the Constitution* (Norman, Okla., 1966); Jackson Taylor Main, *The Antifederalists* (Chicago, 1961).

THE FORMAL ASSUMPTIONS OF THE ANTISLAVERY FORCES

Robert Cover

After 1840 a significant part of all antislavery writing was devoted to analysis of the legal system of the United States and to its bearing on the problems of slavery.[1] There were lawyers of note among the Abolitionists, and the works of William Jay, James Birney, Charles Sumner, Salmon Chase, Robert Rantoul, or Richard Dana bear witness to the professional skill with which such arguments were shaped.[2] However, the story of Abolitionist legal theory by no means stops in the courtroom or with the speculations of established lawyers. Richard Hildreth's book *Despotism in America*, Harriet Beecher Stowe's *Key to Uncle Tom's Cabin*, Thoreau's essays "Civil Disobedience" and "Slavery in Massachusetts," Frederick Douglass's "Speech on the Meaning of the Fourth of July for the Negro," Theodore Weld's *Slavery as It Is* and *The Power of Congress over the District of Columbia*—to mention but a few—bespeak the pervasive concerns of the leaders of the antislavery movement with the legal structures of slavery.

Antislavery was never a unified movement. It is no wonder, therefore, to find a sharp split among different factions of the movement over an issue of such pervasive concern. In its approach to law, the antislavery movement split primarily because of differences over various formal problems in its relation to the legal establishment. The split was between the Garrisonians and a variety of opponents. On the one hand, the Garrisonians steadfastly preached and advocated scrupulous respect for the formalism of the legal system, and understood that formalism largely in the same terms as the leading judges and lawyers of the day. Their opponents, on the other hand, either urged disregard for the formalism of the law or advocated an unorthodox understanding of the nature of the law's formalism. These generalities must be spelled out in detail.[3]

The Garrisonians: Formalism Conceded

The Garrisonians, with Wendell Phillips their chief spokesman, stressed dichotomy between natural and positive law. They accepted the orthodox position that the law as it is and the law as it ought to be present two distinct spheres. Moreover, they agreed that the function of a judge, according to constitutional principles, is the application of positive law—the law as it is. Finally, this group of theorists also accepted as right the obligation of the judge to apply only positive law and to disregard natural law when in conflict with the law as it is. This obligation of judicial obedience was itself derived from natural law justifications of the state—social contract in various forms.

Since William Lloyd Garrison and his followers were above all moralists, it is not surprising to find them among the first to appreciate the consequences of the Constitution for moral choices; that is, they understood the moral weight of presumptive consent attendant on a largely democratic, constitutional compact. It was precisely because they appreciated the inference of moral obligation from constructive consent that they reached their radical prescriptions for action: disobedience, abstention from voting or office holding, and dis-union. Their line of analysis of law was, ironically, similar to that of the most troubled of our federal judiciary: McLean and Story. Wendell Phillips was the most articulate spokesman for the Garrisonian position on these issues, and it is to his work that reference will be made.[4] First, Phillips, like most of the judiciary, perceived the Constitution as, in critical part, a compromise over slavery, a compromise that could, in operation, lead to servitude for millions of human beings. Phillips pointed to five provisions as evidence of this view of the Constitution: the three-fifths clauses, which provided that for both representation and direct taxation a slave would count as three-fifths of a person; the limitation on the power of Congress to prohibit the "migration or importation" of slaves until 1808; the fugitive slave clause; the clause affording Congress the power to suppress insurrection; the clause insuring, upon application from a state, federal assistance in the suppression of domestic violence. Despite the fact that the word slave is circumlocuted everywhere in the Constitution, Garrison and Phillips, no less than Story, argued forcefully that the purpose of these provisions was to effectuate a bargain, the terms of which conferred legitimacy and a measure of protection for slavery. Story called the fugitive slave clause "a fundamental article, without the adoption of which the Union could not have been formed." And Phillips wholeheartedly agreed, denoting the five proslavery clauses as "the articles of the 'Compromise,' so much talked of between the North and South."[5] Indeed, Wendell Phillip's book, *The Constitution: A Pro-Slavery Compact,* consisted of extracts from the then recently published *Madison Papers* and from Elliot's reports of various state ratifying conventions demonstrating that the unabashed intent of the framers was to recognize and protect slavery.

A second point of basic agreement between the Garrisonians and the judiciary concerned the proper limits of the judicial function. Phillips argued that the law as it stood did not permit the judge to apply his own vision of natural law with respect to slavery. More important still, Phillips agreed that the law *should* not permit the judge to apply his own perception of natural law. For authority on the proposition that judges do not have the power, under existing law, to apply their own natural law, Phillips quotes at length Blackstone, Kent, Locke, Chitty, Mansfield, Coke, Scott, Marshall, Iredell, and Baldwin. Story himself could not have done better. As to the wisdom of this constraint, Phillips is eloquent. He fully recognized that the natural law of South Carolina was likely to prove different from his own. Because "nature" no longer spoke with a single voice, only the judge's conscience ultimately determined the source of right. He concluded by quoting Lord Camden: "The discretion of a Judge is the law of tyrants; . . . In the best, it is often times caprice—in the worst, it is every vice, folly and passion, to which human nature is liable."[6]

Finally, the Garrisonians would have agreed wholly with the judiciary that, by external moral criteria, it would be improper for a judge to use judicial power in a manner contrary to agreed rules. The external moral values that Phillips brings to bear are those of good faith and trust. Phillips states that the office holder, at least in a government in which there is some measure of participation, stands in a contractual relationship to those who confer on him his power. To accept power on certain conditions and then fail to live up to the conditions is to deceive those to whom one stands as a sort of fiduciary and to subvert the values that are supposedly served by participatory government—a measure of responsibility to the people on the part of their representatives.[7]

At this point it should be clear that the premises and reasoning of the radical Garrisonians compel a full measure of acquiescence in the judicial refusal to apply natural law concerning slavery. It would, indeed, be impossible for McLean or anyone else to effectuate natural law with respect to slavery while still playing by the rules that Phillips acknowledged were and ought to be in force. Moreover, Phillips also agreed that the Constitution, which by those limits had to be enforced, was in conflict with natural law on the issue of slavery. Phillips did not shrink from the conclusion: "Their only 'paramount obligation,' as judges, is to do what they agreed to do when they were made judges, or quit the bench."[8]

Since the logic of moral discourse leads to an unacceptable result if the choice point is to be between applying natural law and the Constitution, it was necessary to relocate the point of moral choice. If choice is made at the point of participation or abstention, there are no considerations of a formal character or of role limitation that inhibit a "pure" choice on the basis of which alternative more nearly conforms to moral desiderata.

In the second edition of *The Constitution: A Pro-Slavery Compact*, Phillips included a letter of resignation from an obscure Massachusetts justice of the peace to drive home the logic of resignation. This justice, Francis Jackson, wrote, "The oath to support the Constitution of the United States is a solemn promise to do that which is a violation of the natural rights of man, and a sin in the sight of God. . . . I withdraw all profession of allegiance to it [the Constitution], and all my voluntary effort to sustain it."[9]

The Phillips-Garrison view of judicial obligation was not a disinterested one. The struggle for dominance in the antislavery movement was in part between those, like Garrison, who refused to participate in the processes of government and those who wanted a political, even electoral, movement. The jurisprudence of Wendell Phillips served the end of justifying his own faction's position and of impugning the opposition as both morally and legally obtuse. But, of course, the very fact that Phillips found himself on the abstentionist side was in part the result of an intellectual and temperamental preference for the clean logic of a pure moral choice. Such a choice is obscured by confusing the law as it is with the law as it ought to be:

> But alas, the ostrich does not get rid of her enemy by hiding her head in the sand. Slavery is not abolished, although we have persuaded ourselves that it has no right to exist. . . . The Constitution will never be amended by persuading men that it does not need amendment. National evils are only cured by holding men's eyes open, and forcing them to gaze on the hideous reality.[10]

Constitutional Utopians

While the legal theories of the Garrison-Phillips wing of abolitionism have attracted little attention except insofar as they confirmed the diagnosis of acute anti-institutionalism, their opponents in this internal antislavery debate have been seized upon by one dissenting wing of U.S. constitutional law scholarship as prophets of the Fourteenth Amendment and as evidence of the amendment's thrust toward racial equality. Reacting to the apologists for *Plessy* v. *Ferguson,* these dissenting scholars—men like Jacobus tenBroek and Howard Graham—discovered roots for their own constitutional aspirations in the visions of William Goodell, Lysander Spooner, Joel Tiffany, and Alvan Stewart.[11] Just as these scholars in the 1940s and early 1950s appealed to what the Constitution could become, to the highest of the principles that went into it, so their "discovered" progenitors had appealed beyond case law and history to a grand vision of society that they found *in potentia* in many of the phrases of the Constitution.

The argument of tenBroek and of Graham is that the Fourteenth Amendment and its language—"due process," "equal protection," and "privileges and immunities"—cannot be understood except in the context of three decades of abolitionist legal theory aspiring to an antislavery vision of the Constitution and using precisely these phrases in their theories. The "due process" language of the Fifth Amendment and the "privileges and immunities" language of Article

IV were viewed by these Abolitionists as potential sources of an antislavery constitution. Their reincorporation into the Fourteenth Amendment might therefore be best understood as an embodiment of the Abolitionist understanding of the words.

Whatever the merits of this Fourteenth Amendment argument, the ulterior motives of the tenBroek-Graham hypothesis distort somewhat the image of the antislavery constitutional utopians. For this handful of relatively unimportant antislavery thinkers had some meaning for their legal madness. And the meaning related more to theories of obligation than to the substance of the law.

By "constitutional utopians," I am not referring to the many lawyers and writers who appealed to a not-yet-accepted antislavery version of some constitutional issue. The utopians were reacting against such theorists. When Theodore Dwight Weld wrote that Congress had authority and a moral duty to end slavery in the District of Columbia, he appealed to a notion of congressional authority (if not of congressional morality) that was well within the accepted limits of the day.[12] When William Jay castigated the federal government's complicity in the crime of slavery, he did so by contrasting actual federal involvement in slavery with the constitutionally required minimal involvement. He also contrasted the gratuitous complicity with slavery with a vision of what the national government might permissibly do against slavery. Most of Jay's positions on congressional or executive power were well within the mainstream of legal thought of the day. Those few issues on which Jay advanced an unorthodox position were either unimportant or not related to the fundamental problems of distribution of power. On the critical issue of the states' rights to determine their own domestic institutions, Jay and his followers were orthodox in their understanding of the Constitution.[13] To accept William Jay's understanding of the Constitution was to confront the dilemma of conscience posed by Garrison and Phillips. How can one swear fidelity and undertake, by some affirmative act, the obligation of obeisance to a bargain condemning one's fellow men to servitude? True, Jay emphasized how the Constitution holds out the promise of dealing limited blows to slavery, through national legislative action against the trade and against slavery in all islands of national legislative competence. But the slave in Alabama was constitutionally forsaken.[14]

William Goodell, Alvan Stewart, Gerritt Smith, Joel Tiffany, and

most notable, Lysander Spooner, replied that the Constitution out-
laws slavery, even in Alabama.[15] The position that slavery itself was
unconstitutional was so extreme as to appear trivial. TenBroek and
Graham "rediscovered" these theorists because they used certain
phrases that presaged the Fourteenth Amendment. Yet their real
significance in the antislavery movement was the answer they
provided to the formal problems. They searched, not for a legal
theory, but for a way out of the Garrisonian argument with regard to
"obligation." The purpose of the argument was not to prove slavery
unconstitutional (whatever that means in a confessedly utopian
context) but to prove that antislavery men may become judges and
may use their power to free slaves.

Lysander Spooner's opus, *The Unconstitutionality of Slavery,* is
the most complete of the arguments for the utopians. Spooner makes
use of phrases like "due process" and "privileges and immunities" as
pegs on which to hang his theory. But the substance of his argument
is natural law. That substance was largely ignored by tenBroek.[16]
Spooner begins by forcefully asserting that no law in conflict with
natural law is valid and that judges have no obligation to enforce such
naturally invalid law. This natural law operates quite apart from
incorporation by any human constituent process.[17] In form, Spooner
moves on to assume *arguendo* the validity of positive law in conflict
with natural law and to derive the unconstitutionality of such laws by
reference to the U.S. Constitution and related sources alone; but, in
substance, the argument remains infused by the natural law point,
for he relies heavily on an interpretative mechanism that rejects any
construction save one in harmony with natural law.[18]

There is ingenuity in Spooner's work, but it is the haphazard
ingenuity of rule and phrase manipulation, ignoring the "method" of
the judge in any real sense. He rejects any argument based on the
appeal to history and the purposes of the framers; he rejects all
arguments based on the uninterrupted course of applications.[19]
Spooner's Constitution is amputated from any societal context. Garrison condemned it most succinctly: "The important thing is not the
words of the bargain, but the bargain itself."[20]

Alvan Stewart used Spooner's arguments and a host of others in his
challenge to the remnants of slavery in New Jersey. But this New
York maverick had his own unique legal theory, which declared
slavery to be a violation of the due process clause of the Fifth

Amendment. He argued that no slavery was constitutional unless it had come about by due process—presentment by a grand jury of twenty-three and unanimous conviction by a petit jury of twelve. His reading of the constitutional bargain was that the North had agreed to the clauses that seemed to recognize slavery in return for the South's promise that any slavery be due-process slavery. Stewart's argument is remarkable because it does not depend on a single reference to natural law or to a principle affording preference to interpretations that favor natural law. It is an argument founded wholly on constitutional text and requires nothing more than a suspension of reason concerning the origin, intent, and past interpretation of the clause.[21]

The preoccupation of the utopians with a consistent theory of the Constitution outlawing slavery was only one prong of the attack on the judge's dilemma of conscience. Lysander Spooner was willing to treat the problem *arguendo* as one of a judge who had sworn to uphold an *unjust* constitution, even though he believed the Constitution to be properly interpreted as a just, antislavery instrument. Spooner acknowledged that the dominant position seemed to be that such a judge should resign. But he thought the proper analogy was one of a man given a weapon on condition that he kill an innocent and helpless victim. In such a situation, Spooner argued, it is proper to make the promise, keep the weapon and use it, in violation of the condition, to defend rather than attack the victim. To give up the sword, to resign the judicial office, is "only a specimen of the honor that is said to prevail among thieves."[22] Spooner also argued that acceptance of the total invalidity of an oath of office to violate natural law would have a salutary effect on judges: "Judges and other public officers habitually appeal to the pretended obligation of their oaths, when about to perform some act of iniquity, for which they can find no other apology, and for which they feel obliged to offer some apology."[23] Spooner is acute in recognizing the appeal to the oath as an apology, but his prescription, though cutting against the notion of judicial fidelity to positive law, does not refute in any way the Phillips prescription of resignation. The only responsive point on the issue of whether a judge ought to resign is the intimation that it is a waste to refuse to use accessible power for a good purpose, whatever the basis of, or conditions upon, its acquisition.

On the level of theory, then, the issue had been joined by 1845.

The solution to the moral-formal dilemma was resignation, according to one school. According to the other, it was the judicial enforcement of natural law, preferably through a forced reading of positive law instruments, but if need be as an act of naked power. Neither of these solutions promised widespread acceptance by the men who sat on the bench. That practical obstacle had to be confronted by the attorneys who confronted these judges and sought relief from them.

Notes

Excerpted from Robert Cover, *Justice Accused: Antislavery and the Judicial Process* (New Haven, 1975), copyright © 1975 by Robert Cover; reprinted with the permission of Yale University Press.

1. The legal literature of antislavery is of several sorts. One category, not discussed here in any detail, is that of descriptions of slave codes and their administration. The purpose of these works was to use slave law as data, credible data, as to the realities of slavery. The first, and in many ways the best, of these works was George Stroud, *A Sketch of the Laws Relating to Slavery,* first published in Philadelphia in 1827 and reissued in 1856. The best known of this category of work was William Goodell, *The American Slave Code in Theory and Practise* (New York, 1853). Two works that did not concern themselves exclusively with the law of slavery have long sections using legal materials as data for depicting slavery: Theodore Dwight Weld, *American Slavery As It Is* (New York, 1839), a powerful and very influential work, and Harriet Beecher Stowe, *The Key to Uncle Tom's Cabin* (Boston, 1853), an attempt to document the general picture of slavery in the novel published the year before. A second category of antislavery legal work was that of legal arguments on relatively circumscribed issues. These position papers or briefs abound, and range in size, from newspaper columns to books. A few notable examples are: Theodore Dwight Weld, *The Powers of Congress over Slavery in the District of Columbia* (New York, 1838); [William Jay], *The Creole Case and Mr. Webster's Despatch* (New York, 1842); Samuel May, *The Fugitive Slave Law and Its Victims* (New York, 1856); American Antislavery Society, *Fugitive Slave Bill, Its History and Unconstitutionality* (New York, 1850). This last is but one of a number of pamphlets discussing the Fugitive Slave Act with regard to a particular case, in this instance that of James Hamlet. See also Robert Rantoul, "The Fugitive Slave Law," in Luther Hamilton, ed., *Memoirs, Speeches, and Writings of Robert Rantoul* (Boston, 1854). A third category of works on legal issues is the "Constitution and slavery" problem. This literature is discussed below.

   A fourth category, often connected to the third, is the literature on legal obligation and civil disobedience. I have discussed in the text only certain examples of that literature that (a) treat the issue of obligations of magistrates or jurors; (b) were reasonably widely read. Notable examples of works on disobedience that fail to meet the first condition are Henry David Thoreau, "Essay on Civil Disobedience" and "Slavery in Massachusetts," both in *Thoreau's Complete Works* (Boston and New York, 1929). There was also a rich harvest of sermons on obedience and disobedience, many of which are discussed or noted in Stanley Campbell, *The Slave Catchers* (Chapel Hill, 1970), in his discussions of public opinion. Relatively neglected have been the academic, philosophical religious works on obligations by such notables as Francis Wayland. See Edward Madden, *Civil Disobedience and Moral Law in Nineteenth Century American Philosophy* (Seattle, 1968), for an account of these men and their works.

Still another category was that of diatribes against legal institutions or judges for their evil, class-ridden oppression of the downtrodden. These works might use any of the sorts of arguments found in other categories as grist for their mill. Richard Hildreth is my favorite of these authors. Richard Hildreth, *Despotism in America* (Boston, 1854), and, by the same author, *Atrocious Judges: Lives of Judges Infamous as Tools of Tyrants and Instruments of Oppression* (New York, 1856). See my review of this last work in 68 *Columbia Law Review* 1003 (1968). Also in this category is the delightful Theodore Parker, *The Trial of Theodore Parker* (Boston, 1855). A final category of literature is that of reports and accounts of trials or arguments in particular cases. The category is too large for cataloguing here. Many such titles have appeared or will appear in notes in this work.

2. See William Jay, *Miscellaneous Writings on Slavery* (Boston, 1853); Salmon Portland Chase, *Speech in the Case of the Colored Woman Mathilda . . . March 11, 1837* (Cincinnati, 1837); Dwight Dumond, ed., *James Gillespie Birney Letter, 1831–1857* (Gloucester; 1966), pp. 646 ff. See also the argument of Charles Sumner in Roberts v. City of Boston, 59 Mass. (5 Cush.) 198 (1850); Argument of Robert Rantoul in *Sims's Case,* 61 Mass. (7 Cush.) 285 (1851), and before the commissioner in the same affair, see, J. Stone, reporter, *Trial of Thomas Sims on an Issue of Personal Liberty, on the claim of James Potter of Georgia, against Him, as an alleged Fugitive from service. Arguments of Robert Rantoul, Jr. and Charles G. Loring, with the Decision of George T. Curtis, Boston, April 7–11, 1851* (Boston, 1851). For Dana, see Dana, ed., *Speeches in Troubled Times;* see also his speeches in *Sims's Case,* noted above with respect to Rantoul. Other notable advocates included Samuel Sewall, Thaddeus Steven, John Jolliffe, John Parker Hale, Charles Ellis, and T. C. Ware. Politicians whose forensic skills were evident and used in the antislavery cause included Joshua Giddings, Benjamin Wade, and John Quincy Adams.

3. Two works especially useful for understanding the split in antislavery are Gilbert Barnes, *The Antislavery Impulse* (New York and London, 1933), and Aileen Kraditor, *Means and Ends in American Abolitionism* (New York, 1969). Always useful is Dwight Dumond, *Antislavery* (Ann Arbor, 1961).

4. The Garrisonian position was well developed in the pages of the *Liberator* before the publication of the three Phillips works discussed here. But Phillips's treatment is much better and more systematic than the give and take of the columns. Phillips's position is proclaimed in three excellent works: *The Constitution: A Pro-Slavery Compact* (Boston, 1844), which was a masterpiece of compilation of all then-available data on the intentions and opportunities of the framers of the U.S. Constitution with respect to slavery. The work makes use of the then recent publication of Madison's *Notes* and of *Elliot's Debates.* The compilation is persuasive as to the intent of the framers and ratifiers to afford slavery a measure of legitimacy and protection. A year later Phillips published *Can Abolitionists Vote or Take Office Under the United States Constitution?* (New York, 1845), which purported to derive the general abstentionist position from the nature of the Constitution and the obligation to refuse complicity with oppression. Still one year later, Phillips published *A Review of Lysander Spooner's Unconstitutionality of Slavery* (Boston, 1847) [hereafter cited as *Review*], which

not only destroyed Spooner's position, but argued persuasively for resignation by antislavery judges.

5. Phillips, *The Constitution*, pp. vi–vii.
6. Phillips, *A Review of Lysander Spooner's Unconstitutionality of Slavery*, p. 17. The avalanche of authorities is on pp. 18–25.
7. "God does nor require of any of his creatures to juggle their fellows out of the gift of power, and then use that power contrary to their promises, in order to serve humanity. That were to ask 'robbery for burnt offering.'" *Review*, p. 15.
8. Ibid.
9. Phillips, *The Constitution*, 3rd ed., pp. 171–81.
10. Phillips, *Review*, pp. 3–4.
11. Jacobus tenBroek, *Antislavery Origins of the Fourteenth Amendment*, republished as *Equal Under Law* (New York, 1965). H. Graham, "The Early Antislavery Background of the Fourteenth Amendment," 1950 *Wisconsin Law Review* 479 ff. and 610 ff. (1950). In a sense I proclaim the motives of tenBroek and Graham with little documentation though I believe they would embrace my description. tenBroek in his introduction to the new, enlarged edition of his work, praising Brown v. Board of Education, says:

> Equal protection is again emerging from its relative latency to strike down some these vestiges. . . . The work in the name of equality is far from done, perhaps never will be done. . . .
>
> . . . It was to explore the origins and nature of these goals . . . that this book was written (*Equal Under Law*, pp. 15, 26).

12. Theodore Dwight Weld, *The Power of Congress over Slavery in the District of Columbia* (New York, 1838).
13. William Jay, *Miscellaneous Writings on Slavery* (Boston, 1853). See Bayard Tuckerman, *William Jay and the Constitutional Movement for the Abolition of Slavery* (New York, 1893), which is less good on the *movement* than on Jay.
14. Jay, *Miscellaneous Writings*, pp. 207 ff.
15. William Goodell, *Views of American Constitutional Law in Its Bearing Upon American Slavery* (Utica, N.Y., 1844); Alvan Stewart, "A Constitutional Argument on the Subject of Slavery," reprinted in Appendix B of tenBroek, *Equal Under Law;* Joel Tiffany, *The Unconstitutionality of Slavery* (Cleveland, 1849); Lysander Spooner, *The Unconstitutionality of Slavery* (Boston, 1845). Some of this utopian thinking is mixed into the second and third editions of Richard Hildreth, *Despotism in America* (Boston, 1854). See also the argument of Gerritt Smith in *Trial of Henry Allen, U.S. Deputy Marshall, for Kidnapping with Arguments of Counsel and the Charge of . . .* (Syracuse, 1852).
16. tenBroek goes on at some length about the "imaginative" arguments of Goodell, Stewart, and Spooner. Actually, the manipulation of phrases was at all times justified because of the presumed necessity of harmonizing with natural law.
17. Lysander Spooner, *The Unconstitutionality of Slavery* (Boston, 1845), p. 14: " . . . it follows . . . that no law inconsistent with men's natural rights, can arise out of any contract or compact of government: that constitutional law, under any form of government, consists only of those principles of the written constitution that are consistent with natural law, and man's natural rights."
18. "I shall not insist upon the principle of the preceding chapter, that there can be no law contrary to natural right. . . . I shall only claim that in the interpretation it be observed. The most important of these rules . . . is the one that all language must be construed strictly in favor of natural right" (ibid., pp. 15–18).

19. Spooner, *Unconstitutionality of Slavery*, pp. 54–123.
20. As quoted in Kraditor, *Abolitionism*, pp. 195–96.
21. Stewart, *Constitutional Argument*.
22. Spooner, *Unconstitutionality of Slavery*, p. 152.
23. Ibid.

OUTGROWING THE COMPACT OF THE FATHERS:

Equal Rights, Woman Suffrage, and the United States Constitution, 1820–1878

Ellen Carol DuBois

Introduction

Many of the essays in this volume depict the U.S. Constitution as an historically contested arena. In particular, the history of constitutional demands by popular movements provides a counter to the exclusive focus, so beloved by the Reagan administration, on the words and intent of the framers. In the midst of our constitutional Bicentennial, it is especially important for historians to recall the radical constitutional tradition of equal rights that flourished as a part of nineteenth-century republican thought. Women's rights demands were an important aspect of this popular nineteenth-century republicanism. From its inception to the present, the women's rights movement has pursued rights not explicitly mentioned in the Constitution and sought to incorporate them into an expanded understanding of its meaning.

From one perspective, the conviction at the heart of radical republicanism, that an enlargement of "rights" would help create a more egalitarian society, reached its peak with the enactment—and its nadir with the judicial disposition—of the Reconstruction amendments. However, from a women's rights perspective, the radical republican heritage extends much further. Not only did the struggle for political equality for women reach into the twentieth century; but the drive for the Equal Rights Amendment, as well as intense contemporary debate about a whole other realm of rights—sexual and reproductive—keeps constitutional issues about the rights of women alive today.

In this paper on the nineteenth-century movement for women's rights, I have two concerns. One is to integrate women's rights with the other equal rights politics of the nineteenth century—Abolition/ black suffrage and labor reform—into a comprehensive history of radical republicanism. My other concern is to specify the place, and possibilities, of the politics of equal rights in women's history. Concepts of rights, individualism, and equality have had a distinct impact on the way that women have understood themselves and expressed their sense of their proper position in society.

The following overview of nineteenth-century women's rights has three parts. The first section, which covers the antebellum period, establishes that women's rights was linked to other radical equal rights traditions and was widely understood as an alternative to "separate spheres" notions of the subordinate place of women in the social order. With the passage of the Thirteenth Amendment, equal rights politics in general, and the women's rights movement in particular, entered a second, bolder phase and became a constitutional politics. During Reconstruction, the demand for woman suffrage flourished because it was the most forceful way of expressing— and the most powerful tool for achieving—the equality of women with men. At first, women's rights advocates demanded political rights for all without regard to sex or race. Once the Fourteenth and Fifteenth amendments had been ratified without woman suffrage, however, they began to argue for the equality not of individuals but of sexes. Thus began a long process by which ideas about the fundamental difference of women and men began to be subsumed within a woman's rights framework.

The termination of the amendment process in 1870 did not immediately signal the end of hopes for equal political rights for women, but rather heightened struggle over the meaning of the Constitution as amended. This is the subject of the third section. Determined to enforce their egalitarian vision of constitutional rights, women's rights women undertook direct political action. They also began to extend principles of equal rights into the whole realm of "personal rights," of rights over and to one's own body. Women's rights arguments figured significantly in important Supreme Court decisions about the meaning of the Reconstruction amendments. By the mid-1870s, equal rights interpretations of the Constitution had been defeated, and the women's rights movement itself began to move in less democratic, more conservative directions. But the possibility of equal rights politics for transforming women's place had not been exhausted, only temporarily stalled.

The Demand for Women's Political Equality, 1820–1860

The term "women's rights"—meaning the equality of women with men—predates the call for woman suffrage by several decades. Women's rights demands, especially those directed against men's economic power over their wives, were nurtured in the British Owenite movement and brought to the United States by Frances Wright. Wright, a leader in the Jacksonian workingmen's movement, was the first public figure in U.S. history to advocate women's rights. Her lead was followed in this country by Ernestine Rose, a Jewish immigrant from Poland, and by Robert Dale Owen, son of the Owenite movement's leader, Robert Owen. During the 1830s and early 1840s, Rose and Owen advocated a program of women's economic and marital—though not political—rights. They and their comrades lobbied, often successfully, for legal reforms in married women's economic position and for liberalized grounds for divorce, especially for women.[1]

Their women's rights program, with its hostility to the family and its emphasis on women's economic independence, provided an alternative to the ideology of separate spheres that dominated thinking about women's place by 1830. In reaction, separate spheres ideology became more elaborate, more defensive, and more openly political. Catharine Beecher began her influential 1841 treatise on "woman's sphere" by addressing "those who are bewailing themselves over the fancied wrongs and injuries of women in this Nation." The thrust of her argument was to reconcile the general principles of democracy and equal rights with women's "subordinate station" in the family and with their lack of power "in making and administering laws." Beecher quoted Alexis de Tocqueville, who was concerned to refute the "clamor for the rights of woman" in the United States by contrasting it with American women's eager willingness to embrace the limitations of the married state.[2] Despite the intensified debate, however, the impact of the women's right program during the 1830s and early 1840s was limited, above all because most of its advocates were men who had little faith in women's own capacity for reform activism. Without a way to bring women themselves into politics—in other words, without a program for political rights for women—the political force supporting women's rights had to come from other than women, and would therefore be limited.

The notion of political equality for women was so radical that for a long time it was virtually impossible even to imagine woman suffrage. Within the democratic political tradition, the emphasis on independence as a condition for possession of the suffrage worked to exclude women, who were dependent on men almost by definition. Women had an honored place in early republican thought, but they were never considered men's equals, nor was it regarded as appropriate to demand political rights for them. During the 1820s and 1830s, as popular political passions increased, so did the obstacles to the political inclusion of women.[3] Who besides women could provide the "virtue" needed to protect the republic from the rampant but necessary self-interest of men?

The barrier to the proposition of equal political rights for women was broken within a movement that was not initially political, but within which female activism flourished—Abolitionism. Whereas the labor reformers of the 1820s and 1830s advocated women's rights without having much faith in women's own activism, the evangelical movements of the 1830s depended on women's activism.[4] Of the moral reform movements, Abolitionism was the most radical and contributed the most to the emerging sensibility of female self-assertion. The Abolitionists' indictment of the absolute immorality of slaveholding established a much stronger political language than did workingmen's republicanism for describing the tyrannical abuse of power; women quickly put that language to good use in indicting men's tyranny over them.[5] As arguments against the institution of chattel slavery, abstract ideas about equality and individual rights gained real social meaning. In particular, Abolitionists paid attention to the misuses of the slave's body, thus illuminating themes of sexual and marital abuse among free women as well.

In its first decade, radical abolitionism repudiated the political arena as fundamentally corrupt and the Constitution as inherently proslavery; that hostility to politics helped women's activism to flourish within the movement. But, as Eric Foner has made clear, Abolitionism had eventually to reconcile itself with popular reverence for the Constitution, with the republican political tradition in its radical form. The rise of political abolitionism in the 1840s temporarily increased women's isolation from politics but eventually lessened it. When the American Anti-Slavery Society split in 1839, political abolitionists, largely male, were on one side, and women abolitionists, mostly Garrisonian, were on the other.[6]

Within a decade, however, that seeming impasse had generated the demand for woman suffrage. The woman who articulated the proposition that women should have the same political rights as men had equally strong links to female and to political abolitionism. She was Elizabeth Cady Stanton, protégé of Lucretia Mott, cousin of Gerrit Smith, and wife of Henry B. Stanton. She came to understand that a fundamental change in women's political status was the key to their comprehensive equal rights. Just as her husband was participating in the development of a political and constitutional approach to antislavery, she was inventing a political and constitutional approach to women's rights. In the summer of 1848, while Henry Stanton was organizing the Free Soil Party in Buffalo, New York, Elizabeth Cady Stanton called together the first women's rights convention, in Seneca Falls.

The Seneca Falls "Declaration of Sentiments and Resolutions"—an adaptation of the Declaration of Independence—had as its central idea protest against the denial to women of "this first right of a citizen, the elective franchise, thereby leaving her without representation in the halls of legislation, . . . oppressed on all sides." The declaration went on to enumerate the whole range of women's grievances, including women's civil death in marriage, their lack of rights to their own wages, their taxation without representation, and their treatment under divorce and guardianship laws that favored husbands over wives. Despite the comprehensive significance of women's disfranchisement, which the declaration demonstrated, the convention's participants hesitated before resolving that "it is the duty of the women of this country to secure to themselves their sacred right to the elective franchise."[7] As women they were wary of such a clear-cut assertion of sexual equality, and as Abolitionists they were suspicious of, and hostile to, politics. But the logic of women's rights led straight to political equality, and the woman suffrage resolution at Seneca Falls—the first formal assertion of the equal rights of women to the political franchise—prevailed.

The demand for political equality could inspire a women's rights movement among women from 1848 on because political democracy was simultaneously a widely held belief and a radical assertion when applied to women. Political equality for women rested on the popular republican tradition that insisted on equal rights for all, with the franchise the crowning jewel of individual freedom. Women's rights advocates could speak of their demands in terms of the "rights, for which our fathers fought, bled, and died," seeking only to claim women's place in the glorious American political experiment. They enjoyed the confidence of appealing to a virtually hegemonic republican tradition. "We do not feel called upon to assert or establish the equality of the sexes" declared a statement issued by the Second National Women's Rights Convention in 1851 (though its authors believed fervently in that equality). "It is enough for our argument that natural and political justice . . . alike determine that rights and burdens—taxation and representation—should be co-extensive; hence, women as individual citizens . . . liable to be . . . taxed in their labor and property for the support of government, have a self-evident and indisputable right, identically the same right that men have, to a direct voice in the enactment of those laws and the formation of that government." Made possible by the spread of women's reform activism, the demand for woman suffrage was strengthened by the increasing attraction that popular politics began to have for women, as well as for men, during the 1850s.[8] From then on, women's rights began to move into the American political mainstream.

As the demand for woman suffrage became linked with a widely held republican faith, it also expressed the desire of some women for a radically different position in society than women's traditional one. Woman suffrage carried with it the unmistakable message of women's desire for independence, especially from men within the family. "The Right of Suffrage for Women is, in our opinion, the cornerstone of this enterprise," resolved the 1851 women's rights convention, "since we do not seek to protect woman, but rather to place her in a position to protect herself." A moderate version of the theme of independence emphasized the importance of individual self-development for women, much as Margaret Fuller had in her 1845 manifesto, *Woman in the Nineteenth Century.* The more radical arguments for women's political independence suggested that men's and women's interests were not only distinct but also antagonistic. Elizabeth Cady Stanton could always be counted on to ring that note. She believed that "the care and protection" that men give women was "such as the wolf gives the lamb, the eagle the hare he carries to the eyrie!!"[9]

Underlying both versions of the claim that women needed greater independence from men was the notion of women as individuals. "We believe that woman, as an accountable being, can not innocently merge her individuality in that of her brother, or accept from him the limitations of her sphere," explained Ann Preston at the 1852 Westchester Convention in Pennsylvania.[10] The notion that women's individuality, like men's, was a moral and political absolute ran counter to widely held ideas that women's selflessness, their service to others, was the ethical and emotional core of the family. Moreover, the emphasis on individuality implicitly undermined the first premise of separate spheres ideology: the idea of categorical sexual difference, that is, that all women differed from all men insofar as women were the same as each other. Because of its venerable republican heritage and because of its ability to express women's growing desire for independence and individuality, the demand for woman suffrage attracted many women—especially writers, physicians, and other pioneering professionals—who had never before identified themselves with women's rights.

The new focus on political equality did not narrow the scope of the women's rights movement but enlarged it, particularly to include the issue of wives' subordination to their husbands. Ideologically, the women's rights consensus that centered around woman suffrage emboldened egalitarians like Ernestine Rose and Stanton to elaborate the implications of individual rights principles for the family. Women's position in marriage was criticized, in language borrowed from Abolitionism, as a violation of the most elementary individual right, the right to control the uses of one's body. Throughout the 1850s Lucy Stone spoke repeatedly against the common law of marriage because it "gives the 'custody' of the wife's person to her husband, so that he has a right to her even against herself." When contracting her own marriage, she protested against all manifestations of coverture by taking the unheard-of step of refusing her husband's name. During the decade legislative gains gave married women rights to their own earnings and property, rights that constituted a fundamental challenge to the economic inequalities of marriage.[11]

Finally, at the Tenth National Woman's Rights Convention in 1860, Stanton made equal rights criticisms of the marriage relation explicit by reintroducing the old Owenite demand for liberalization of divorce laws. What was important about Stanton's resolutions was not her vehement indictment of the miserable underside of women's married lives—previous women's movements had targeted domestic violence, and Stanton used those traditions in attacking the "legalized prostitution" of coerced marital intercourse and unwilling maternity. What was new was that Stanton based her indictment of women's position in marriage on the supremacy of individual rights, and on the systematic violation in marriage of "the inalienable right of all to be happy," and that she advocated divorce and remarriage, not resignation, as the solution to women's marital misery. The philosophical basis for her position was utilitarian and radically individualist. The relation of marriage had "force and authority," she argued, only to the degree that it made the individuals in it happy. In essence, she contended that marriage had no independent standing as an institution and certainly no moral supremacy over the rights and inclinations of the individuals who entered into it. Inasmuch as women's lives were so much more circumscribed by marriage than were men's, unhappy marriages were infinitely more destructive to wives than to husbands, and on that ground freedom to leave a bad marriage and to form a better one would benefit women more than men.[12]

Participants in the 1860 convention engaged in a heated debate over Stanton's resolutions. Antoinette Brown Blackwell, the first ordained woman minister in the United States, argued that marriage as an institution established the limits of the principles of individual rights—that it was a relation in which the participants incurred "obligations," not only to their children but also to each other, that they could not morally forfeit. As for divorce as a solution to women's marital misery, Blackwell believed that "the advantage, if this theory of marriage is adopted, will not be on the side of woman, but altogether on the side of man." The issue at the heart of the 1860 debate—that fact that women are equally at economic risk in and outside marriage—continues to plague feminists today.[13] But even in the mid-nineteenth century, Stanton's equal rights approach established basic principles that Blackwell had to concede, in particular, the principle of woman's right to self-determination over her own body.

The debate over divorce reached a stalemate in 1860, with all women's rights leaders agreeing that the issue of women's position in the family belonged on their platform but disagreeing about whether the principle of individual rights was the best guide to resolving it. The issue was not picked up again for over a decade, at which time the women's rights movement was simultaneously exploring the collective grievances of women and insisting, with unparalleled militancy, on equal rights as the only framework for addressing them. Meanwhile the events of the Civil War had given new meaning and possibility to the movement's foremost demand, political rights, from which the subtheme of personal rights was derived. Political equality had been the first principle of the women's rights movement for almost two decades, but it was the historical consequences of the Civil War that began to make it a political possibility.

Women's Rights and Universal Suffrage, 1863–1869

In the wake of the Civil War, equal rights was elevated to the level of constitutional principle. The radical politics of the period focused on constitutional change. Its exponents regarded natural rights in the most egalitarian light, considered the right to vote a natural right, and urged the mobilization of national power and sovereignty to enact and ensure the equal access of all to that right.[14] The faith in constitutional revision and interpretation among believers in equal rights during Reconstruction was virtually unlimited, for if amending the Constitution could abolish slavery, what could it not do? The women's rights movement, already committed to an egalitarian and political version of individual rights, shared deeply in that reverent, yet activist, attitude toward the Constitution. Much as debates over women's rights during the 1840s and 1850s had focused on the meaning of the Bible, in the 1860s and 1870s they focused on the Constitution as their fundamental text.

Thus in 1863 congressional radicals turned to the women's rights movement for support in passing the first of the Reconstruction amendments, the constitutional abolition of slavery. Women's rights leaders, enthusiastic advocates of "A NEW CONSTITUTION in which the guarantee of liberty and equality to every human being shall be so plainly and clearly written as never again to be called in question," were eager to help and organized a campaign of popular support, the first such effort on behalf of a proposed constitutional amendment. They collected over 400,000 signatures—Robert Dale Owen, now head of the American Freedmen's Inquiry Commission, worked closely with them—and Senator Charles Sumner gave them much of the credit for the ultimate passage of the Thirteenth Amendment.[15]

Once slavery was abolished, the political status of the former slaves became the crucial constitutional question. Black suffrage was the key, both to the freedmen's own future and to the fortunes of the Republican Party. Women's rights leaders were determined to take advantage of the constitutional crisis that swirled around black suffrage. In their work on behalf of the Thirteenth Amendment, they took every opportunity to point out that the principle of unconditional emancipation led directly to that of universal enfranchisement. In Stanton's memorable metaphor, the black suffrage issue opened the "constitutional door," and women intended to "avail ourselves of the strong arm and blue uniform of the black soldier to walk in by his side."[16]

Reconstruction strengthened the belief that the right to vote was a natural right. The right to suffrage was either the supreme natural right, as Sumner argued, or the necessary protection of all other natural rights, as George William Curtis contended at the New York Constitutional Convention in 1867. In either case popular suffrage, as the sovereign power, was inherent, not bestowed. "For God gave [the right of suffrage] when he gave life and breath, passions, emotions, conscience, and will," declared Parker Pillsbury. "It was man's inalienable, irrepealable, inextinguishable right from the beginning." As Stanton consistently put it, the republican lesson of the war was that popular sovereignty, the equal political rights of all individuals, preceded and underlay governments and nations, constitutions and laws.[17]

The belief that the right to vote was the individual's natural right made the case for woman suffrage much stronger, more self-evident than it had ever been. "In considering the question of suffrage," Stanton declared in 1867,

> there are two starting points: one, that this right is a gift of society, in which certain men, having inherited this privilege from some abstract body and abstract place, have now the right to secure it for themselves and their privileged order to the end of time. . . . Ignoring this point of view as untenable and anti-republican, and taking the opposite, that suffrage is a natural right—as necessary to man under government, for the protection of person and property, as are air and motion to life—we hold the talisman . . . to point out the tyranny of every qualification to the free exercise of this sacred right.[18]

Given those premises, it was only necessary to appeal to the natural rights women held in common with all other persons. Rather than argue that women had a special need or capacity for the franchise, women's rights advocates regarded any mention of race or sex as suspect, as a reference to the inferiority of women and Negroes. "To discuss this question of suffrage for women and ne-groes, as women and negroes, and not as citizens of a republic," Stanton argued, "implies that there are some reasons for demanding this right for these classes that do not apply to 'white males.' " The Reconstruction-era approach to women's enfranchisement, race and sex were, in Olympia Brown's words, "two accidents of the body" unworthy of constitutional recognition. "The terms 'male' and 'fe-male' simply designate the physical or animal distinction between the sexes," explained Ernestine Rose, who had always insisted that the distinction of sex was the enemy of women's freedom. "Human beings are men and women, possessed of human faculties and understanding, which we call mind; and mind recognizes no sex, therefore the term 'male,' as applied to human beings—to citizens— ought to be expunged from the constitution and laws as a last remnant of barbarism."[19]

While the Republican Party discussed the constitutional disposi-tion of black suffrage, women's rights leaders insisted that the nation be reconstructed not on the basis of special cases designed for "anomalous beings" but on the fundamental principle of universal suffrage. "To bury the black man and the woman in the citizen," they organized the American Equal Rights Association, with the goal of incorporating black suffrage and woman suffrage into the over-arching demand for universal suffrage.[20]

The Reconstruction-era tendency to regard the difference of sex, and of race, as "incidental" simultaneously advanced and retarded the women's rights movement. Undoubtedly it lent a certain abstraction to the discussion of women's rights, which can be measured by the paucity of discussion of concrete grievances—sexual, economic, domestic—from women's rights platforms in those years. Yet the emphasis on the equal rights of all individuals carried with it the militant confidence of absolute principle and the intention to abolish female subordination as totally as slavery.

One strength of the Reconstruction-era approach was that it focused more attention on black women than ever before—or after—in the long drive for woman suffrage. A framework that disregards race and sex in favor of our common humanity and individual rights ironically can include, even focus on, black women, whereas a discourse that separates out, and too often counterposes, blacks and women tends to obscure the existence of those persons who are both. No doubt some of the Reconstruction-era emphasis on black women was a way to introduce women's rights into a political dialogue that was largely about race, but it was not all so opportunistic. Sojourner Truth spoke frequently from the women's rights platform in the 1860s and, despite the terrific pressure not to delay the freedmen's enfranchisement, was in favor of holding out for universal suffrage. Frances Dana Gage, a white advocate of women's rights active in the Bureau of Refugees, Freedmen, and Abandoned Lands, appeared often at women's rights conventions, where she argued for political rights for black women. Even Stanton, whose capacity for invidious racial distinctions would soon become clear, now directed her arguments to the condition of black women. A few Reconstruction-era women's rights activists began to explore what it might mean to put black, not white, women at the center of the movement's concerns. Women's capacity for resistance, not their weakness, could be emphasized. Thinking of the freedwomen she knew, Gage envisioned "the strength, the power, the energy, the force, the intellect, and the nerve, which the womanhood of this country will bring to bear" once enfranchised.[21]

Given the Republican Party's determination to draw the line at black suffrage, however, the political claims of women and of freedmen were increasingly antagonistic. Within reform circles, former allies—Elizabeth Cady Stanton and Wendell Phillips, Susan B. Anthony and Frederick Douglass—divided bitterly over whether to base Reconstruction on black suffrage or on universal suffrage. Each faction staked its claim on different grounds. The champions of black suffrage spoke in terms of freedmen's historically specific needs as a group and of the ballot as an instrument for their protection. Douglass's position was that when women were "dragged from their houses and hung upon lamp-posts"—he meant white women—their need for the ballot would be as great as that of the black man.[22]

By contrast the universal suffrage argument of the women's rights movement was more individualist and lacked the urgent power of contemporary crisis. Possession of the ballot, its proponents claimed, benefitted the victims of race and sex discrimination alike by raising the individual out of degradation and dependence. Susan B. Anthony developed that line of argument, frequently linking enfranchisement with the liberating aspects of free wage labor. "I want to inquire whether granting woman the right of suffrage will change anything in respect to the nature of our sexes," Douglass asked her. "It will change the nature of one thing very much, and that is the dependent condition of woman," she answered. "It will place her where she can earn her own bread, so that she may go out into the world an equal competitor in the struggle for life." Anthony, the only self-supporting Reconstruction-era women's rights leader, revived and restated the 1830s artisan republican case for political rights in feminist terms, a tendency reinforced by the women's rights movement's tactical alliance with postwar Democrats.[23]

The failure of the universal suffrage campaign in the face of the political realities of Reconstruction can be read in the language of the Fourteenth Amendment. The amendment included the first reference in the Constitution to the distinction of sex and to the inferiority of women by specifying the number of "male citizens" as the basis of congressional representation. The comparison with the Constitution's three-fifths clause, written eighty years earlier, is obvious. Just as the founders were unwilling to admit that the slave's status contradicted the general principles of natural rights, Reconstruction-era politicians were unwilling to acknowledge the strength of women's political claims. In both cases, language was introduced that insulated the subordinate group's status from constitutional interference. Senator Sumner told Stanton that he "wrote over nineteen pages of foolscap to get rid of the word 'male' and yet keep 'negro suffrage' as a party measure intact; but it could not be done." Women's rights leaders denounced the Fourteenth Amendment as a "desecration." "If that word 'male' be inserted as now proposed," Stanton predicted to her cousin Gerrit Smith, "it will take us a century at least to get it out again."[24]

The Fifteenth Amendment represented a more powerful defense of the freedmen's political rights, but that only underlined the Republicans' refusal to include discrimination by sex with that by race, color, and previous condition of servitude in the constitutional guarantee of political rights. Even Ernestine Rose, an especially strong advocate of equal rights, had to admit at this point that the universal suffrage approach had failed women and that they might do better to find new grounds for their claim for political rights. "Congress has enacted resolutions for the suffrage of men and brothers. They don't speak of the women and sisters," she declared. "I propose to call [our movement] Woman Suffrage; then we shall know what we mean." Women's rights leaders abandoned the American Equal Rights Association and formed a new organization, the National Woman Suffrage Association (NWSA), to assert a new version of their demand.[25]

The impact of the defeat of universal suffrage began to generate new kinds of arguments for women's political rights. Previously the case for suffrage had consistently been put in terms of the individual rights of all persons, regardless of their sex and race. Angered by their exclusion from the Fifteenth Amendment, women's rights advocates began to develop fundamentally different arguments for their cause. They claimed their right to the ballot not as individuals but as a sex. The distinction of sex, they argued, was not irrelevant but central to social organization; whereas earlier they had opposed its political recognition as a "desecration," now they called for it. The reason women should vote was not that they were the same as men but that they were different. That made for a rather thorough reversal of classic women's rights premises. In an 1869 speech by Stanton, described in the *History of Woman Suffrage* as "a fair statement of the hostile feelings of women toward the amendments," the shift from one kind of argument to the other is obvious. "The same arguments made in this country for extending suffrage from time to time, to white men, . . . and the same used by the great Republican party to enfranchise a million black men in the South, all these arguments we have to-day to offer for woman," Stanton contended, "and one, in addition, stronger than all besides, the difference in man and woman." Stanton had always ridiculed such arguments as "twaddle." Now even she based her case on the contrast between "masculine" and "feminine" elements. "There is sex in the spiritual as well as the physical and what we need to-day in government, in the world of morals and thought, is the recognition of the feminine element, as it is this alone that can hold the masculine in check," she asserted.[26]

The shift from arguments based on the common humanity of men and women to arguments based on fundamental differences between the sexes has had a parallel in virtually every feminist epoch. That makes it all the more important to identify the historically specific character, sources, and impact of such transitions when they occur. The various versions of "womanhood" that began to appear as the women's rights movement's demand shifted from universal suffrage to woman suffrage had their roots in Reconstruction politics as well as in contemporary intellectual trends.

The argument that women should be enfranchised to bring the "feminine element" into government had a decidedly nationalist edge, which reflected the Fifteenth Amendment's transfer of control over the right of suffrage from the state to the national level. Part of the argument for black suffrage was that enfranchising the freedmen would keep the Republican Party in power, thus preserving the victories of the war and strengthening the nation. In arguing that the "feminine element" would elevate national life and "exalt purity, virtue, morality, true religion," woman suffrage partisans were trying to match that nationalist argument and go it one better. Enfranchising the freedmen only promised partisan advantage; enfranchising "woman" would uplift the nation at its very heart, the family. An 1869 woman suffrage convention resolved that the "extension of suffrage to woman is essential to the public safety and to the establishment and permanence of free institutions" because "as woman, in private life, in the partnership of marriage, is now the conservator of private morals, so woman in public life, in the partnership of a republican State, based upon Universal suffrage, will become the conservator of public morals." Here the tendency to see in women a fundamentally different social force than in men served a particularly nationalist ideological purpose. "With the black man you have no new force in government—it is manhood still," Stanton argued, "but with the enfranchisement of woman, you have a new and essential element of life and power." Led by Stanton and Anthony, the NWSA distinguished itself among suffrage organizations by its emphasis on national, as opposed to state, action to enfranchise women. Even though it sometimes worked to amend state constitutions, the NWSA's watchword was "national protection for national citizens."[27]

The new suffrage arguments also contained a strong theme of race antagonism, a reaction to the strategic antagonism between black suffrage and woman suffrage. Whereas the advocates of universal suffrage had claimed comradeship between men of the disfranchised and despised classes and all women, woman suffrage advocates now claimed that the enfranchisement of black men created "an aristocracy of sex" because it elevated all men over all women. Woman suffragists criticized the Fifteenth Amendment because "a *man's* government is worse than a *white* man's government" and because the amendment elevated the "lowest orders of manhood" over the "higher classes of women." The racism of such protests was expressed in hints of sexual violence, in the suggestion that women's disfranchisement would mean their "degradation," "insult," and "humiliation."[28] Those overtly racist arguments reflected white women's special fury that men they considered their inferiors had been enfranchised before them.

Beginning in the early 1870s, trends in social scientific thought also encouraged the move from equal rights arguments to essentialist ones. Of particular importance to women's rights partisans was the special role attributed to "woman" by positivists, such as Auguste Comte, in the organicist solutions they proposed for social conflict. "The great questions now looming upon the political horizon can only find their peaceful solution by the infusion of the feminine element in the councils of the nation," declared an 1872 woman suffrage resolution. "Man, representing force, would continue . . . to settle all questions by war, but woman, representing affection, would, in her true development, harmonize intellect and action, and weld together all the interests of the human family."[29]

Such new intellectual currents, decidedly scientific and secular, merged with much older and more conservative ideas about sexual difference and female nature. Isabella Beecher Hooker, half-sister of the renowned advocate of female domesticity, Catharine Beecher, began to assume a leadership role among suffragists in 1870. She used the arguments her sister had developed in opposition to women's rights thirty years before to argue *for* political equality for women. She stressed the importance of political equality for mothers because it would permit them to better carry out their responsibilities to their children. "Mothers for the first time in history are able to assert . . . their right to be a protective and purifying power in the political society into which [their] children are to enter." Other suffrage leaders of the period made allied arguments. Phebe Hanaford, an ordained minister, called for woman suffrage on religious grounds, because of the "moral influence that the participation of women in government would have upon the world." Paulina Wright Davis, once a moral reform activist, urged woman suffrage as an antidote to men's corruption, sexual and political alike.[30] "Motherhood," "purity," Christian civilization, and women's duties—all were notions that had traditionally been posed against the demand for women's rights; now they were being assimilated into it.

By the end of the 1870s, such arguments would dominate woman suffrage ideology. The impact of that ideological change was complex. The demand for woman suffrage, that it claimed the vote for women as women, permitted the cultivation of sex-consciousness far more than had the equal rights and universal suffrage approach. The call for woman suffrage, therefore, was much more effective in forging women into a group with a common status and with a common demand—a group that would form the popular basis for a women's rights movement. Yet the emphasis on sexual difference steered the women's rights movement away from its egalitarian origins; the movement would ultimately become more compatible with conservative ideas about social hierarchy.

Woman Suffrage and the Meaning of the Reconstruction Amendments, 1870–1878

By inscribing the freedmen's political rights firmly in the Constitution, the ratification of the Fifteenth Amendment threatened to bring the process of constitutional revision, and the strategic possibilities of winning women's political rights, to an end. When the amendment passed Congress in February 1869, it created what looked like a strategic dead end for woman suffrage. Then in October, a husband and wife team of Missouri suffragists, Francis Minor and Virginia Minor, came up with a different approach to the Reconstruction amendments: an activist strategy for winning woman suffrage that relied on what was already in the Constitution, rather than requiring an additional amendment.[31]

The Minors argued that the Constitution, properly understood, already provided for women's political rights; women were already enfranchised and had only to take the right that was theirs.[32] Their argument rested on the link in the pending Fifteenth Amendment between national supremacy and equal political rights. Although the first section of the Fourteenth Amendment had defined national citizenship, the second section had left suffrage under the control of the individual states. The Fifteenth Amendment shifted that control to the national level, thus intensifying the nationalizing aspect of the Fourteenth Amendment and extending its scope to the franchise. Much of the subsequent woman suffrage case was based on that relationship between the two amendments.

The Minors believed that the initial premises of the Constitution, greatly strengthened by the Reconstruction amendments, supported their case. They cited the Constitution's preamble to substantiate their claim that popular sovereignty preceded and underlay constitutional authority. To establish the supremacy of national citizenship, they cited various provisions of Article I, the supremacy clause of Article VI, and the first section of the Fourteenth Amendment. The weakest point of their argument—but also its linchpin—was the assertion that suffrage was a right of national citizenship. The Fifteenth Amendment was still pending, but they found an alternate constitutional basis in a frequently cited 1823 case, *Corfield* v. *Coryell,* which had found the elective franchise to be one of the "privileges and immunities" protected by Article IV.[33]

Although the Minors' constitutional argument was new, their underlying assumptions were consistent with the Reconstruction-era approach to women's rights. Their argument perfectly expressed the era's radical political philosophy that this article has been tracing: a combination of natural rights, popular democracy, national sovereignty, and extreme reverence for the Constitution. But the Minors provided a new, militant, activist stance for woman suffragists, a stance that rested on the premise that women had merely to take a right that was already theirs. That approach, which came to be called the "New Departure," became the strategic basis for suffragists' actions during most of the 1870s.[34] In many ways, the New Departure period was one of the most radical in the history of women's rights, both in its tactical militancy and in its larger vision of female emancipation. From the larger perspective of constitutional history, the New Departure became part of the conflict over the meaning of the Reconstruction amendments, a struggle that extended far beyond the courts, although that is where it was resolved.

The tactics that the Minors advocated were a combination of direct action and litigation. "I am often jeeringly asked," Virginia Minor explained, " 'If the constitution gives you this right, why don't you take it?' " So she urged women to try to vote and, if they were stopped, to sue those officials who refused to register them. In fact, women in the spiritualist center of Vineland, New Jersey, had successfully voted as early as 1868; that they attempted to vote and were permitted to do so by election officials suggests how widespread, even popular, the assumptions that underlay the New Departure were. The passage of the Enforcement Act to strengthen the Fifteenth Amendment in May 1870 seems to have encouraged many more women—in California, New Hampshire, Michigan, and elsewhere—to regard the right to vote as already theirs. That year black women went to the polls in South Carolina, encouraged to do so by federal government agents.[35]

In early 1871, the NWSA drew up a resolution formally advising women of their "duty . . . to apply for registration at the proper times and places, and in all cases when they fail to secure it to see that suits be instituted in the courts having jurisdiction and that their right to the franchise shall secure general and judicial recognition." A group of women in the District of Columbia tried, but were not permitted, to register in 1871. Susan B. Anthony and fifteen of her friends in Rochester, New York, succeeded in voting in 1872, only to be arrested a few weeks later for violating the Enforcement Act, the very law that they believed protected their rights. As the number of women attempting to vote grew, their cases began to move through the judicial system.[36]

Then a second direction was opened up in the New Departure strategy. In January 1871 Victoria Woodhull, already a notorious figure and one heretofore not associated with the organized woman suffrage movement, appeared before the House Judiciary Committee to speak on behalf of political equality for women. Woodhull had been invited to address the committee by one of its members, Benjamin Butler, a Massachusetts Republican who was seeking to lead his party into the 1870s under the twin banners of labor reform and woman suffrage. Woodhull had her own links to the radical labor movement through her leadership in the International Working-men's Association. Like the Minors, Woodhull argued that women were already enfranchised under the Constitution. But instead of calling for the courts to vindicate her constitutional interpretation, she proposed that Congress pass a declaratory act clarifying the constitutional right of all United States citizens, including women, to vote. In other words, she proposed a way to pursue the New Departure that was more overtly political than the Minors' tactics of direct action and litigation.[37]

Woodhull's constitutional argument that the right to vote was inherent in national citizenship was even stronger than the Minors'. Woodhull asserted that the newly ratified Fifteenth Amendment established the "right of any citizen of the United States to vote," a right that could not be abridged by state law "neither on account of sex or otherwise." In a speech supporting the Woodhull memorial, Judge A. G. Riddle agreed that the Fifteenth Amendment must be understood to assume "the right of the citizen to vote as already existing, and it specifies classes, as persons of color, of certain race, and of previous servitude, as especially having the right to vote." He did not believe it should be read as authorizing the disfranchisement of classes not mentioned—that is, women. As a right of national citizenship, the suffrage was subject to the same protections as all other such rights.[38]

With other advocates of the New Departure, Woodhull believed that the relationship between the Fourteenth and Fifteenth amendments made voting a right of national citizenship. Her constitutional case had other elements to it, which bore the mark of her own distinctive thought. "Women, white and black, belong to races, although to different races," she explained, and "the right to vote can not be denied on account of color." Therefore, "all people included in the term color have the right to vote, unless otherwise prohibited." She also contended that "women, white and black, have from time immemorial groaned under what is properly termed in the Constitution 'previous condition of servitude.'" Thus, when the Thirteenth Amendment abolished slavery, it also abolished the subordinate condition of women.[39]

Inasmuch as she was cooperating with Butler, Woodhull's sudden emergence as an advocate of woman suffrage was a product of an intense struggle within the Republican Party over its future now that the freedmen had been enfranchised and, what was essentially the same thing, over the meaning of the Reconstruction amendments. Some Republicans initially supported Woodhull's initiative. After her memorial, Republican leaders in the House gave suffragists a room in the Capitol from which to lobby, a move Anthony suspected was a "Republican dodge." However, the dominant Republican faction did not support Woodhull and used her memorial as an opportunity to voice its opposition to the New Departure in the courts, where various New Departure cases were pending. In response to the New Departure's expansive and egalitarian construction, the House Judiciary Committee's Majority Report, authored by John Bingham, argued that the Fourteenth Amendment neither elevated national over state citizenship nor added anything new to it but merely strengthened the federal government's ability to protect already existing "privileges and immunities." Moreover, the report disagreed with Woodhull's interpretation of the Fifteenth Amendment, that it implied a prohibition on any limitation to the suffrage other than those explicitly indicated.[40]

Woodhull is, of course, remembered more as a sexual radical than as a constitutional scholar of woman suffrage, but the two politics have the same philosophical roots. Her leadership in the women's rights movement during the 1870s reveals the link between women's political equality and the women's rights critique of women's subordination in marriage, a connection not openly made since the 1860 debate on divorce. Woodhull's "free love" ideas were based on the same philosophy of individual rights as her suffrage arguments. She asserted that individuals had the inalienable right to make and to dissolve sexual relations as they desired. The right of sexual self-determination was derived from what Woodhull characterized as "our theory of government, based upon the sovereignty of the individual." Her most famous declaration of "free love" was expressed in constitutional terms and infused with natural rights assumptions. "Yes, I am a Free Lover," she responded to a heckler at one of her speeches. "I have an *inalienable, constitutional* and *natural* right to love whom I may . . . to *change* that love *every day* if I please, . . . and it is *your duty* not only to *accord* [my right], but, as a community, to see that I am protected in it."[41]

Applied to marriage, to sexuality and reproduction, "the sovereignty of the individual" began to take on a corporeal dimension, to become the right of the individual to determine the uses of her or his body. According to a controversial 1871 suffrage resolution that reflected Woodhull's influence, "the right of self ownership [is] the first of all rights." (Paulina Wright Davis delivered that resolution, and there was a great flap after the convention as to whether she "knew" what she had "said.")[42] The new emphasis on rights to one's "person" was an inevitable development of the individual rights tradition once it had been taken into a women's movement and women had brought it to bear on their deep discontent with their sexual and reproductive lives within marriage.

In Woodhull's writings and speeches, "self sovereignty" remained relatively abstract, but in Stanton's accomplished hands it turned into a much more concrete program for women's sexual rights. In addition to her advocacy of divorce law liberalization, Stanton came to imagine that women might have rights with respect to their maternity. To describe such rights—which in the 1870s had no name but which would later be called "birth control" and, even later, "reproductive rights"—Stanton used the term "self sovereignty." Beginning in 1871 she convened small groups of women—including one in Salt Lake City—to urge that wives "learn and practice the true laws of generation" in order to have fewer children. "We are to be the sovereigns of the world but woman must first understand her true position," Stanton explained. "Woman must at all times be the sovereign of her own person." "Whenever we stay in a town two days I talk one afternoon to women alone," she wrote to a friend. "The new gospel of fewer children and a healthy, happy maternity is gladly received."[43]

The free love issue was raised first by Woodhull's opponents, notably in the *Christian Union,* which Henry Ward Beecher edited. Rather than take on her constitutional case for women's political equality, her critics attacked her personal life and claimed that, as a divorced and sexually active women, she was too disreputable to speak for her sex. Stanton clearly understood the political functions of such attacks. Woodhull, she wrote, "has done a work for women that none of us could have done. She has faced and dared men to call her names that make women shudder. She has risked and realized the sort of ignominy that would have paralyzed any of us who have longer been called strong-minded." "We have had women enough sacrificed to this sentimental, hypocritical prating about purity," Stanton wrote to Lucretia Mott. "This is one of man's most effective engines for our division and subjugation."[44] The attacks did destroy Woodhull, and both her political credibility and her sanity were eventually ruined. On the eve of the 1872 presidential election, she was arrested by federal marshals for violating the just-passed Comstock law. Less than a month later, Susan B. Anthony was also arrested by federal marshals—for "criminal voting," an act based on the same ideas as those advocated by Woodhull. In retrospect, those events demonstrate what was not yet clear to the New Departure suffragist: federal power could as easily be the enemy as the protector of individual rights, depending on political forces.

Meanwhile, following the lead of the 1871 Bingham report of the House Judiciary Committee, Republican judges began to rule against cases brought by New Departure suffragists. The first major New Departure case to reach the courts was the suit brought by Sara Spencer and seventy other women against election officials in the District of Columbia for refusing to register their votes. In October 1871 Judge Cartter of the Washington, D.C., U.S. District Court found against the women. His ruling was based more on ideological grounds than on constitutional ones, and it indicated how the general fear of political democracy was working against woman suffrage and against the expansive and egalitarian interpretation of the Reconstruction amendments with which it had associated itself. "The claim, as we understand it," Cartter explained,

> is, that [women] have an inherent right, resting in nature, and guaranteed by the Constitution, in such wise that it may not be defeated by legislation. . . . The right of all men to vote is as fully recognized in the population of our large centres and cities as can well be done. . . . The result in these centres is political profligacy and violence verging upon anarchy. . . . The fact that the practical working of the assumed right

would be destructive of civilization is decisive that the right does not exist.[45]

The next stage in the judicial history of the New Departure was *Bradwell* v. *State* in which Myra Bradwell challenged the Illinois bar's refusal to admit her to practice before it. The case was brought to the U.S. Supreme Court by Matthew Carpenter, Republican senator from Wisconsin. Carpenter argued for Bradwell's right to practice law just as suffragists were arguing for women's right to vote—on the grounds that the Fourteenth Amendment pledged the national government to protect women's rights equally with those of all other citizens. There was considerable historical irony in Carpenter's brief. Although he used the structure of New Departure arguments, Carpenter went to great lengths to distinguish Bradwell's right to practice law, which he argued was one of the rights protected under the Fourteenth Amendment, from women's right to vote, which he argued was not. He made the distinction in order "to quiet the fears of the timid and conservative."[46]

The Court's ruling on *Bradwell* came in conjunction with its first major interpretation of the Fourteenth Amendment, the famous Slaughterhouse Cases. In the Slaughterhouse Cases, the Court declared, by a bare five to four majority, that the amendment created no new national rights and did not establish national citizenship as supreme over state citizenship. Those were virtually the same arguments that Representative Bingham had made in the House Judiciary Committee's Majority Report rejecting Woodhull's petition. Then the Court moved on to the *Bradwell* case, and with only Chief Justice Salmon P. Chase dissenting, applied the same principle to reject the argument that Bradwell's right to be admitted to the bar was protected by the Fourteenth Amendment.[47]

A few months after the *Slaughterhouse* and *Bradwell* decisions, Anthony's case, *United States* v. *Anthony,* was heard before the U.S. Circuit Court in Canandaigua. (Anthony had so thoroughly canvassed her home county of Monroe, explaining her case to potential jurors, that the venue of the trial had to be changed.) Judge Ward Hunt, a Roscoe Conkling appointee, earned himself a special place of infamy in the annals of women's rights by depriving Anthony of her constitutional rights and directing the jury to find her guilty. Hunt rejected Anthony's arguments that national citizenship was supreme over state citizenship and that voting was a right of national citizenship, and he cited the *Bradwell* and *Slaughterhouse* decisions to support his opinion. Regarding the Fifteenth Amendment, he argued that it applied only to disfranchisement on grounds it "expressly prohibited" and that it did imply a prohibition of discrimination by sex. Anthony saw that the implications of such opinions reached beyond woman suffrage to the whole framework of political rights. She predicted with stunning accuracy that "if we once establish the false principle, that United States citizenship does not carry with it the right to vote in every state in this Union, there is no end to the petty freaks and cunning devices that will be resorted to, to exclude one and another class of citizens from the right of suffrage."[48]

Hunt kept Anthony's case from going to the Supreme Court. Appropriately, the case that allowed the Supreme Court to rule once and for all on the New Departure was Virginia Minor's suit against the Missouri election official who refused to accept her ballot. Since the claim that the Fourteenth Amendment created a national citizenship that superseded state citizenship had already been dismissed in the *Slaughterhouse* and *Bradwell* cases, *Minor* v. *Happersett* focused exclusively on voting as a right of citizenship. The suit treated that assertion as so obvious, so basic to the entire meaning of the Civil War and Reconstruction, as to be virtually unchallengeable: "We claim, and presume it will not be disputed, that the elective franchise is a privilege of citizenship within the meaning of the Constitution of the United States." Yet the Court was "unanimously of the opinion that the Constitution of the United States does not confer the right of suffrage upon any one."[49]

In 1875, much as Anthony had predicted, the Court began to undermine the voting rights of the freedmen along lines that reflected its dismissal of New Departure interpretations of the Fifteenth Amendment with respect to woman suffrage. In *United States* v. *Reese* and in *United States* v. *Cruikshank*, the Court deprived black men of their right to vote by narrowing the prohibitions of the Fifteenth Amendment, first to disfranchisement that was the direct result of state action, and then to racial disfranchisement only when the grounds were explicitly stated. The judicial fate of the woman suffrage New Departure had laid the legal groundwork for those decisions in several ways. The precedent of rejecting the constitutional arguments for woman suffrage by interpreting the Fifteenth

Amendment as intended to forbid only disfranchisement by race made it much easier to disfranchise the freedmen on grounds, such as education, income, or residence, that were surrogates for race. Furthermore, the Court's decisions in the New Departure cases severed the Fourteenth and Fifteenth amendments—they separated the right to vote from federal powers of enforcement and from the affirmative statement of national citizenship in the Fourteenth Amendment. That left voting rights dependent solely on the Fifteenth Amendment and, therefore, much more vulnerable. In *Minor* v. *Happersett*, the Court ruled conclusively that the right of suffrage was not a necessary attribute of national citizenship, and from there it was a very short step to permitting the whole range of indirect devices for de facto disfranchisement of the freedmen.[50]

Afterword

In 1878, three years after the defeat of its New Departure strategy by the Court's decision in the *Minor* case, the NWSA began pursuing a different strategy for winning women's political rights: a constitutional amendment, patterned after the Fifteenth Amendment, exclusively to prohibit disfranchisement by sex. Earlier an amendment had been proposed that included both a general assertion that "the Right of Suffrage in the United States shall be based on citizenship, and shall be regulated by Congress" and the specific prohibition against "any distinction or discrimination whatever founded on sex." The 1878 amendment, which was eventually adopted as the Nineteenth Amendment, did not make any general assertions about the right to vote but simply prohibited disfranchisement by sex. The small difference of wording indicated a much larger difference of political atmosphere; it revealed the reformulation of the demand for woman suffrage to coincide with an age in which political democracy was contracting rather than expanding. Not only had many reformers, woman suffragists included, turned against black voters, seeing them as a source of ignorance and corruption, but white workers, angry over their own subordination, had also shown their capacity for violence and social disorder.[51] To what larger political propositions could woman suffrage be attached in such an era?

At the NWSA's 1878 Tenth Washington Convention, where the new woman suffrage amendment was introduced, Reconstruction-era assertions that all individuals deserved the vote, irrespective of sex or race, were mixed with categorical arguments about what women as women could be expected to do with the vote, both to protect themselves and to benefit the larger society. But it was the essentialist arguments that fit best with the new, antidemocratic spirit behind woman suffrage. That link was expressed by Elizabeth Boynton Harbert, a representative of the new generation of suffragists. Harbert emphasized two themes in her speech at the 1878 convention: that "the ballot in the hands of women would prove a help, not a hindrance" in lowering taxes and reasserting the power of property; and that women had a distinct "mother instinct for government" that was the best reason for trusting them with the vote. The two arguments were fundamentally linked inasmuch as women could be relied on to represent the forces of order and stability in government as in the family. Other suffragists of the late 1870s made similar connections. Characteristically, they based their arguments on woman's special capacity to halt the growing power of "vice," a concept that expressed the fear of working-class power by mixing it with the powerful specter of unleashed sexuality.[52]

Harbert's speech contrasted with an impassioned speech, entitled "National Protection for National Citizens," that Stanton gave at the same convention. Although the convention was meant to inaugurate a grand campaign for the proposed woman suffrage amendment, Stanton delivered a stubborn defense of the New Departure, particularly of the principle of popular sovereignty, which held that political rights were inherent, not bestowed. To her what was at stake in the NWSA's rejection of the New Departure was not simply woman suffrage, but a larger egalitarian interpretation, both of the Constitution and of national purpose. Stanton's interpretation of the Constitution emphasized the power of the federal government, especially its power to enforce equal rights. Federal action could realize true equality because its impact was "uniform" and "homogeneous" on all citizens; it had the power to level. Against that egalitarian definition of national supremacy, Stanton contrasted the growing use of national power "to oppress the citizens of the several States in their most sacred rights," for instance by undermining the separation of church and state.[53]

Stanton certainly understood that her interpretation of the Constitution as a document that committed the nation to the protection of equal rights had been defeated. In the future, the Constitution would be used to defend the rights of property, not persons. But for that reason, the defeat of equal rights constitutionalism would necessarily be temporary. "A century of discussion has not yet made the constitution understood," Stanton asserted. "It has no settled interpretation. Being a series of compromises, it can be expounded in favor of many directly opposite principles." Above all, she took heart because "the numerous demands by the people for national protection in many rights not specified by the constitution, prove that the people have outgrown the compact that satisfied the fathers."[54]

Notes

This article appears in the *Journal of American History* 74, no. 3 (December 1987), and is reprinted with permission.

1. Celia Morris Eckhardt, *Fanny Wright: Rebel in America* (Cambridge, Mass., 1984), pp. 1–3, 282–83; Barbara Taylor, *Eve and the New Jerusalem: Socialism and Feminism in the Nineteenth Century* (New York, 1983), pp. 1–18, 65–70.
2. Catharine E. Beecher, *A Treatise on Domestic Economy, for the Use of Young Ladies at Home, and at School* (Boston, 1841), pp. 4, 6–7, 9.
3. Linda K. Kerber, *Women of the Republic: Intellect and Ideology in Revolutionary America* (Chapel Hill, N.C., 1980), pp. 11–12; Ellen Carol DuBois, *Feminism and Suffrage: The Emergence of an Independent Women's Movement in America, 1848–1869* (Ithaca, N.Y., 1978), pp. 40–47; Ellen Carol DuBois, "Radicalism of the Woman Suffrage Movement: Notes Toward the Reconstruction of American Feminism," *Feminist Studies* 3 (Fall 1975): 63–71.
4. Sean Wilentz, *Chants Democratic: New York City and the Rise of the American Working Class, 1788–1850* (New York, 1984), p. 248; Mary P. Ryan, *Cradle of the Middle Class: The Family in Oneida County, New York, 1790–1865* (New York, 1981), pp. 105–44; Carroll Smith Rosenberg, "Beauty, the Beast and the Militant Woman: A Case Study in Sex Roles and Social Stress in Jacksonian America," *American Quarterly* 23 (October 1971): 562–84; Nancy A. Hewitt, *Women's Activism and Social Change: Rochester, New York, 1822–1872* (Ithaca, N.Y., 1984), pp. 97–138.
5. See especially the writings of Angelina Grimké and Sarah Grimké. Sarah, for example, repudiated the "flattering language of man since he laid aside the whip as a means to keep woman in subjection." Sarah M Grimké, *Letters on the Equality of the Sexes and the Condition of Woman: Addressed to Mary S. Parker, President of the Boston Female Anti-Slavery Society* (Boston, 1838), p. 17.
6. Eric Foner, *Free Soil, Free Labor, Free Men: The Ideology of the Republican Party before the Civil War* (New York, 1970), pp. 73–102; Aileen S. Kraditor, *Means and*

Ends in American Abolitionism: Garrison and His Critics on Strategy and Tactics, 1834–1850 (New York, 1967), pp. 39–77.

7. "Declaration of Sentiments and Resolutions," in *The Concise History of Woman Suffrage*, ed. Mari Jo Buhle and Paul Buhle (Urbana, Ill., 1978), pp. 94–98.

8. "Syracuse National Convention, Syracuse, New York, September 8–10, 1852," in *Concise History of Woman Suffrage*, p. 117; "Second National Convention, Worcester, Massachusetts, October 15–16, 1851," in ibid., p. 112; Lori D. Ginzburg, "'Moral Suasion Is Moral Balderdash': Women, Politics, and Social Activism in the 1850s," *Journal of American History* 73 (December 1986): 601–22.

9. "Second National Convention," p. 112; Margaret Fuller Ossoli, *Woman in the Nineteenth Century and Kindred Papers Relating to the Sphere, Condition and Duties of Woman* (Boston, 1855), p. 96; Elizabeth Cady Stanton, "Address at Seneca Falls," in *Elizabeth Cady Stanton, Susan B. Anthony: Correspondence, Writings, Speeches*, ed. Ellen Carol DuBois (New York, 1981), p. 33.

10. Elizabeth Cady Stanton, Susan B. Anthony, and Matilda Joslyn Gage, eds., *History of Woman Suffrage*, vol. I: 1848–1861 (Rochester, N.Y., 1881), p. 364.

11. "Syracuse National Convention," p. 123; "Second National Convention," p. 107; Henry B. Blackwell and Lucy Stone, "Protest," in *Concise History of Woman Suffrage*, pp. 151–52; Norma Basch, *In the Eyes of the Law: Women, Marriage, and Property in Nineteenth-Century New York* (Ithaca, N.Y., 1982), pp. 162–99.

12. Smith Rosenberg, "Beauty, the Beast and the Militant Woman"; "Debates on Marriage and Divorce, Tenth National Woman's Rights Convention, May 10–11, 1860," in *Concise History of Woman Suffrage*, pp. 170–89.

13. "Debates on Marriage and Divorce," p. 182. For a modern feminist study of the negative consequences of divorce law liberalization for women, see Leonore Weitzman, *The Divorce Revolution: The Unexpected Social and Economic Consequences for Women and Children in America* (New York, 1985), pp. 357–401.

14. David Montgomery, *Beyond Equality: Labor and the Radical Republicans, 1862–1872* (New York, 1967), pp. 80–81; Judith Baer, *Equality Under the Constitution: Reclaiming the Fourteenth Amendment* (Ithaca, N.Y., 1983), p. 59.

15. Elizabeth Cady Stanton, Susan B. Anthony, and Matilda Joslyn Gage, eds., *History of Woman Suffrage*, vol. II: 1861–1878 (Rochester, N.Y., 1881), p. 85.

16. Elizabeth Cady Stanton, "'This Is the Negro's Hour,'" in *Concise History of Woman Suffrage*, p. 219. Stanton used the same "door" metaphor, but with racist overtones, to ask whether "the representative women of the nation . . . had better stand aside and see 'Sambo' walk into the kingdom first."

17. "Woman's Rights Convention, New York City, May 10, 1866, including Address to Congress adopted by the Convention," in *Concise History of Woman Suffrage*, p. 226; Stanton, Anthony, and Gage, eds., *History of Woman Suffrage*, II: 206, 281, 291.

18. Stanton, Anthony, and Gage, eds., *History of Woman Suffrage*, II: 185.

19. Ibid., pp. 185, 241, 356.

20. Ibid., pp. 174, 185.

21. Ibid., pp. 193, 197, 211–13, 274.

22. DuBois, *Feminism and Suffrage*, pp. 53–104; "Debates at the American Equal Rights Association Meeting, New York City, May 12–14, 1869," in *Concise History of Woman Suffrage*, p. 258.

23. Ida Husted Harper, ed., *The Life and Work of Susan B. Anthony*, 3 vols. (Indianapolis, Ind., 1898–1908), vol. I: 324; Stanton, Anthony, and Gage, eds., *History of Woman Suffrage*, II: 404.

24. Elizabeth Cady Stanton, *Eighty Years and More: Reminiscences, 1815–1897* (New

York, 1898), p. 242; Alma Lutz, *Created Equal: A Biography of Elizabeth Cady Stanton* (New York, 1940), p. 134.

25. "Debates at the American Equal Rights Association Meeting," p. 273.

26. Elizabeth Cady Stanton, "Address to the National Woman Suffrage Convention, Washington, D.C., January 19, 1869," in *Concise History of Woman Suffrage*, pp. 249–56; William Leach, *True Love and Perfect Union: The Feminist Reform of Sex and Society* (New York, 1984), p. 147; Stanton, Anthony, and Gage, eds., *History of Woman Suffrage*, II: 318.

27. Stanton, Anthony, and Gage, eds., *History of Woman Suffrage*, II: 384; "Resolutions and Debate, First Annual Meeting of the American Equal Rights Association, New York City, May 10, 1867," in *Concise History of Woman Suffrage*, p. 240; Elizabeth Cady Stanton, Susan B. Anthony, and Matilda Joslyn Gage, eds., *History of Woman Suffrage*, vol. III: 1876–1885 (Rochester, N.Y., 1886), pp. 73–77.

28. Stanton, "Address to the National Woman Suffrage Convention," p. 252; Stanton, Anthony, and Gage, eds., *History of Woman Suffrage*, II: 359, 387.

29. Leach, *True Love and Perfect Union*, pp. 292–322; Stanton, Anthony, and Gage, eds., *History of Woman Suffrage*, II: 493. See also Elizabeth Cady Stanton, "Proposal to Form a New Party, May, 1872," in *Elizabeth Cady Stanton, Susan B. Anthony*, p. 167.

30. Isabella Beecher Hooker, Susan B. Anthony et al., *An Appeal to the Women of the United States by the National Woman Suffrage and Educational Committee* (Hartford, Conn., 1871); Stanton, Anthony, and Gage, eds., *History of Woman Suffrage*, II: 398, 436.

31. Stanton, Anthony, and Gage, eds., *History of Woman Suffrage*, II: 407–10.

32. Ibid. For further discussion of the Minors' arguments, see Louise R. Noun, *Strong Minded Women: The Emergence of the Woman Suffrage Movement in Iowa* (Ames, Iowa, 1969), pp. 168–69.

33. Stanton, Anthony, and Gage, eds., *History of Woman Suffrage*, II: 407–10; Corfield v. Coryell, 6 F. Cas. 546 (E.D. Pa. 1823) (No. 3, 230).

34. On the New Departure, see Stanton, Anthony, and Gage, eds., *History of Woman Suffrage*, II: 407–520, 586–755. See also Harper, ed., *Life and Work of Susan B. Anthony*, I: 409–48.

35. Stanton, Anthony, and Gage, eds., *History of Woman Suffrage*, II: 410; III: 586; Paulina W. Davis, comp., *A History of the National Woman's Rights Movement for Twenty Years . . . from 1850 to 1870* (New York, 1871), p. 23; Eleanor Flexner, *Century of Struggle: The Woman's Rights Movement in the United States* (Cambridge, Mass., 1975), p. 371.

36. Harper, ed., *Life and Work of Susan B. Anthony*, I: 378, 409–65; Stanton, Anthony, and Gage, eds., *History of Woman Suffrage*, II: 407–520.

37. Stanton, Anthony, and Gage, eds., *History of Woman Suffrage*, II: 443–48; Dale Baum, "Woman Suffrage and the 'Chinese Question': The Limits of Radical Republicanism in Massachusetts, 1865–1876," *New England Quarterly* 56 (March 1983): 60–77; Emanie Sachs, *"The Terrible Siren": Victoria Woodhull (1838–1927)* (New York, 1928), p. 146.

38. Stanton, Anthony, and Gage, eds., *History of Woman Suffrage*, II: 444, 448–58, esp. p. 455.

39. Ibid., p. 445. The argument that women, as part of races, have the rights of races, combines the powerful ring of common sense and tremendous naivete for the legal niceties; thus it suggests that Victoria Woodhull had a role in writing her own argument and was not merely reading words written for her by Benjamin Butler or other male politicians and lawyers. That is the one of the many common

and unsubstantiated assertions made by historians about Woodhull. See, for example, Elisabeth Griffith, *In Her Own Right: The Life of Elizabeth Cady Stanton* (New York, 1984), p. 149.

40. Harper, ed., *Life and Work of Susan B. Anthony,* I: 381; Stanton, Anthony, and Gage, eds., *History of Woman Suffrage,* II: 461–64.

41. Victoria C. Woodhull, *A Speech on the Principles of Social Freedom, Delivered in New York City, November 20, 1871, and Boston, January 3, 1872* (London, 1894), pp. 23–24

42. *Woodhull and Claflin's Weekly,* 27 May 1871, p. 3.

43. "For Women Only," *Des Moines Daily Register,* 29 July 1871; Elizabeth Cady Stanton to Martha Coffin Wright, 19 June 1871, box 60, Garrison Family Collection (Sophia Smith Collection, Smith College, Northampton, Mass.).

44. Paxton Hibben, *Henry Ward Beecher: An American Portrait* (New York, 1927), p. 235; "Lady Cook and Victoria Woodhull," *Chicago Daily Socialist,* 21 March 1911. (The author wishes to thank Mari Jo Buhle for the citation. For another version of the quotation, see Lutz, *Created Equal,* p. 228.) Stanton to Lucretia Mott, 1 April 1872, Elizabeth Cady Stanton Papers (Vassar College, Poughkeepsie, N.Y.).

45. Stanton, Anthony, and Gage, eds., *History of Woman Suffrage,* II: 597–99.

46. Bradwell v. State, 16 Wallace 130 (1873); quoted in Stanton, Anthony, and Gage, eds., *History of Woman Suffrage,* II: 615–22.

47. Slaughterhouse Cases, 16 Wallace 36 (1873); William E. Forbath, "The Ambiguities of Free Labor: Labor and the Law in the Gilded Age," *Wisconsin Law Review* 4 (1985): 767–89. Stanton, Anthony, and Gage, eds., *History of Woman Suffrage,* II: 622–26. While arguing for the relevance of the Fourteenth Amendment to the Bradwell case, Senator Matthew Carpenter submitted a brief to the Court *against* the relevance of the amendment in the Slaughterhouse Cases because he opposed a construction so "broad that it would invalidate desirable government regulation." Slaughterhouse Cases, 21 U.S. Supreme Court Reports Lawyer's Edition (1873): 399–401.

48. United States v. Anthony, 24 F. Cas. (C.C.N.D.N.Y. 1873) (No. 14,459); quoted in Stanton, Anthony, and Gage, eds., *History of Woman Suffrage,* II: 641, 675–79.

49. Minor v. Happersett, 21 Wallace 162 (1875): quoted in Stanton, Anthony, and Gage, eds., *History of Woman Suffrage,* II: 717–42, esp. 719, 742. Chief Justice Salmon P. Chase, the lone dissenter in Bradwell v. State, had died and had been replaced by Chief Justice Morrison R. Waite.

50. United States v. Reese, 92 U.S. 214 (1876); United States v. Cruikshank, 92 U.S. 542 (1876).

51. Stanton, Anthony, and Gage, eds., *History of Woman Suffrage,* II: 333; III: 14, 25, 75. For comments on the railroad strikes of 1877, both for and against the strikers, see ibid., III: 72–73.

52. Stanton, Anthony, and Gage, eds., *History of Woman Suffrage,* III: 73–77; Steven M. Buechler, *The Transformation of the Woman Suffrage Movement: The Case of Illinois, 1850–1920* (New Brunswick, N.J., 1986), pp. 108–17; Christine Stansell, *City of Women: Sex and Class in New York, 1789–1860* (New York, 1986), pp. 203–9.

53. Stanton, Anthony, and Gage, eds., *History of Woman Suffrage,* III: 80–92.

54. Ibid., pp. 87–88.

MARXISM AND THE U.S. CONSTITUTION:

Changing Views of the Communist Party, U.S.A., 1926–1956

Paul Mishler

> Every constitutional crisis in American history has been, of course, merely the juridical form taken by great social struggles, conflicts of classes, contradictions between fundamental class interests.
>
> —Earl Browder,
> general secretary of the Communist Party[1]

The U.S. Constitution is the preeminent document of U.S. politics. As a symbol of our historical traditions, its significance is shared only by the Declaration of Independence and perhaps the Emancipation Proclamation. More importantly, in drafting the Constitution in 1787, the framers set down the formal political structure through which bourgeois democracy in this country would develop. Thus how radicals have analyzed the role of the Constitution in the history and political structure of this country has been a distillation of their perspectives on the problems of U.S. politics in general.

The development by U.S. Communists of a Marxist analysis of the Constitution was part of an attempt to reconcile the desire for revolutionary social transformation with the limits imposed by the structures of constitutional government and by the ideological reverence with which the Constitution was held by the people of the United States. The focus of this essay is the change in the Communist Party's perspective on the Constitution that occurred in the mid-1930s. The central feature of this new perspective was the understanding of the creation, and continuing importance, of the Constitution and its role in U.S. politics as a historical process in which popular struggle had an important impact. The importance of this change was that it provided a framework for political radicals to struggle for change within the capitalist system at the same time as they maintained their opposition to the system as a whole.

During the 1920s, the Communist Party viewed the particulars of U.S. history and political life, and the contradictory developments within our institutions, as insignificant compared to the role the entire "superstructure" played as a mask for class power. Their negative view of the Constitution was thus only one aspect of a more general analysis of bourgeois democracy. However, by the latter part of the 1930s Communists had begun to discuss the Constitution as a historical document whose meaning had changed in response to the pressures exerted by popular democratic struggles. The Constitution was now seen as an expression of the struggle between complex class forces, with this class struggle having an impact on how the Constitution was used and interpreted over the course of U.S. history.

Between 1926 and 1936 the Communist Party had viewed the Constitution as having little or no relevance to the U.S. working class. It was seen as a document that had been created to serve the interests of the newly empowered ruling class of the 1780s, in order to protect this class from the demands of the eighteenth-century lower classes. The 1928 election platform of the Workers' (Communist) Party expressed this view succinctly:

> The Constitution of the United States was drawn up by the big bankers, big landowners, and rich merchants of 1787, admittedly against the working masses. As Madison, the "Father of the Constitution," put it, the Government ought to *protect the minority of the opulant against the majority.*[2]

Further on in this platform the Communist attitude toward U.S. political life is summed up in the statement that the "present big business democracy of the United States is in reality nothing but a dictatorship of the capitalists."[3] But the Communist Party also looked to the 1770s for lessons for revolutionaries of the twentieth century. Their view was that the two central documents of the revolutionary period—the Constitution and the Declaration of Independence—were fundamentally in conflict. Like previous generations of U.S.

radicals, they saw the Declaration of Independence as representing the radical wing of the Revolution and the Constitution as a conservative attempt to undo its promises.

The Communist Party began its reevaluation of U.S. political and ideological traditions in the mid-1930s as a result of changes in political strategy mandated by the Seventh Congress of the Communist International in 1935. Responding to the victory of fascism in Germany and Italy and the danger of its spreading elsewhere in Europe, the Communist International argued that alliances among the Communist Party and other democratic forces within each country were now necessary. Overcoming the divisions among working-class political organizations, and especially between Communist and Socialist parties, was central to this strategy. In addition, in a new development in the Comintern perspective, the various Communist parties were to ally with antifascist sections of the bourgeoisie in defense of bourgeois democracy. By 1934, the Communist Party in the United States had pioneered in adopting this strategy because of its experience in organizing against the effects of the Depression, in organizing industrial unions, and in the youth movement. The adoption of the new Comintern line gave the sanction of the International Communist movement to the practical lessons being drawn by Communists in the United States.

The political defense of democracy required by the new line had an analytical corollary in the need to develop a Marxist interpretation of the role of the democratic tradition in the United States. This was symbolized by the best-known Communist slogan of the period, "Communism is twentieth-century Americanism."

Bourgeois democracy, in fact, had been taken for granted by Communists as the political form most suited to a capitalist economy. It needed no defense from the Communists because they assumed, as had other radicals before them, that history moved only in a progressive direction. Therefore they thought that socialist democracy was the only possible historical successor to capitalist democracy. But the victory of the Nazis in Germany and the growth of fascist or fascist-type movements elsewhere (including in the United States), showed that history could go backward as well.[4]

Georgi Dimitroff, the central proponent of the Popular Front strategy in the international Communist movement, pointed out the importance of claiming the legacy of the historical struggles for democracy in his main report to the Seventh World Congress of the Communist International in 1935:

> Communists who . . . do nothing to enlighten the masses on the past of their own people, in a historically correct fashion . . . , who do nothing to *link up their present struggle with its revolutionary traditions and past*—voluntarily relinquish to fascist falsifiers all that is valuable in the historical past of the nation, that the fascists may bamboozle the masses.[5]

The development by U.S. Communists of a new analysis was rooted in their changing perspective on the two central battles in the history of democracy in the United States, the War for Independence, and the Civil War. It was here that the party found the basis of a Marxist approach to the Constitution and its use in the working-class struggles of the twentieth century.

In particular, Communist writers focused on the political aftermath of these wars. They argued that it was during such periods of political consolidation that the cleavages of U.S. society were illuminated most clearly. At these points, the key struggles were over the social character of the victories won on the battlefield and the incorporation of these victories into the political structure. In other words, while the wars themselves were carried out with the cooperation of a broad multiclass alliance, the postwar political struggle over the distribution of power within the victorious alliance determined which class would receive the lions' share of the political and social spoils. This approach had much in common with that of bourgeois historians; what was different was the attempt to formulate an analysis that would legitimate the role of revolutionaries living and working in the twentieth century.

In an article entitled "Whose Revolution Is It?" written in 1926 to commemorate the 150th anniversary of the Declaration of Independence, Bertram D. Wolfe appealed to his readers to claim the legacy of the bourgeois democratic revolution of 1776. He disputed the claims put forward by "many working-class writers" that the Revolution of 1776 did not live up to glowing promises of the Declaration of Independence and therefore had not accomplished anything.[6] He argued that "it is time that the American working class begins to 'discover America' and its body of native revolutionary traditions."[7]

What is particularly interesting about Wolfe's analysis is that, except for a brief defense of the Bill of Rights, he barely mentions the Constitution. His concern is to use the experiences of the Revolution to defend by inference, Soviet revolutionary practice. Thus after arguing that the causes of the Revolution lay in the economic interests of the incipient North American bourgeoisie, he turns to the issues raised by the Revolution itself. The central argument here is that after the war, the victorious "patriots" established a revolutionary class dictatorship:

> The truth of the matter is that our revolution of 1776 was carried out as a class dictatorship with all the accompaniments of force and revolutionary terror that the ruling class historians of today attack in the case of Soviet Russia and that the polite liberals deplore.[8]

Similarly, Earl Browder, writing just before the adoption of the Popular Front, explicitly counterposed the revolutionary stance of the Declaration of Independence to the conservativism of the Constitution:

> These men [the "patriots" of the Revolution], in their own time, faced the issues of their day, cut through the red tape of precedent legalism and constitutionalism with a sword, made a revolution, killed off a dying and outworn system, and opened up a new chapter in world history. . . . The Declaration of Independence was for that time what the Communist Manifesto is for ours.[9]

Turning to the Constitution, Browder wrote: "After the *counter-revolution* engineered by Alexander Hamilton had been victorious and established itself under the *Constitution* in 1787, a period of reaction set in."[10]

The focus on the progressive nature of the Declaration of Independence, to the exclusion of the Constitution, continued into the late 1930s. Twelve years after Wolfe's article, Francis Franklin wrote on the same subject:

> The Declaration of Independence indicated the conscious maturity of the movement for national unification and for the self-determination of the American people. All the tasks so boldly enunciated by this Declaration have still not been realized. Therefore, July Fourth can be celebrated only by *renewed* declaration of the effort to realize in their entirety its aims of freedom and equality. The Communist Party, inheritor of the revolutionary democratic tasks of the great molders of the American people, proudly proclaims its determination to fulfil these tasks.[11]

Like Wolfe, Franklin saw the postrevolutionary period as a time of fierce struggle between the counterrevolutionary Federalists and the democratic-revolutionary Jeffersonians. But while he accepts Jefferson's support of the Constitution, Franklin highlights the struggle for the inclusion of the Bill of Rights. In the end, he says, it was the Bill of Rights that was the key popular victory in the period of postrevolutionary consolidation. It is therefore the Declaration of Independence and the Bill of Rights that are the parts of the U.S. revolutionary past that are worthy of support, not the Constitution itself: "Under modern conditions, only socialism can afford an economic base capable of giving permanent support to the fundamental principles of Americanism as contained in the Declaration of Independence and the Bill of Rights."[12]

The view of the Constitution adopted by Communists during the Popular Front was an elaboration and extension of their earlier analysis rather than a complete negation of it. What was new, however, was the recognition that the struggle for democracy was an issue in which the working class had a stake.

Now the Constitution was seen as an arena of struggle, not simply a superstructural expression of capitalist domination. Communists looked to the debates over constitutional issues for expressions of the shifting nature of class alliances, alliances in which the working classes could advance their position. Most importantly, they saw that these alliances changed at particular historical junctures in which the crises of class society emerged ever more sharply. Earl Browder wrote in 1937:

> The Constitution that emerged was thus a compromise. It was a compromise between conflicting regional interests of the bourgeoisie; it was a compromise between two antagonistic social-economic systems, the slave system of the Southern plantation owners and the budding capitalism of the Northern merchants and manufacturers; and *most basic of all . . . it was a compromise between aristocratic and democratic principles of government.*[13]

Here the importance of democratic principles is connected to an analysis that takes into account differences in the interests and political role of different sections of the bourgeoisie. The democratic elements of the Constitution, such as the Bill of Rights, are viewed as victories won by the lower orders of the postrevolutionary period against the machinations of the Hamiltonian Federalists, the "economic royalists" of their day.

Furthermore, unlike in his earlier statement, in which he saw the "counterrevolution" of the Constitution as the conclusion of the revolutionary process, in the post-Popular Front writings Browder is much more optimistic. By 1937 he no longer believed that the revolutionary period ended with a counterrevolutionary Constitution. Rather, Jefferson's victory of 1800, he said, was a defeat for the aristocrats and a victory for the people.[14]

In his discussion of what he called the "American tradition," Browder connected the struggles of the past with those of the present. After describing the crises of the Revolutionary and Civil War periods, he claimed that he country was now (1937) facing a third major crisis, one that

> arises from the fact that political power, as expressed in the democratically registered will of the majority, is challenged by economic power, as expressed in our economic royalists—the small group of rich families which owns and controls 95 per cent of our productive economy. Our economic royalists are moving to destroy our political democracy, which has been undermined by losing its economic foundations.[15]

The development of a Marxist analysis of the Civil War and Reconstruction periods played an even greater role in developing a historical view of the Constitution and its ongoing role in U.S. politics. For the Communists, two issues arose in this era that were central to the possibilities for, and limits on, democracy in the United States: the role of the bourgeoisie in the struggle for democracy, and the critical role of Afro-Americans in the battle for this democracy. Furthermore, this was one of those historical junctures in which social and class conflict broke into the open and illuminated the role that struggle could play in defining the legal and political institutions of a society.

By the late 1920s both the Communist Party, U.S.A., and the Communist International had defined the struggle for Afro-American equality as a crucial feature of the overall class struggle in the United States. In making this argument, the Communists wanted to avoid nationalism, which emphasized racial oppression to the exclusion of class oppression, *and* the approach of the pre-World War I Socialist Party, which made the "Negro question" subordinate to the class question. In formulating their approach, Communist writers began to look into the history of Afro-Americans in order to find justification for their own Marxist strategy. While much attention has been paid to the mechanical application of Soviet nationality theory to the United States in the form of the demand for a Black nation in the South, in fact the Communists took up the struggle for Afro-American equality in every facet of their work. The Scottsboro case, in which the Communist Party organized a mass defense movement in support of nine Alabama Afro-American boys who were being framed on a rape charge was turned into an international *cause célèbre*. Furthermore, their efforts to organize sharecropper unions united poor rural blacks and whites in some parts of the South for the first time. These are just two examples of the ways which Communists tried to make white workers concerned about the issues faced by blacks.[16]

As in the case of the Communist analyses of the Revolution, the analyses of the Civil War done prior to the Popular Front focused on its essentially bourgeois nature. For example, in 1927 "A.L." wrote an introduction to a selection of Marx's writings on the Civil War which argued that, for Marx, the continuing existence of slavery was central to the struggle between the northern bourgeoisie and the southern planters. Marx had argued that the Union could not be preserved and the northern capitalists could not command the ascendent position unless the slaves were freed. While this might seem obvious, historians had been assiduously avoiding this point, concentrating instead on the issues of political control over the government and the constitutional issues involved in the struggle over "states' rights." For the Progressive historians, the purely economic conflicts between northern industrialists and southern agrarians were the key. "A.L." goes on to point out that in Marx's analysis, made during the 1860s, the military failures of the first two years of the Civil War were shown to be a direct result of the limitations of the bourgeois nature of the struggle. Thus Marx wrote to Engels, "The manner in which the North carries on the war is only to be expected from a bourgeois republic where swindle has been on the sovereign throne for so long."[17]

While "A.L." did not deal with the constitutional changes that emerged from the northern victory, the Communist Party's 1928 election platform explicitly stated that the failure of the Civil War and

Reconstruction was the result of the refusal of the bourgeoisie to guarantee black rights. The Constitution, which before the Civil War was flawed by its legalization of slavery, became a sham afterward because the new amendments did not guarantee freedom for the former slaves:

> The famous Fourteenth and Fifteenth amendments of the Constitution amount but to a scrap of paper. They never were carried out for a moment. The Supreme Court has upheld State laws which disenfranchised the Negroes. Sheer force prevents the Negro from exercising his so-called political rights. The Federal Government has never made any attempt to reduce the representation from those Southern States which violate the Constitution, as Section Two of the Fourteenth Amendment to the Constitution provides. . . . *Lynch law is the law over Negroes. The terror of the Ku Klux Klan is the constitution for the Negroes.*[18]

The most important Communist analysis of this period that was written from the perspective of the Popular Front was James S. Allen's *Reconstruction: The Battle for Democracy,* published in 1937. In it Allen developed a view of the post-Civil War constitutional battles that was more complex than that outlined in the 1928 election platform.

In 1932 Allen had written on the relationship between the struggle for Afro-American equality in the twentieth century and the development of an analysis of the Civil War and Reconstruction:

> It is inevitable that the pressing nature of the Negro question today, the problems met with in clarifying the Communist position on this question, should lead us back to the Civil War and Reconstruction since it was there that much of the ground work was laid for the present oppression of the Negroes.[19]

In *Reconstruction: The Battle for Democracy,* Allen argued that the Fourteenth and Fifteenth amendments were the "quintessence of the greatest victories of Reconstruction," but "remain promissory notes upon which the Negro people still have to collect."[20] The reason lies in the nature of the class coalition that led the country during and after the Civil War. The struggle between the "Radical Republicans" and the more conservative sections of the Republican Party over the policies of Reconstruction was between business-oriented and more democratic sections of the party: "The complicated device attached to the Constitution as the Fourteenth Amendment was a compromise measure. It displays more adequately than any other legal action taken at this time the conflicting tendencies in the bourgeois democracy."[21]

The compromise was the inclusion of what Allen called "the now infamous 'due process of law' clause for the protection of corporations."[22] This clause was framed to afford maximum protection to corporations, not to protect the democratic rights of former slaves. Allen quotes Roscoe Conkling, a prominent Republican of the time, as saying that the Fourteenth Amendment was a "golden rule" to "curb the many who would do to the few as they would not have the few do to them":

> The golden rule was supplied, the Supreme Court had only to take the hint. It decided that the phrase applied to "corporate" as well as natural persons. From 1868 to 1912, the Supreme Court rendered 604 decisions based on the Amendment, of which 312 concerned corporations. There were 28 appeals to the Court involving Negro rights under the Fourteenth Amendment, of which 22 were decided adversely.[23]

What was new about Allen's analysis was that it focused on the ways in which political struggle between classes and class alliances shaped the institutional framework of bourgeois democracy. It was not that the perspective on the Constitution developed by the Communist Party during the Popular Front period repudiated the critique of the failures of capitalism that was central to earlier analyses. Rather, by seeing constitutional change as the outcome of political struggle, the possibilities of effecting change in the political system within a constitutional framework was enhanced.

In formulating this historical perspective, the Communist Party tried to avoid both the errors of social democracy and their own earlier sectarianism. Thus they did not see the capitalist state as a neutral institution or believe that socialism in the United States could be instituted solely through legislative means. Instead, they argued that the extent to which the political institutions of capitalist society proved responsive to popular demands was determined by the militancy of the struggle carried out by the working class and its allies.

The influence of this historical approach remained strong even after the end of the New Deal, the coming of the Cold War, and the repression of the post-World War II period. Although the development of this analysis was associated with Earl Browder's leadership, it survived its repudiation and his expulsion from the party in 1946. At least one of the factors in ousting Browder was his overestimation of the ability of bourgeois democracy to reform itself to the point where socialism would no longer be necessary.

The political context of the post-World War II period proved how mistaken Browder had been. During the late 1940s and through the 1950s the Communist Party, as well as the rest of the Left, faced the onslaught of the heightening Cold War and its domestic ramifications: witch-hunts, blacklists, and legal repression. A debate developed in the party over the meaning of the repression in the context of the traditions of U.S. politics. It took the form of a discussion of whether fascism was coming and whether constitutional guarantees could still be relied upon to protect against repression.

What is particularly interesting is that all sides in this discussion took a pro-Constitutional view. There is very little in the published debates that returns to the perspective of the 1920s—that the Constitution represented the structure within which bourgeois domination operates. In fact, this view did not reemerge until the 1960s, when it was part of the New Left critique of liberalism and a response to the new wave of repression that marked the end of that decade.

But in the 1950s most Communists saw the repression as an aberration of U.S. political life. The Constitution not only provided tools with which to defend the party and the Left, but the commitment of the U.S. people to the Constitution was seen as an important protection for the movement. Even those Communists who saw incipient or existing fascism in the repression did not reject the Constitution per se. Instead they argued that the U.S. ruling class had broken its own rules. Indeed, the belief that the Constitution was a democratic document may have been strongest among this group because it saw repression as a major change in the U.S. political tradition. They were much less willing to admit that repression could take place within the confines of bourgeois democracy and yet not represent a wholesale transformation to fascism.[24]

As early as 1948, many Communists, concerned about the conservative turn in the foreign and domestic policy, felt that the coming period would be characterized by a right-wing, or possibly fascist, trend. Eugene Dennis's report to the Fourteenth Convention of the Communist Party in 1948 was entitled "The Fascist Danger." In it he said, "Only those who have eyes but will not see can be blind to the increased danger of fascism in America. Yet in some quarters the danger is denied, while in others it is not understood."[25]

Yet even though the Communists warned about the danger of fascism, they did not believe that the repression directed against them represented fascism in practice. Rather, they saw the period beginning with the end of the war as one of fierce struggle between forces moving toward fascism and the democratically minded people. The relationship between this analysis of the possibilities of fascism and the attitude that Communists should take toward bourgeois democracy was set out in an article by William Z. Foster in 1954:

> The Party must particularly answer the specific question as to whether or not these trends have now brought about such a qualitative weakening of bourgeois democracy in this country that we can be said actually to be in the beginnings of fascism. . . .
>
> If this danger is overestimated it can lead to an abandonment, as hopeless, of practical means of struggle . . . and if the danger is underestimated, this can cause a Rightist failure to arouse the workers and their allies to fight a political menace which, if neglected, can become catastrophic for them.[26]

Foster argued that there was indeed a danger of fascism, but that it was not inevitable.[27] This conclusion was based on the party's analysis of the particular historical strengths and weaknesses of bourgeois democracy during the 1950s. As Mark Logan wrote in *Political Affairs* in 1954:

> There is a *real* constitutional crisis. The bourgeoisie does not yet *formally* outlaw and illegalize the Bill of Rights and the Constitution. It continues to operate behind the smokescreen of "due process." It still attempts to give "legal" sanction to all of its illegal encroachments.[28]

In order to assess the state of bourgeois democracy the party returned to the historical analysis of the bourgeois democracy that had been developed during the late 1930s. Now, however, the focus was the Bill of Rights. As with the previous analysis of the Constitution, they no longer saw the Bill of Rights as solely an eighteenth-century document, but as living representation of class and social struggles. Arnold Johnson wrote in 1949:

> The mass of American people know that the Bill of Rights is not a mere piece of paper to be put in the archives or to be destroyed. It is a

document which embodies the struggles of the mass of the people against the most reactionary and Tory elements of the ruling class. The full meaning of the struggle of the people for the Bill of Rights today can be best understood by appreciating the historical struggles and battles which have become part of that document.[29]

Furthermore, the struggle over the inclusion of the Bill of Rights was now seen as central to the final ratification of the Constitution, since constitutional government without the protection of the Bill of Rights would have been a reversal of the struggles first waged between reactionaries and democrats in the 1780s: "[T]he American people refused to accept the Constitution as a legal framework until the ruling classes recognized that the Bill of Rights could not be denied to the masses who had carried through the Revolution."[30]

During the 1950s the struggle for black equality continued to be important to the Communists' view of the Constitution. The emphasis on the Bill of Rights was explicitly connected to the Constitutional amendments dealing with the rights of Afro-Americans. "The Bill of Rights was strengthened with the Thirteenth, Fourteenth, and Fifteenth Amendments. The actual realization of the fundamental rights in these amendments is still on the agenda for today."[31]

The 1954 Supreme Court decision outlawing segregation in public education confirmed the decisive role played by mass struggle in shaping the Constitution. While the Communist Party viewed the Supreme Court as primarily a conservative institution, it was still capable of responding to mass pressure. "The Supreme Court," wrote George Blake, "is an instrument of the ruling class, and its decisions throughout our history bear the imprint of that relationship, as well as the general alignment of class forces prevailing at each period."[32] Thus the Communists saw *Brown* vs. *Topeka Board of Education* as proof that, in the last analysis, a mobilized population could shape the political decisions of the country, even in a period such as the 1950s. To quote Logan again:

The recent decision of the Supreme Court on segregation in education, historic in its significance as a victory for the Negro people in particular, bears directly upon and highlights special features of the crisis of bourgeois democracy and the many pathways of struggle before the American working class and their allies. The Supreme Court decision was wrested from the bourgeoisie by intensive, prolonged and heroic struggles on the part of the Negro people, aided by the American working class as a whole.[33]

One result of the Communist Party's growing acceptance of the importance of the Constitution as a framework for popular struggle was a lessening of the party's critique of bourgeois democracy. The implications of this change were particularly apparent in the party's analysis of the role played by the Constitution in the transition to socialism in the United States. By the mid-1950s, the party had commited itself to a constitutional transition to socialism that explicitly precluded the almost insurrectionary perspective of the 1920s.

The reasons for this lay not only in the development of the more positive outlook on the Constitution, but also in the need to rely on the legal protections of the Constitution and Bill of Rights during a period of repression. Thus in 1956 Eugene Dennis, then general secretary of the party, reported to the National Committee on the possibility of building a mass socialist movement in the United States. Given the criticisms of Stalin made at the Twentieth Congress of the Communist Party of the Soviet Union, as well as the position of Communists in the United States during the 1950s, Dennis argued that Communists had to see the transition to socialism in the United States *within* the U.S. political framework. In answer to some members criticisms, as well as that of those opposed to the Communists, he wrote:

> [W]e American Communists do *not* advocate force and violence. We do *not* consider civil war inevitable nor in any way desirable. We desire and seek constitutional and democratic solutions to current and fundamental problems. We favor and advocate a peaceful and democratic transition to Socialism.[34]

However, even while the Communist Party had moved to the point of seeing the Constitution as containing the possibility for radical social transformation, it was not on the ground that the political structure of the United States had lost its class content, or that the peaceful transition to socialism could be assured by the intentions of Communists. Thus Gil Green argued in 1956 that whether socialism would come to the United States peacefully or not would depend on the actions of the ruling class:

> The Communists, therefore, do not advocate the use of force and violence in the achievement of either their immediate or ultimate aims.

On the contrary, they desire to accomplish necessary social change by winning the majority of the people for these, and by creating conditions in which the majority can exercise its will without infringement. Whether this is possible or not depends not on the Communists, but upon whether people can prevent the monopolists from unleashing violence against them.[35]

The view of the Constitution as a historically defined arena of struggle is now held by many on the Left today, particularly radical lawyers. Its disadvantage is that it may lead us to overvalue legalist interpretations at the expense of understanding the crucial role played by mass struggle in all social change. Its advantage is that it shows us both the limits and the possibilities for changing the political order, as well as how the Left can claim the mantle of defending traditional U.S. liberties against the unconstitutional actions of ruling-class politicians, at home and abroad.

Notes

I would like to thank Geraldine Casey, Attorney Mark S. Mishler, and Gil Green for their help in preparing this article.

1. Earl Browder, "The Constitutional Crisis" (radio broadcast, NBC, 1 September 1937), in Earl Browder, *The People's Front* (New York, 1938), p. 222.
2. *The Platform of Class Struggle: The National Platform of the Workers' (Communist) Party, 1928* (New York, 1928), p. 34.
3. Ibid., p. 36.
4. I am indebted to Gil Green for this point. He is currently a member of the Central Committee of the Communist Party, U.S.A., and was, during this period, the general secretary of the Young Communist League of the United States and a member of the Executive Committee of the Communist International (after 1935).
5. Georgi Dimitroff, *United Front Against Fascism* (New York, 1935), p. 78.
6. Bertram D. Wolfe, "Whose Revolution Is It?" *Workers' Monthly* (official organ of the Workers' Communist Party of America) 5, no. 9 (July 1926): 387.
7. Ibid., p. 392.
8. Ibid., p. 390.
9. Earl Browder, "Who Are the Americans?" in Earl Browder, *What Is Communism?* (New York, 1936), p. 16.
10. Ibid., p. 17.
11. Francis Franklin, "July 4th—Birthday of American Democracy," *The Communist* 17, no. 7 (July 1938): 630.
12. Ibid., p. 642.
13. Earl Browder, "The Revolutionary Background of the U.S. Constitution," *The*

Communist (September 1937), in Browder, *The People's Front,* p. 252; emphasis added.

14. Earl Browder, "The American Tradition," in ibid., p. 236.

15. Ibid.

16. See Earl Browder, "The Revolutionary Way Out," in *Communism in the United States* (New York, 1935), for a description of Communist perspectives on the struggle for Afro-American equality. In particular, Browder emphasizes that the demand for national self determination in the southern black belt was only a context for the struggle for black equality in all facets of life. He also pointed out the differences between the Communist perspective and those of the Socialists and black nationalists.

17. A.L., "Introduction" to Karl Marx, "The Civil War in North America," *The Communist* 7, no. 2 (April 1927): 101.

18. *The Platform of Class Struggle,* p. 50.

19. James S. Allen, "Distorters of the Revolutionary Heritage of the American Proletariat: The Traditions of Civil War and Reconstruction," *The Communist* 11, no. 12 (December 1932): 1104.

20. James S. Allen, *Reconstruction: The Battle for Democracy* (New York, 1937), p. 209.

21. Ibid., p. 83.

22. Ibid.

23. Ibid., p. 84.

24. I am indebted to Gil Green for corroborating this point. Green, a defendent in the Smith Act trials and an underground leader of the party, told me about the political ramifications of this debate. The decision as to whether the party should go underground, or how much of the party should concentrate on clandestine organization, was based on the definition of the political state of the country.

25. Eugene Dennis, "The Fascist Danger," *Political Affairs* 31, no. 4 (April 1952): 15.

26. William Z. Foster, "Is the U.S. in Early Stages of Fascism?" *Political Affairs* 33, no. 11 (November 1954): 5.

27. Ibid., p. 14.

28. Mark Logan, "The Working Class and the Nation," *Political Affairs* 33, no. 8 (August 1954): 31.

29. Arnold Johnson, "The Bill of Rights and the Twelve," *Political Affairs* 28, no. 7 (July 1949): 11.

30. Henry T. Goodwin, "On the Fight for Legality," *Political Affairs* 33, no. 11 (November 1954): 45.

31. Johnson, "The Bill of Rights," p. 16.

32. George Blake, "The Supreme Court Will Not Have the Last Word," *Political Affairs* 31, no. 3 (March 1952): 17.

33. Logan, "The Working Class and the Nation," p. 30.

34. Eugene Dennis, "For a Mass Party of Socialism," *Political Affairs* 35, no. 6 (June 1956): 5.

35. Gil Green, *The Enemy Forgotten* (New York, 1956), p. 315.

THESIS AND ANTITHESIS:
Section 7 of the NLRA, the First Amendment, and Workers' Rights

Staughton Lynd

For U.S. workers, the Constitution is a source of both hope and frustration.

On the one hand, the Constitution appears to guarantee the rights to speak, petition, and assemble, the right to be free of unreasonable searches and seizures, and the right not to be punished until proven guilty. These are rights that U.S. workers would very much like to have in their working lives. These seeming assurances of the First, Fourth, and Fifth amendments give rise to the strongly held feeling, "I got my rights."

Yet, as it turns out, workers do not have these rights. A worker employed by a private corporation does not have on-the-job constitutional rights because the Constitution applies only to governments, not to private employers. Workers in the public sector often have fewer rights than their private sector counterparts.

In coming years, workers and workers' advocates face a double task, first of arguing for public ownership, and second of arguing for dramatic extensions in the rights of employees. We cannot avoid the first of these tasks, because capitalism is collapsing in basic industries such as steel. But we cannot be content to promote the first task alone, because without an expansion of employees' rights, the spread of public ownership could prove a very mixed blessing. Under any imaginable form of government or quasi-government ownership, just as in the private sector, workers' rights to leaflet, petition, assemble, organize, picket, boycott, and strike will need express legal protection. This is the lesson of Polish Solidarity and of the British coal miners' strike.[1] Indeed, it is also a lesson of twentieth-century socialism taken as a whole.

The puzzle is, how best to provide that protection.

At first glance, it might seem that the advent of public ownership would inevitably mean that public sector labor law, including the First Amendment, rather than private sector labor law, expressed in statutes like the National Labor Relations Act (NLRA) and Railway Labor Act, will govern labor relations in affected enterprises.

At first glance, too, this might seem to be a good thing. A constitutional amendment might appear to offer more protection than a mere statute. Further, the erosion of workers' rights in the private sector, while ostensibly protected by Section 7 of the NLRA,[2] has prompted widespread skepticism about the act itself. At least since the adoption of the Taft-Hartley amendments in 1947, private sector employees have generally not been protected when they tried to boycott, to strike in solidarity with workers in another industry, to refuse to cross other workers' picket lines, to strike in violation of a collective bargaining agreement, to strike because of imminent danger to health and safety, to communicate with government agencies about practices of the employer believed to be unlawful, and to strike (or even picket) without union authorization.

However, on reflection neither question is as simple as it might at first appear.

The government or quasi-government ownership that will predictably come into being in an increasing number of enterprises can take many forms: the centralized administration of an entire industry, in the manner of the British coal industry, is only one among many models. TVA, Conrail, National Legal Services, and the planned Steel Valley Authority in the Pittsburgh area offer other possibilities. National financing can be combined with decentralized administration, as in the case of Legal Services. Facilities acquired by government can be administered by a public corporation, as in the case of Conrail and TVA.

As a result, a quasi-public enterprise may be governed not by public labor law but by the NLRA or Railway Labor Act. It is so with Conrail (where the Railway Labor Act and statutes creating Conrail govern). It is so with Legal Services (where the NLRA applies).

Thus the NLRA, rather than the Constitution, may govern the

labor relations of steel mills and other means of production acquired by the government. And this may be a good thing, because the Constitution does not protect certain rights essential to workers, above all the right to strike.

Historically, the First Amendment was not intended to protect the rights of wage workers (who, of course, did not exist in large numbers at the time the amendment was adopted). Rather, the amendment sought to safeguard the rights of property-owning middle-class citizens to read, speak, meet, and publish, prior to the formation of public policy. These rights are also critical for workers. But they are not *all* the rights required by wage workers, who, unlike middle-class persons, must ordinarily *act* together in order to make themselves heard. If workers in our society elected those whose economic decisions affect their daily lives, it might be sufficient for workers to have only First Amendment rights; but since economic decision-makers are not elected, workers must use methods more forceful than mere speech.

The First Amendment on its face does not protect rights such as the right to strike and the right to mass picketing. The amendment protects speech, both by individuals and by groups, and protects speech on subjects other than conditions of work (as Section 7 does not). Both the First Amendment and Section 7 protect the right to associate, and rights to group speech, such as leafletting and informational picketing. But only Section 7 protects concerted *activity* as such, so that in a situation where the First Amendment might be found not to be applicable because workers were engaged in "more than speech," Section 7 could still apply. On balance, Section 7, far more precisely than the First Amendment, delineates the kinds of rights that workers must have to protect themselves under any form of management, private or public.

The fact that the language of the First Amendment does not exactly fit or cover the rights that workers require—particularly the right to strike—helps to explain why public employees enjoy fewer rights than their private sector counterparts despite the availability of the First Amendment. As a result, there is good reason to take another look at Section 7 and to ask whether the right to engage in "concerted activity for mutual aid or protection" can be reanimated.

This article will therefore examine Section 7, and its relation to the First Amendment, in the following ways. In the first section, I will emphasize that both Section 7 and First Amendment rights are "communal rights," quite unlike the individualistic, property-based rights typical of our society. The second section will show that Section 7 speech rights were intended by the sponsors of the NLRA to be functional equivalents in the workplace of First Amendments rights in the larger society. In the third section, I will show how the Supreme Court during the years 1937–47 drew on the First Amendment in developing the case law as to speech rights in the workplace. Finally, in the fourth section I will suggest that (1) unions should abandon the practice of agreeing not to strike during the duration of a collective bargaining agreement, and (2) that the NLRA should be amended to cover public as well as private workplaces.

The right to engage in concerted activity for mutual aid or protection, and the rights protected by the First Amendment, are "communal rights" appropriate to a socialist society

If a new society is struggling to be born from the womb of capitalist society, one would expect to find a rudimentary world view and a corresponding new conception of right. The new kind of right would not be conceptualized as individual property, nor would it presuppose that one person's gain was inevitably another's loss. It would articulate, in however preliminary a form, the values of community, compassion, and solidarity.

The right to engage in concerted activity

I suggest that the right of workers "to engage in concerted activities for . . . mutual aid or protection," now guaranteed by federal labor law,[3] is an example of a communal right. More than any other institution in capitalist society, the labor movement is based on communal values. Its central historical experience is solidarity, the banding together of individual workers who are alone too weak to protect themselves.[4] Thus, there has arisen the value expressed by the phrase, "An injury to one is an injury to all." To be sure, at times particular labor organizations, and to some extent trade unionism in general, fall short of this communal aspiration. Yet it is significant that trade union members still address one another as "Brother" and "Sister" and sign their correspondence "Fraternally yours." These conventions evidence an underlying attitude and practice fundamentally different from that in business and even in academia, where one person's job security subtracts from, or at most is separate from, another's.

There is nothing metaphysical or indeterminate about this right. It articulates the historical experience of rank-and-file workers. It is, if anything, more specific in content than most legal rules. No one has ever doubted that "concerted activity" meant strikes, picketing, the formation of labor organizations, and related activities. And it is clearly not a right akin to an individual's ownership of property. On the contrary, it is a right to act together, to engage in activity commonly and most effectively undertaken by groups.

This in no way endorses the National Labor Relations Act, in which the right is presently embodied. On the one hand, the protection of concerted activity in Section 7 of the NLRA makes it "perhaps the most radical piece of legislation ever enacted by the United States Congress."[5] On the other hand, the American Civil Liberties Union predicted at the time the act was passed that it would "impair labor's rights in the long run, however much its authors may intend precisely the contrary."[6] I have felt for some years that this assessment by the ACLU was correct:

> [I]t took a lot of backtracking by the Supreme Court to get there, but maybe that was part of the prediction, at least in its more sophisticated form: no matter how the law was written, once you had the government that far into controlling the labor movement, given the nature of power in American society, it was going to wind up controlling the labor movement for the sake of business.[7]

But from my point of view, the historical miscarriage of the NLRA makes it more and not less important to "celebrate and seek to restore to its intended vigor the right to engage in concerted activity for mutual aid or protection."[8]

It may not be immediately clear why this right is so different from other rights. The best approach to understanding the special features of this right is to examine the underlying forms of struggle from which the right is derived. Consider the following example.

After Anna Walentynowicz was discharged from her job as a crane operator in the Lenin shipyard in Gdansk, Poland, in August 1980, her workmates struck demanding her reinstatement. Other ship-yards struck in sympathy. In two days the workers at the Lenin yard had won their demands. Walentynowicz and Lech Walesa were reinstated and the Polish government promised to build a monument honoring workers killed in the strike of 1970. The strike would have ended in failure, however, had it not been for the intervention of two individuals, Walentynowicz and her friend Alina Pienkowska. As Walentynowicz tells the story:

> Alina Pienkowska and I went running back to the hall to declare a solidarity strike, but the microphones were off. The shipyard loud-speakers were announcing that the strike was over and that everyone had to leave by six P.M. The gates were open, and people were leaving.
>
> So Alina and I went running to the main gate. And I began appealing to them to declare a solidarity strike, because the only reason that the manager had met our demands was that the other factories were still on strike. I said that if the workers at these factories were defeated, we wouldn't be safe either. But somebody challenged me. "On whose authority are you declaring this a strike? I'm tired and I want to go home." I too was tired, and I started to cry. . . .
>
> Now, Alina is very small, a tiny person, but full of initiative. She stood up on a barrel and began to appeal to those who were leaving. "We have to help the others with their strikes, because they have helped us. We have to defend them." Somebody from the crowd said, "She's right!" The gate was closed.[9]

The strike that gave birth to Polish Solidarity followed.

I believe that this piece of history embodies a good deal of what legal workers for a new society care about. In Gdansk, one worker was fired and a whole shipyard walked off the job in protest. Although one recounts this as if it were an everyday occurrence, I have never known a university faculty to do this for a colleague who had been fired or denied tenure. It does, however, occur regularly in the labor movement. Ed Mann tells of an incident in Youngstown in the late 1960s:

> We had a man killed in the open hearth. . . . He had seven days to go to retirement. Two or three months before that I'd filed a grievance, requesting that certain safety features be adopted. The grievance was rejected out of hand. He was killed by a truck backing up. One of the

items on the grievance was that trucks backing up have a warning system.

The guy gets killed. Everybody liked him. He'd worked there . . . how many years? . . . you know. All right, I led a strike. I had to scream and holler, drag people out by the heels, but I got them out, shut the place down.[10]

In Gdansk, after the first yard struck in protest, workers at other shipyards also left their jobs. As is often the case in wildcat strikes, the workers developed their own demands, in addition to demanding Walentynowicz' reinstatement. When the question was posed whether the Lenin yard strikers should stay out on behalf of the demands of other shipyards, Anna Walentynowicz took the position that only if the Lenin workers continued their strike on behalf of the workers at the other shipyards would they be "safe." Clearly she was saying that workers, to secure their rights, need above all else to preserve their solidarity.

This distinctive experience of solidarity, underlying the right to engage in concerted activity, has three unusual attributes. First, the well-being of the individual and the well-being of the group are not experienced as antagonistic. Justice Sandra Day O'Connor has written that "the concepts of individual action for personal gain and 'concerted activity' are intuitively incompatible."[11] This is the view from the outside, the view of someone who has not experienced the wage worker's elemental need for the support of other workers. Judge Learned Hand came much closer to the reality in a passage written soon after the enactment of Section 7:

> When all other workmen in a shop make common cause with a fellow workman over his separate grievance, and go out on strike in his support, they engage in a "concerted activity" for "mutual aid or protection," although the aggrieved workman is the only one of them who has any immediate stake in the outcome. The rest know that by their action each one of them assures himself, in case his turn ever comes, of the support of the one whom they are all then helping; and the solidarity so established is "mutual aid" in the most literal sense, as nobody doubts. So too of those engaging in a "sympathetic strike," or secondary boycott; the immediate quarrel does not itself concern them, but by extending the number of those who will make the enemy of one the enemy of all, the power of each is vastly increased.[12]

I have heard a rank-and-file steelworker use almost identical language in trying to persuade fellow workers to support each other's grievances. What is counterintuitive to Justice O'Connor's argument is the common sense of those engaged in the struggle.

Second, the group of those who work together—the informal work group, the department, the local union, the class—is often experienced as a reality in itself. Thus, Hand's rationale misses something crucial to the right to engage in concerted activity. I do not scratch your back only because one day I may need you to scratch mine. Labor solidarity is more than an updated version of the social contract through which each individual undertakes to assist others for the advancement of his or her own interest.

In a family, when I as son, husband, or father, express love toward you, I do not do so in order to assure myself of love in return. I do not help my son in order to be able to claim assistance from him when I am old; I do it because he and I are in the world together; we are one flesh. Similarly in a workplace, persons who work together form families-at-work. When you and I are working together, and the foreman suddenly discharges you, and I find myself putting down my tools or stopping my machine before I have had time to think—why do I do this? Is it not because, as I actually experience the event, your discharge does not happen only to you but also happens to *us*?

Justice Brennan's majority opinion in *NLRB* v. *City Disposal Systems, Inc.* portrays this experienced reality of the working group. The case dealt with a truck driver who refused to drive an unsafe truck.[13] Nobody was with Brown, the driver, when he told two supervisors that the truck in question, No. 244, "has got problems and I don't want to drive it."[14] One of the supervisors went on to tell Brown that "[w]e've got all this garbage out here to haul and you tell me about you don't want to drive." Brown responded, "Bob, what are you going to do, put the garbage ahead of the safety of the men?" Thus Brown, although he was quite alone, put his case as a matter of "the safety of the *men*," because this is how he experienced it. And in fact, Brown initially had become aware of the problems with the truck when, two days earlier, he had been driving a different truck and, because of its brake problems "truck No. 244 nearly collided with Brown's truck";[15] when that happened, Brown and the driver of No. 244 together brought it to the employer's repair facility. Accordingly, Justice Brennan is profoundly right when he says in *City Disposal* that when Brown invoked the clause in the collective bargaining agreement permitting a driver to refuse to drive an unsafe truck, he did "not stand alone" but brought "to bear on his employer the power and resolve of all his fellow employees."[16] When James Brown refused to drive a truck he believed to be unsafe,

> he was in effect reminding his employer that he and his fellow employees . . . had extracted a promise from City Disposal that they would not be asked to drive unsafe trucks. He was also reminding his employer that if it persisted in ordering him to drive an unsafe truck, he could reharness the power of that group to ensure the enforcement of that promise. *It was just as though James Brown was reassembling his fellow union members to reenact their decision not to drive unsafe trucks.*[17]

Finally—and again in dialectical tension with the attribute just emphasized—the solidarity of workers articulated in the right to engage in concerted activity can and must be individually exercised. The Walentynowicz story contains this theme, too. When Walentynowicz was asked, "On whose authority are you declaring this a strike?" she began to cry. But her friend, now acting completely alone, stood up on the barrel and finished the job.

Any conception of the right to concerted activity that might make the rights to strike and to picket less capable of exercise by individuals flies in the face of legislative history. In the late nineteenth and early twentieth centuries, workers were understood to be free to quit work or to picket individually (however ineffectual that might be), but were found liable under conspiracy or common law tort theories if they performed the same acts jointly. The intent of the Clayton and Norris-LaGuardia acts was to protect activities by groups that were assumed to be protected when practiced by individuals. Both laws expressly protected striking, and Norris-LaGuardia protected picketing as well, whether undertaken "singly or in concert."[18]

Section 7 of the Wagner Act, enacted only three years after the passage of Norris-LaGuardia, protected "concerted activity" against the private employer but failed to add that individual exercise of the same right was also protected. There is not the slightest evidence to suggest that this omission indicated any change in the conception of right as expressed in Norris-LaGuardia. Nonetheless, for many years the National Labor Relations Board and the Supreme Court took advantage of the omission, finding "statutory protection for an activity engaged in by two employees while the very same activity engaged in by one remains unprotected,"[19] and creating the concept of the right to engage in concerted activity for mutual aid or protection as a "collective right" that can be exercised by individual workers only with the approval of their union representatives. These doctrines are contrary to the legislative history and policy of the statute. Robert Gorman and Mathew Finkin conclude an authoritative survey as follows:

> [T]here are not two abstract and distinguishable categories of action—individual action for self-interest and collective action for mutual interest—one which Congress chose not to protect and the other which Congress chose to protect, but rather a continuum of individual activity—of individuals choosing to speak and act on their own behalf, singly and in small and large groups. Thus, the narrow reading of the Act proceeds upon a false dichotomy, for at the core of the freedom of the individual to protest in a group necessarily lies the freedom of the individual to protest at all.[20]

In *City Disposal,* the Supreme Court acknowledged the Gorman-Finkin critique and accepted it in situations where a union has been recognized and a collective bargaining agreement has been negotiated. The majority opinion points out that the language of Section 7 protects the rights "to join, or assist labor organizations . . . and to engage in other concerted activities," although both joining and assisting are "activities in which a single individual can engage."[21] Brown's individual refusal to drive an unsafe truck was, according to the Court, "integrally" related to the group activity that had created the union and brought into being a contract protecting the right to refuse to drive an unsafe truck:

> When an employee joins or assists a labor organization, his actions may be divorced in time, and in location as well, from the actions of fellow employees. Because of the integral relationship among the employees' actions, however, Congress viewed each employee as engaged in concerted activity. The lone employee could not join or assist a labor organization were it not for the related organizing activities of his fellow employees. Conversely, there would be limited utility in forming a labor organization if other employees could not join or assist the organization once it is formed. Thus, the formation of a labor organization is integrally related to the activity of joining or assisting such an organization in the same sense that the negotiation of a collective-bargaining agreement is integrally related to the invocation of a right provided for

in the agreement. *In each case, neither the individual activity nor the group activity would be complete without the other.*[22]

This extraordinary opinion comes close to suggesting that even without a collective bargaining provision articulating the right to refuse unsafe work, such refusal might be an "efficient substitute" for filing a "formal" grievance.

The right to engage in concerted activity for mutual aid or protection is the paradigm communal right. Neither a narrowly individual nor a merely collective right, it is a right derived from the actual character of working-class solidarity and accordingly a right that foreshadows a society in which group life and individual self-realization mutually reinforce each other.

The First Amendment

As I initially formulated this idea a few years ago, I may have seemed to say that the right to engage in concerted activity is the *only* communal right and that all other rights, including the rights associated with the First Amendment, are individualistic property rights.

The late Edward Sparer read my words this way and understandably protested. "It would be unfortunate," he wrote,

if Lynd is too readily accepting a narrow conception of such rights as speech and dissent. Such rights do not necessarily subtract from or function separately from "the right to engage in concerted activity for mutual aid." Indeed, the former rights are indispensable to the maintenance of the latter right. Where would the right of working people to unionize and strike be without the right to free speech?[23]

Sparer made the same point in this way:

While it is easy to understand how one person's right to separately possess property limits another person's separate possession of property, I fail to see how one person's exercise of, for example, free speech and dissent *necessarily* limits another person's. Quite the contrary; the exercise of these latter rights can increase the next person's ability to exercise them.

Pondering Sparer's words, it gradually became clear that the rights represented by the First Amendment might themselves be seen as what I have called "communal rights," more like the right to engage in concerted activity than individualistic property rights.

For one thing, I knew that when Congress enacted Section 7 of the Wagner Act the sponsors of the legislation analogized Section 7 rights to First Amendment rights. Picketing in particular was regarded as protected *speech*. Moreover, during the early years of the Wagner Act's administration, the NLRB and the Supreme Court articulated a single developing body of doctrine for both Section 7 and First Amendment cases, applying essentially the same test whether speech was regulated by a private employer or by the state.

Then I came across a remarkable passage from one of Thomas Jefferson's letters in which he memorably portrayed the self-contradictory character of intellectual property:

> If nature has made any one thing less susceptible than all others of exclusive property, it is the action of the thinking power called an idea, which an individual may exclusively possess as long as he keeps it to himself; but the moment it is divulged, it forces itself into the possession of every one, and the receiver cannot dispossess himself of it. Its peculiar character, too, is that no one possesses the less, because every other possesses the whole of it. He who receives an idea from me, receives instruction himself without lessening mine: as he who lights his taper at mine, receives light without darkening me.[24]

These words suggested that the communal search for truth is no more compatible with the right to private property than is the concerted activity of workers for mutual aid or protection.

Finally, I looked again at the text of the First Amendment itself:

> Congress shall make no law respecting an establishment of religion, or prohibiting the free exercise thereof; or abridging the freedom of speech, or of the press; or the right of the people peaceably to assemble, and to petition the Government for a redress of grievances.

Insofar as the First Amendment specifies to whom the rights it enumerates belong, the rights belong not to individuals but to "the people." The two clauses concerning religion describe arguably communal rights: the right not to be forced to support a particular denomination, and the right to be free to meet in religious assemblies of any persuasion without state interference. The free speech clause is linked with freedom of the press, which even in the eighteenth century required a group of persons for its exercise. Finally, it is difficult even to imagine an individual exercising alone the rights to assemble and petition.

All of this suggests that if the rights associated with the First Amendment can be viewed as communal rights, it might be possible to celebrate and defend them along with the communal rights of workers, without weakening the critique of rights associated with private property. First Amendment rights would then be seen not as "bourgeois rights," to be cast aside along with private property, but as communal rights prefiguring the qualities of a future, better society.

The modern history of the law concerning allegedly seditious political speech—the only branch of First Amendment doctrine considered here—provides important evidence in the search for the communal content of the First Amendment. As with the right to engage in concerted activity, we find the conception—alien to the general thrust of existing law and difficult even to express—that certain rights represent *both* affirmations of public values *and* protection for individual self-realization. This part of First Amendment doctrine also suggests that an individual's exercise of certain freedoms can best be safeguarded not by likening them to property, but simply by emphasizing the importance to the community that the rights should flourish.

The modern history of seditious speech law begins with a cluster of Supreme Court opinions written just after World War I. In March 1919 Justices Holmes and Brandeis, writing for a unanimous Court, upheld the convictions of socialists (including Eugene Debs) who had spoken out against the war. In November 1919, in a case presenting essentially similar activity, Justice Brandeis joined the first of Justice Holmes' famous First Amendment dissents.[25]

Interestingly, the "speech test" employed by the Justices did *not* change. Justice Holmes used the same "clear and present danger" speech test to send Debs to jail that he used less than a year later to argue against sustaining the conviction of Abrams. What changed was the weight Holmes gave to uninhibited political speech as a public value.[26] When Holmes first suggested the phrase "clear and present danger," he saw it as a distillation of the law of criminal attempt; he used it to assess purported speech crimes as he would have used it in any other criminal case. During the summer of 1919, however, Holmes appears to have been persuaded by Zechariah Chafee, among others, that free speech was a preeminent community value and that the First Amendment was "a declaration of national policy in favor of the public discussion of all public questions."[27] As a result, in his dissent in *Abrams* v. *United States,* Holmes implicitly distinguished between the ordinary criminal prosecution of an individual and a prosecution for speech "where private rights are not concerned."

The subsequent opinions of Justice Brandeis, culminating in his concurrence in *Whitney* v. *California* in 1927,[28] expressly set forth the dual character of First Amendment rights. Political speech is a public value because it is necessary to democratic self-government: "The fundamental right of free men to strive for better conditions through new legislation and new institutions will not be preserved, if efforts to secure it by argument to fellow citizens may be construed as criminal incitement to disobey the existing law."[29] But free speech and assembly are also "fundamental personal rights."[30] Accordingly, an adequate description of the First Amendment must incorporate both its public and private aspects. Except for the recurrence of the male pronoun, Brandeis' characterization seems difficult to improve upon:

> The right of a citizen of the United States to take part, for his own or the country's benefit, in the making of federal laws and in the conduct of the Government, necessarily includes the right to speak or write about them; to endeavor to make his own opinion concerning laws existing or contemplated prevail; and, to this end, to teach the truth as he sees it.[31]

One striking theme of Brandeis' pronouncements is his insistence that the rights at issue are just as real and important as property rights. "I cannot believe," he wrote, "that the liberty guaranteed by the Fourteenth Amendment includes only liberty to acquire and to enjoy property."[32] The power of the courts to strike down an offending law, he stated, "is no less when the interests involved are not property rights, but the fundamental personal rights of free speech and assembly."[33]

The critique of traditional rights rhetoric and the character of what I term "communal rights" converge at this point. It does not make a right more real, or more protected, to make an analogy to the rights to property and say that it is "vested." The rights to speak, associate, assemble, and petition will be protected only as long as they are valued by society; the best of speech tests will be readily circumvented if that valuation fades. This does not mean that we should cease to struggle for the speech tests that are most protective of political speech and speech in the workplace. Still less does it mean that because these rights depend on social consensus for their enforcement, the First Amendment is superfluous as a legal right. The First Amendment as social and moral value and the First Amendment as legal right stand in symbiotic relation to one another. The value requires the right to be legally enforceable, and the right requires continuing nurture of the value so that the political will that the right be enforced will not cease to exist.

Section 7 was intended to protect in the private workplace the same rights of speech, petitioning, and assembly that are protected by the First Amendment

The draftsmen and sponsors of the early incarnations of Section 7 inherited a generation of bitter struggle on behalf of free speech for working people. In the course of that struggle, the Supreme Court held that the president of the American Federation of Labor might constitutionally be enjoined from causing to be published the word "unfair."[34] The Court also prohibited mass picketing, in the face of free speech claims, because it conveyed a "necessary element of intimidation." Lower federal courts enjoined "abusive language," "annoying language," "indecent language," "bad language," "opprobrious epithets," and particular words such as "traitor" and "scab." One injunction ordered the officers of the United Mine Workers "and all other persons whomsoever" to cease a variety of verbal acts, including "issuing any instructions, written or oral" and "issuing any messages of encouragement or exhortation." Another injunction, verging on the sacrilegious, outlawed "persuasion in the presence of three or more persons."

These court actions were halted by the Norris-LaGuardia Act of 1932, which forbade federal courts from enjoining "[g]iving publicity to the existence of, or the facts involved in, any labor dispute, whether by advertising, speaking, patrolling, or by any other method not involving fraud or violence."[35] Picketing, in particular, was conceptualized as protected speech.

Something of the passion which accrued to the struggle over the right to picket is suggested by the committee report submitted together with the final version of the Norris-LaGuardia Act on February 4, 1932. The report condemned an injunction issued by the United States District Court for the Northern District of Iowa on March 29, 1930. The injunction was directed at picketing to publicize the existence of a strike. The injunction forbade

> printing, publishing, issuing, circulating, and distributing, or otherwise communicating, directly or indirectly, in writing or verbally to any person, association of persons, or corporation, any statement or notice of any kind or character whatsoever, stating or representing . . . [that] there is a strike.[36]

The committee report summarized: "In other words, their mouths were absolutely closed and 'free speech' was forbidden." Referring to the same injunction on the Senate floor, Senator Norris stated that it absolutely and completely denied "the fundamental right of human liberty and freedom," and that a worker who disobeyed it "would be doing only what every human being has a right to do!"[37]

The National Labor Relations Act intended no change in the Norris-LaGuardia Act's understanding of concerted activities. The committee report submitted with the first draft of the bill expressly declared that Section 4 (which in later drafts became Section 7)

> restates the familiar law already enacted by Congress in Section 2 of the Norris-LaGuardia Act [and other statutes]. . . . The language restrains employers from attempting by interference or coercion to impair the exercise by employees of rights which are admitted everywhere to be the basis of industrial no less than political democracy. A worker in the field of industry, like a citizen in the field of government, ought to be free to form or join organizations, to designate representatives, and to engage in concerted activities.[38]

This authoritative exposition of the National Labor Relations Act, even more clearly than the report which accompanied Norris-LaGuardia, thus made an analogy between Section 7 rights and the rights outside the workplace that were protected by the First Amendment.

In addition to Section 7 and Section 13, the National Labor Relations Act protected the right to strike by defining the "employ-

ees" protected by the act so as to include workers on strike. Responding in 1939 to the first wave of proposals for restrictive amendments
to the National Labor Relations Act, Senator Wagner had this to say
about the right to strike:

> [T]he amendments proposed by Senator Burke would have the effect,
> among other things, of placing restraints upon the right to strike. No
> such proposal can strengthen or improve the Labor Act because it is
> antagonistic to the whole spirit and purpose of the law. The spirit and
> purpose of the law is to create a free and dignified workingman who had
> the economic strength to bargain collectively with a free and dignified
> employer in accordance with the methods of democracy. The abolition
> or curtailment of the right to strike is a denial of the principles of
> democracy and a substitution of the methods of the authoritarian state.
> The design of the National Labor Relations Act is to reduce the number
> of strikes by eliminating the main wrongs and injustices that cause
> strikes. The imposition of legal restrictions upon the right to strike,
> instead of removing these wrongs, would merely deprive the worker of
> his inalienable right to protest against them.[39]

Peaceful picketing, it is clear, was also expressly designated for
protection by Section 7.

In sum, then, the words "concerted activities for . . . mutual aid or
protection" were used in the Norris-LaGuardia and National Labor
Relations acts with the intent of shielding activities like strikes and
peaceful picketing from court orders and employer retaliation; these
activities were to be protected whether undertaken by one person or
by many; and the rights thus recognized were felt to be fundamental
rights, akin to the rights protected by the First Amendment, and so
deserving of protection for their own sake.

The law of Section 7 and of the First Amendment was developed by
the Supreme Court in the years 1937–47 as a single body of doctrine,
further constitutionalizing Section 7 protections

From 1937, when the Supreme Court held the Wagner Act constitutional in *Jones & Laughlin*,[40] to the enactment of the Taft-Hartley
amendments in 1947, the Court attached great importance to work-

ers' rights. During this period the Court was responding to the continuing surge of CIO organization. Some of the cases which came to the Court sought protection for workers' rights to organize, associate, strike, picket, and leaflet without interference by the state. In other cases, essentially the same rights were threatened by the employer.

The first group of cases were First Amendment cases, while the second group of cases required clarification of Section 7 of the Wagner Act. The Supreme Court responded to the issue presented by articulating a single developing body of doctrine for both sets of cases. Labor cases which presented the First Amendment problem of permissible interference by the state prompted the Court to articulate the "public forum" and "overbreadth" doctrines, and to revive the concept of "clear and present danger." And in clarifying the scope of speech rights under Section 7, the National Labor Relations Board, sensitive to the Court's attitude, pointed to First Amendment parallels in the Court's contemporaneous decisions on "fighting words," leafletting as a form of speech, and the irrelevance of the regulator's motive. The Court, in *Republic Aviation,* its leading case on employee speech rights vis-à-vis the employer, in effect protected employee speech on private property except when likely to pose a clear and present danger of disrupting production.[41] In these decisions, the Court faithfully reflected one of the purposes of the Wagner Act: to recognize "rights which are admitted everywhere to be the basis of industrial no less than political democracy."

The Supreme Court early declared the rights protected by Section 7 to be "fundamental." This vague if resonant language still left to the NLRB the problem of what exactly Section 7 did and did not protect. Congress deliberately worded Section 7 broadly "lest the courts emasculate specific provisions or employers find practices not specifically covered which impede the progress of self organization."[42] As the Court stated in *Republic Aviation Corp.* v. *NLRB:*

> The Wagner Act did not undertake the impossible task of specifying in precise and unmistakable language each incident which would constitute an unfair labor practice. On the contrary, that Act left to the Board

the work of applying the Act's general prohibitory language in the light of the infinite combinations of events which might be charged as violative of its terms.[43]

Thus it fell to the NLRB to create a federal common law of Section 7 rights, including speech rights.

The NLRB looked for guidance to then contemporaneous Supreme Court decisions interpreting the First Amendment. Although the lack of state action prevented First Amendment adjudication from being directly applicable to cases involving employer discipline, the NLRB properly viewed these decisions as expressions of policy which should be followed under Section 7. This was the more natural since many of the advances in general First Amendment theory during the period 1937–47, such as the articulation of the "public forum" and "overbreadth" concepts, as well as the Supreme Court's increased use of the clear and present danger test, were associated with labor cases.

For instance, in *Thornhill* v. *Alabama,* the Court dealt with an anti-picketing statue applied to pickets who "appear to have been on company property." Holding the statute facially overbroad and hence unconstitutional, the Court declared broadly the "[i]n the circumstances of our times the dissemination of information concerning the facts of a labor dispute must be regarded as within that area of free discussion that is guaranteed by the Constitution."[44] Strictly speaking, the Court was referring only to state action in restraint of speech. But the language of *Thornhill* was and still is invoked as a statement of public policy which should inform the resolution of employee speech cases in any setting.

What *Thornhill* and the other First Amendment cases told the Board was that just as speech outside the workplace was protected except where the government could show a clear and present danger, so speech at work should be protected save where it disrupts production; hence, an employer's no-solicitation rule is overbroad if it conclusively prohibits speech during nonworking hours when a workplace is a public forum.

Since 1947, the Court has drastically curtailed both the Section 7 and the First Amendment rights of workers.[45] Any adequate use of these related bodies of doctrine to protect workers' rights should go back to the law as it stood during and just after World War II, and build on that law, rather than on the decisions that have come down since.

Workers need a synthesis of the specific protections provided by Section 7 with the constitutional status of rights protected by the First Amendment

The labor movement rightly blames the current feeble state of Section 7 on conservative decisions by the courts and the NLRB, on the Taft-Hartley amendments, and on the intransigence of union-busting employers. But the most grievous damage to Section 7 has been inflicted by the labor movement itself. Nothing in the law requires unions to agree to a no-strike clause in a collective bargaining agreement. Yet from the very first CIO contracts with General Motors and U.S. Steel in 1937, the CIO routinely gave away this most important right, which the law sought to protect. We lack experience on the basis of which to evaluate what the NLRA might look like if unions had refused to surrender the right to strike in collective bargaining, or if they were to do so in the future. My guess is that the statute would at once appear more attractive in that new context.

The problem remains that rights protected by Section 7 lack the special status of rights protected by the Constitution. The Supreme Court has held that the real purpose of Section 7 was not to protect workers' rights for their own sake, but rather to help workers form unions in the mass production industries, which in turn would promote labor peace. Using this rationale, the Court has found that once a union has been recognized, workers' rights can lawfully be abridged, despite the seemingly unambiguous language of Section 7. It is as if the Declaration of Independence contained only the expression, "Governments are instituted among men, deriving their just powers from the consent of the governed," omitting both the preceding affirmation that governments exist "to secure" certain inalienable rights, and the claim that if government ceases to protect those rights "it is the right of the people to alter or abolish it." What the Supreme Court has held is that workers' rights exist to bring unions into being, and once unions exist the rights are no longer needed.

It would promote respect for Section 7 rights as fundamental rights, akin to constitutional rights, if the NLRA were amended to apply to *all* workers. There is no logical reason that the NLRA applies to airline pilots but not to air traffic controllers, or to nurses but not to teachers. The limitation of Section 7 to the private sector reflects an outmoded distinction between private and public sectors of the economy. Today, the decisions of all large economic entities have public consequences, while at the same time workers in all enterprises require the same basic rights. By universalizing Section 7 rights, we could make them rights of a constitutional nature, protecting workers against oppression from all sides.

Notes

This article is based on the following previously published articles, material from which is reprinted with permission: "The Right to Engage in Concerted Activity after Union Recognition: A Study of Legislative History," 50 *Indiana Law Journal* 720–56 (1975); "Employee Speech in the Private and Public Workplace: Two Doctrines or One?," 1 *Industrial Relations Law Journal* 711 (Winter 1977); "Communal Rights," 62 *Texas Law Review* 1417–41 (May 1984). Full citations will be found in these articles.

1. In August 1980 the Gdansk strikers demanded (among other things): (1) "To accept trade unions as free and independent of the party, as laid down in Convention No. 87 of the ILO. . . "; (2) "To guarantee the right to strike, and the security of strikers and those who help them"; (3) "To respect freedom of expression and publication, . . . and to take no measures against independent publications. . . . "; (4) "To re-establish the rights of people who were sacked after the strikes in 1970 and 1976 and of students who have been excluded from institutions of higher education because of their opinions, (b) to free all political prisoners . . . , (c) to cease repression against people for their opinions."
2. Section 7 of the NLRA, 29 U.S.C. Section 157, states: "Employees shall have the right to self-organization, to form, join, or assist labor organizations, to bargain collectively through representatives of their own choosing, and to engage in other concerted activities for the purpose of collective bargaining or other mutual aid or protection."
3. 29 U.S.C. Section 157 (1982).
4. See, e.g., A. Lynd and S. Lynd, *Rank and File: Personal Histories by Working Class Organizers* (Boston, 1973), hereinafter cited as *Rank and File*.
5. K. Klare, "Judicial Deradicalization of the Wagner Act and the Origins of Modern Legal Consciousness, 1937–1941," 62 *Minn. L. Rev.* 265, 265 (1978).
6. C. Daniel, *The ACLU and the Wagner Act* (Ithaca, 1980), p. 75 (quoting letter from ACLU director Roger Baldwin to Senator David Walsh [20 March 1934]).

Baldwin expressed similar concerns in letters to Secretary of Labor Frances Perkins and Chairman of the Labor Advisory Board Leo Wolman (ibid., p. 34). Mary Van Kleeck, chairman of the ACLU's subcommittee on labor and policy, wrote Senator Robert Wagner: "I have serious doubts about the inevitable trends of [the Act's] administration" (ibid., p. 71).

7. MARHO, *Visions of History* (New York, 1983), p. 157 (interview with the author).
8. Lynd, "Government Without Rights: The Labor Law Vision of Archibald Cox," 4 *Indus. Rel. L.J.* 483, 495 (1981).
9. Jane Atkinson, "The Woman Behind Solidarity: The Story of Anna Walentynowicz," *Ms.* (February 1984): 96 (used by permission).
10. *Rank and File*, p. 281, quoting Ed Mann.
11. NLRB v. City Disposal Systems, Inc., 104 S. Ct. 1505, 1517 (1984) (O'Connor, J., dissenting).
12. NLRB v. Peter Cailler Kohler Swiss Chocolates Co., 130 F.2d 503, 505–506 (2d Cir. 1942).
13. NLRB v. City Disposal Systems, Inc., 104 S. Ct. 1505 (1984).
14. Ibid., at 1509.
15. Ibid., at 1508.
16. Ibid., at 1511.
17. Ibid., at 1511–12; emphasis added.
18. Norris-LaGuardia Act, ch. 90, Section 4, 47 Stat. 70, 70–71 (1982) (current version at 29 U.S.C. Sections 51, 104 (1982)).
19. R. Gorman and M. Finkin, "The Individual and the Requirement of 'Concert' under the National Labor Relations Act," 130 *U. Pa. L. Rev.* 286, 329 (1981).
20. Ibid. at 344–45.
21. 104 S. Ct. at 1511 n.8.
22. Ibid., at 1512; emphasis added.
23. E. Sparer, "Fundamental Human Rights, Legal Entitlements, and the Social Struggle: A Friendly Critique of the Critical Legal Studies Movement," 36 *Stan. L. Rev.* 509 (1984) at 527, 530.
24. See G. Wills, *Inventing America: Jefferson's Declaration of Independence* (New York, 1979), pp. 234–35, quoting letter from Jefferson to Isaac McPherson, 13 August 1813.
25. Abrams v. United States, 250 U.S. 616, 624 (1919) (Holmes, J., dissenting).
26. See D. Raggan, "The Emergence of Modern First Amendment Doctrine," 50 *U. Chi. L. Rev.* 1205, 1311–17 (1983).
27. Z. Chafee, "Freedom of Speech in War Time," 32 *Harv. L. Rev.* 932, 934 (1919).
28. 274 U.S. 357, 372 (1927) (Brandeis, J., concurring).
29. Pierce v. United States, 252 U.S. 239, 273 (1920) (Brandeis, J., dissenting).
30. Whitney, 274 U.S. at 374 (Brandeis, J., concurring).
31. Gilbert v. Minnesota, 254 U.S. 325, 337–38 (1920) (Brandeis, J., dissenting).
32. Ibid., at 343.
33. Whitney, 274 U.S. at 374 (Brandeis, J., concurring).
34. Bucks Stove & Range Co. v. Gompers, 221 U.S. 418, 439 (1911).
35. 29 U.S.C. Section 104(e) (1970).
36. U.S., Congress, Senate, *Report No. 163*, 72d Cong., 1st sess., 1932, pt. 1: 7.
37. U.S., Congress, Senate, *Congressional Record*, 72d Cong., 1st sess., 1932: 4502.
38. U.S., Congress, Senate, *Report No. 1184*, 73d Cong., 2d sess., 1934: 4.
39. *The Wagner Act: After Ten Years*, ed. L. Silverberg (1945), p. 31.
40. 301 U.S. 1 (1937).
41. 324 U.S. 793 (1945).
42. J. Gross, *The Making of the National Labor Relations Board: A Study in Economics,*

Politics, and the Law (Albany, 1974), p. 133, quoting series of memoranda by P. Levy.

43. 324 U.S. at 798.
44. 310 U.S. 88, 94, 102 (1940).
45. Space is lacking to document this generalization, with which most labor and left-oriented scholars would agree. See, e.g., James B. Atleson, *Values and Assumptions in American Labor Law* (Amherst, 1983), on Section 7, and J. Pope, "Labor and the Constitution: From Abolition to Deindustrialization," 65 *Texas L. Rev.* 1071 (May 1987), and S. Kupferberg, "Political Strikes, Labor Law, and Democratic Rights," 71 *Va. L. Rev.* 685 (June 1985). I do not mean to deny that there have been particular decisions in the years since 1947 that are protective of workers' rights. Examples are NLRB v. City Disposal Systems, Inc., 104 S. Ct. 1505 (1984), where an individual worker's refusal to drive an unsafe truck under the pertinent clause of the collective bargaining agreement was "concerted activity"; and NAACP v. Claiborne Hardware Co., 458 U.S. 886 (1982), where a blacks' boycott of white enterprises with the objective of obtaining civil rights was protected speech.

THE CONSTITUTION AND THE CIVIL RIGHTS MOVEMENT:
The First Amendment— and the Fourteenth

Anne Braden

Most of us do not pay much attention to the Constitution until we need it.

It was that way with me. I heard about it in school, read the Bill of Rights, and grew up sure that I had the right to say anything I wished (within bounds of good taste), and go anywhere I wanted to go.

But I grew up white in racist Alabama society, and in a fairly privileged section of it at that. So it was not until later that I discovered that what I thought were rights were privileges conferred by the fact that I was part of the dominant group—and that when I broke with that group and challenged its rules (in those days, racial segregation), the privileges would be snatched away. At age 30, I found myself and my husband Carl charged with sedition—that is, conspiring to overthrow the government of Kentucky, where we lived—and possibly facing years in prison, simply because of actions we had taken against segregation.

The "evidence" was that we had "subversive" books in our house, associated with "subversive" people, attended "subversive" meetings, and opposed the nation's foreign policy, which we thought was driving us toward a World War III.

It was then that I really discovered the Bill of Rights, especially the First Amendment, and rather fell in love with it. We had a right to do these things, I maintained firmly; the Constitution said so. Our lawyers argued that eloquently in court.

It didn't do much good. This was the early 1950s, and anything went. The prosecutor's office raided our house and took away truckloads of books. The Fourth Amendment said they couldn't, but they did. When my husband was tried, one of the most damaging pieces of evidence against him was a news article he had written saying unemployment was rising in our city in the late 1940s (thus, according to the prosecutor, saying that the U.S. economic system didn't work). The First Amendment said he had freedom of the press, but the jury didn't care. Another fatal piece of evidence was a petition he had circulated against the atom bomb. The First Amendment said he had the right to petition the government, but that didn't matter either. He was sentenced to fifteen years in prison.

His appeal to the higher courts was based on the Bill of Rights, but he didn't win on that ground. The courts did in fact reverse his conviction two years later, dropping the charges against me as well, but they said it was because the federal government had preempted the field of sedition with the Smith Act and therefore a state could not bring that charge. In other words, it was the federal government that should have put us in jail for reading books, going to meetings, writing news articles, and circulating petitions.

But in the meantime we had made use of the First Amendment to convince many people that what the state was doing was wrong. In that same period—the time of witch-hunts against Communists, and anyone called Communist—other people were doing the same thing, taking their case to the fourth branch of government—the people—insisting that it was in the interests of the country that the constitutional guarantees of human rights be upheld. This work in the court of public opinion began to dissipate the atmosphere of hysteria. It was undoubtedly this change that made it possible for the courts to rule in our favor in the sedition case, even though on narrow technical grounds.

Through this experience I began to understand that although the Constitution does not guarantee any right that cannot be taken away if those in power decide to do so, it does provide a weapon with which we can fight for our rights. It provides a way to do that in the arena where most battles are won or lost anyway: in the struggle for the hearts and minds of men and women—that is, in the political arena. Thus it is not a guarantee; it is an organizing tool.

The Civil Rights Movement

I saw this pattern played out on a larger canvas later as the modern civil rights movement developed and shook first the South and then the entire nation, changing patterns of race relations forever and breaking up a literal police state in the South.

It was just a year after our sedition case began that the historic bus boycott was launched in Montgomery, Alabama. Fifty thousand black people decided to walk instead of ride because they would accept second-class citizenship no longer. Their principal inspiration was a religious one: a conviction that they were children of God and by virtue of that fact entitled to certain rights.

But they had also learned from their lawyers that the Constitution said they had those rights. This was an added incentive to keep on walking. Speakers said it was a violation of God's law to cooperate with evil, and that segregation was evil. But they also said it was a violation of the nation's law. Sometimes they quoted the Constitution as saying that "all men are created equal," which of course it doesn't. But an important concept had been implanted in the minds of those who struggled: the concept that there are written documents in our heritage, the Declaration of Independence and the Constitution, that say that we have certain rights, and that therefore it is right to struggle for them.

The court action that challenged segregation on the Montgomery buses went hand-in-hand with the people's mass movement, and they complemented each other. After a year, the courts ruled that bus segregation violated the Constitution. That decision forced city officials to give in to the movement's demands, and black people in Montgomery might never have won without it. But there would never have been a court victory, or even a court action, if it had not been for the masses of people in the streets of that city—people whose action inspired the country and won the support of large sections of the population, white as well as black. Again, the Constitution was used as an organizing tool.

By the time of the historic March on Washington in 1963, this tool was being used to inspire action throughout the South and to win public support throughout the country. So when Dr. Martin Luther King, Jr., addressed the 250,000 people who took part in that march, he struck a responsive chord when he began:

In a sense, we've come to our nation's capital to cash a check. When the architects of our republic wrote the magnificent words of the Constitution and the Declaration of Independence, they were signing a promissory note to which every American was to fall heir. This note was a promise that all men, yes black men as well as white men,[1] would be guaranteed the unalienable rights of life, liberty, and the pursuit of happiness. . . . Instead of honoring this sacred obligation, America has given the Negro people a bad check, a check which has come back marked "insufficient funds". . . .

Between the mid-1950s and the time King spoke these words, black activists (and a growing number of white allies) had been trying to cash that check in communities across the South. They had sat in at segregated lunchcounters and restaurants, picketed theaters, tried to register to vote in Mississippi courthouses, and to march in the streets of Birmingham, Alabama, Albany, Georgia, and elsewhere. For all that, they were attacked by police with billy clubs, cattle prods, and dogs, brutally beaten, and put in jail by the thousands. Some were murdered.

But as their courage won the respect of the nation, lawyers appeared from all over the country and said: "Of course you have a right to do these things. It says so in the Constitution." And when masses of demonstrators were arrested, the lawyers developed a technique of taking the cases out of the state courts, where local racist judges presided, and "removing" them (using a federal statute passed in 1866 to protect the constitutional rights of blacks in the South after the Civil War) to federal court, where justice was supposed to reside.

And a President had been elected, John F. Kennedy, who owed a great deal to the nation's black voters, since he had won the White House because he was smart enough to telephone Coretta Scott King in 1960 expressing concern because her husband was in jail in Georgia. Kennedy told the nation that the Constitution would be enforced; he ordered the Justice Department to help beleagured southern civil rights workers. Thus organizers in southern communities soon found that they could call the Justice Department collect when they were in trouble and have the charges quickly accepted, or call its representatives at home in the middle of the night and get a friendly reception.

The facts, however, are that very few of these appeals to the

Constitution, the federal courts, and the U.S. executive agency charged with enforcing the nation's laws permanently established any of the rights guaranteed in the Constitution. Many of the cases removed to federal court eventually got tossed back to the states. And for civil rights workers on the southern front lines, it became less and less enchanting to have collect calls accepted in the middle of the night by high government officials when no protection ever came and when FBI agents watched police and vigilante attacks and beating in community after community, taking notes but doing nothing. They said they had no jurisdiction over state law enforcement. After the Civil War, amendments to the Constitution gave the federal government precisely such jurisdiction. But its agents in the 1960s did not want to assume it, so they didn't.

There were exceptions. Sometimes a federal judge who really believed in the Constitution would act—for example, Judge Simon Sobeloff of the Fourth Circuit Court of Appeals, who stopped mass trials of demonstrators in Danville, Virginia, in 1963, and Judge Minor Wisdom of the Fifth Circuit, who wrote a historic three-judge decision enjoining Ku Klux Klan activities in Bogalusa, Louisiana, in 1965. And sometimes a local federal judge would uphold the rights of civil rights workers.

But for the most part change came not because the courts and the federal government decided to uphold the Constitution but because masses of people were in the streets. Their presence created tumultuous situations that led public officials to decide that they had better give a little to keep a lot, that concessions had to be made. Thus in many communities between 1960 and 1964, business leaders sat down with public officials and said, "We've got to desegregate." Soon national officials were saying the same thing. Public accommodations in the South began to open up, and by the time Congress enacted landmark legislation in 1964 saying they had to do so, it was really just writing changes that already been won in the streets into the law of the land.

Similarly, when civil rights leaders went into federal court in 1965 to challenge a clearly unconstitutional injunction that forbid them marching from Selma to Montgomery, the court ruled in their favor. But by that time thousands of people had descended on Alabama from all over the nation; there was obviously going to be turmoil if they were not allowed to march.

That march was a major factor in winning passage of the Voting Rights Act of 1965, a law that should not have been necessary since the Fifteenth Amendment already guaranteed the right to vote. The amendment was only implemented after a number of people had died demanding that right in Mississippi and Alabama. These martyrdoms aroused people all over the country, to the point that they were prepared to disrupt the nation if necessary to get the right to vote enforced. And the Voting Rights Act itself was little more than a scrap of paper until people throughout the South filed more suits and took more direct action to enforce it, a process that is still going on today.

And once again, although the words of the Constitution did not really guarantee human rights, the document was being used as an organizing tool. The main value of those removal actions—taking mass arrests out of the state courts—was as a delaying action. They got people out of jail for the moment, and movements that otherwise would have been crushed aborning were able to go on organizing and taking their cause to the people. Thus during the 1960s a whole body of humane law found their way onto the books, measures that benefited white as well as black Americans.

And the *words* of the Constitution continued to inspire action. Many people who are old enough get goose pimples when they remember watching Dr. King on television, as he spoke at Masonic Temple in Memphis on April 3, 1968, in a sequence that was broadcast over and over again after he was murdered the following evening. It was at the height of the Memphis garbage strike; one march had ended in violence and Dr. King had returned to Memphis on Wednesday to lead another march the following Monday. A court injunction had been issued to stop that march, and a multitude of people had come out on the evening of April 3 to hear Dr. King. And there we saw him on TV, his thundering voice again arousing masses of people to action.

"I call upon you to be with us when we go out on Monday," he said. "We have an injunction, and we're going into court tomorrow morning to fight this illegal unconstitutional injunction. All we say to America is 'Be true to what you said on paper.' "

And then Martin, in the pattern of the Baptist preacher, repeating over and over a key phrase like a chorus in an oratory, said: "*Somewhere I read* of freedom of assembly. *Somewhere I read* of freedom of speech. *Somewhere I read* of freedom of the press. *Somewhere I read* that the greatness of America is the right to protest for right."

And the people rose to their feet and cheered, ready to risk jail and physical attack to march again.

That march never happened. Instead people from across the country marched in the streets of Atlanta at Martin's funeral. For a time after that the movement pushed ahead, and for several years into the 1970s the changes it had generated were being written into legislation, administrative policies, and court decisions. But the overriding feature of the late 1960s and early 1970s was the combination of cooptation of the movement, where that would work, and extreme repression where it would not; totally unconstitutional Cointelpro operations that split and sometimes destroyed organizations; and a powerful propaganda campaign that told the nation that blacks had gone too far too fast. All this temporarily derailed the movement and gradually pushed the country into an almost-180-degree turn away from the commitment to humane values that had been growing in the 1960s. This created an atmosphere hostile to human rights that still plagues us into the 1980s.

The civil rights movement of the 1960s made remarkable strides toward winning its basic goals: an end to segregation enforced by law, the right to vote, and the right to organize. But it was just beginning to move into the arena of economic justice, where the Constitution offers little guidance, when it was blunted, and it remains an unfinished revolution.

Despite that, it stands in our history as a classic instance in which people took hold of rights that the Constitution gave them on paper, used them as an organizing tool, and by their action widened those rights somewhat, not only for those who were part of the movement but for the entire nation.

The Fight Against Anticommunism

Meantime, some of us who were active in the civil rights movement were also using the First Amendment as a weapon in an important additional battle, the fight against the mindless anticommunism that constantly threatened to divide, weaken, and de-bilitate the movement.

The civil rights movement arose during the so-called silent 1950s, when Cold War abroad and witch-hunts at home had devastated social justice movements across the country. That movement, more than any other factor, broke the pall of the 1950s, set people working for justice again, and dissipated the fear engendered in those years. But the civil rights movement was profoundly affected by the atmosphere those fears had created.

Long before the days of Joe McCarthy, southern segregationists called anyone who opposed them a "Communist." There was some factual basis for this, since the U.S. Communist Party had long been in the forefront of demands for racial justice. But the real underpinning of the racists' cry of "red" was the stubbornly held belief that civil rights were a "foreign" concept, Communism was a "foreign" ideology, and therefore anyone who advocated racial justice was a Communist. Thus they labelled *every* civil rights organization red, even anticommunist ones. The national witch-hunt of the 1950s enabled the racists to tie their kite to a nationwide whirlwind and pose as guardians of the national security, rather than as defenders of a corrupt southern status quo. This gave them a degree of legitimacy and influence that they would not otherwise have had.

There was another factor that made certain organizations prime targets of this attack. At some point the nation's power structure had apparently decided that it was not going to be able to stop the mass movement of blacks demanding basic rights. So the next best bet was to contain it, to confine its thrust to the simple issue of segregation, and to prevent it, if possible, from moving on to a more thorough critique of the society, especially its economic conditions. That was a futile aim: the movement always acted out of a larger, although sometimes sketchily defined, vision of a totally new society, and its later shift to an attack on basic social and economic structures was inevitable. But in the early 1960s, those in power thought that they could prevent this by isolating people and organizations that linked the issues of racial justice, economic justice, and world affairs. And since it was the older organizations—those that had arisen in the 1930s and 1940s and had managed to survive the witch-hunts of the late 1940s—that tended to make these linkages, it was these that came in for special attack.

A further target of the racists was white people in the movement—southern segregationists had always explained them away by declaring them "Communists." Interracial organizations were considered especially dangerous, since those in power sensed that if the racism that has historically divided black from white was seriously undermined, power relationships would change.

I was white, and I was part of one of those older organizations, the Southern Conference Educational Fund (SCEF), and it was interracial. So I and the people I worked with became major targets of the "Communist" cry. (The National Lawyers Guild, which gave massive assistance to the southern movement, was another special target.) The attacks came mainly from those legislative investigating committees that still roamed the land, subpoenaing suspect individuals, labelling people, making headlines, spreading fear, and ruining lives: the House Un-American Activities Committee (HUAC), the Senate Internal Security Subcommittee (headed by James O. Eastland of Mississippi), and similar committees modeled after the federal ones in virtually every southern state—FUAC in Florida, LUAC in Louisiana, etc.

These committees tended to scratch each other's backs. For example, in the early 1950s, Senator Eastland had brought his committee south to attack SCEF, and issued a report saying that the real purpose of that organization was to "promote Communism in the South." His documentation was a report HUAC had issued ten years earlier of SCEF's predecessor organization. Various state committees then quoted Eastland's report as their documentation for similar condemnations of SCEF, and HUAC in turn quoted the state committees to issue a new attack. In the meantime, various racist organizations leaped on all these reports and quoted them widely in speeches, press releases, and leaflets, which was always good for headlines in the South.

The constant cry of "red" frightened away many potential allies of the civil rights movement, especially white ones. People who might have braved cattle prods and jail shied away from being called traitors to their country. And within the movement itself, some people—perhaps understandably—decided that the better part of wisdom was to stay away from groups that bore the heaviest brunt of this attack.

All this was destructive. One early activist in the Student Nonviolent Coordinating Committee (SNCC) later summed up its effect: "The first thing, someone said be careful about associating with such-and-such a group. And somebody else said be careful about that organization. And then somebody said there might be Communists in *our* group. I didn't even know what a Communist was, and then somebody called *me* a Communist. We were all looking at each other and wondering 'which rock are they under'? We wasted months that way before we decided to forget all that and go after segregation."

Those of us who were targets of such attacks decided we had to fight back. Not just to establish our own right to be a part of a movement that we believed in, but—much more important—to combat the fear and division that was weakening the entire movement. And the weapon we used in our fight back was the First Amendment.

We maintained that because of the First Amendment, the witch-hunting committees had no right to exist. We said that the Constitution gave Congress (and, by virtue of the Fourteenth Amendment, the state legislatures) the right to investigate *only* to gather information it needed to enact legislation or oversee existing legislation; and that since the First Amendment prohibited them from passing legislation that would limit the right of citizens to believe, associate, speak, or organize, they had no right to investigate in this area.

In 1958, my husband was one of a number of civil rights activists called before HUAC in Atlanta. He told the committee that his beliefs and associations were none of their business and cited the First Amendment as his justification. Three years later he was sentenced to prison for a year for that assertion (as was Frank Wilkinson, who at that time was organizing the National Committee to Abolish HUAC). That case gave us a larger platform from which to carry on the fight against the witch-hunting committees, and we proceeded to use it. We organized workshops, talked to people one-on-one and in groups, wrote pamphlets, leaflets, and position papers. SCEF held a conference in Chapel Hill in 1961 on "Freedom and the First Amendment," which was one of the first large interracial gatherings of the period. Soon many people in the movement were talking about the need to end the witch-hunt and its committees.

Later, in 1963, when the Louisiana Un-American Activities Committee raided the SCEF office in New Orleans and had its director, Jim Dombrowski, arrested for "subversive" activities, Arthur Kinoy and the groups of lawyers who later formed the Center for Constitutional Rights went into federal court and got this prosecution stopped; this was the monumental Dombrowski decision. In layman's language, that decision held that where a state and its agencies threaten First Amendment rights, the federal courts have an obligation to step in and stop the injustice *before* it happens.

This decision proved useful in cases involving other civil rights activists: it opened the way to having charges dropped immediately, rather than after the long process of conviction and appeal—when reversal and vindication would come long after the movement that was the target of the attack had been destroyed. The decision also helped us to eliminate Kentucky's sedition law when we were indicted for the second time in the late 1960s.

So that was one victory for the First Amendment that we won in the courts. But in this battle, as in others, our main victory was again in the court of public opinion. The changed atmosphere in the 1960s did as much as the Dombrowski court action to defeat the Kentucky sedition law. And even the Dombrowski decision was later whittled away and weakened by subsequent court decisions. For SCEF, the main value of the Dombrowski fight was that it kept our leaders out of jail at a critical moment and enabled the organization to go on with its work of encouraging white participation in the civil rights movement.

And the courts never upheld the right my husband and others asserted before HUAC—the right to remain silent on the grounds of the First Amendment. But we won that battle in the court of public opinion also, and HUAC was abolished in 1975; its fangs had already been pulled, because people simply were not afraid of it anymore. That came about because many people stood up and said no to HUAC, just as people throughout the South said no to segregation. The National Committee to Abolish HUAC led the campaign to defang and abolish the committee, and a major part of that campaign was the southern civil rights movement. That movement said no.

In fact, the beginning of the end for HUAC was probably those 1958 Atlanta hearings, because at that time two hundred black southern leaders issued an open letter demanding that the committee stay out of the South. It was an audacious challenge at a time when HUAC still struck fear into many hearts. Martin Luther King Jr., later braved an avalanche of criticism to denounce HUAC when my husband and Frank Wilkinson went to prison, pointing to its violation of First Amendment rights and its use on behalf of segregation. In the mid-1960s, when HUAC threatened to investigate SNCC, that organization voted overwhelmingly not to cooperate.

Perhaps the most important thing the civil rights movement won by its decision to stand up against the witch-hunt was an understanding of how the irrational anticommunism of the 1950s boxed people in and closed the door to the exploration of new ideas. Bob Moses, the courageous organizer of the Mississippi movement, put it eloquently in a 1963 statement to the National Student Congress, which I quoted in a widely circulated pamphlet I wrote, titled *HUAC: Bulwark of Segregation:*

> The Negro seeks his own place within the existing institutional framework, but to accommodate him society will have to modify its institutions—and in many cases make far-reaching fundamental changes. . . . The function of the white American is not so much to prepare the Negro for entrance into the larger society . . . but to prepare society for the changes it must make to include Negroes. . . . In coming years, it will be more and more crucial to discuss, debate. . . . Movements for social change require freedom of speech and association.

In those days we called our battle against the witch-hunt and its committees a fight for "civil liberties." The Rev. Fred Shuttlesworth of Birmingham and other courageous black leaders, including Dr. King, incorporated that appeal into their organizing activities; for them, civil liberties and civil rights were indivisible.

Looking back, I think this name for our battle was not entirely accurate. What we were really fighting was the Cold War legacy of anticommunism, the anticommunism that closed doors and minds to the kind of discussion, debate, and exploration Bob Moses said was essential. The concept of civil liberties—the fact that there was on paper, in our Constitution, a First Amendment—was the weapon we used to carry that battle into the marketplace of public opinion.

The First Amendment—and the Fourteenth

During that year in the early 1960s when my husband was in prison for defying HUAC, I spent much time traveling the South talking to people about the witch-hunting committees and their danger to the civil rights movement. For several years afterward, this continued to be a part of my work with SCEF. I talked to groups large and small, black and white. And I remember vividly my recurring theme. Over and over I said: "In an unjust society, the First Amendment is really all we need. It's our right to speak, our right to print, our right to assemble and petition—that is, our right to organize. If we have that, we can change anything."

In more recent years, I've come to believe that this statement, although it sounded good, was not totally accurate.

This came home to me dramatically in the early 1980s when I sat in the editorial offices of the Louisville, Kentucky, newspapers with a delegation of black and white community leaders; we had come to explain to the editorial writers why we did not think a national Klan leader should be allowed to speak at a local high school in September. It was a school where black students had been harassed steadily in the aftermath of turmoil that followed the institution of an extensive desegregation busing plan. We felt that a Klan rally at the beginning of the school year would create a clear and present danger to the students attending the school.

During the discussion one editorial writer looked at me accusingly and said, "But Anne, how can you of all people say the Klan should not have a First Amendment right to speak? You, who have had to struggle for your own right to speak?"

Before I could answer, Mattie Jones, a grass-roots leader in Louisville's black community, interrupted. She had long been the target of Klan death threats, which had recently increased. "Look," she said, "I'm for freedom of speech. But I want to know what protection I have when the Klan comes to my house in the middle of the night. What amendment is going to protect me?"

The editorial writer did not answer, and the meeting soon broke up. But as we left an answer dawned on me, and I said: "You know, Mattie, there is an amendment to protect you. It's the Fourteenth Amendment, and it was put in the Constitution for that very purpose. It says you are entitled to 'equal protection of the laws,' and a whole bunch of laws were passed after the Civil War to implement it."

Mattie was skeptical. She knew as well as I that those laws had never really been enforced. But I thought about that later as I mulled over the debate then raging—and still raging—among people of good will in this country as to whether First Amendment rights extend to violent racist groups that have proved their purposes in blood.

There are many complex aspects to this question. What is the line between speech and action? Is it really only symbolic speech when a cross is burned, since the purpose is intimidation and there are laws against threatening and intimidating people? Is a march by robed Klansmen a legitimate expression of freedom of assembly when it has been proven over and over again that racist violence follows such action?

And was it really a parallel situation to what social justice advocates faced with HUAC when that same committee, led by a white liberal, finally investigated the Klan in the mid-1960s? Many of us in the civil rights movement opposed that investigation. We thought it would give renewed legitimacy to HUAC, and having opposed HUAC's investigation of civil rights groups we thought we had to be consistent. Thus I was startled a few years ago when Pat Bryant, a young black activist of the 1980s who was organizing against resurgent Klan activity in North Carolina, spoke of the "1960s hearings on the Klan." He said he had read the proceedings and found them useful for the current struggle: for one thing, they identified apparently respectable citizens who had used their businesses as fronts for Klan activity and were probably still doing so.

Pat was surprised when I told him I had opposed those hearings. It occurred to me, twenty years too late, that maybe there *was* a legitimate legislative purpose for *those* hearings. We had always said Congress could investigate in order to oversee existing legislation. There was indeed existing legislation, passed after the Civil War, to stop Klan violence, and it was not being enforced in the 1960s. This was something quite different from HUAC investigating organizations struggling to enforce constitutional rights, and maybe we should have said so at the time (although HUAC was not the proper committee to do it).

And then there is a whole body of international law on this subject. United Nations covenants call on signatory nations to outlaw racist "propaganda," and at least ninety nations, including many that revere free speech—although not the United States—have ratified them.[2] The outlawing of "propaganda" would seem to be a clear contradiction of our First Amendment. But is it possible that we have reached a stage in human history—after tragic evidence of the fruits of racism in Nazi Germany and today's South Africa—when civilized nations must say racism itself is a crime, just as murder and its advocacy are crimes? Or, indeed, that racism *is* murder?

These are not easy questions. They are not answered by a glib assumption that the First Amendment must be absolute no matter what, that this will in some way make everything all right. I was *not* correct twenty-five years ago when I said the First Amendment is "all we need." That presupposed a society in which everyone starts even; it assumes that when ideas compete in the marketplace, justice will prevail.

But that assumption is not compatible with our history, in which people did not start even. The central fact of our history is not its democratic tradition, but its racist one. The country was founded on racism—on the assumption that it should be run by whites for the benefit of whites, and that the lives of people of color did not matter. A civil war had to be fought before we could even *begin* dealing with that wrong, and more amendments had to be added to the Constitution. And even those amendments did not protect black people in the South, so that in response to the violence, murder, and mayhem perpetrated by the Klan during Reconstruction, civil rights laws had to be enacted.

Some of these laws, literally interpreted, actually seem to contradict the First Amendment. For example, 18 U.S.C., Section 241, says that it is a crime for "two or more persons" to "conspire to injure, oppress, threaten, or intimidate any citizen in the free exercise or enjoyment of any right or privilege secured to him by the Constitution or laws of the United States." It seems to me that the very *existence* of organizations like the Klan constitutes a conspiracy to "injure, oppress, threaten, or intimidate" other citizens—since their sole purpose is to "injure and oppress" people of color by depriving them of equal rights and opportunities. Yet the First Amendment, as usually interpreted, says they have a right to exist. To be more specific, the very holding of that Klan rally at the Kentucky high school "threatened and intimidated" black students (and their white allies). Yet a federal judge, when we asked him to enjoin the rally, ruled—not unexpectedly—that the First Amendment guaranteed the Klan the right to meet.

The civil rights laws enacted after the Civil War were called "anti-Klan laws." Within a few years, there were thousands of prosecutions under these laws. But finally terror prevailed, the federal government withdrew from the South, and the laws lay unused for almost a century, until civil rights lawyers in the 1960s dusted them off and tried to get them enforced again.

In the last decade, despite all the gains of the civil rights movement, racist violence has again increased dramatically. Many people are thus asking—and rightly so—whether violent racist groups can be tolerated in a civilized society

The Fourteenth Amendment clearly guarantees all citizens "equal protection of the laws." But to make that guarantee real for people of color in a racist society, is it possible that rights enunciated in the First Amendment must be abridged for those who would stop such protection by violence? It just may be that there is a real contradiction between the First and Fourteenth amendments.

If we see the Constitution not as an end in itself, not just a beautiful document, but as what history has shown it to be—a weapon which people can use in the struggle to make justice a reality—we have to face that contradiction squarely. In some situations, we may have to decide which of these amendments should prevail at a particular time, to the end that human rights are broadened in a still fundamentally racist society.

Notes

1. My personal opinion is that King meant women too, even if the writers of the Declaration of Independence did not.
2. Article 20 of the International Covenant on Civil and Political Rights says, "Any advocacy of national, racial, or religious hatred that constitutes incitement to discrimination, hostility, or violence shall be prohibited by law."

   Article 4 of the International Convention on the Elimination of All Forms of Racial Discrimination obligates ratifying nations to "declare illegal and prohibit organizations, and also organized and all other propaganda activities, which promote and incite racial discrimination."

PART 3

Separation of Powers and the Structure of the Constitution

At the heart of the U.S. Constitution are the related doctrines of separation of powers and checks and balances. As President Reagan said at a Bicentennial celebration, these doctrines represent "the genius of our constitutional system."[1] Yet there has been little study or discussion of the relationship between these concepts and the development of capitalism in the United States. Theorists have focused on the proper role of each of the branches of government, leaving unattended the role of the Constitution's structure in social and economic relations.

This section therefore addresses the relationship between constitutional structure and U.S. capitalism. Neil Mullin delves beneath the debate on the role of judicial review to develop a hypothesis about function that it plays in maintaining the economic and political system. He argues that if the relative autonomy of the bourgeois state from the economic structure of capitalist society is to be maintained, there must be mechanisms that will prevent one sector of the capitalist class, operating in its own narrow short-term interests, from dominating the state. Judicial review has survived and flourished precisely because it serves as the arbitrator between competing factions of the ruling class, framed in language of national unity.

Similarly, Ed Greer, Vine Deloria, Jr., and Walter LaFeber look beyond the liberal/conservative debate to examine the relation between constitutional structure and society. In the arena of foreign affairs, the Constitution was deliberately structured to divide and

191

limit state power. Congress was given the power to authorize the use of force, while the Executive was given the authority to command the troops. The Executive was to negotiate treaties, but the Senate had to ratify them. Clearly, this structure has broken down in the twentieth century—witness the unilateral use of force by Executive action. LaFeber locates the underlying reason for the rise of the imperial presidency in the transformation of U.S. society between 1890 and 1920. It was the changing nature of U.S. capitalism that lay behind the demise of constitutional restraints on U.S. power abroad, as an increasingly imperialist United States aggressively asserted itself around the world.

Vine Deloria also looks at structural changes in the constitutional system. The early constitutional understanding treated Native American groups as quasi-independent nations—thus Congress was given the power to regulate commerce "with the Indian tribes" and federal power to deal with the Indians was based primarily on the treaty power. Yet, as Deloria demonstrates, in the nineteenth century those original conceptions broke down. Indians became a part of the domestic body politic. The reasons for this change are fundamentally the same as those analyzed by LaFeber: rising U.S. power. The result is also similar: the demise of whatever constitutional restraints existed on congressional power over the Indians, who were left in a "no-man's land of political existence," there being virtually no limitation on the federal government's exercise of naked political power over the tribes.

Ed Greer looks at another problem created by the changing U.S. economic and social structure. Monopoly capitalism has led to increased government regulation of economic and social relations. Like the rise of imperialism abroad, that development has transformed traditional concepts of the separation of powers. Instead of Congress enacting laws and the Executive enforcing them (traditional theory), post-New Deal legislatures have delegated broad authority to administrative agencies, which in effect both make and enforce the law. These administrative agencies were supposed to regulate the excesses resulting from unbridled competition, but, as Greer points out, the underlying dynamics of the economy have consigned such regulation to failure.

Clearly, then, the transformation of the United States from a nation of small competitive farmers and manufacturers to one of monopoly capitalists has wrought dramatic changes in the structure of U.S. government.

This section therefore shows the need to analyze our constitutional structure not as mythology or as a static worship of something decreed in 1787, but as these structures operate today. Such an analysis has several important political implications. First, as progressives critique and understand these structures in their social and economic context, their impact on political movements will become clear. Second, once these structures are demystified, more realistic appraisals of their importance and usefulness become possible. Finally, we learn how far mainstream political thought has departed from some aspects of the original constitutional vision. In such areas as foreign affairs, for example, it is the progressive movement that best expresses the original constitutional understanding, making it both appropriate and vital to use our constitutional symbols to develop and inspire our vision of an anti-imperialist United States.

Note

1. *New York Times,* 18 September 1987.

JUDICIAL SUPREMACY, EDWIN MEESE, AND THE RELATIVE AUTONOMY OF THE STATE

Neil Mullin

The Durability of Judicial Supremacy

A lot has been written about dinosaurs lately. Perhaps one of the hottest of the paleontological debates concerns whether dinosaurs were sluggish, cold-blooded reptilian types flopping about like so many crocodiles in the swamps, or active, mobile, warm-blooded creatures skittering across the ancient landscape. In answering such questions, paleontologists work backward from fossilized remnants. In millions of years of natural selection, for example, duck-billed dinosaurs developed chunky feet, not the broad webbing needed by lake-dwellers. Contrary to prevailing wisdom, therefore, it is now thought that duck-billed dinosaurs trotted around on dry land; that was their environment.[1]

Political systems also are governed by a system of natural selection that may be read backward in order to reconstruct the economic environment in which certain political principles or institutions developed. If we find, for example, that a certain political phenomenon has stubbornly prevailed under capitalism over a period of many decades, it makes sense to ask whether that phenomenon does not reflect a very basic structural need of the system. Put another way, in the economic environment of a capitalist system, certain political institutions, such as slavery and exclusion of women from the industrial workforce, die out, while other institutions, such as universal suffrage, survive. It is reasonable to ask why: what underlying features of the capitalist soil feed one political institution but starve another?

One political phenomenon of the U.S. constitutional system stands out as a long-term survivor: the doctrine of judicial supremacy and judicial review. By "judicial review" we mean the power of the federal court system to examine and declare unconstitutional acts and orders of Congress and of the executive branch of the federal government and of all branches of state government. By "judicial supremacy" we mean the doctrine holding the U.S. Supreme Court to be the final arbiter of constitutional issues, the court whose declarations on the constitution are binding upon all other branches of the state and federal governments.

This essay suggests a hypothesis that explains the durability of that doctrine as being a function of very basic underlying structures of a capitalist system. In addition, it appears that many of the features of the U.S. constitution are also functions of the same structural prerequisites that have given rise to the doctrine of judicial supremacy and judicial review.

Recent history gives us a good place to start.

Attorney General Meese, Andrew Jackson, and the Supreme Court

In October 1986, the attorney general of the United States, Edwin Meese, III, gave a speech in New Orleans, in which he sharply criticized the U.S. Supreme Court.[2] He asserted that the Court's interpretations of the Constitution were not the "supreme law of the land" and added that government officials should be guided by their own views of that document rather than always deferring to the Court. While a Supreme Court decision "binds the parties in the case and also the executive branch for whatever enforcement is necessary, such a decision does not establish a 'supreme law of the land' that is binding on all persons and parts of government, henceforth and forevermore."

Meese claimed that the Court had overblown its own role by seeming "to equate the judge with the lawgiver," and criticized a tendency by some Senators and others to place judicial rulings "on a par with the Constitution itself." Meese took particular issue with the Supreme Court's 1958 ruling that Governor Orval E. Faubus of Arkansas was bound by the Court's 1954 prohibiton, in *Brown* v. *Board of Education,* of school segregation even though Faubus had not been a party to the decision.[3] In the 1958 case, the Court has written that the "Federal judiciary is supreme in the exposition of the law of the Constitution, and the principle has ever since been respected by this Court and the country [and is] a permanent and indispensable feature of our constitutional system."

Meese's attack on the role of the Supreme Court drew an angry retort from liberal Americans. The American Civil Liberties Union denounced Meese's "invitation to lawlessness."[4] Laurence H. Tribe, an expert in constitutional law at Harvard Law School, said the "Mr. Meese's position represents a grave threat to the rule of law because it proposes a regime in which every lawmaker and every government agency becomes a law unto itself. . . ."[5] The *New York Times* condemned Meese's "contempt of court,"[6] and Stanford law professor Paul Brest wrote an article entitled "Meese, the Lawman, Calls for Anarchy."[7]

At first glance, it appears that the battle between Meese and liberal America is simply a result-oriented, political debate in the shallow sense—Meese is miffed about specific decisions by the Court favoring school desegregation, abortion rights, rights of the criminal defendant, etc., so he attacks the Court in a demogogic way in order to achieve other results. If the shoe were on the other foot, the liberals would be attacking judicial supremacy and Meese would be condemning liberal anarchy—or so it might be argued. Indeed, the U.S. left and liberal community has, in times past, attacked the Supreme Court in Meesian terms, when the Court's rulings have unremittingly favored the wealthy and powerful. The reader is invited to compare *Government by Judiciary* by Louis Boudin (attack from the left) with the more recent *Government by Judiciary* by Raoul Berger (attack from the right).[8]

But there is more going on in the battle between Meese, the Supreme Court, and liberal America than a battle over specific Supreme Court decisions. In fact, that conflict reflects a fundamental problem with the footing of the U.S. political and economic system. Indeed, Meese's remarks, uncensored by the President, have an unusually radical quality: he attacks an institutional feature of the

Supreme Court that has been in place for almost two centuries—the doctrine of judicial supremacy. He could have limited himself to criticizing specific decisions. It has always been a feature of mainstream politics to accept as sound the basic economic and political structure and to call for policy adjustments only. It is reasonable to ask if some *fundamental* tension propelled the attorney general to launch a radical attack at a time when the Court has generally favored his political views and when it promises, because of conservative changes in its composition, to become even more disposed toward such views.

The most important evidence that the battle between Meese and his opponents reflects a fundamental issue is historical and doctrinal. It is beyond the scope of this piece to detail the history of the doctrine of judicial supremacy and review, but the following can be summarized: (1) What Meese is saying is not new; throughout the history of the United States there has been a strong tension between executive branch opponents of judicial supremacy and judicial proponents of that doctrine;[9] (2) for nearly two centuries the Supreme Court has adhered to the doctrine that it is the supreme expounder of the Constitution and has gone to great lengths, doctrinally, to justify that principle; and (3) throughout the world, all capitalist nations have tended to develop judicial review mechanisms and have moved in the direction of judicial review supremacy—such has been the case even in nations having strong traditions of parliamentary supremacy.[10]

Some brief historical examples will help to illustrate the historical presence of the judicial supremacy debate. Consider the following words:

President Andrew Jackson, speaking about the Supreme Court's decision upholding the propriety of a national bank: "It is maintained by advocates of the bank that its constitutionality in all its features ought to be considered as settled by precedent and by the decision of the Supreme Court. To this conclusion I cannot assent. . . . If the opinion of the Supreme Court covered the whole ground of this act, it ought not to control the coordinate authorities of this government. The Congress, the Executive, and the Court must each for itself be guided by its own opinion of the Constitution. . . . The opinion of the judges has no more authority over Congress than the opinion of Congress has over the judges; and, on that point, the President is independent of both."

President Abraham Lincoln, speaking, inter alia, of the Supreme Court's pro-slavery Dred Scott decision: "I do not forget the position, assumed by some, that constitutional questions are to be decided by the Supreme Court; nor do I deny that such decisions must be binding in any case, upon the parties to a suit, as to the object of that suit. . . . At the same time, the candid citizen must confess that if the policy of the government, upon vital questions affecting the whole people, is to be irrevocably fixed by decisions of the Supreme Court, the instant they are made, in ordinary litigation between parties in personal actions, the people will have ceased to be their own rulers, having to that extent practically resigned their government into the hands of that eminent tribunal."

The tension between the executive branch and the judiciary with respect to the issue of judicial supremacy has resounded throughout our history. Whether it is the liberal Franklin Roosevelt decrying a Court that would not implement state-capitalist measures for achieving economic stability, or the conservative Meese, the issue of judicial supremacy has been a constant in U.S. constitutional history. And during the past two centuries, the Supreme Court, using legal fictions where necessary, has firmly upheld its role as the constitutional arbiter whose rulings are final and binding upon all branches of government, state and federal.

In formulating a hypothesis about the source of the judicial supremacy tension, it is useful to make some basic economic points about U.S. society.

Stabilizing a Government on Shifting Ground

The convention that drew up the U.S. Constitution was torn with ideological conflicts that to a large degree reflected conflicts within the monied and propertied ruling class of the time.[12] The concrete problem that the convention had to solve was how to build the structure of a stable national government upon such shifting ground. More precisely, the problem was how to create a political system that would not simply mirror the deep splits within ruling circles, and, by allowing opposing sects to seize control of different branches of government, end up with governmental paralysis and instability.

The solutions achieved in the Constitution were brilliant and far more stabilizing than the parliamentary structures created by the European bourgeois revolutions of the same era. And an essential part of the solution was the concept of judicial supremacy.

A capitalist class is not a monolithic, self-conscious entity. It exists through competition that splinters it into commercial, financial, industrial, and agricultural sectors, monopoly and nonmonopoly sectors, state-capital and private-capital sectors,[13] and so on. Everything in a capitalist society becomes commodified, rendered an object for sale, and that process also splinters and fragments the capitalist class. Sex is commodified by the pornography industry. That segment collides head-on with the commodifiers of religion. Each such segment reaches for political power and judicial legitimation; the pornographers cloak themselves in the First Amendment and those who sell God speak the language of the antisodomy statutes and strict regulation of abortion.

How can such a fragmented class maintain itself in power against external and internal enemies? It must develop a state apparatus that mediates and arbitrates its internal conflicts, a political system that forces its government figures to look beyond the narrow interests of a segment or fraction of the class (in common political parlance, the "special interest group") to the long-range good of the entire class.

To accomplish that task, a capitalist state must, in the words of the late Nicos Poulantzas, become *relatively autonomous* of its economic mooring. The state, while fulfilling the long-range needs of the capitalist class, must not become paralyzed by the specific narrow needs of its competing sectors. The balance is delicate. If the state becomes too autonomous, seats of government may be captured by noncapitalist sectors, and legislation, as well as executive and judicial decisions, may undermine capitalist security. European governments with a large Communist and Socialist parliamentary presence cannot engage in unbridled capitalist economic development. On the other hand, if the state is not autonomous enough, it will become paralyzed, as indeed the U.S. Congress has become with respect to, for example, energy policy, and the health of the system will again suffer.

The need to structure a relatively autonomous state capable of mediating and arbitrating among the various fractions and segments of the capitalist class does not present itself openly as part of the political ideology. Political figures who come from the monied class and/or whose futures are funded by that class do not generally conceive of themselves as servants of wealth. Rather, the need for a relatively autonomous state is presented as the need to serve one's nation rather than one's self—the need to serve the public not the private sector. Ask not what your country can do for you; ask what you can do for your country.

In the legal setting, relative autonomy translates easily into the language of judicial supremacy. We are a government of laws (the general capitalist interest), not individuals (special interests). We have a Supreme Court that is the final arbiter (the general interest) of constitutional disputes between or among the other branches of government (special interests). If the system requires a national bank, but special state-level interests are offended by that institution, the supreme arbiter will arbitrate that issue, Andrew Jackson notwithstanding.

With some exceptions, it was in the rarified language of national (i.e., class) unity that the Constitution was elaborated and it was that conceptual framework that gave rise to our tradition of judicial supremacy.

James Madison and Relative Autonomy

In *The Federalist Papers* James Madison provides us with a clear example of the translation of the need for the Poulantzian relatively autonomous state into the language of national unity. Madison first of all recognizes the need to develop a political system that by its very structure will militate against the tendency of the capitalist class to fragment: "Among the numerous advantages promised by a well-constructed Union, none deserves to be more accurately developed than its tendency to break and control the violence of the *faction*."[14] In Madison's view, the subordination of the government to a "faction" (i.e., a segment) of the ruling class had to be structured out of the new government.

Madison argued that "factionalism" is inherent in the "nature of man," and noted that the goal must therefore be to control the effects of factionalism rather than to root out the causes of it. In one incredible passage, the ideological garb drops away from Madison's language and the problem of "factions" is presented in clear class terms:

> The most common and durable source of factions has been the verious [sic] and unequal distribution of property. . . . A landed interest, a manufacturing interest, a mercantile interest, a moneyed interest, with many lesser interests, grow up of necessity in civilized nations, and divide them into different classes, actuated by different sentiments and views. The regulation of these various and interfering interests forms the principle task of modern legislation and involves the spirit of party and faction in the necessary and ordinary operations of government.

Having identified the various competing fractions of the ruling class, Madison asks how the government can rise above these special interests. His words presage the role of the Supreme Court as the supreme arbiter and expounder of constitutional law and underscore his view of the legislature as a body potentially subordinated to narrow interests of specific sectors of the ruling class:

> No man is allowed to be a judge in his own cause, because his interest would certainly bias his judgment. . . . With equal, and nay with greater reason, a body of men are unfit to be both judges and parties at the same time; yet what are many of the most important acts of legislation but so many judicial determinations concerning . . . the rights of large bodies of citizens. And what are the different classes of legislators but advocates and parties to the causes which they determine.

Madison did not want a simple democracy giving voice to every fragment and section of the ruling class. He wanted a device that would mediate such diverse interests and sort out the general interest of the entire class. He wanted a delegated government that could "refine and enlarge the public views by passing them through the medium of a chosen body of citizens, whose wisdom may best discern the true interest of their country [i.e., the general interest of their class] and whose patriotism and love of justice will be least likely to sacrifice it to temporary or partial considerations [i.e., special interests of particular segments of the capitalist class]."

Alexander Hamilton, also writing in *The Federalist Papers,* wanted a federal judiciary structured to rise above any narrow interest that might achieve dominance in the legislative or executive branches.[15] The "independence of judges" is essential to safeguard against "injury to the private rights of particular classes of citizens by unjust and partial laws." The "firmness of the judicial magistry . . . operates as a check upon the legislative body . . . who, perceiving that obstacles to the success of an iniquitous intention are to be expected form the scruples of the courts . . . qualify their attempts."

For Hamilton and Madison, legislatures (both state and federal) were institutions that would be seized, and at times dominated, by factional interests. An independent judiciary was seen as an institution that could, by virtue of the life tenure of its judges, break free of narrow interests and play a role in preserving the public and national interests—i.e., the general capitalist interest.

Marbury v. Madison and Its Progeny

In 1801 William Marbury and three others applied to the Supreme Court for an order directing Secretary of State James Madison to issue to Messrs. Marbury *et al.* a document called a "commission," appointing them justices of the peace for the District of Columbia. President Adams had, prior to the expiration of his term, already appointed the complainants to the position of justice of the peace, the Senate had confirmed them, and the commissions had been prepared and stamped with the seal of the United States. But before the commissions could be physically delivered to their recipients, there was a change of administration. Enter President Jefferson. His newly appointed Secretary of State refused to deliver the commissions to appointees of the prior administration. Hence Marbury's lawsuit.

Marbury did not sue Madison in a lower court and arrive in the Supreme Court by way of appeal. Instead, relying on an act of Congress that gave individuals the right to seek certain writs directly in the Supreme Court, Marbury sought relief there. The Court ruled that the statute upon which Marbury premised jurisdiction was unconstitutional; it simultaneously established the doctrine that the Supreme Court was the supreme arbiter and expounder of constitutional law and as such had the right to declare acts of Congress unconstitutional and therefore void.

In so ruling, the Court echoed Madison's distrust of the legislature. Those who would deny the Supreme Court the power to review and overturn an act of Congress "would be giving to the legislature a practical and real omnipotence . . . it thus reduces to nothing, what we have deemed the greatest improvement on political constitutions, a written constitution."[16]

Marshall argued, with an illogicality that has been repeated for decades since, that because, according the Article VI, the Constitution is the supreme law of the land, and because, according to Article III, the Supreme Court must decide, *inter alia,* cases arising under the Constitution, therefore the Supreme Court must have the power to declare an act of Congress unconstitutional.

Obviously, there were many alternative interpretations that Marshall ignored. The most intellectually honest position he could have taken was that the Constitution simply does not address the issue of how an unconstitutional legislative act shall be remedied. Given that admission, it would have been appropriate for Congress to initiate an amendment addressing that issue and it would have been proper for the Court to abide by that political process. Another alternative would have been to argue that unconstitutional legislation had to be dealt with politically: the executive could refuse to enforce an unconstitutional law and the people could refuse to elect (or could seek impeachment of) promulgators of such unconstitutional laws.

There was also the possibility—this time explicitly rejected, but again on the basis of a legal fiction—that the Court could render to Congress and the executive advisory opinions aimed at stopping unconstitutional laws during the enactment process.

What is important for our purposes is that Chief Justice Marshall's conclusion that the Court had the power, under the Constitution, to declare a law unconstitutional was not a conclusion compelled by logic. It was therefore compelled by something else—the need for a relatively autonomous national government capable of checking factional tendencies in the elective branches of the federal government and in state governments.

Judicial Review and Supremacy as a Vehicle for Capitalist Modernization

As discussed above, the doctrines of judicial review and judicial supremacy arose from the need to form a national government that had the capacity to distance itself from the splintering and selfish tendencies of the ruling class. Without organizing such a relatively autonomous mechanism of power, that class would not have been able to move toward capitalist modernization at the expense, if necessary, of specific backward sectors of that same class.

It is therefore not surprising, that some of the most powerful judicial restatements of the notion of judicial supremacy and review have been made when the national government has been fighting for the general capitalist interest against backward monied interests: This has happened with respect to the entry of women, blacks, and other racial/ethnic groups into the workforce, and with respect to the development of active state intervention in economic production and capital accumulation.

Perhaps the most powerful move toward capitalist modernization in the United States has been the shattering of the semifeudal racial barriers to universal wage labor. That trend, which was in the general interests of capitalist economic growth, met with opposition in state governments and the federal legislature from forces wedded to a precapitalist caste system in the South. That collision in turn forced the reassertion of the national (general class) interest in the garb of constitutional/judicial supremacy.

In *Cooper* v. *Aaron*, one of the cases singled out by Attorney General Meese for condemnation, the Supreme Court faced an entire state political institution—the state of Arkansas—that would not honor the Court's ruling, in *Brown* v. *Board of Education*, that the power of the state government may not be used to bar black children from public schools attended by whites.

In November 1956, Arkansas passed an amendment to its state constitution commanding the Arkansas General Assembly to oppose "in every Constitutional manner the un-constitutional desegregation decisions of . . . the United States Supreme Court." Arkansas also passed a "pupil assignment law" that relieved schoolchildren from compulsory attendance at racially mixed schools.[17]

On September 2, 1957, the day before nine black students were scheduled to attend a white high school, the governor of Arkansas dispatched units of the Arkansas National Guard to block their entry.

The local school board, which had arranged the black youngsters' attendance, petitioned a federal district court, asking for permission to delay the implementation of the court's desegregation order in the light of the pro-segregation forces now polarizing around the state governor: "The effect of [the governor's] action . . . was to harden the core of opposition to the Plan and cause many persons . . . to believe there was some power in the State of Arkansas which, when exerted, could nullify the Federal law."

On September 25, 1957, the President dispatched federal troops to the Arkansas high school, and black students were admitted. Sometime thereafter, the issue of whether the lower federal court should postpone desegregation, in light of the state government's hostility, reached the Supreme Court.

The need for capitalist development was in this case translated into the need for the Court to assert the supremacy of its decision in *Brown* v. *Board of Education* over local power: "As this case reaches us it raises questions of the highest importance to the maintenance of our federal system of government. It necessarily involves a claim by the Governor and Legislature of a State that there is no duty on State officials to obey federal court orders resting on this Court's considered interpretation of the United States Constitution."

In response to the Arkansas challenge, the Court, equating the supremacy of the Constitution with its own supremacy, fired off a chain of tautologies and fictions to "prove" its role:

> [W]e should answer the premise of the actions of the Governor and Legislature that they are not bound by our holding in the Brown case. It is necessary only to recall some basic constitutional propositions which are settled doctrine.
>
> Article 6 of the Constitution makes the Constitution the "supreme Law of the Land." In 1803, Chief Justice Marshall, speaking for a unanimous Court, referring to the Constitution as "the fundamental and paramount law of the nation," declared in the notable case of Marbury v. Madison (US) 1 Cranch 137, 177, 2 L ed 2d 60, 73, that "It is emphatically the province and duty of the judicial department to say what the law is." *This decision declared the basic principle that the federal judiciary is supreme in the exposition of the law of the Constitution, and that principle has ever since been respected by this Court and the Country as a permanent and indispensable feature of our constitutional system.* It follows that the interpretation of the Fourteenth Amendment enunciated by this Court in the Brown case is the supreme

law of the land, and Art. 6 of the Constitution makes it of binding effect on the States "any Thing in the Constitution or Laws of any State to the Contrary notwithstanding."[18]

Again, while the Constitution names itself as the supreme law of the land, it does not name the Supreme Court as the supreme expositor of the Constitution. That idea was generated not by logic or force of precedent, but by the need for national forms of political power that were free of the narrow interests that might control the elective branches of government. The Court's periodic incantation of "basic constitutional propositions" that are "settled doctrine" does not transform the legal fiction into reality and does not explain the existence of that fiction.

Another example—this one negative—of the role of the supremacy/review doctrine in the assertion of the capitalist interest in modernization can be found in the Franklin Roosevelt era.

That regime, more than any prior one, moved legislatively in the direction of state monopoly capitalism, in the form of federal limitations upon unplanned and unrestrained competition in the private sector. The Supreme Court failed at first to endorse this national drive toward modernization, and between January 7, 1985, and May 25, 1936, it handed down twelve decisions that declared Roosevelt's modernizing legislation to be unconstitutional.[19] In so doing, the Court aligned itself with narrow industrial interests against the interest in long-term stability embodied in the New Deal legislation. Thus instead of helping the national government to become autonomous by lending a constitutional gloss to the modernization efforts, the Court played the opposite role—and triggered a constitutional crisis. An important commentator of the period, Edward S. Corwin, echoing Jackson and Lincoln and prefiguring Meese, condemned "the doctrine of the *finality* of its [the Supreme Court's] reading of the Constitution." Corwin called for a "clear recognition that the National legislative organ, Congress and the President, are vested not only with the *power* but with the *duty* to read the Constitution for themselves."[20]

In February 1937, Roosevelt embarked on a legislative plan (ultimately not implemented) that would have allowed him to appoint up to six additional justices to the Supreme Court. Shortly thereafter the Court, sensing defeat, reversed itself and began to uphold the constitutionality of Roosevelt's New Deal laws. The system stabilized and the court-packing crisis ended.

Conclusion

When the Court grants constitutional legitimacy to a modernizing effort and declares governmental overreaching by special groups unconstitutional, it is playing the role envisioned by Madison: it is helping the national government to maintain its autonomy and allowing the system to stabilize and grow. When the Court adopts an opposite role and aligns itself with narrow factions against a national drive toward modernization, the system becomes unstable.

This essay has focussed on the judicial supremacy/review doctrine as a function of relative autonomy, but it is worth noting that the entire constitutional framework has, historically and structurally, played the role of rendering the federal or national government autonomous of narrow fractions of the dominant class. For example, the fact that the President is elected not by the legislature but through a national, popular vote forces him (or her) to recognize broad and diverse interests of capital, rather than the specific sectors that from time to time dominate the legislature. In addition, such national elections allow the system to maintain its autonomy by promoting a charismatic national leader who is capable—by virtue of a national popular consensus—to rise above and confront narrow interests.

Other factors that maintain autonomy include an electoral system that denies representation even to strong pluralities, a federal legislative scheme with long terms of office, a constitutional framework that makes amendments almost impossible, and a term-long tenure for the President even when that President lacks the confidence of the Congress. All of the foregoing factors tend to give the federal government a life of its own, a degree of freedom from pressure by specific factions of the dominant class. And in the modern era, such features are more necessary than ever to capitalist stability and growth.

Indeed, in the modern world of capitalist politics, Madison's fear about the factional potential of the political branches of government has been fully realized. Politics itself has become commodified:

politicians are packaged and marketed like toothpaste. Candidates who need enormous campaign funds are more likely than ever to become beholden to specific interests of narrow factions. Congress is faced with enormous and highly financed lobbying efforts. The office of the President is also increasingly subject, through the campaign and election process, to control by narrow segments of the ruling class which are at odds with the segments that control the legislative branches of the federal government.

By enacting a series of laws and regulations that govern the manner in which campaign contributions may be made, Congress has in effect recognized the seriousness of its loss of autonomy, its capitulation to specific economic interests. In such a setting, the stabilizing function of judicial supremacy has never been of greater importance.

Yet the same forces that render the elective branches increasingly susceptible to factional domination to some degree undermine the judicial stabilizing function by politicizing, in the narrow sense, the process of selecting federal judges. The Nixon and Reagan years have given us federal judges who are ideologically wedded to tendencies opposed to modernization. If the trend continues, we can expect the kind of destabilization that characterized the federal government in 1935 and 1936.

To summarize, the doctrines of federal review and judicial supremacy are products of the systemic need for autonomy. To the extent that the Supreme Court puts its constitutional imprimatur on federal efforts to modernize, to that extent the system is stabilized. And because capitalist modernization necessitates the elimination of precapitalist caste systems, as well as of crude forms of exploitation and competition, the Supreme Court has at times appeared to be progressive, endorsing popular struggles for equality and against exploitation. The autonomy required by this system is, however, a *relative* autonomy and, in the final analysis, the federal system will provide constitutional protection for individual rights only to the extent required by the agenda of the dominant classes.

Notes

1. See Robert T. Bakker, *The Dinosaur Heresies* (New York, 1986), pp. 146–59.
2. Stuart Taylor, Jr., "Meese Says Rulings by U.S. High Court Don't Establish Law," *New York Times,* 23 October 1986, p. A.1–20.
3. Cooper v. Aaron, 358 U.S. 1 (1958); Brown v. Board of Education, 347 U.S. 483 (1954).
4. Stuart Taylor, Jr., "Liberties Union Denounces Meese," *New York Times,* 25 October 1986, p. A.17.
5. Ibid.
6. Editorial, "Mr. Meese's Contempt of Court," *New York Times,* 26 October 1987, p. IV-22.
7. Paul Brest, "Meese the Lawman Calls for Anarchy," *New York Times,* 2 November 1986, p. IV-23.
8. Louis Boudin, *Government of Judiciary* (1932; rept. ed. New York, 1965); Raoul Berger, *Government by Judiciary* (Cambridge, Mass., 1977).
9. See Charles Grove Haines, *The American Doctrine of Judicial Supremacy* (New York, 1959).
10. Mauro Cappalletti, *Judicial Review in the Contemporary World* (Indianapolis, 1971); Wolfe, *The Rise of Modern Judicial Review* (New York, 1986).
11. Haines, *The American Doctrine of Judicial Supremacy,* pp. 332–35 and pp. 374–75.
12. See Lawrence Kaplan, "The Origins of the Constitution: Thoughts on a Marxist Paradigm," in this volume.
13. Nicos Poulantzos, *Political Power and Social Classes* (London, 1975), pp. 84–85; see also Paul M. Sweezy, *The Theory of Capitalist Development* (New York, 1942), pp. 294–99.
14. *The Federalist No. 10* (James Madison) in *The Federalist Papers,* ed. Clinton Rossiter (New York, 1961), pp. 77–84. I want to thank Lawrence Kaplan of the City University of New York for his suggestion about the parallel between Madison's *Federalist No. 10* and the Poulantzian concept of autonomy as a vehicle for overcoming a fractional class.
15. *The Federalist No. 78* (Alexander Hamilton), in ibid., pp. 464–72.
16. Marbury v. Madison, 1 Cranch 137 (1803) at 176–180.
17. Cooper v. Aaron, 358 U.S. 1 (1958).
18. Ibid, at 17–18; emphasis added.
19. Benjamin F. Wright, *The Growth of American Constitutional Law* (Chicago, 1942), p. 180.
20. Edward S. Corwin, "Curbing the Court," in *American Constitutional History: Essays by Edward S. Corwin* (Cambridge, Mass., 1970), pp. 126 ff.

ADMINISTRATIVE LAW AND CHRONIC UNDERREGULATION IN THE MODERN STATE

Edward Greer

Government regulation emerged as a political response to problems associated with the capitalist market economy, yet in substantial measure it has failed to resolve these problems. In the face of this failure, a conservative response has emerged that demands deregulation and a return to the untrammeled market. But this essay insists that a more accurate and useful approach to the regulatory system is one that focuses on the opposite problem: underregulation. The reality is that chronic underregulation (which in turn derives from the structure of the largely private political economy) is the real problem. After summarizing the development of modern administrative law, the essay delineates the multiplicity of ways in which the reality of regulation is but a pale shadow of what is proclaimed.

Regulation in the "Expanded State"

Our current constitutional system, a product of the New Deal, is very different from that envisaged by its framers. During the New Deal, the structure and functioning of the federal government was radically transformed by the creation of over one hundred new federal agencies. In addition—and of more significance to the law—the New Deal legitimated government regulation.

The New Deal juridical revolution was a necessary consequence of the redistribution of political power in the United States, itself the result of a new class compromise. In particular, monopoly capital was forced to share—under the impetus of a mighty labor insurgency—political power with other capitalist strata, and was also obliged to admit some portions of the working class into a share—albeit a subordinate one—of governance. Expressed more abstractly, the hegemonic class of monopoly capital incorporated real interests of other classes into public policy and created an "expanded state."[1]

Before the New Deal, the leading constitutional paradigm was that Congress legislated, the courts judged, and the President administered. Each had absolute power in its own sphere, but if it entered another sphere its actions were illegitimate and void. This constitutional construction left administrative agencies, such as the Interstate Commerce Commission, which combined powers from all three branches, in a status of reduced legitimacy and power. Indeed, they were contemptuously referred to as the so-called "headless 'fourth branch' of government."[2]

The practical consequence of this was that the validity of delegating broad rule-making and adjudicatory power to administrative agencies at first came under assault. In particular, government reforms that served the working masses (such as child-labor and minimum-wage statutes) were in constant danger of being held invalid by the Supreme Court. Nevertheless, after a few years of the New Deal's "expanded state," the issue of the permissibility of delegating power to unelected bureaucratic bodies disappeared from constitutional discourse. The new administrative agencies were accepted as the solution to the ills of capitalism: the crisis of the Depression had both demanded and allowed this substantial restructuring of government.

The federal courts now began to devote the largest single part of their energies and policy outputs to questions of administrative law, which moved from the periphery to the core of the legal system. As so reconstructed, the legal system took on the social function of attempting to answer popular demands for reform that neither the private market nor older government structures could accomplish.

The Administrative Procedure Act of 1946 encapsulated the new legal framework for government regulation. The act was perceived by lawyers as the embodiment of an essentially just framework within which there could be a fair resolution of disputes among interest groups. This system would end class conflict and create the good society. But this celebration of the U.S. legal system had scarcely declared itself before events overtook it.

As long as the post-World War II economy was expanding, the New Deal system could work. To its credit, the legal system was able to overcome the political deadlock around the Jim Crow system by declaring it in violation of the Constitution. Heady with this genuine accomplishment, liberal activist jurists hoped to turn the courts into an instrument of ongoing social reform. However, the enterprise of fixing the ills of society was a utopian project. Riding for a brief moment on the crest of the civil rights movement, parts of the liberal legal establishment tried to advance a program of democratic participation and substantive fairness in administrative law. The courts soon abandoned this enterprise, although they remained reluctant to undo prior reforms.

The reason the judiciary has been unable to continue down the road of judicial reform lies in the larger U.S. political economy, specifically its steep decline since the defeat of U.S. imperialism in Vietnam. As conservative ideologist Samuel P. Huntington (serving as rapporteur to the Trilateral Commission) bluntly stated, increasing participation by previously marginal social groups threatens to overload "the political system with demands which extend its functions and undermine its authority."[3] It is simply too expensive to provide a full panoply of social entitlements and due process hearings for the entire population.

The mystery of the so-called crisis of administrative law is thus readily fathomable as a manifestation of the economic costs that society as presently constituted cannot bear. As the administrative law system reaches this limit, public policy (including that of the courts and agencies) becomes increasingly short-sighted and mean-spirited. A new consensus has therefore emerged that administrative law is at an impasse.

It would be, I think, a silly and futile intellectual exercise to try to understand the main trends of administrative law doctrine over the past fifty years without looking at exogenous causes in the political economy. I do not think that this Marxist position (which argues that there are boundary conditions imposed on the legal subsystem by the political economy) implies a rejection of the existence of an immanent legal logic.[4] But I do think that it is a mistake for radical legal scholars to focus their intellectual energies on an immanent ideological critique (i.e., a "deconstruction") of bourgeois legal claims of doctrinal coherence of the law. It is impossible to use such a debate to develop a coherent radical program of political action.[5]

The Realities of Regulation

Administrative agency actions, like those of government generally, fall into two broad categories: rule-making and adjudication. The ubiquitous regulations promulgated by regulatory bodies profoundly affect our daily lives.

The courts have come to devote an ever increasing proportion of their energies to judicial review of "public law" matters. Even areas that are traditionally matters of private law, such as torts, have been effected by government regulations which set legal standards of care in designing products.

Our society has begun to choke on bureaucratic oversight, as record-keeping and reporting obligations proliferate. For instance, formal federal agency adjudications outnumber the total caseload of the federal courts by a factor of ten. And in turn, for each of these formal agency adjudications, there are perhaps a hundred less formal ones.

Nevertheless, despite their immense number, such regulatory actions are still rare. The overwhelming mass of social behavior, even that which is formally within the parameters of "regulated" activity, is not subject to enforcement. It is this gap between the vast universe of theoretically regulated activity and the actual practice of oversight that must be analyzed.

To understand the magnitude of this chasm, the case of the Internal Revenue Service (unquestionably one of the strongest and most activist of the federal agencies) comes to mind. As a practical matter, any person can disobey the tax laws with only a miniscule likelihood of punishment (there are only three hundred criminal convictions a year).[6] And there are millions of substantial violators. A full one-eighth of those who are required to do not even bother to file returns. And these nonreporters, together with the more significant group of underreporters, are jointly responsible for an average annual revenue shortfall equal to the annual federal budget deficit! In fact, the nonfilers are responsible for only 5 percent of the uncollected revenues, with the vast bulk due to nonreporting of various forms of profit.[8]

Part of the explanation for this underenforcement of the Internal Revenue Code is that the ability of the propertied strata to resist enforcement is great. The other part, of course, is that the population is generally averse to further increases in government regulation and supervision of their lives. This sentiment which is tied to a correct understanding that ever increasing state supervision of daily life is not a viable or desirable path for society, acts as a general limiting factor on all forms of government regulation. Thus there is no effective "general will," in Rousseau's sense, to accomplish social reform through government regulation.

In a less abstract manner, we can understand such underenforcement by examining several structural features of the regulatory process.

The most important obstacle to enforcement is the fact that an agency cannot act to correct a violation unless it is apprised of its existence. This is ordinarily a very difficult threshold to cross. The information-gathering necessary for effective public control of private matters is comparable to that needed by public planners under nonmarket socialist conditions. As everyone now understands, this kind of detailed knowledge is generally not available.

Agency information-gathering occurs through three basic mechanisms: (1) first-party self-reporting by the violator, (2) second-party reporting by the victim, or (3) third-party investigation by the agency itself. Let us examine each in turn.

(1) To compel self-reporting, two conditions must be met: a legislative mandate and data to report. Both may be hard to come by. Indeed, it was not until the New Deal judicial revolution that the constitutionality of legislation mandating self-reporting was established. Given the popular unease regarding governmental surveillance, even in an "expanded state," such statutory authorization is difficult to accomplish—we need only look at Congress's veto of the Federal Trade Commission rule requiring dealers to disclose major known defects in used cars to recognize the problem. As one senator commented, "This rule will increase paperwork [and] the cost of cars to consumers."[9]

Similarly, self-reporting is meaningless unless there is data to report, and such data often does not exist. Thus when the FDA went back to review drugs that had been placed on the market before the legislation requiring them to be efficacious as well as safe, it had to review 3,400 prescription drugs, a process that took twenty-two years.[10] Currently, a lack of data is a major factor blocking the regulation of toxic chemical exposures. Similar difficulties exist with respect to most environmental and high-technology regulations.[11]

When there is no underlying data and the statute or agency requires the regulated industry to create it, special problems occur, most notably the development of erroneous data.[12] (It is also possible for the agency to collude with the regulated party to defer enforcement while awaiting the creation of data that is not really essential.)[13]

Once the reporting is mandated and the data exists, another problem develops. The objective of the self-reporting requirement, after all, is to compel a party that is not willing to comply voluntarily with the underlying substantive rule to provide the data that the agency can then use to make it comply. But this is obviously a one-step regress. And sure enough, where there is serious opposition to the substantive rule, there is generally a similar pattern of non-reporting.

While the issue has not been studied exhaustively, the available anecdotal evidence suggests that large corporations (and, *a fortiori,* small businesses) are typically in noncompliance with federal reporting requirements. For instance, General Motors did not provide required information to the National Highway Transportation Safety Agency about its X-model brakes; Smith-Kline did not report to the FDA about Selacryn; and the Chrysler Corporation did not keep accurate records on employee injuries required under OSHA.[14]

So common is false reporting of this sort that it is a central part of the discovery effort of product-liability attorneys. When detected, the reporting violations are often so deliberate and egregious as to constitute criminal fraud.

(2) The main alternative to the wrongdoer confessing is for the victim to report the crime to the authorities. But this is only feasible if the victim has knowledge of the wrong and it is commonplace, in the contemporary world of complex technical causation, for the large majority of victims to be ignorant and quiescent. Thus, for instance, a

Massachusetts health department ruling which required manufacturers of urea-formaldehyde foam insulation to remove it at their expense and substitute an inert insulating material was upheld—to quite considerable news coverage—but of ten thousand homeowners affected, fewer than four hundred applied under the administrative removal program, and perhaps one hundred pursued nonexclusive common-law tort remedies.

Similarly, Massachusetts has perhaps the strongest lead paint statute in the nation. It provides for strict liability and recovery based on government inspection reports certifying the presence of lead paint on the premises. Where there is a willful violation, the landlord is liable to automatically trebled damages and criminal penalties. Nevertheless, after fifteen years of this exemplary law, it is estimated that fewer than 2 percent of the state's rental units have been de-leaded. This is true even though two thousand children a year are identified with blood lead levels above the clinical injury threshhold.[15] The reasons for this outcome—as with unenforceable housing codes throughout the country—is apparent.

If the private tort system, which has the advantage of the kinds of economic incentives congenial to a capitalist society, fails to bring claims, we can imagine how rare is pure civic-minded reporting to government agencies. Thus, for example, out of an estimated 60,000 annual cosmetic-related injuries, fewer than 400 are reported to the FDA.[16]

(3) If neither the perpetrator nor the victim come forward, the government agency can investigate and discovery on its own accord. But this too is a rarity, with the norm being noninspection.

Thus, to return to our initial example of the federal income tax, only 1.5 percent of returns are audited each year. On an annual basis, only 3 percent of government contractors subject to the Walsh-Healey Act are inspected; and even when violations are found, reinspections occur in only 25 percent of cases.[17] Similarly, in its first five years of existence OSHA was able to inspect only 7 percent of covered workplaces.[18]

This pattern holds almost wherever one looks. For instance, a spot inspection of airlines revealed that 20 percent had violations in the handling of passenger's food, yet inspections have not increased.[19] While 6 percent of inspected lots of imported foods (which have come to encompass a full 25 percent of the fruits and vegetables we consume) are found to have illegal pesticide residues, the FDA inspects only 1 percent of these lots each year.[20]

In short, most violations, in most contexts, continue to exist.

Even when a violation is detected, an agency enforcement adjudication resulting in an effective sanction is far from likely. Indeed, in most regulatory contexts it is rare.[21] Thus, confronted with firm evidence of ethylene dibromide (EDB) in imported mangoes, the EPA determined that it would not act since it was entitled to "consider [the adverse] impact on foreign economies."

Agencies in this respect function much like courts, which also are far stronger in words than deeds when it comes to enforcing social legislation in the "expanded state." One sees this phenomenon vividly in the sharp discounting of damages that is a hallmark of class actions.[22]

In every arena, as the political power of the regulated group increases, the likelihood of adverse governmental action declines. Such is the nature of a class society.

Conclusion

Government regulation, a generation ago proclaimed as the new constitutional solution to the contradictions of capitalism, comes today to be writ small as the job of remedying "market failure." Visibly failing even that radically diminished task, the Right is calling for it to be cast out entirely. The Left, however, suggests that full enforcement be attempted even if it would entail dramatic changes in property and social relations, and correlative reinterpretation of the Constitution itself.

Notes

1. See Christine Buci-Glucksmann, *Gramsci and the State* (Atlantic Highlands, N.J., 1980) for a theoretical explanation of the concept of the "expanded state."
2. President's Committee on Administrative Management, *Administrative Management in the Government of the United States* (1937), p. 36.
3. Michel Crozier et al., *The Crisis of Democracy* (New York, 1975), p. 114. As Claus

Offe puts it, there has developed a "disparity between the volume of [social] claims and the government's steering capacity" (*Contradictions of the Welfare State* [1984], p. 68).

4. Thus I think that Leon Lipson is in error in asserting that "the most fundamental characteristic of a Marxist theory of law is that it purports to look at law from outside law, to disdain the immanent jurisprudence, to relate law to something else that is regarded as being logically or dynamically prior to law." See "Is There a Marxist Theory of Law? Comments on Tushnet," in J. Roland Pennock and John W. Chapman, eds., *Marxism,* Nomos series 26 (Brooklyn, N.Y., 1983), p. 189.

   Furthermore, all legal interpretation necessarily requires an element outside of "law" so that there *cannot* be any "immanent legal logic" which could uniquely determine juridical outcomes. See Thomas C. Grey, "Advice for 'Judge and Company,' " *The New York Review of Books,* 12 March 1987, pp. 32–35.

5. This is why the Conference on Critical Legal Studies winds up having to devote its energies to defending itself from powerful attacks from all sides of "nihilism." See, e.g., John Stick, "Can Nihilism Be Pragmatic?," 100 *Harvard Law Review* 332 (1986).

6. The average sentence is thirty months. See *New York Times,* 19 September 1984.

7. Ibid., 7 June 1984, 18 March 1982, 19 September 1984.

8. Ibid., 10 April 1982.

9. *New York Times,* 19 May 1982; see also 27 May 1982. Of 210 co-sponsors of the veto resolution, 186 had received contributions from the National Automobile Dealers Association (ibid., 12 May 1982).

10. *New York Times,* 16 September 1984. One-third of these drugs were withdrawn as inefficacious.

11. The National Research Council found available data insufficient to allow even a partial health assessment of 90 percent of chemicals, 66 percent of pesticides, 84 percent of cosmetics, and 81 percent of food additives (ibid., 3 March 1984).

12. For an example from my own air-pollution enforcement experience, see Edward Greer, *Big Steel: Black Politics and Corporate Power in Gary, Indiana* (New York, 1979), p. 189.

13. An example of this variant was EPA's deferral of enforcement of the PCB regulations along a Texas pipeline. In the face of harshly worded Congressional oversight charges that the agency had sat on its hands for eighteen months even after knowing about the PCB-laden pits, the EPA's director of compliance for toxic substances responded that it was awaiting the completion of additional studies. "We wanted more information; that's why we waited" (*New York Times,* 17 March 1987).

14. For the first, see *New York Times,* 23 August 1984; in a later proceeding the brakes were not found to be unsafe. For the second, see *New York Times,* 13 June 1984, 14 December 1984; the FDA's recommendation of felony charges was overruled by the Justice Department on the ground of an insufficiency of evidence of intentional misconduct. For the third, see *New York Times,* 31 January 1987.

15. *Boston Globe,* 20 January 1987, 5 March 1987.

16. *New York Times,* 19 September 1984.

17. Ibid., and 2 January 1970.

18. Mark Rothstein, *Occupational Safety and Health Law* (1978), p. 68. A meticulous empirical study shows that where inspections were concentrated, OSHA—despite the scorn heaped on it by the reactionaries—was moderately successful in reducing injuries (John Mendeloff, *Regulating Safety* [Cambridge, Mass., 1979], pp. 94–120).

19. *New York Times,* 7 December 1984.

20. Ibid., 4 December 1986.
21. Over a five-year period, only fifteen contractors were penalized for violating the Walsh-Healy Act (ibid., 2 January 1970), while among several thousand instances of illegal imported food residues, only a handful led to collected fines (ibid., 4 December 1986). As counterfeit goods of all sorts increasingly enter domestic trade (now $20 billion a year worth of drugs, surgical machine parts, brakes, eyeglasses, engines, etc.), this aspect of the problem grows apace (see ibid., 24 October 1984).
22. Thus even before an unusually liberal judge and after liability had been established, the antibiotics antitrust class action settled for one-sixth of damages (Charles W. Wolfram, "The Antibiotics Class Actions," *American Bar Foundation Research Journal* (1976): 251, 356. The corporate defendants in the Agent Orange case concluded that they got off very cheaply (Peter H. Schuck, *Agent Orange on Trial* [1986], pp. 166, 180).

THE CONSTITUTION AND U.S. FOREIGN POLICY:
An Interpretation

Walter LaFeber

Perhaps the best single sentence defining the Constitution was, appropriately, penned by the "father" of the document in 1792. In such "charters of liberty" as the Constitution, James Madison wrote, "every word . . . decides a question between power and liberty." He hoped that "being republicans," Americans would be "anxious to establish the efficacy of popular charters, in defending liberty against power, and power against licentiousness."[1] Some 180 years later, while writing one of the few extended analyses of the relationship between the Constitution and foreign policy, Louis Henkin noted that in one critical area Madison's insight had been tragically neglected. No greater power existed than the United States', and specifically the President's, ability to destroy all civilization, but books "that deal with the Constitution say little about American foreign relations," Henkin lamented, and those dealing with foreign policy have "roundly ignored" the "controlling relevance of the Constitution."[2]

In truth, the neglect of the connection between foreign affairs and the observance of constitutional principles is relatively new. From the time of *The Federalist* (whose opening essays stress the foreign policy problems that threatened the new nation's liberties and security) and the 1792–93 Hamilton-Madison debate over the President's powers in the global arena, through the bitter "imperialist" versus "anti-imperialist" debates of 1898–1900, Americans argued over appropriate foreign policy while keeping the Constitution closely in view, and fought over constitutional principles with acute awareness

221

of how those principles affected their international affairs. By World War II, however, the debate had dramatically changed. Scholars led by Edward S. Corwin repeatedly raised the danger of conducting foreign policy without due regard for constitutional restraints, but Congress, the courts, and above all the Executive neglected Corwin's warnings. In the top-secret National Security Council document 68 of April 1950, a paper that became the blueprint for U.S. policy after 1950, the Truman administration argued that "the integrity of our system will not be jeopardized by any measures, covert or overt, violent or non-violent, which serve the purposes of frustrating the Kremlin design."[3] That prophecy turned out to be mistaken within a generation, but after a brief flurry of concern about the Cold War's effect on "the integrity of our system" during the 1970s, the debate and the politics reverted to the assumptions of 1950. Nor to this point (Autumn 1987), has the Reagan administration's Iran-contra scandal shown any signs of expanding—as it should—into a national debate over the relationship between foreign policy, on the one hand, and accountable power and the preservation of constitutional rights on the other.

The turn from Madison's sensitivity for the delicate balance between power and liberty to NSC-68's assumption that the foreign-policy ends justify the means occurred not in the early days of the Cold War but between 1890 and 1920. Supreme Court Justice George S. Sutherland uttered the most famous blessing on the turn in 1936 when he wrote the majority opinion in *United States* v. *Curtiss-Wright Export Corporation* (which will be discussed further below). But Sutherland's decision had been shaped two decades earlier and, resembling most such blessings, it only affirmed behavior that had long been practiced. Imperial presidencies, weak congresses, and cautious courts, which have been endemic to modern U.S. foreign policy formulation, appeared at the turn of the century as the nation's foreign relations became global rather than largely continental, were driven more by corporate than by agrarian interests, and were tracked by telegraphs and airplanes instead of by couriers and stagecoaches. These changes radically challenged the constitutional forms that had governed the continental foreign policy for a century. The Presidency and the courts met this challenge simply and directly: they largely severed foreign policy from traditional constitutional restraints by declaring that international and domestic relations could be dealt with separately. As Supreme Court decisions from 1890 to 1936 announced, Americans were to view their overseas and home policies as distinct. Actions in the world arena were not to affect liberties at home, at least not unduly.

The framers of the Constitution believed such a separation between foreign and domestic realms to be both artificial and dangerous. In their view, the inability of individual states to cooperate in foreign policy had produced continual crises throughout the 1780s. The effect was also reciprocal: the inability to control overseas trade (which could bring badly needed specie into the country), or to protect the western settlements, had produced dangerous internal unrest. Shays Rebellion in western Massachusetts and the threat of western settlements leaving the confederation to join adjacent British or Spanish empires dramatized the dangers.[4] The equal danger, of course, was that in creating a central government capable of dealing with European powers, a monster would be created that could also suppress individuals and states. But that possible connection had to be dealt with, not wished away. Madison, for one, had closely studied the connection. In conclusions drawn during 1786–87, in "Vices of the Political System of the United States" (a paper that later became three of *The Federalist* essays), the Virginian attacked the states for their encroachment on "federal authority" and their "trespasses . . . on the rights of each other." In nearly every example he provided of such "transgressions," foreign policy issues such as the Atlantic trade or imperial competition over western lands were involved.[5] Nothing more directly contributed to the calling of the 1787 Convention than the spreading belief that under the Articles of Confederation Congress could not effectively and safely conduct foreign policy.[6]

But Madison also later warned that "perhaps it is a universal truth that the loss of liberty at home is to be charged to provisions against danger, real or pretended, from abroad."[7] In the South Carolina legislature's debate on the new Constitution, Pierce Butler, who had participated in the Philadelphia meetings, outlined the extensive discussion that had occurred on the war-making powers. Butler indicated that the debates had little to do with efficiency and much to do with accountability and the maintenance of checks and balances in a republican system. The President did not receive exclusive power to make peace or war because it meant "throwing into his hands the influence of a monarch, having an opportunity of involving his country in a war whenever he wished to promote her destruction."[8] Butler had learned that lesson the hard way: he had been the delegate who wanted to vest all war powers in the President. That kind of thinking had led Madison and Elbridge Gerry to move that Congress have the power to "declare" war. The motion was followed by Gerry's acid remark that he "never expected to hear in a republic a motion to empower the Executive alone to declare war."[9]

Madison had earlier explained his view to the delegates: "Constant apprehension of war has the . . . tendency to tender the head too large for the body. A standing military force, with an overgrown Executive will not long be safe companions to liberty." In giving his version of the giddy-minds-and-foreign-quarrels theme, Madison believed that "the means of defense against foreign danger have been always the instruments of tyranny at home. Among the Romans it was a standing maxim to excite a war, whenever a revolt was apprehended. Throughout all Europe, the armies kept up under the pretext of defending, have enslaved the people."[10] Hamilton emphasized the point in *Federalist 8:* "Safety from external dangers is the most powerful director of national conduct. Even the most ardent love of liberty will, after a time, give way to its dictates." He shrewdly noted the irony: "To be more safe, [citizens] at length become willing to run the risk of being less free."[11]

Hamilton and Madison argued that the Constitution's provisions could protect liberty at home while they also safeguarded U.S. interests abroad. That belief later produced divisions between Federalists and Anti-federalists. At no time, however, did either side disconnect foreign and domestic policies. Both groups agreed on the proper priority to be given to these policies: liberty and order at home led to an effective overseas policy. Madison stated the postulate in the Virginia Ratifying Convention while debating Patrick Henry: "Does [Henry] distinguish between what will render us secure and happy at home, and what will render us respectable abroad? If we be free and happy at home, we shall be respectable abroad."[12]

The argument over this proper balance between extending power abroad and maintaining liberty at home shaped much of the political debate during the quarter-century that followed the Constitution's ratification. When George Washington issued his Neutrality Proclamation as the Anglo-French war erupted in early 1793, Madison and

Hamilton clashed over the President's right to make such policy. Both focused on the effect the proclamation would have on the separation of powers and, as Hamilton termed it, on "republican propriety and modesty."[13] Madison's "Helvidius" letters comprised one sustained attack on the dire effects of Washington's act, which "seems to violate the forms and spirit of the Constitution" by exalting executive powers in foreign affairs.[14] By the end of the decade even leading Federalists were reluctant to claim too much for executive power. In 1795, James Kent argued that "war only can be commenced by an act or resolution of Congress." During the Undeclared War with France three years later, Hamilton himself admitted that President John Adams could repel attacks but not order reprisals without congressional approval.[15]

Federalists used the crisis with France to pass the Alien and Sedition acts in an attempt to silence political opponents. Jefferson and Madison responded with the Kentucky and Virginia resolutions. The two men attacked what they perceived to be the attempt by the national government to use a foreign policy crisis to violate the constitutional rights of individuals and states. Assuming that the federal government's powers resulted "from the compact to which the states are parties," the Virginia legislature's resolutions outlined a constitutional process that would prevent the Adams administration from using foreign policy crises to justify a witch hunt.[16]

In his distinguished study of the rapid expansion of presidential power between 1789 and 1820, Abraham Sofaer concluded that the Founders established modern presidential practices in those years "with a high degree of awareness as to the potential consequences." The practices included John Adams leading Americans into their first major post-1783 war without a formal declaration; Jefferson's loose construction of his executive powers in order to purchase and govern Louisiana; and "the earliest analogue to the Gulf of Tonkin Resolution," when Madison extracted from Congress vague powers which he used to subvert and then seize West Florida. But Sofaer also asked whether "anything has changed since those early times." He believed that the "answer is definitely yes. . . . Our first Presidents were overtly deferential to Congress," whereas more recent chief executives were not. The first Presidents, moreover, never made two claims much heard after 1940: that the executive "may use whatever raw power he had—monetary, diplomatic and military—in the national interest"; and that he held inherent powers as chief executive and commander-in-chief that "are beyond legislative control. No early President suggested that Congress was significantly limited in the control it potentially had over assigned executive powers."[17]

The nature of U.S. foreign policy interests until the Civil War helps explain such presidential deference. Those interests usually had several characteristics. First, they touched large numbers of Americans in ways that cut across functional groups and even involved entire regions of the country. Second, they were not to be located on the other side of the globe or in secret military installations, but across the next river or mountain range where lands and ports claimed by Indians, Mexicans, or Europeans were coveted. Those characteristics not only closely linked foreign policy with the immediate, individual rights of Americans, but made large numbers of them aware of the link. They believed that they were able to shape the nation's foreign affairs. That link and belief appeared in many forms. Jefferson, for example, explicitly connected expansion with domestic happiness: "I am persuaded no constitution was ever before so well calculated as ours for extensive empire and self-government."[18]

Other Americans, especially those in New England, vigorously disagreed with such reasoning. After Jefferson's 1803 foreign policy success, when he purchased all of Louisiana, Fisher Ames, a conservative Federalist Party member from Massachusetts, lamented that "Our country is too big for union, too sordid for patriotism, too democratic for liberty."[19] A Federalist leader in Congress, Josiah Quincy, despised the "extensive territory" created by the Louisiana Purchase and warned that it could turn "liberty" into "licentiousness." The Constitution, Quincy declared in the debate on whether to admit Louisiana as a state, "was never constructed to form a covering for the inhabitants of the Missouri," and the "mixed, though more respectable, race of the Anglo-Hispano-Americans who bask on the sands in the mouth of Mississippi." Give them statehood, Quincy warned, and "the bonds of this Union are virtually dissolved."[20]

Having survived both Quincy's challenge and the war with Great Britain between 1812 and 1814, in 1829 an aged Madison turned Quincy's reasoning on its head to make an ominous prophecy about the constitutional system. He feared that expansion would stop and that "in 100 years" (or 1929), the rapidly growing population would outstrip the available land. Society would then polarize between the wealthy and the "indigent laborers." The "institutions and laws of the country" could be put to the ultimate test.[21] Such pessimism was not new: it could be traced to Madison's belief in 1786–88 that the high rate of population increase (which he accurately calculated) and the turn from farming to "manufactures" could create a political crisis.[22] The difference between his warnings in the 1820s and those forty years earlier was not that the new Constitution could help cushion the society against the effects of radical social change, but that the Constitution itself, and the liberties it helped guarantee, rested on an expansionism that when exhausted would force a rethinking of the entire system.

President James K. Polk apparently did not know of Madison's forebodings. In any case, Polk's mind, resembling the minds of some later Presidents, did not run to the theoretical or concern itself with consequences associated with possible limits of growth. To appease political factions which had elevated him from a failed Tennessee gubernatorial candidate to the presidency, and to satisfy his own understanding of U.S. manifest destiny, Polk increased the nation's territory by nearly 50 percent. He instigated a war with Mexico by making territorial demands and, when the demands went unanswered, sending U.S. forces into a disputed area and forcing a response from Mexican troops. Alleging that American blood had been spilled on American soil, Polk pried a war declaration from Congress. Abraham Lincoln, then a young Whig Party congressman who disliked most of Polk's Democratic program, warned that if the President succeeded with his scheme to have a war by invading a neighboring nation, "see if you can fix any limit to his power in this respect." In Lincoln's view, Polk, by taking away Congress's right to exercise its war-declaring power properly and with accurate information, had committed "the most oppressive of all Kingly oppressions" feared by the Constitutional Convention.[23]

The war against Mexico for land in the Southwest and ports on the Pacific launched the most frenetic fifteen-year-era in U.S. diplomatic history until the Cold War. The years 1846 to 1861 were frenetic precisely because so many Americans believed the survival of their own liberty and property interests depended on following certain foreign policies. Polk first discovered this dangerous link when he asked for funds to buy peace with Mexico. The House of Representatives responded with the Wilmot Proviso, which prohibited slavery in any territory taken by a treaty with Mexico. The President, either through ignorance or willfulness, refused to see the link: "What connection slavery had with making peace with Mexico it is difficult to conceive."[24] For both slave owners who needed fresh territory (and the congressional representation that arose out of that territory), and free-soil interests, however, the "connection" meant everything. As Arthur Bestor has observed, "Territorial expansion drastically changed the character of the dispute over slavery by entangling it with the constitutional problem of devising forms of government for the rapidly settling west." Foreign policy sharpened the already thorny question of congressional authority in the newly acquired territories.[25]

That Americans took no more adjacent continental territory after 1854 is irrelevant. Given southern filibusterers, an All-Mexico Movement, Young America, a drive for Cuban annexation led by both northeastern and southern factions, new involvements in Central America, and even the application of the Monroe Doctrine's principles to Hawaii, the questions between 1846 and 1861 were not whether but when, where, and how U.S. expansion would strike next. The corollary question was whose interest that expansion would benefit. The answer to those questions would decide who could determine the most critical constitutional issues far into the future. In this context, the *Dred Scott* decision of 1857 was a powderkeg. Supreme Court Chief Justice Roger Taney ruled that slavery could exist in any of the territories, North as well as South, and that the U.S. government had to protect slavery in those territories. If Taney's decision held, then—as Lincoln and others argued—U.S. expansion anywhere could automatically carry with it the expansion of the slave-state interests. On that issue, Stephen A. Douglas, who was determined not to allow his simple policy of rampant expansionism to be complicated by the *Dred Scott* decision, took a position that split the Democratic Party. Into the breach moved Lincoln and the Republicans. They were committed in the long run to overturning *Dred Scott* by making fresh appointments to the Supreme Court, and in the short run to containing the slave states by denying them the annexation of Cuba.

In late 1860, Lincoln slashed the knot tied in the 1780s by Madison and the other Founders. The newly elected (but not yet inaugurated) President refused to allow expansion to be used to maintain a possible constitutional balance. The result was civil war. Lincoln had to face this ultimate issue when Senator John Crittenden of Kentucky pieced together a compromise that protected slavery where it existed and then, in the pivotal provision, prohibited it north of the old Missouri Compromise line of 36°30' but protected slave interests in all other territory "now held, or hereafter acquired." Warning that, if this compromise passed, the South would attempt to being Cuba into the Union as slave territory within a year, Lincoln declared there was only one solution: "A prohibition against acquiring any more territory."[26] The Crittenden Compromise was killed. And so, during the next four and one-half years, were 600,000 Americans.

The nation that emerged from civil war had lost interest in further landed expansion. William Seward's success in maneuvering the Senate into purchasing Alaska from Russia was accompanied by a congressional resolution opposing any further acquisition of territory. By 1890 the official U.S. census concluded that the line separating the frontier from more settled areas had ceased to exist. Although a continued high birth rate and record numbers of immigrants were filling the country, no important push for further annexation of territory appeared. Now the focus changed. As the first century of U.S. foreign policy had been characterized by a landed expansion that involved many Americans and occurred largely on contiguous territory, so the next century's foreign policy was to be dominated by economic and military interests that involved relatively few Americans (although it did affect powerful interest groups), and was often carried out far from the North American continent. In the 1895 edition of his classic *American Commonwealth,* James Bryce believed (somewhat mistakenly) that ever since the 1840s "external relations have very rarely . . . affected internal political strife"; nor did they "occupy the public mind. . . . I mention them now as the traveller did the snakes in Iceland, only to note their absence."[27]

Just three years after Bryce published those words, however, foreign policy again dominated the public mind. But the questions were now radically different from the "external relations" of the pre-1861 period. Since the Civil War, Americans had been simultaneously blessed and damned by their new industrial and mechanized agricultural complexes—blessed in that they suddenly acquired wealth that made them the world's greatest economic power by the early twentieth century, damned in that the efficient complexes so glutted the nation with goods that they drove prices down and unemployment up. Out of this crisis, which became dangerously acute during the long 1873–97 economic depression, arose new U.S. interests in Asian, Latin American, and African markets, as well as the military power needed to protect the developing overseas lifelines.[28] The War of 1898 and President William McKinley's dispatch of U.S. troops to the mainland of China in 1900 brought home to many Americans that a constitution written in the age of horses and muskets might need altering to fit wars controlled by transoceanic cables and fought with machine guns.

The alteration was already underway. In 1890 the Supreme Court decided *In Re Neagle*. Although the justices were actually ruling on the President's power to provide them with personal bodyguards (a question about which they were hardly disinterested), they went much further. Declaring that the President could provide such protection, the Court, in a 6–2 vote, argued that his duties were not limited to carrying out treaties and congressional acts according to their express terms, but rested on broad implied powers, including "the rights, duties, and obligations growing out of the Constitution itself, our international relations, and all the protection implied by the nature of the government under the Constitution."[29] With that decision, the Court recognized immense and indefinite presidential power. Bryce might have had the decision in mind five years later when he noted that in foreign affairs, which require "promptitude and secrecy," the President "is independent of the House, while the Senate, though it can prevent his settling anything, cannot keep him from unsettling everything." He can "embroil the country abroad or excite passion at home."[30]

Bryce nevertheless believed that the constitutional system remained "singularly unfitted" for ruling the overseas dependencies that were needed for the new foreign policy. The older system only provided for bringing in the areas as self-governing states, he argued. Another problem existed for the Constitution if further territorial expansion occurred: "Eight millions of recently enfranchised negroes (not to speak of recent immigrants from Europe) are a heavy enough load for the Anglo-Americans to carry on their shoulders without the ignorance and semi-barbarism of the mixed races of the tropics."[31]

No one more worried over the constitutional crisis developing out of the new foreign policy than Captain Alfred Thayer Mahan. The nation's most influential military strategist, intellectual godfather of the new U.S. navy, a widely read publicist who stressed the need for overseas economic and military expansion, lionized in the most powerful European circles, and a close adviser of such powerful figures as Presidents William McKinley and Theodore Roosevelt, Mahan struck at the core of the problem in an 1897 essay. He bitterly complained that "any project of extending the sphere of the United States, by annexation or otherwise, is met by the constitutional lion in the path, which the unwilling or the apprehensive is ever sure to find." A remarkable part of this onslaught was his use (without attribution) of Madison's famous idea in *Federalist 10.* The Virginian had argued that in the new Constitution dangerous factions were to be controlled by extending the sphere within which they had to operate. These factions, based especially on economic and political interests, were to be spread over a vast territory (or "sphere") so that they could not easily combine to seize governmental power. Mahan was updating Madison's classic rationale for continental expansion and applying it to the overseas expansion of the 1890s. But even more remarkable was the naval officer's attack on the constitutional restraints that, as Bryce had noted, inhibited a great rush overseas. "Law is the servant of equity," the Captain argued. "While the world is in its present stage of development, equity which cannot be had by law must be had by force, upon which ultimately law rests, not for its sanction, but for its efficacy."[32] Getting down to cases, Mahan privately voiced his concern to Theodore Roosevelt about the "insoluble political problem" that prevented the annexation of the Hawaiian Islands. He then advised that the assistant secretary of the navy "do nothing unrighteous; but as regards the problem, take them first and solve afterwards."[33]

Mahan's "lion" was effectively removed from the path of U.S. expansion by the War of 1898 and the ingenuity of President McKinley, who first raised the hidden-hand Presidency to a political art form.[34] McKinley stretched the constitutional restraints on his power until they assumed an entirely new shape. In 1897–1898 he stopped several congressional attempts to "declare" war on Spain; then in April 1898 he himself led the way to war and destroyed the Senate's attempt to bind his hands with a resolution attached to the declaration of war that automatically recognized the Cuban revolutionary regime. At no time did McKinley want to have to deal with revolutionaries. Six weeks into the war, U.S. territorial holdings suddenly moved thousands of miles across an ocean when McKinley, uncertain that he could obtain the necessary two-thirds Senate vote to pass a treaty of annexation for Hawaii, obtained the islands with a joint congressional resolution requiring a mere majority of both houses. The President unilaterally committed U.S. forces and prestige to the distant Philippines, then moved to contain native Filipino forces until they fired on U.S. troops. McKinley used the outbreak of the fighting to push the Philippine annexation treaty through a rebellious U.S. Senate by one vote. In the Caribbean he treated newly conquered Puerto Rico as neither a state nor a full-fledged colony; for the first time in U.S. history, a treaty acquiring territory held out no promise of future citizenship. Cuba became a U.S. protectorate through the Platt Amendment, which allowed Cubans to have the problems of day-to-day governing and left the U.S. government holding the right of military and economic intervention whenever its officials desired. In 1900 the President landed five thousand troops in China, not only—as had past Presidents—to protect American lives and property abroad, but to join an international contingent in Peking that directly intervened in Chinese internal affairs. Peking officials responded by declaring war on the United States. It was a considerably more fitting response than Congress's, which said nothing to McKinley about the spectacle of U.S. troops fighting in the capital of China.

A small group of "Anti-imperialists" did oppose the President's policies between 1898 and 1900, especially his attempt to control the Philippines. They expressed many objections, but their concern about the Constitution was primary. The Anti-imperialists did not believe that the document's powers could be stretched so far across water, and used so broadly by the President, without snapping fundamental constitutional restraints. The nation, they feared, could then be transformed from a republic into a centralized colonial empire. As E.L. Godkin, editor of *The Nation,* warned, "Unquestionably, our present Constitution was not intended for a conquering nation with several different classes of citizens."[35] The wealthy Boston Anti-imperialist Moorfield Storey prophesied that if McKinley and the Republican Party could justify "conquest and despotic methods in the Philippines and Porto Rico" on the grounds that the inhabitants were racially and morally unfit for self-government, "it is only to be expected that the same doctrine will be applied at home."[36] Storey was not inaccurate in arguing that the Constitution overseas could not be so easily separated from the Constitution at home. As states disfranchised millions of black voters, Roosevelt, Albert K. Beveridge, Henry Cabot Lodge, and others argued bluntly (in Beveridge's words), that "There are people in the world who do not understand any form of government . . . [and] must be governed. . . . And so the authors of the Declaration [of Independence] themselves governed the Indian without his consent."[37]

The Supreme Court ignored Storey's warning and instead ratified the imperialists' view of the Constitution's malleability in the Insular Cases, a series of decisions that began to be handed down in 1901. By slim majorities the Court held that the Constitution did not apply to the countries seized from Spain in 1898 until Congress "incorporated" them into the Union. Meanwhile the government in the "unincorporated" territories was whatever Congress wanted it to be. The Court declared some "fundamental" rights might exist in "unincorporated territories," but they seemed few and largely unspecified.[38] In a brief opposing the McKinley policy, the Anti-imperialists argued unsuccessfully that "the real question is not whether the Constitution extends over the island of Porto Rico . . . but whether it extends over the Executive and Congress when they are engaged in enacting laws" for Puerto Ricans. The Anti-imperialists also insisted that "the Constitution follows the flag," but after the Insular Cases, Secretary of War Elihu Root quipped, "Ye-es, as near as I can make out the Constitution follows the flag—but doesn't quite catch up with it."[39]

Concern for reconciling foreign policy actions with constitutional powers had become so slight that in 1903, when Roosevelt took a ten-mile strip for an isthmian canal in Panama and annexed it through a treaty (duly ratified by the Senate), neither the nature of U.S. ownership nor the legal status of the inhabitants was determined in any detail.[40] Secretary of State John Hay justified U.S. control of the Canal Zone by claiming "titular sovereignty," a claim so vague that it allowed the Panamanians to turn it against the United States and, after a long and sometimes bloody struggle, finally acquire full sovereignty for themselves in 1978.[41]

In the fast-changing realm of U.S. foreign affairs, the Constitution was undergoing its own far-reaching transformation between 1890 and 1905. One change could be described as a centrifugal-centripetal effect: as U.S. military and economic power moved outward, political power consolidated at home. The expansion of U.S. power abroad has historically had such a centripetal political effect, but with the possible exception of the early Cold War years, never was it as striking as in the 1890 to 1905 era that ushered in modern U.S. foreign policy. Not only did McKinley and Roosevelt master Congress, but using the new telegraphic networks and exploiting their commander-in-chief power to the full, the chief executives also pulled power into their own hands by minutely supervising the movements of their military commands and controlling information made available to the public.[42] Louisville newspaper editor (and ardent Democrat) Henry Watterson perfectly, if overdramatically, captured how the economic-political crises of 1873–97 had led to foreign expansion—and then to "Caesarism" by 1898–1900:

> We escape the menace and peril of socialism and agrarianism, as England escaped them, by a policy of colonization and conquest. . . . It is true that we exchange domestic dangers for foreign dangers; but in every direction we multiply the opportunities of the people. We risk Caesarism, certainly; but even Caesarism is preferable to anarchism. . . . In short, anything is better than the pace we were going before these present forces [of 1898] were started into life.[43]

The second historic transformation was a direct cause of this "Caesarism." This change resolved the terrible tension emerging between the new foreign policy and the traditional Constitution by separating the former from the latter. Mahan's "lion in the path" was reduced not merely to a watchdog, but a chained kitten. *In Re Neagle* forged the first link in that chain by accepting the theory of inherent presidential power in international affairs. The Insular Cases created another link by ratifying McKinley's conquests and allowing the U.S. government to rule the conquests as it saw fit. Theodore Roosevelt further severed presidential powers from constitutional restraints when, in 1904–1905, he ordered the U.S. navy to protect U.S. interests by stopping an internal revolution in Santo Domingo. Roosevelt justified his action by referring to unspecified "police" powers. He then signed a treaty giving his officers control of Santo Domingo's main revenue source, the customs houses. When the U.S. Senate rejected the treaty on the ground that it wanted no part of a de facto Rooseveltian protectorate, TR circumvented the Senate's constitutional powers by negotiating an executive agreement. He justified this and other presidential actions with a "stewardship" theory: "My insistence upon the theory that the executive power was limited only by specific restrictions and prohibitions appearing in the Constitution or imposed by the Congress under its Constitutional powers."[44]

Neither the theory nor such executive agreements was new. The view of implied presidential powers held by Hamilton (whom Roosevelt and his friend Henry Cabot Lodge highly praised in their own writings on U.S. history), anticipated TR's denial that a President could act only when permitted by specific authorization. Executive agreements were important in foreign policy at least as early as the 1817 Rush-Bagot pact, which demilitarized the U.S.-Canadian border. New, however, was the claim made by post-1897 Presidents that the stewardship theory allowed extraordinary enlargement of the commander-in-chief powers overseas (such as using U.S. troops in China or for "police" activities in the Caribbean). New also was the extensive use of executive agreements. Roosevelt alone used the device in 1904 in Santo Domingo, in 1907 to deal with a dangerous immigration dispute with Japan, and in 1905 and 1908 to resolve a growing U.S.-Japanese confrontation in Asia.[45] The Senate's ability to control presidential power through its right to participate in treaty-making was being systematically undercut.

The historic transformation in the relationship between the Constitution and foreign policy was analyzed by the widely known political scientist and university president Woodrow Wilson in 1908. In his *Constitutional Government in the United States*, Wilson argued that between 1865 and 1898 domestic questions, and thus congressional power, were at the front of the nation's politics. But the 1898 war "changed the balance of the parts," for diplomatic questions became paramount and "in them the President was of necessity leader." Wilson spelled out the constitutional implications: "The initiative in foreign affairs, which the President possesses without any restriction whatever [sic], is virtually the power to control them absolutely." The Constitution's theories might be traced back to Newton's and Montesquieu's ideas that politics could be "turned into mechanics," but Wilson disagreed: Government "is accountable to Darwin, not to Newton. It is modified by its environment, necessitated by its tasks, shaped to its functions by the sheer pressure of life." The environment had radically altered in the 1890s, and, as Darwinian thought decreed, the new presidential functions necessarily evolved. Henceforth the President alone "must . . . be one of the great powers of the world," and therefore not be of "ordinary physique and discretion," but chosen "from among wise and prudent athletes—a small class." With considerable insight, Wilson guessed that such changes would occur "not by any reconstruction of the system," but by modification in "our national consciousness" that would allow the power to be quietly relocated.[46]

As Wilson's writing exemplified, a strong doubt about the inability of the traditional constitutional system to deal with global issues was eating away at the system's checks and balances. Seventy-five years earlier, Tocqueville had declared that "especially in the conduct of their foreign relations . . . democracies appear to me decidedly inferior to other governments." He had wondered about the consequences when U.S. diplomacy would have to do more "acting" and less "abstaining."[47] Now that the "acting" had become global, the concern grew. In 1891 Wilson tried to deal with the growing problem by bluntly stating in public lectures that it must be that the President "*exercises* the power, and *we obey*."[48] In 1913 the passage of the Seventeenth Amendment, requiring Senators to be elected directly by the people instead of by state legislatures, increased the concern. In *Federalist 64* John Jay had justified the Senate's treaty powers by claiming that the members would be carefully chosen by the states' "select assemblies," and the body would be small enough to preserve secrecy and promote wisdom. By World War I neither the source nor the size of the Senate's membership fit Jay's argument.

But perhaps nothing more discredited the role of democracies, representative assemblies, and constitutional restraints on foreign policy than the world war itself. On the eve of U.S. entry into the conflict, Wilson gave a soon-to-be famous interview in which he warned that once Americans became involved in fighting, "They'll forget there ever was such a thing as tolerance." The President thought that "the Constitution would not survive [the war]; that free speech and the right of assembly would go."[49] Historians have held Wilson personally responsible to some extent for the wartime intolerance and postwar Red Scare that wracked U.S. society.[50] But later Presidents, their advisers, and widely read journalists saw both the

Red Scare and the Senate's defeat of the League of Nations Covenant as the tragic results of a war effort corrupted by an ill-informed and unrestrained democracy. One of Wilson's young advisers, Walter Lippmann, looked back on the shattering experience and concluded that before the war the international system had been at peace because strong leaders had kept their nation's democratic impulses under control. By 1917, however, the demands of total war allowed the growth of those impulses until they broke "the institutional frameworks of the established governments." The executives in the western nations "lost control of the war." Lippmann believed that "the consequences were disastrous and revolutionary." War could no longer be waged "for rational ends." He lamented that "the people have acquired power which they are incapable of exercising. . . . A mass cannot govern."[51]

There were to be dissenting views. In 1947, Professor Edward S. Corwin asked why Americans had once lived under a "Constitution of right," but now endured a *"Constitution of Powers,* one that exhibits a growing concentration of power" in fewer, and especially presidential, hands. He answered that this was largely the *"Constitution of World War I"* now *"adapted to peacetime uses in an era whose primary demand upon government is no longer the protection of rights but the assurance of security."*[52] Corwin believed that the 1917–20 years were seminal because they created a dangerously centralized security state. Lippmann viewed the era as crucial because it proved that "the people" were incapable of shaping rational foreign policy. Corwin's argument was powerful, but Lippmann's proved more persuasive.

During the 1920s, U.S. officials more privately carried out a foreign policy well away from the raucous political arena in which the Congress had passed the Espionage and Sedition acts and the Senate had killed Wilson's dream of a League. The important business of diplomacy was accomplished not by negotiating treaties on which the Senate could act, but by quiet arrangements made by private bankers in New York, London, Berlin, and Tokyo. War-devastated Western Europe was rebuilt, and the German economy saved, at a 1924 conference at which the U.S. government had only an observer—although behind the scenes, and well away from Capitol Hill, officials from State, Commerce, and Treasury worked intimately with the private financiers.[53]

In 1929, the private money markets that buttressed the formal diplomatic arrangements (such as the 1924 Dawes Plan for rebuilding Europe, or the Washington treaty system of 1921–22 for the Far East), collapsed and pulled down the diplomatic superstructure with them. In the 1930s the United States turned inward; "domestic questions," as Wilson termed them in 1908, again became paramount. Congressional power came to the forefront. The Senate's defeat of President Franklin D. Roosevelt's plan to join the World Court, the Neutrality acts, which restricted the Executive's foreign policy alternatives between 1935 and 1939, and the President's delicate handling of foreign economic initiatives illustrated the turn that had occurred in the chief executive's treaty powers, war powers, and commander-in-chief powers. But it was short-lived turn. By 1940–41, as the spreading war threatened the United States, Roosevelt began recentralizing power in the White House. Sometimes, as in the Lend-Lease legislation of 1941, he showed deference to Congress. More often, as when he executed the destroyers-for-bases deal in 1940, or when he secretly ordered U.S. convoys for British ships in 1941, and apparently even angled for German attacks on U.S. vessels that would force the nation into war, he did so with little or no deference to those restraints.[54] The centrifugal-centripetal effect again appeared, and this time it was to have a long life.

Ironically, during the short-lived resurgence of congressional influence in the mid-1930s, the Supreme Court handed down the landmark decision that justified expansive presidential power in foreign affairs. In *U.S.* v. *Curtiss-Wright Export Corporation et al.,* the Court upheld the President's right to prohibit the United States' sale of arms and munitions to specific belligerents in Latin America, especially because Roosevelt had done so pursuant to congressional authorization. But Justice George Sutherland, speaking for the majority, went well beyond those specific facts. He finished the process that had been initiated by, among other events, *In Re Neagle,* Mahan's advice, and the McKinley–Theodore Roosevelt–Wilson initiatives, by explicitly separating the Constitution's relationship to domestic policy from its relationship to foreign relations. He accomplished this judicial legerdemain with three short and highly questionable statements: (1) the federal government's "powers of external sovereignty" antedated the Constitution and came from the British King in the Revolution; (2) therefore "federal power over external affairs [is] in origin and essential character different from that over internal affairs"; and (3) "in this vast external realm . . ., the President alone has the power to speak or listen as a representative of the nation." To emphasize the last point Sutherland declared that there is "the very delicate, plenary and exclusive power of the President as the sole organ of the federal government in the field of international relations—a power which does not require as a basis for its exercise an act of Congress." The Justice did think that this "exclusive power" had to be "exercised in subordination to the applicable provisions of the Constitution." What those provisions might be he did not mention.[55]

During that next year (1937), Sutherland also wrote the majority opinion in *U.S.* v. *Belmont,* which held that an executive agreement was the equivalent of a treaty, and that in certain cases a President's will could replace state law. In these two cases, Sutherland allowed the President's power in foreign affairs to float as freely from its constitutional moorings as possible, short of doing away with the moorings altogether. It was, Louis Henkin reflected, "a singular constitutional theory: the powers of the United States to conduct relations with other nations do not derive from the Constitution!"[56] Sutherland's unique interpretation of history, including his belief that the central government's sovereignty in foreign affairs was fully formed at the first moment of independence, has been effectively challenged by many later scholars, but his interpretation has lived on.[57]

Other aspects of the decision are also of importance. Sutherland, it should be stressed, did not first advance these arguments in 1936. A U.S. Senator and a member of the Foreign Relations Committee before he was appointed to the Court, Sutherland had written an article in 1910 and a book nine years later in which he rigidly distinguished between "our *internal* and our *external* relations." An ardent conservative, he attacked those who would interfere in affairs best left to individual states (such as the states' right to pass or, as Sutherland preferred, not pass child labor laws), but he argued that in "external matters" the states had "no residuary powers."[58] He thus solved the key problem facing other conservatives who were also ardent nationalists (Mahan, McKinley, Theodore Roosevelt, Lodge), and who somehow wanted strong national powers in foreign affairs but protection for certain states' rights from those awesome powers in domestic affairs—perhaps the central constitutional problem facing the United States as it became a global power between the 1890s and 1920.

But Sutherland's solution trapped him and others who assumed that the two arenas of foreign and domestic affairs could be so neatly separated. The trap began to close in his 1910 article when he had to argue that if the government was to carry out the Constitution's admonition to "provide for the Common Defense," the means needed to realize the charge could not be denied: "Always the end is more important than the means."[59] The end-justifies-the-means argument opened Sutherland to later charges of advocating "executive totalitarianism,"[60] raised questions about the course of U.S. conservatism, and left hanging the most important question: the possible outcome if his pivotal belief that foreign and domestic affairs could be neatly separated turned out to be mistaken. The trap continued to close on Sutherland when, during the 1914 to 1920 years, he gave vent to a vigorous patriotic nationalism and his longtime belief in personal rights while simultaneously working for U.S. entry into the war and attacking slackers who were "compromised by a hyphen" in their Americanism.[61] He came to despise Wilson, especially the President's foreign economic policy (which included a low tariff that hurt the beet sugar industry in Sutherland's home state of Utah). But how Wilson was supposed to conduct a strong foreign policy without also controlling overseas economic policy the Utah Senator did not discuss.[62] Sutherland's view of "external relations" was narrow, oversimplified, and based on a false separation of foreign and domestic affairs.

But that view has nevertheless been dominant in constitutional-foreign policy relationships. The popular slogan, "Politics stops at the water's edge," encapsulated the hope that diplomacy could be separated from domestic politics. Bipartisanship in foreign policy peaked between 1947 and 1950 when it helped produce the Marshall Plan and U.S. membership in the North Atlantic Treaty Organization. But even during those years the separation could not be total. The most graphic example occurred in 1947 when President Harry S. Truman, bucking strong political opposition, formulated his Truman Doctrine, which has everafter brilliantly solved the central question of how a President can obtain a domestic consensus for his foreign policy. Nine days after he announced the doctrine in 1947, however,

Truman felt it necessary to start the first peacetime security program for government employees in U.S. history. An emergency abroad could not be stopped at the water's edge.[63] Truman rode the crest of the resulting consensus until stalemate in the Korean war, the possibility of a long inconclusive struggle with China, and the Soviet Union's explosion of its first atomic bomb opened the administration to virulent attack.

One result was a search for Communists in government that turned into the McCarthyite witch hunt. Secretary of State Dean Acheson fought back with a blunt statement that would no doubt have surprised most of the Founders: "Not only has the President the authority to use the armed forces of the United States in carrying out the broad foreign policy of the United States and implementing treaties, but it is equally clear that this authority may not be interfered with by the Congress in the exercise of powers which it has under the Constitution."[64] Louis Hartz provided the proper perspective on what was occurring: "The issue is deeper than foreign policy, for the world involvement has also brought to the surface of American life great new domestic forces. . . . It has redefined, as communism shows, the issue of our internal freedom in terms of our external life."[65] That link, despite Mahan's, Sutherland's, and Acheson's attempts to smash it, held.

Presidential power was briefly curtailed in 1952 when the Supreme Court ruled in the steel seizure case that Truman had gone beyond his authority by moving to take over strike-bound steel mills to ensure the steady production of war material. The commander-in-chief provision, Justice Robert Jackson declared, did not endow the President with the "power to do anything anywhere, that can be done with an army or navy."[66] The validity of Jackson's assertion, however, was tested within a decade. The Cuban missile crisis of 1962 edged the world toward a final catastrophe. In the words of a distinguished scholar, Richard Neustadt, the crisis dramatized how "technology has modified the Constitution: the President, perforce, becomes the only man in the system capable of exercising judgment under the extraordinary limits now imposed by secrecy, complexity, and time."[67] The combination of available technology, presidential decisiveness, and a general consensus on the need to contain Communism anywhere on the globe appeared most dramatically when President Lyndon Johnson ordered 550,000 troops to Vietnam in

1967–68. When Congress finally resisted Johnson's policy, it was told by a top administration official that "to declare war," as the term was used in the Constitution, was "an outmoded phraseology" in the present international arena.[68]

Another measure of presidential power was revealed when investigation showed that in 1930 the United States had made 25 treaties and 9 executive agreements, but by 1972 had signed 947 treaties and 4359 executive agreements.[69] *Curtiss-Wright* reappeared to provide precedent. In the early 1970s, a 1941 Treasury Department memorandum surfaced that concluded that the Sutherland decision raised "a serious question whether the Congress can constitutionally limit the President's powers" in foreign relations. In 1971, Acheson testified that the 1936 case allowed the President to withhold any information from Congress if he believed that it affected national security interests. Others argued that the case allowed withholding information the Executive deemed important to national security, even if that information was obtained without warrant through electronic surveillance of defendants whose rights might be affected.[70]

As the Vietnam experience demonstrated, Congress had difficulty controlling presidential actions once troops were committed to distant alliances and battlefields. To remedy this weakness, in 1973 the House and Senate passed the War Powers Act, which placed some limits on, and made more accountable, the President's commander-in-chief powers. By then the Vietnam War had come home to the United States through rioting, inflation, and political polarization. Congress responded with a flurry of activity that tried to limit executive initiatives at home as well as overseas. Secretary of State Henry Kissinger declared that "the decade-long struggle in this country over executive dominance in foreign affairs is over. The recognition that the Congress is a coequal branch of government is the dominant fact of national politics today."[71] The Supreme Court seemed less certain. Even though it allowed the publication of the Pentagon Papers and ordered President Richard Nixon to release his White House tapes, the Court based its rulings on narrow grounds that raised the possibility that future Presidents could fare better than Nixon if they could persuasively argue that information had to be withheld on national security grounds.[72]

In 1983 the Supreme Court struck down the power of Congress to control certain presidential actions through the so-called legislative veto. If it were applied to the War Powers Act, the Court's decision would remove perhaps the most important congressional restraint on the President's power to dispatch and keep troops abroad. As executive authority in foreign policy surged, President Ronald Reagan refused to recognize the War Powers Act's provisions explicitly, although he by and large abided by them.[73] Meanwhile, the *Curtiss-Wright* case was cited to support broad presidential powers, even by justices—such as William Rehnquist—who were usually considered to be wary of such broad construction.[74] Some observers feared that Rehnquist's opinion carried presidential powers beyond the issue of how congressional and state rights were affected by the 1936 decision to the manner in which Sutherland's reasoning was being used to infringe on individual rights.[75] Experts also worried that the President's dependence on public opinion poll support, and the knowledge that historically support of his actions increased during foreign policy crises, had created a "plebiscitary presidency" that unilaterally acted in foreign policy, regardless of constitutional provisions, whenever a "fix" was needed for higher ratings in the polls.[76]

The rise of international terrorism in the 1980s made many Americans, including congressional leaders, willing to give the President the plenary powers justified by Sutherland. Republican Senate Majority Leader Robert Dole of Kansas urged repealing the War Powers Act because terrorism made it outdated. Arguing a kind of situational politics, Dole wanted the President to have automatic support to fight terrorism "as the Constitution prescribes and as the situation demands." Dole's view of the need for constitutional restraints seemed quite different, however, from the beliefs that had shaped the 1973 act or the 1787–88 debates and decisions about the interconnectedness of foreign and domestic policies. Theodore Lowi, on the other hand, noted how the Reagan administration was taking a number of decisions to increase mail, electronic, and physical surveillance, as well as to justify breaking and entering to find evidence, in the name of ending terrorism. Lowi believed Sutherland's line between the domestic and foreign powers had become dangerously, but inevitably, blurred.[77]

A number of these questions demand scholarly investigation (and in some instances, political action). Three areas for future research seem especially important. The first is how and why conservatives and many liberals have attempted to separate foreign and domestic policies when such a separation has increasingly become artificial and dangerous. Conservatives have often sought the separation to justify a weak central government at home and strong executive power abroad, while some liberals have reversed those priorities. Both sides have ignored how, for example, military budgets ranging from $50 to $300 billion have made such distinctions unreal in the post-1945 era. A second area for research is how the President and his supporters have been able not only to blunt attempts to curb executive power, but in pivotal instances have actually used those attempts to increase it. Eisenhower's handling of the Bricker Amendment movement (which unsuccessfully tried to limit the President's ability to make executive agreements), in 1953–54, and recent Presidents' circumventing of the War Powers Act come to mind in this context. A third area for future work requires a wedding of social and diplomatic history: why have Americans, with their supposed love affair for the Constitution and especially its protection of individual liberties, been so willing to drop that affair for involvements overseas? Perhaps one reason for such willingness is the irrelevance of public opinion and, often, of congressional opinion in the making of foreign policy. The presidency has usually shaped those opinions, not vice-versa, and we need more systematic studies to explain how and why this has occurred.

Nearly two centuries ago Madison worried that liberty at home might be lost because of danger, "real or pretended," abroad. In 1787–89 the Founders had given the President flexibility to conduct foreign policy, but they also provided other branches of the government with checks on executive power and extended guarantees to individual rights that might be threatened by that power. Madison reaffirmed the importance of those checks when he wrote as "Helvidius" in his 1792–93 debate with Hamilton. Especially since the 1890s, no equally effective "Helvidius" has appeared. That is strange, because there have been no historical cycles in the development of executive power in foreign affairs, but only the steady, consistent accretion of authority by the President. That accretion became most notable in the 1890 to 1920 era, when the United States became a great world power.[78] Imaginative Presidents, agreeable courts, compliant Congresses, and cooperative scholars have removed and chained Mahan's "lion."[79] Sutherland, drawing on arguments formed in the 1890 to 1920 era, provided the most important historical and judicial justification for taking the critical step of separating foreign and domestic affairs. The acceleration of centralized and often unchecked foreign policy powers in the 1960s, 1970s, and 1980s makes that separation, and especially its effect on individual liberties, questionable and dangerous. Historical perspective also demonstrates that those decades must be understood in the context of post-1890 U.S. foreign policy, and not merely in the context of the Cold War. Madison had hoped to use expansion to prevent the establishment of irresponsible centralized power. But in the late twentieth century, after a century of overseas expansionism, the extension of U.S. power created the kind of centralization Madison wanted to prevent.

Notes

This article appeared, with minor revisions, in the *Journal of American History* 74, no. 3 (December 1987).

1. Gaillard Hunt, ed., *The Writings of James Madison*, 9 vols. (New York, 1906), 6: 83–85.
2. Louis Henkin, *Foreign Affairs and the Constitution* (Mineola, N.Y., 1972), p. vii.
3. *Foreign Relations of the United States, 1950* (Washington, 1977), 1: 235–92. Throughout, NSC-68 is concerned with the difficulty a democracy faces in fighting a cold war against a totalitarian state, but then resolves it in this manner (see esp. pp. 242–44, 252–56, 291–92).
4. Frederick W. Marks, III, *Independence on Trial: Foreign Affairs and the Making of the Constitution* (Baton Rouge, 1973), esp. chapters 3,4; Merrill Jensen, *The New Nation: A History of the United States During the Confederation, 1781–1789* (New York, 1950), p. 171.
5. Madison's papers for this study are usefully drawn together in Robert A. Rutland, ed., *The Papers of James Madison* (Charlottesville, Va., 1962–), 9: 345–58.
6. Jack N. Rakove, "Solving a Constitutional Puzzle: The Treatymaking Clause as a Case Study," *Perspectives in American History*, n.s. 1 (1984): 268.
7. Quoted in Arthur Schlesinger, Jr., *The Imperial Presidency* (Boston, 1973), p. ix.
8. Max Farrand, ed., *The Records of the Federal Convention of 1787*, 4 vols. (New Haven, 1966), 3: 250.
9. Ibid., 2: 318.
10. Rutland, ed., *Papers of Madison*, 10: 86–87.
11. *The Federalist Papers*, with an introduction by Clinton Rossiter (New York, 1961), p. 67. All references to *The Federalist* will be to this edition.
12. Hunt, ed., *Writings of Madison*, 5:146. In the Virginia Ratifying Convention, Antifederalist George Mason agreed with Madison on this point (after misrepresenting Madison's views). See Robert A. Rutland, ed., *The Papers of George Mason, 1725–1792*, 3 vols. (Chapel Hill, 1970), 3: 1065.

13. Harold C. Syrett and Jacob Cooke, eds., *The Papers of Alexander Hamilton*, 15 vols. (New York, 1961–69), 15:135; also ibid., pp. 33–43.

14. Irving Brant, *James Madison*, 6 vols. (Indianapolis, 1941–61), 3: 375, 382; Hunt, ed., *Writings of Madison*, 6: 138–88.

15. Charles Lofgren, "War-Making Under the Constitution: The Original Understanding," *Yale Law Journal* 81 (March 1972): 672–97, 700.

16. A convenient source is Henry Steele Commager, ed., *Documents of American History*, 7th ed., 2 vols. (New York, 1963), 1: 178–84; Madison's view in *The Federalist No. 39* anticipates the assumptions of the Virginia Resolution; see Rutland, ed., *Papers of Madison*, 10: 379–80.

17. Abraham D. Sofaer, "The Presidency, War, and Foreign Affairs: Practice Under the Framers," *Law and Contemporary Problems* 60 (Spring 1976): 36–37. The essay and conclusions are based on Sofaer's longer work, *War, Foreign Affairs, and Constitutional Power: The Origins* (Cambridge, Mass., 1976), esp. pp. 56, 377–78.

18. Alexander DeConde, *This Affair of Louisiana* (New York, 1976), p. 254.

19. Julian P. Boyd, "Thomas Jefferson's 'Empire of Liberty,'" *Virginia Quarterly Review* 24 (Autumn 1948): 553.

20. Edmund Quincy, *Life of Josiah Quincy of Massachusetts* (Boston, 1868), pp. 216–217; "Speech on the Admission of Louisiana as a State," in Josiah Quincy, *Speeches Delivered in Congress of the United States by Josiah Quincy* (Boston, 1874), pp. 196, 216.

21. Hunt, ed., *Writings of Madison*, 9: 358–60.

22. Rutland, ed., *Papers of Madison*, 9: 76–77; Hunt, ed., *Writings of Madison*, 5: 170.

23. Quoted with analysis in Richard N. Current, ed., *The Political Thought of Abraham Lincoln* (Indianapolis, 1967), pp. 43–44.

24. Milo M. Quaife, ed., *The Diary of James K. Polk During His Presidency, 1845 to 1849*, 4 vols. (Chicago, 1910), 2: 75.

25. Arthur Bestor, "The American Civil War as a Constitutional Crisis," *American Historical Review* 69 (January 1964): 338.

26. David Potter, *Lincoln and His Party in the Secession Crisis* (New Haven, 1942), p. 223.

27. James Bryce, *The American Commonwealth*, 3rd ed., 2 vols. (New York, 1895), 2: 521–22.

28. The best succinct analysis of these changes and the effect on the new foreign policy are Thomas McCormick, *China Market: America's Quest for Informal Empire, 1893–1901* (Chicago, 1967); and Charles S. Campbell, *The Transformation of American Foreign Relations, 1865–1900* (New York, 1976), chapters 5–6, 8, 16.

29. In Re Neagle, 135 U.S. 64 (1890).

30. Bryce, *American Commonwealth*, 1: 54.

31. Ibid., 2: 531.

32. A. T. Mahan, *The Interest of America in Sea Power, Present and Future* (Boston, 1898), pp. 256–57, 268; ibid., pp. 227–28.

33. Robert Seager, II, and Doris D. Maguire, eds., *Letters and Papers of Alfred Thayer Mahan*, 3 vols. (Annapolis, 1975), 2: 506. Mahan never lost his impatience with legal restrictions and lawyers; see ibid., 3: 411.

34. The best analysis is Lewis L. Gould, "William McKinley and the Expansion of Presidential Power," *Ohio History* 87 (Winter 1978): 5–21; the phrase is from Fred I. Greenstein, *The Hidden-Hand Presidency: Eisenhower as Leader* (New York, 1982).

35. Robert Beisner, *Twelve Against Empire: The Anti-Imperialists, 1898–1900* (Chicago, 1985), p. 216.

36. William B. Hixson, Jr., "Moorfield Storey and the Struggle for Equality," *Journal of American History* 55 (December 1968): 539.

37. Walter L. Williams, "U.S. Indian Policy and the Debate over Philippine Annexation," *Journal of American History* 66 (March 1980): 819–20.

38. Henkin, *Foreign Affairs and the Constitution,* pp. 268–69.

39. Beisner, *Twelve Against Empire,* p. 216; James Edward Kerr, *The Insular Cases: The Role of the Judiciary in American Expansionism* (Port Washington, N.Y., 1982), pp. 40–41.

40. James Bryce, *The American Commonwealth,* 2 vols. (New York, 1910), 2: 580.

41. This struggle is outlined in Walter LaFeber, *The Panama Canal: The Crisis in Historical Perspective* (New York, 1979).

42. Robert Beisner, *From the Old Diplomacy to the New, 1865–1900,* 2nd ed. (Arlington Heights, Ill., 1985), pp. 88, 138–39.

43. Richard Hofstadter, *The Paranoid Style in American Politics and Other Essays* (New York, 1965), pp. 180–81.

44. Quoted with a useful analysis in Henkin, *Foreign Affairs and the Constitution,* pp. 371–72.

45. Lawrence Margolis, *Executive Agreements and Presidential Power in Foreign Policy* (New York, 1986), pp. 9–11.

46. Woodrow Wilson, *Constitutional Government in the United States* (New York, 1908), pp. 48–49, 56–58, 58–59, 77–80. An excellent context for this point is given in Michael Kammen, *A Machine That Would Go of Itself: The Constitution in American Culture* (New York, 1986), pp. 18–20.

47. Alexis de Tocqueville, *Democracy in America* (The Henry Reeve Text), 2 vols. (New York, 1948), 1: 234.

48. Arthur Link, ed., *The Papers of Woodrow Wilson* (Princeton, 1966–), 7: 352; emphasis in original.

49. Arthur S. Link, "That Cobb Interview," *Journal of American History* 72 (June 1985): 11–12.

50. Harry N. Scheiber, *The Wilson Administration and Civil Liberties, 1917–1921* (Ithaca, N.Y., 1960), p. 27.

51. Walter Lippmann, *Essays in the Public Philosophy* (New York, 1955), pp. 14–18.

52. Edward S. Corwin, *Total War and the Constitution* (New York, 1947), p. 172; emphasis in original.

53. Useful accounts of this process are Carl Parrini, *Heir to Empire: U.S. Economic Diplomacy, 1916–1923* (Pittsburgh, 1969), superb on the bankers-government relationships; Michael Hogan, *The Private Structure of Cooperation in Anglo-American Economic Diplomacy, 1918–1928* (Columbia, Mo., 1977); Melvyn Leffler, *The Elusive Quest: America's Pursuit of European Stability and French Security, 1919–1933* (Chapel Hill, 1979); and, most recently, Frank Costigliola, *Awkward Dominion: American Political, Economic, and Cultural Relations with Europe, 1919–1933* (Ithaca, N.Y., 1985).

54. Warren F. Kimball, ed., *Churchill and Roosevelt: The Complete Correspondence,* 3 vols. (Princeton, 1985), 1: 229–30.

55. U.S. v. Curtiss-Wright Export Corp., et al., 299 U.S. 305, 318, 319, 320 (1936). A good brief discussion of Sutherland's earlier view is in Kammen, *A Machine That Would Go of Itself,* p. 257.

56. Henkin, *Foreign Affairs and the Constitution,* p. 19.

57. For critiques, see Charles A. Lofgren, "*U.S. v. Curtiss-Wright Export Corporation:* An Historical Reassessment," *The Yale Law Journal* 83 (November 1973): 1–32; Louis Fisher, "Evolution of Presidential and Congressional Powers in Foreign Affairs," ms. (1984), p. 5; Louis Fisher, *Constitutional Conflicts Between Congress and the President* (Princeton, 1985), pp. 109–10; Harry N. Scheiber, "Federalism

and the Constitution: The Original Understanding," in *American Law and Constitutional Order: Historical Perspectives,* ed. Lawrence M. Friedman and Harry N. Scheiber (Cambridge, Mass., 1978), p. 86.

58. George Sutherland, "The Internal and External Powers of the National Government," *Senate Documents, Document No. 417,* 61st Cong., 2nd sess., 8 March 1910, pp. 1, 12.

59. Ibid., p. 5.

60. Joel Francis Paschal, *Mr. Justice Sutherland: A Man Against the State* (Princeton, 1951), pp. 226–30.

61. Ibid., pp. 217–20.

62. Ibid., p. 62.

63. A good introduction to this connection is Richard M. Freeland, *The Truman Doctrine and the Origins of McCarthyism: Foreign Policy, Domestic Politics, and Internal Security, 1946–1948* (New York, 1972).

64. Henkin, *Foreign Affairs and the Constitution,* p. 307.

65. Louis Hartz, *The Liberal Tradition in America: An Interpretation of American Political Thought Since the Revolution* (New York, 1955), p. 5.

66. An excellent analysis is Maeva Marcus, *Truman and the Steel Seizure* (New York, 1977). The context is provided in Henkin, *Foreign Affairs and the Constitution,* p. 307.

67. Richard Neustadt, *Presidential Power: The Politics of Leadership* (New York, 1968), pp. 212–14.

68. U.S., Congress, Senate, *Congressional Record,* 90th Cong., 1st sess., 21 August 1967, pp. 23390–91.

69. George Ball, *Diplomacy for a Crowded World: An American Foreign Policy* (Boston, 1976), pp. 208–09.

70. Lofgren, *"U.S. v. Curtiss-Wright,"* p. 4.

71. "Address by Henry Kissinger to the American Society of Newspaper Editors, 'U.S. Foreign Policy: Finding Strength Through Adversity.'" *Department of State Bulletin* 72 (5 May 1975): 562.

72. Henkin, *Foreign Affairs and the Constitution,* p. 254, has a useful discussion of the concurring opinions in the Pentagon Papers case, especially in the footnote section, p. 487.

73. Fisher, "Evolution of Presidential and Congressional Powers," pp. 1–2.

74. Ibid., p. 4; Dames & Moore v. Regan, 153 U.S. 661, 118 (1981).

75. Margolis, *Executive Agreements and Presidential Power,* p. 62.

76. Theodore J. Lowi, *The Personal President: Power Invested, Promise Unfulfilled* (Ithaca, N.Y., 1985), p. 175.

77. Ibid., p. 174; Dole's quote is from *Washington Post,* 23 April 1986, p. A23.

78. In a useful analysis of the period from 1890 to 1920, John E. Semonche asserts that "the Supreme Court's special task was to determine whether a fundamental law, fashioned in a much simpler time, could accomodate these new exertions of governmental power." See *Charting the Future: The Supreme Court Responds to a Changing Society, 1890–1920* (Westport, Conn., 1978), p. ix.

79. Important here are Henkin, *Foreign Policy and the Constitution,* pp. 6–7; Fisher, "Evolution of Presidential and Congressional Powers," p. 24; and the 1986 decision in Dellums et al., v. Smith, where the U.S. Court of Appeals for the Ninth Circuit refused to question the President's support of the Nicaraguan contras. I am indebted to Max Miller and Jules Lobel for a copy of this and related opinions, as well as for advice on this and other points in the essay.

BEYOND THE PALE:
American Indians and the Constitution

Vine Deloria, Jr.

The Indians and the Original Constitutional Understanding

The American Revolution was clearly foreseeable after 1740, when the British Parliament approved the Naturalization Act for the American colonies. This law declared that a citizen of one colony was presumed to be a citizen of every other colony for the purpose of preventing the erection of trade and political barriers between and among colonies. Traditional European considerations, such as family, inherited status, and ethnic origin, were submerged in the larger and more comprehensive idea of the citizen who gladly gave his consent to be governed, in exchange for the right to choose who would perform the governing functions. Thereafter it was assumed that new participants in the body politic—with the major exception of the slaves—whether transferred to it en masse (as in the annexation of the southwest) or arriving as individuals (as with the people disembarking at Ellis Island from the many ports of Europe), would become part of the great melting pot, surrendering their group and personal characteristics for the opportunity to play a part in the larger drama.

The sole exception to this idea of voluntary social contract, in the eyes of the constitutional fathers, were the Indian tribes. These were regarded as hostile nations, inhabiting the frontier and having considerably more in common with European colonial rivals than with the huddled masses clustered along the Atlantic seaboard. *The*

Federalist Papers viewed Indians as a matter of foreign policy. Hamilton suggested that "the savage tribes on our Western frontier ought to be regarded as our natural enemies," the natural allies of the Europeans, "because they have most to fear from us, and most to hope from them."[1] And he felt that the Indian situation was not a problem for the individual colonies: "The territories of Britain, Spain, and of the Indian nations in our neighborhood do not border on particular States, but encircle the Union from Maine to Georgia. The danger, though in different degrees, is therefore common. And the means of guarding against it ought, in like manner, to be the objects of common councils and of a common treasury."[2] Indians, in their corporate political capacity, were placed outside the federal union, and the Constitution makes only sparse and vague references to them. Congress is to regulate commerce "with the Indian tribes," while "Indians not taxed" are excluded from the enumeration for congressional representation and direct taxation. Yet there is no specific phrase outlining federal-Indian relationships and few clues concerning how the United States is to deal with its hostile frontier neighbors.

Over two hundred different amendments to the Constitution have been proposed since it was adopted and twenty-five have been ratified, but not one has dealt with American Indians, either to propose new powers for the federal government or to clarify the existing exercise of political power. But it is no secret that federal Indian law exists and represents a large and complex body of data. And there is no question that American Indians are a part of the body politic and have been so for many decades. In federal-Indian relations, history and the inevitable need to improvise have become important influences in resolving disputes that have had no other means of solution. The fact remains, however, that American Indians are largely outside the Constitution, receive few protections from the arbitrary actions of the federal government, and suffer considerably from a lack of status within the constitutional framework.

How American Indians reached this no-man's land of political existence is instructive. During its first four decades of independence the United States dealt with Indian tribes as quasi-independent nations, its sole fear in this regard being its fear that the European nations might exploit the nebulous status of the tribes to foment warfare on the frontier. Thus, for example, at the beginning of the Revolution, the American commissioners signed a mutual defense treaty with the Delawares in which they promised to admit an Indian state, headed by that tribe, upon the successful conclusion of the war.[3] In addition, the Indian tribes generally supported England during the War of 1812, and the Treaty of Ghent, which concluded the hostilities, made it incumbent upon the warring parties to place their Indian allies on the same political footing with respect to each other that they had enjoyed prior to the conflict. Treaty commissioners traveled up the rivers of the West to make peace with the western tribes, and in the process asked them to recognize the United States as the primary sovereign to which they pledged allegiance.[4]

If Indian political existence was admitted by the United States, the Indian claim to ownership of the lands on which the tribes lived was not. Following the lead of the European nations, which had unilaterally asserted legal ownership of North American lands on the tenuous justification that they had "discovered" them, the United States from the beginning believed that Indian lands were subject to its final disposition. While most of the treaties for the purchase of land from the Indians were upheld, there was never any question that the United States was simply clearing Indians out of areas that it believed it owned outright.

The Supreme Court articulated this idea extensively in *Johnson* v. *McIntosh* (1823),[5] and its reasoning should be read and understood in conjunction with the Monroe Doctrine, issued that same year, in which the United States defined its role in international affairs and pledged to close the hemisphere to further European colonial adventures. In *Johnson* v. *McIntosh* the Court said that while it was indeed pretentious to claim that merely sailing by a land vested legal title in the discoverer, this doctrine was accepted by all civilized nations and formed the basis for U.S. assertions that Indian lands ultimately belonged to the United States. Since the United States had succeeded to the discovery claims of Great Britain upon the successful conclusion of the Revolution, the Court saw no reason not to require that all land titles originate in actions by the United States, and ruled that titles alleging to come from Indians without the approval of the United States be considered void. When this doctrine was coupled with the Monroe Doctrine, Indian tribal properties became a matter of domestic policy. In effect, Indian *property* was the subject of federal control, whereas Indian *political existence* remained outside the reach of the federal government—except where it chose to embark on a path of conquest and incorporate Indians within it.

Since no wars of conquest against the tribes were launched by the federal government, no opportunity existed to bring Indians within the constitutional framework. Indeed, exactly the opposite situation occurred. In 1802 the state of Georgia secured a pledge from the federal government to clear state land of Indian titles in exchange for the state's ceding longstanding colonial charter claims to western land. This compromise was necessary because the federal government recognized the validity of colonial charters and it was therefore national policy to establish the federal government as the owner of western land in the public domain. But by the late 1820s, when the federal government had not made any significant strides in extinguishing the Indian titles, the state took matters into its own hands and began passing laws that extended state jurisdiction over the lands that had been guaranteed to the Cherokee Indians by federal treaty.

The Indians appealed to the federal government for assistance, but their pleas fell on deaf ears. The resulting political crisis was profound because it involved the constitutional relationship between the states and the federal government on the one hand, and the actions of the federal government, on behalf of the constituent states, through the treaty process on the other. The situation was unique, at once profoundly political and yet confusing in the constitutional sense of confusing the boundaries at which the national government and state sovereignty met.

In two definitive cases spawned by this situation, Chief Justice John Marshall attempted to formulate a conceptual framework within which the conflict could be resolved. Receiving little response from the federal government, the Cherokees filed an action against the state of Georgia in the Supreme Court (as the court of original jurisdiction), claiming that they were a foreign nation and therefore entitled to seek assistance from the Court. But in *Cherokee Nation* v. *Georgia*,[6] Marshall turned away the Indian effort by describing the Cherokees, and by implication all other Indian tribes, as "domestic dependent nations." He apparently believed that by excluding Indians from the status of foreign and independent political entities, he could avoid the controversy altogether.

Among the arguments raised against the Cherokees was the suggestion that if the tribe was truly an independent nation, its only proper recourse was to wage war against Georgia and repel the invasion of its land. From the point of view of federalism, and certainly from the constitutional perspective, this suggestion was spurious and indicated only that the justices had no conception of exactly where Indians fit into the constitutional framework. It also suggested that the states had reserved for themselves the power to make war on their neighbors, or at least to create conditions under which the federal government would be obligated to wage war on their behalf. The course of action that the federal government was to take was thus unclear, since it had pledged its honor to the Cherokees but was responsible to its constituent states as well. Ultimately it was not the "nationhood" of the Cherokees that posed the problem, but the delicate balance between the federal and state governments under the Constitution. Regretfully, there was no place in this relationship for "domestic dependent nations."

The *Worcestor* case,[7] a year later, is the classic example of stalemate among the federal branches of government. A group of missionaries, under the leadership of the Rev. Samuel Worcestor, entered Cherokee country under the auspices and sponsorship of the federal government and submitted themselves to the Cherokee law (which had been guaranteed to the Indians by their treaties with the United States but were prohibited by recent Georgia law). Arrested and convicted of violating state law, the missionaries appealed to the Supreme Court, arguing that they were agents of the United States; they thereby raised the question of the supremacy of federal over state law. The Court, caught in this dilemma, upheld the law and actions of the federal government, and ordered the release of the missionaries. Andrew Jackson, upon hearing the decision, is reported to have said the Chief Justice Marshall could enforce his own decree. The executive branch refused to move, the missionaries were held in prison in Georgia, and the Cherokees eventually had to sign a treaty agreeing to leave the southern states and move to Oklahoma.

The two Cherokee cases provided a framework for dealing with the Indian tribes by excluding them from the category of "foreign nations." Since there was no category of "domestic dependent nations," the result was to affirm federal power over the Indians but without describing any corresponding set of responsibilities and, more importantly, without outlining any standards by which the action—or nonactions—of the federal government could be judged. The Constitution was relevant to American Indians only to the degree that the courts could identify where the responsibility for the Indians existed; yet there was nothing in the Constitution that required the federal government to fulfill its responsibilities in this regard.

In 1834 Congress passed two major pieces of legislation that sought to develop an institutional structure for the ill-defined relationship between the federal government and the Indian tribes. The first statute sought "to regulate trade and intercourse with the Indian tribes," while the second was intended to "provide for the organization of the department of Indian Affairs."[8] The two statutes taken together did not attempt to take control over the lives and property of Indians but sought to establish certain rules of conduct that had to be followed by traders who wished to deal with the Indians and to clarify the conditions under which federal jurisdiction was to be enforced in Indian country. If the Indian tribes were indeed wholly within the reach of the Constitution, then these laws were rather feeble efforts to bring constitutional principles to bear upon the situation. On the other hand, if these statutes were the natural result of a good faith effort to fulfill treaty promises, they make a great deal more sense. We might, in fact, interpret the Indian treaties as having self-operating articles that go into effect immediately, and articles that require some additional action of the legislative branch if they are to be realized. The two 1834 statutes would easily fall into the latter category, and in this sense they were responsible—and constitutional—actions.

However, Congress also seemed to assert that it had some kind of residual power that could be used to protect the Indian tribes. This power derived from the fact that some tribes had treaties with the federal government while others, lacking that status, were expected to have treaty relations sometime in the future. Yet even this power was derived not from broad plenary grants under the Constitution but from treaty responsibilities willingly assumed. The congressional report accompanying this legislation described the situation that Congress confronted:

> With the emigrant [Indian] tribes we have treaties, imposing duties of a mixed character, recognizing them in some sort as dependent tribes,

and yet obligating ourselves to protect them, even against domestic strife, and *necessarily retaining the power to do so*. With other tribes we have general treaties of amity; and with a considerable number we have no treaties whatsoever.[9]

About all we have at this point is a general admission that Congress has *some kind* of responsibility when it deals with Indian matters. But there is no clear constitutional duty to do much of anything.

The Conflict Between Indians as Semi-Autonomous Tribes and the New View of Indian Policy as Purely Domestic Policy

In 1871 Congress prohibited any further treatymaking with Indians. This change signaled a practical realization that the tribes did not have the military power to turn aside any determine effort by the United States to destroy them through armed conflict, as well as the demand by the administrative agencies of the government for a more restricted contest in which Indian programs could be administered. Holding out the possibility of treatymaking only inhibited the tribes' acceptance of programs for civilization and assimilation which the Department of the Interior was responsible for providing. The prohibition against treaties did not, however, nullify or abrogate any existing treaties, and since each tribal group with treaty relations had its own history of dealing with the United States, little was accomplished by terminating quasidiplomatic relations with the Indians. In fact, by eliminating the possibility of negotiating on points of serious conflict, Congress created a feeling of betrayal among the Indians and vested dictatorial powers in the Indian agents, who were no longer seen as advocates for the tribes but as antagonists who sought to force immediate change and destroy tribal customs and practices.

The conflict between the old treaty relationship, with its necessity for bargaining, and the new restrictive status of Indians as captive wards of the Indian agent quickly became clear. In 1881, Crow Dog, a minor chief of the Brule Sioux on the Rosebud Indian Reservation in Dakota Territory, killed Spotted Tail, the principal chief of the Brules and a long-standing advocate of peaceful relations with the United States. Spotted Tail, who had once been imprisoned for a year by the

United States, no longer thought it possible for the Sioux to maintain themselves as an independent people and was often inclined to compromise with the Indian agent in order to preserve his eroding position as the leading chief at the agency. This attitude antagonized the more traditional Sioux and contributed significantly to his death.

Crow Dog's relatives made peace with Spotted Tail's family after the ancient custom of the tribe, offering compensation for the injury their kinsman had done, and the Brules were satisfied that the quarrel had been settled. But non-Indian public opinion was outraged at the idea that one Indian could murder another and simply pay for his misdeeds with gifts, and pressure mounted to try Crow Dog for murder in the territorial court. He was indicted, tried, convicted, and sentenced to death at the court in Deadwood, Dakota Territory. The judge allowed Crow Dog to return home and settle his family affairs, specifying the time when he should return and surrender himself. On the designated day, after walking through a terrible Dakota blizzard, Crow Dog appeared at the courthouse door. This feat, and the inherent integrity of the man, galvanized public opinion in his favor and an appeal on his behalf was taken to the Supreme Court.

In *Ex Parte Crow Dog*,[10] the Court once again had to deal with the vague boundary lines between the constitutional inclusion and exclusion of Indians. Title XXVIII of the Revised Statutes of the United States dealt with Indian matters and was a compilation and summary of the laws covering the government of Indian Country. Section 2145 extended the general laws of the United States as to the punishment of crime to the Indians. It seemed to extend the reach of congressional power over the Indians to include the internal functioning of their communities. But Section 2146 declared that

> the preceding section shall not be construed to extend to [crimes committed by one Indian against the person or property of another Indian, nor to] any Indian committing any offence in the Indian country who has been punished by the local law of the tribe, or to any case where by treaty stipulations the exclusive jurisdiction over such offences is or may be secured to the Indian tribes respectively.[11]

The court found several treaty articles that preserved domestic law, including criminal law, to the tribe, and it could not find, directly or by implication, that the United States had extended its jurisdiction over the Sioux or that the Sioux had consented to U.S. jurisdiction in such a broad and pervasive sense. So a writ of habeas corpus was issued and Crow Dog was freed to return to his reservation.

The *Crow Dog* case was a reasonably clear delineation of the principle that in certain respects, and for certain negotiated purposes, Indian tribes were both outside the U.S. Constitution and beyond the reach of the legislative powers of Congress. But this was to change, and again public outrage influenced the course of events. In 1885 Congress passed the Seven Major Crimes Act,[12] which extended territorial (hence federal) law over the Indian reservations with respect to the crimes of murder, manslaughter, rape, arson, assault with intent to kill, burglary, and larceny. The Seven Major Crimes Act did not mention any treaty provisions and did not cite Revised Statutes 2145 and 2146 as being specifically repealed or amended; it did not even mention the Sioux Indians. Yet its popular interpretation, coming on the heels of the publicity surrounding the Crow Dog case, was that it resolved the problem of Indian local self-government where serious criminal activity was concerned by applying the white man's law.

Sioux Indians have long believed that the Seven Major Crimes Act was an unconstitutional intrusion into their political affairs. In 1885, however, when the Sioux knew little about the white man's way of life, they had no way to challenge the act. And in 1889, when the Sioux agreed to the dissolution of their large reservation, the government promised that *all* the provisions of the 1868 treaty and 1877 agreement, insofar as they were not incompatible with the provisions of the 1889 negotiations, would be brought forward and reaffirmed. Presumably this would have once again given the Sioux jurisdiction over their internal affairs and would have excluded them from the provisions of the Seven Major Crimes Act. This is the argument of some Sioux political leaders today, although it is not favored by the federal government.

This line of reasoning—that the tribes are not affected by federal legislation dealing with self-government —has some solid historical precedent behind it. Less than a decade after the passage of the Seven Major Crimes Act, a Cherokee citizen named Talton was convicted of murder by a Cherokee court. He petitioned for a writ of habeas corpus on the ground that the Cherokee grand jury that had indicted him was composed of an insufficient number of jurors, so that he had been deprived of his rights under the Fifth Amendment. Presumably this was a direct challenge to the constitutionality and applicability of the Seven Major Crimes Act, since that statute had declared in no uncertain terms that *all* Indians were covered by its provisions.

In almost identical language to *Crow Dog,* the Supreme Court, in *Talton* v. *Mayes,*[13] reviewed the treaty and statutory history of the Cherokee–United States relationship and turned aside Talton's plea for release, stating the "the crime of murder committed by one Cherokee Indian upon the person of another within the jurisdiction of the Cherokee nation is, therefore, clearly not an offence against the United States, but an offence against the local laws of the Cherokee nation."[14] And, the Court explained, Cherokee rights of self-government were not delegated by Congress and consequently were not powers arising from and created by the U.S. Constitution. "It follows," the Court concluded, "that as the powers of local self-government enjoyed by the Cherokee nation existed prior to the Constitution, they are not operated upon by the Fifth Amendment, which, as we have said, had for its sole object to control the powers conferred by the Constitution on the National Government."[15]

It would appear that the *Talton* case spoke directly to the issue of the nature of the federal relationship with the Indians and with congressional power to deal with Indians in their corporate, national existence. But neither the Seven Major Crimes Act, nor any other act or expression of Congress (apart from the history of the diplomatic relationship between the tribe and the United States), was mentioned. Provided with a golden opportunity to clarify Indian status within the constitutional framework, the Court studiously avoided the issue and instead placed Indians beyond the reach of most existing federal Indian law. The constitutional test of the Seven Major Crimes Act occurred in an entirely different context and produced one of the most astounding decisions ever to be written by the Supreme Court.

The Rise of Congressional Extra-Constitutional Plenary Powers in Dealing with Indians

By the mid-1880s necessity and expediency ruled conduct on the Indian reservations in the western states and territories. In addition to the large, assertive Plains tribes, which had well-defined treaty rights, smaller groups scattered in isolated regions of the West also came under federal protection and supervision. The President issued executive orders to set aside small tracts for these groups and an effort was made to assist them in adjusting to the barren land where they were made to live. It was as a result of an incident on one of these federally created reservations that the Seven Major Crimes Act was tested.

Kagama (alias Pactah Billy) and Mahawaha (alias Ben) murdered Iyouse (alias Ike) on the Hoopa Valley Reservation in northern California. Since California had long been a state and the Indian reservations within it were minor and neglected outposts of the federal supervisory administrative apparatus, the question arose as to whether the federal district courts had jurisdiction over the case. In *United States* v. *Kagama*,[16] the Supreme Court showed an amazing reluctance to offer any definitive statement on the federal relationship with Indians. "The Constitution of the United States is almost silent in regard to the relations of the government which was established by it to the numerous tribes of Indians within its borders,"[17] the Court declared. It then cited the enumeration clauses of Article I and the Fourteenth Amendment, and moved on to the commerce clause:

> This clause is relied on in the argument in the present case, the proposition being that the statute under consideration is a regulation of commerce with the Indian tribes. *But we think it would be a very strained construction of this clause, that a system of criminal laws for Indians living peaceably in their reservations, which left out the entire code of trade and intercourse laws justly enacted under that provision, and established punishments for the common-law crimes of murder, manslaughter, arson, burglary, larceny and the like, without any reference to their relation to any kind of commerce, was authorized by the grant of power to regulate commerce with the Indian tribes.*[18]

This analysis is nothing short of breathtaking. For over a century Congress had acted on the assumption that it was fulfilling its delegated power to regulate commerce with foreign nations, among the several states, and with the Indian nations. Federal Indian legislation had proceeded cautiously, step by step, to add provisions to federal laws that would ensure peaceful trade relations with the Indians. It had established trading houses and factories, it had licensed traders, and it had prevented anyone from dealing with the Indian tribes in land matters without a federal presence to ensure fairness and honesty in the transaction. Even criminal laws in the territories had been carefully worded to reflect the need for a peaceful domestic setting within which trade with the Indians could be conducted.

Yet in this decision, the Supreme Court swept aside over a century of federal legislation and stated that it was unable to see in either the enumeration or commerce clauses "any delegation of power to enact a code of criminal law for the punishment of the worst class of crimes known to civilized life when committed by Indians."[19] The Court then proceeded to analyze U.S. political institutions in geographical terms, spelling out the idea that the United States had primacy in Indian matters because of its ownership of the lands of the continent, an ownership derived originally from the Doctrine of Discovery, with its corresponding requirement that both Indian titles and Indian political status had to be respected by the sovereign asserting political control and protection over the tribes. The Court seemed to deal with the subsequent history of the federal relationship with the Indians by noting that "from their very weakness and helplessness, so largely due to the course of the Federal Government with them and the treaties in which it has been promised, there arises a duty of protection, and with it the power."[20] Finally, the opinion concluded:

> The power of the General Government over these remnants of a race once powerful, now weak and diminished in number, is necessary to their protection, as well as to the safety of those among whom they dwell. It must exist in that government, because it has never existed anywhere else, because the theatre of its exercise is within the geographical limits of the United States, because it has never been denied, and because it alone can enforce its laws on all the tribes.[21]

What did the *Kagama* decision really say? It suggested that by the mere ownership of land, the U.S. government had acquired a power outside the Constitution that allowed it to deal arbitrarily with Indians under the guise of "protecting" them, such protection being necessary both because of the bad-faith dealings by the very government that was supposed to protect them *and* because of treaty promises. In short, the Court was in complete confusion, to such a degree that it could not find a constitutional phrase upon which to base its decision. *Kagama* cited extra-constitutional reasons for holding a congressional statute to be constitutional, a doctrine of staggering implications for Indians and the federal government alike. But *Kagama* did much more. It was the formal, albeit confused, announcement that henceforth there would be *no* constitutional limitation on the federal government in its dealings with Indian tribes. *Kagama* abandoned the requirement that congressional acts bear some detectable relationship to a phrase in the Constitution and announced a new doctrine: that if a subject in some way relates to Indians, it is a valid exercise of congressional authority. Although there must presumably be a good reason given for any congressional act, even the most tenuous explanation was to be acceptable.

Power Without Limits

By citing land ownership rather than the constitutional delegation of power in *Kagama*, the Court laid down the conditions for the exercise of plenary legislative power by Congress and plenary interpretive power by the federal courts in the following century. If there was no limit on Congress's ability to pass Indian legislation, there was also no limit on the manner in which the federal courts could torture words to reach a satisfactory decision in an Indian case. The first formal articulation of this plenary and extra-constitutional power came in *Lone Wolf* v. *Hitchcock* (1903).[22] The Kiowa, Comanche, and Apache tribes had signed a treaty with the United States in 1867 in which Article 12 promised that no future cessions of land would be considered valid unless the agreement was signed by three-quarters of the adult male members of the tribes.

In the early 1890s Congress authorized the Jerome Commission to treat with the tribes in the allotment of their land and the cession of the "surplus" to the United States for settlement by white home-steaders. Through a variety of slippery devices, a substantial number of Indians signed the agreement but the three-quarters requirement was not met, even when the Bureau of Indian Affairs had the luxury of manipulating the figures by changing the age of adulthood and otherwise tampering with Indian signatures.

Lone Wolf, a Kiowa chief, filed for a temporary injunction to prevent the secretary of the interior from carrying out the provisions of the federal statute that purported to ratify the agreement. Since the agreement had been materially altered by Congress after numerous hearings, Lone Wolf argued that the final version of the act was not only a violation of the 1867 treaty, but also bore no relationship to the agreement that members of his tribe had signed. Lone Wolf was turned down at the lower court levels and appealed to the Supreme Court. By the time the case arrived at the highest tribunal, the argument had been refined to a simple Fifth Amendment claim, in addition to the treaty provision—in effect, the violation of the treaty was also a violation of Fifth Amendment rights.

The Supreme Court engaged in sophistry of the highest order in posing the question that it wished to answer. In response to the argument that the treaty established the conditions under which future land cessions would be considered valid, a promise the Indians had dearly paid for, the court argued:

> To uphold the claim would be to ajudge that the indirect operation of the treaty was to materially limit and qualify the controlling authority of Congress in respect to the care and protection of the Indians, and to deprive Congress, *in a possible emergency, when the necessity might be urgent for a partition and disposal of the tribal lands, of all power to act, if the assent of the Indians could not be obtained.*[23]

Here, under the guise of "care and protection"—the criteria (established in *Kagama*) for the exercise of the proprietary power over land and presumably its Indian inhabitants—the Court found that Congress had the power to act "in a possible emergency, when the necessity might be urgent for a partition and disposal of the tribal lands." But what was the emergency in this case? Congress had dallied with the act through several sessions, and apart from the pressing crowd of Sooners and Boomers camped outside the Indian lands demanding that they be opened to settlers, there was no emergency at all—unless there was a real possibility that the federal government would refuse to protect the Indians from the settlers, which itself would be a violation of the doctrine of *Kagama* as well as every statute passed by Congress since the inception to the Republic.

Under both *Kagama* and the Doctrine of Discovery, the United States was charged with the protection of the Indians from foreign powers and from the acts of its own citizens and constituent states.

Andrew Jackson had blatantly refused to provide this protection, but in other instances the federal government had made an effort to fulfill its responsibilities. The only possible scenario in which the emergency powers of Congress to violate the 1867 treaty provisions could be justified would be invasion by a foreign country. If such an invasion was halted in geographic proximity to the Kiowa, Comanche, and Apache lands, and one of the conditions demanded by the successful invader was that part or all of the Indian land be divided or the invader would continue its conquest of the United States and/or destroy the Indians completely, then the treaty could be violated. But without a crisis of this magnitude, it is inconceivable that the Supreme Court could conjure up a scenario to justify violating the treaty.

In this instance, as in the *Kagama* case—and in distinct contrast to *Crow Dog* and *Talton*—there was no appeal to a constitutional phrase. There was not even an elementary geography lesson to disguise the naked assertion of force through judicial application. "Presumably," the Court lamely remarked, "such power will be exercised only when circumstances arise which will not only justify the government in disregarding the stipulations of the treaty, but may demand, in the interest of the country and the Indians themselves, that it should do so."[24] But the Court was not very enthusiastic about calling the case under consideration one of those times. It immediately followed this argument with an extensive quotation from the *Kagama* case which emphasized the helplessness of the Indians, a condition the Court itself was immeasurably increasing. It also cited a recent decision, *Cherokee Nation* v. *Hitchcock*,[25] in which it had held that "full administrative power was possessed by Congress over Indian tribal property."[26]

Moving from that concept, which had never been a part of federal Indian law, the Court finally resorted to a nonsensical euphemism worthy of a swindler of the first magnitude. "In effect," the Court said, "the action of Congress now complained of was but an exercise of such [administrative] power, *a mere change in the form of investment of Indian tribal property.*"[27] The Court could not, it declared, find bad faith on the part of Congress, and it advised the Indians that "if injury was occasioned, which we do not wish to be understood as implying, by the use made by Congress of its power, relief must be sought by an appeal to that body for redress and not to the courts."[28]

In short, negotiations with Congress, a modified form of treaty-making, was the only relief available to the Indians. The federal courts would not presume to make any unfavorable comment on the actions of Congress, no matter how bizarre those actions might seem to be.

From the 1890s until the present, the Indians have had no constitutional protection against the actions of the federal government. Traditional checks and balances do not apply. Thus while tribal rights have been traditionally protected if they have been phrased in terms of federal prerogatives, so that the federal exercise of power is shielded from intrusions by the states, whenever Indian rights appear to conflict with federal statutes, the courts have pretended that the Congress, when considering legislation, has carefully considered whether the provisions of a bill were in conflict with the existing rights of the tribes. In fact, however, congressional hearings rarely mention that Indian treaty rights stand in the way of power dams, superhighways, or use of resources. Litigation is thus wholly and completely arbitrary. Sometimes the courts rule that Congress did intend to supercede the Indian right and sometimes they rule that it did not.

Two cases dealing with Sioux Indian claims illustrate the no-man's land in which Indian tribes live. In pressing their claims for compensation for the illegal confiscation of the Black Hills of South Dakota, the Sioux argued all of the moral phraseology which *Kagama* and *Lone Wolf* seem to encourage. But the Court of Claims nimbly skipped through the jurisprudential landscape and rejected every argument. When the Sioux said that they were helpless and in an inferior bargaining position, the Court responded:

> While it had been the practice and policy of the United States Government during the many years of tension between the whites and the Indians to negotiate with them by treaty convention and to settle differences, if possible by treaty, those treaties did not absolutely abrogate the right to the Government to regulate the Indians or, when necessary, to legislate contrary to or inconsistently with a treaty. *The primary consideration must be the good of the country and the duty the Government owes to all its citizens, not only the obligation that arose as a result of a previous treaty with the Indians or the duty that was created in the United States by virtue of its superior bargaining position in relation to a weak and defenseless people.*[29]

In other words, neither treaty or admitted weakness is a sufficient ground for the court to uphold Indian rights.

The Sioux also argued that they were "wards" of the federal government, in the fashion of the Marshall decisions, and that the government was morally and legally bound to follow the rules of fiduciary trust which obtain in a ward-guardian relationship. But the court promptly responded:

> While it has often been said by this court and the Supreme Court that the general relationship of the Government to the Indians of the United States is *similar* to that of a guardian and a ward, it has never been held that such a general relationship amounts to a legal guardian-ward relationship in the absence of some specific language to that effect in a treaty, agreement, or act of Congress. *In the absence of such specific language, the general relationship of the United States to the Indians has been that of a strong and powerful sovereign to a comparatively weak and defenseless people.*[30]

So the circle completes itself, and there is no way that Indians can require the federal government to act responsibly, let alone according to its constitutional mandate.

The manipulations of the Black Hills land question illustrate the confusion over past transactions between the Indians and the federal government. Since 1979, the federal courts have been asked to resolve the issue of whether the United States constitutionally "took" the Sioux lands and whether just compensation is to be given the Sioux. The irony of this situation is that the concensus of both the Supreme Court and the Claims Court is that the Black Hills were in fact "unconstitutionally" taken from the Sioux. But while the Indians assumed that the federal government could not do something unconstitutional, and that any action declared such would be null and void, the reverse has been the case. "Unconstitutional" in an Indian setting seems to mean that something horribly distasteful has occurred, but that it is nevertheless permanent and irreversible.

There is no solution to the constitutional exclusion of Indians as federal Indian law is presently understood. At best the courts have begun to devise a test to determine in what capacity Congress may be said to have acted. Thus in *Three Tribes of Fort Berthold Reservation* v. *United States*,[31] the Court of Claims, confronted with the question of the nature of the congressional action in taking tribal lands, stated:

It is obvious that Congress cannot simultaneously (1) act as trustee for the benefit of the Indians, exercising its plenary powers over Indians and their property, as it thinks is in their best interests, and (2) exercise its sovereign power of eminent domain, taking the Indians' property within the meaning of the Fifth Amendment to the Constitution. In any given situation in which Congress has acted with regard to Indian people, it must have acted either in one capacity or the other. *Congress can own two hats, but it cannot wear them both at the same time.*[32]

The Court of Claims then suggested that the proper test would be that "where Congress makes a good-faith effort to give the Indians the full value of the land and thus merely transmutes the property from land to money, there is no taking. This is a mere substitution of assets or change of form and is a traditional function of a trustee."[33]

The suggested test is, however, nothing of the sort. It merely manipulates the idea of trustee/guardian, which is a relationship that has already been disclaimed unless a treaty, agreement, or statute specifically states that the federal government is assuming such an obligation. The test also waits until Congress has acted and then suggests a means by which such action can be interpreted as a legal and authorized act. Nothing exists in law to prevent Congress from injuring tribal rights, and nothing requires that either Congress or the courts link actions of Congress to a constitutional power specifically delegated to the federal government.

Indians therefore remain beyond the pale of the constitutional framework. And unless and until there is some positive move by the federal government to accept limitations on its exercise of naked political power over the tribes, Indians will remain a people without a status and, more importantly, without the ability to protect themselves from the continuing exploitation visited upon them by the U.S. people and their government. That two centuries of constitutional law have not solved this problem is eloquent testimony to the fact that there are indeed limitations on the degree to which our federal documents meet every contingency.

Notes

1. *The Federalist No. 24* (A. Hamilton), *The Federalist Papers*, ed. J. Cooke (Middletown, Conn., 1961), p. 156.
2. *The Federalist No. 25*, p. 158.
3. Treaty of 17 September 1778, 7 Stat. 13.
4. See Treaties of 1815, i.e., Treaty with the Osage, 12 September 1815: "The parties, being desirous of re-establishing peace and friendship between the United States and the said tribes or nations, and of being placed in all things, and in every respect, on the same footing upon which they stood before the war . . ."
5. 8 Wheat. 543.
6. 5 Pet. 1.
7. 6 Pet. 515 (1832).
8. 4 Stat. 729 and 4 Stat 735.
9. U.S., Congress, House, 23rd Cong., 1st sess., 20 May 1834, H. Rept. 474, p. 2; emphasis added.
10. 109 U.S. 556 (1883).
11. Ibid., at 558.
12. 23 Stat. 385.
13. 163 U.S. 376 (1896).
14. Ibid., at 381.
15. Ibid., at 384.
16. 118 U.S. 375 (1886).
17. Ibid., at 378.
18. Ibid., at 378–79; emphasis added.
19. Ibid.
20. Ibid., at 384.
21. Ibid., at 384–85.
22. 187 U.S. 553.
23. Ibid., at 564; emphasis added.
24. Ibid., at 556.
25. 187 U.S. 294.
26. 187 U.S. 553 at 568.
27. Ibid.
28. 231 U.S. 28 (1913).
29. 146 F. Supp. 229 (1956) at 235–36; emphasis added.
30. Ibid., at 237; emphasis added.
31. 182 Ct. Cls. 543 (1968).
32. Ibid., at 553; emphasis added.
33. Ibid.

PART 4

Race, Sex, and Class: Tensions and Dilemmas in Individual Rights

All of the essays in this part address the ambiguity and tensions inherent in the rights that are part of our constitutional system. In the first essay, Randall Kennedy stresses that civil rights are not fixed and determined, either by the original intent of the framers or by the fundamental structures of U.S. society. Instead they are the product of human choice, and the choices adopted thus far have been contradictory. For example, as Kennedy points out, the Supreme Court "allowed affirmative action to exist in public higher education as long as it sufficiently camouflaged itself." For Kennedy, the final interpretation is not to be found in the Constitution but in "We the People." His essay should be read with those of Kinoy, DuBois, Mishler, and Braden in mind.

In the next essay, Rhonda Copelon argues that the Supreme Court's protection of reproductive and sexual autonomy through the right of privacy is double-edged. The right to privacy has thus far constrained the ability of the state legislatures to criminalize abortion, and to a limited extent has protected sexual privacy. But it has also reinforced the distinction between public and private that is an essential mechanism of the patriarchal order. The liberal idea of privacy is that it is a negative right to be free from state interference. That idea reinforces the separation of the personal from the political and relegates woman's issues to the private sphere. Copelon argues for a more radical idea of privacy, one grounded in a positive affirmative right to self-determination and equality.

Owen Fiss also addresses a basic tension caused by the public/private distinction, this time in the First Amendment. That amendment prohibits public interference with the right of private actors to say what they please. While such a public/private dichotomy may have been appropriate in the Jeffersonian era, it breaks down where large monopolistic television stations control our main form of mass communication, where giant private shopping malls replace the public streetcorner as a popular meeting place. As Fiss points out, positing freedom of speech solely in terms of a negative right of private actors to be free from state interference may, in modern society, conflict with our goal of facilitating the communication of ideas.

The public/private distinction runs throughout liberal theories of rights. The Supreme Court's reliance on the narrow privacy concept in reproductive and sexual freedom cases, its unwillingness to interfere with the monopolistic media in the First Amendment area, and its refusal to abandon the state-action doctrine in the area of civil rights all stem from the public-private distinction.

Margaret Burnham's essay also focuses on the contradictory nature of the constitutional struggle. For her, *Brown* v. *Board of Education* represents "both a momentous theoretical victory and a practical quagmire." Similarly, she demonstrates the landmark achievements of the civil rights movement in the First Amendment area, but notes that the Supreme Court spoke more with "ambivalence and reluctance than clarity and consistency." At the end, her essay challenges the "much touted elasticity of the [constitutional] document." While recognizing the need for engaging in constitutional struggle, she argues that it would be foolhardy to continually seek constitutional reform "at the expense of a more promising search for extra-constitutional definitions of twentieth-century equality."

Staughton Lynd also deals with the contradictions of the First Amendment, this time in the labor arena. In important respects, his article dovetails those of Fiss and Burnham. As with Fiss, Lynd urges a reconsideration of the public/private distinction, noting that the "decision of all large economic entitities have public consequences." He therefore argues for "constitutionalizing" Section 7 of the National Labor Relations Act (NLRA), recognizing a fundamental right of collective activity. He would also like to conceptualize a new type of right, one that would extend beyond the individualistic notion of constitutional rights to a "communal right to engage in concerted activities for mutual aid or protection." It is interesting to compare Lynd's "communal right," protected by the NLRA and the First Amendment, with Burnham's conclusion that the civil rights movement resulted in a "critical new consciousness that the right to organize was the linchpin of the free speech right." Thus both the labor and civil rights movements posed the same "revolutionary" reading of First Amendment rights, as a "collective right" to resist oppression and exploitation.

In the final essay in this section, David Rudovsky addresses the tension between providing constitutional safeguards for the accused and the proper enforcement of criminal laws. He argues that, contrary to conservative rhetoric, the enforcement of constitutional limitations on the police can be reconciled with the proper enforcement of the law, and that the constitutional protection of the accused must not be abandoned because it is an important aspect of our democratic rights in general. That protection is critical, not merely in capitalist societies, but in socialist societies as well.

RACE AND THE FOURTEENTH AMENDMENT:
The Power of Interpretational Choice

Randall L. Kennedy

The Fourteenth Amendment, like every other significant provision in the U.S. Constitution, is as politically progressive or conservative as an interpreter determines that it shall be. Its meaning is largely up for grabs. There does exist some degree of consensus that allows radically antagonistic parties—say, William Rehnquist and William Kunstler—to know at least what the other refers to when he speaks of the Fourteenth Amendment. An important element of that understanding is the text, the relevant portion of which, for the purpose of this essay, declares that no state shall deny to any person "the equal protection of the laws."[1] But the point at which quotation gives way to interpretation is also the point at which consensus ends and controversy begins.

Widespread but misconceived anxieties about constitution adjudication make it important to recognize that an interpreter has power over the constitutional text. One anxiety, deftly played upon recently by conservatives, is the fear of judicial tyranny. Opposed to the liberal politics of some federal judges, conservatives have effectively invoked the specter of the "imperial judiciary" in order to discredit the federal judiciary's reformist accomplishments of the period from the mid-1950s to the mid 1970s. An effective strategy in this campaign has been to charge that federal judges have supplanted constitutional values with their own subjective desires. More specifically, conservatives claim that judges have made law rather than applied it, thereby subverting democracy by arrogating to themselves—an elite corps of decision-makers beyond the discipline of elections—the authority to set social policies that should be determined primarily by the "political" branches of government. Politically influential conservatives—I think here particularly of Attorney General Edwin Meese—concede that the federal judiciary should restrain majoritarian decision-making within certain bounds. They insist, however, that in determining those bounds judges should refer principally, if not exclusively, to the original meaning of constitutional texts—the meaning, for instance, that the framers of the Fourteenth Amendment sought to convey in 1868, as distinct from the meanings that jurists today might prefer to implant.

A very different anxiety is the fear that the Constitution is one of many aspects of American life that stands as a bulwark against the sort of radical measures that need to be taken if the United States is to be transformed from a nation mired in overlapping forms of social hierarchy into an egalitarian democracy. This apprehension is felt even with respect to matters involving race relations, the very area in which constitutional development is widely perceived as having reached its most impressive heights. Keenly aware that protections for slavery comprised an essential aspect of the patchwork of compromises that gave birth to the original Constitution, some progressives—I think here particularly of Derrick Bell—contend that racism was impressed into the nation's fundamental structures from the outset and that the most that can be attained by resort to reformist politics, including litigation, is some degree of protection against the worst excesses of racial prejudice. Even the Fourteenth Amendment, once regarded as a charter of black freedom, is now regarded by some progressives as a flawed platform, the usefulness of which will always be limited by the circumstances of its origins as an expedient created more to satisfy the requirements of white politicians than the full and true needs of the former slaves.

What relates these politically divergent perspectives is a disparagement of judicial choice in constitutional adjudication. Conservatives seem to believe that "good" judges can and should restrain their own personal preferences and merely apply the policy choices made by the framers of the text in question. This belief is flawed, however, as both description and aspiration. It fails as description because the process of determining original intent calls upon the interpreter to make controversial choices that will inevitably reflect an attitude toward the substantive issue at stake. And the endeavor to confine choice by reference to the intentions of white men situated in the eighteenth or nineteenth century should be rejected as aspiration because, if followed, it would quite likely portend the nullification of legal achievements that support the rights of racial minorities and others whose interests in previous centuries generally had a lower level of priority than obtains today.

What should also be rejected, however, is the despairing assertion that racism is a power beyond the reach of choice, the position that the United States will always be, first and last, a white man's country. Racism is obviously a remarkably powerful, resilient, and mysterious force, but it is not supernatural. It too is a product of human interaction, and is subject to human control.

Interpreting the Constitution in the context of concrete disputes is the principal medium through which the Justices of the Supreme Court make political choices that control the direction of constitutional development. To accomplish their interpretive task, the Justices rely on a wide variety of sources, including the constitutional text, the history surrounding the framing of the text, judicial precedent, arguments about the relationship of a particular part of the Constitution to the structure of the document as a whole, personal moral and political commitments, estimations of what "society" considers to be "reasonable," "fundamental," or "necessary," and all sorts of other sources, including personal knowledge and prejudices, to which people ordinarily turn when making important decisions. Although the Justices ritualistically maintain (particularly at their confirmation hearings) that they merely discern constitutional meanings, history shows that they do far more than that: they actually *create* constitutional meanings. They do not simply apply the Constitution; they make and re-make it repeatedly.

An instructive example of the judicial construction and reconstruction of constitutional meaning is the history of what the Court, interpreting the Fourteenth Amendment, has prohibited as invidious racial discrimination. In creating lines that distinguish acceptable government policies from those deemed to be intolerably racist, the Court has confronted a variety of problems, including (1) how to evaluate classifications that expressly burden a given group on the basis of race; (2) how to evaluate racial classifications that purport to impose burdens neutrally; (3) how to evaluate racial classifications that appear to be private rather than public in character; (4) how to evaluate decisions that are challenged as racist but that are made pursuant to classifications that are silent as to race; and (5) how to evaluate classifications that affirmatively discriminate in favor of designated racial minorities.

1

Government classifications that expressly burden a given group on the basis of race have exerted an important formative influence on the evolution of judicial interpretation of the Fourteenth Amendment. This sort of classification was invalidated by the Court the first time it interpreted the amendment in a race relations context. In 1879, in *Strauder* v. *West Virginia*,[2] the Court reversed the conviction of a black man tried before an all-white jury that had been impanelled under a state law that explicitly excluded blacks (and women) from jury service. Interpreting the Fourteenth Amendment's delphic command that no state shall deny to any person "the equal protection of the laws," the Court construed this language to mean that "the law in the States shall be the same for the black as for the white."[3] Applying this interpretation to the case at hand, the Court then concluded that:

> The very fact that colored people are singled out and expressly denied by a statute all right to participate in the administration of the law, as jurors, because of their color . . . is practically a brand upon them, affixed by the law, an assertion of their inferiority, and a stimulant to that race prejudice which is an impediment to securing to individuals of the race that equal justice which the law aims to secure to all others.[4]

Strauder is widely and properly viewed as one of the Court's most significant pronouncements against racial oppression. However, it articulated certain limitations and facilitated the creation of yet others that have significantly cramped an array of affirmative responses to racial oppression. *Strauder* posits sameness of treatment as an essential demand of the Fourteenth Amendment: ". . . the laws in the states shall be the *same* for the black as for the white." This idea surely represented an improvement over the legal norms that existed in the antebellum United States: chattelization of slaves and the statutory exclusion of free blacks from a wide range of public activity. Prior to the Civil War, for instance, only one state (Massachusetts) allowed blacks to sit on juries. Yet equating legal equality with sameness of treatment has discouraged the creation of a more substantive conception of racial justice.

Strauder does not require that blacks actually sit on juries trying black defendants, only that the state refrain from explicitly barring blacks on the basis of race. But ever since the Civil War at least some blacks have maintained, with good reason, that given the intensity and pervasiveness of white Negrophobia, racial equality requires something more than simply the cessation of racial exclusion; equality in the administration of justice requires that black defendants be entitled to a jury on which there is at least some black representation. The Supreme Court, however, has repeatedly refused to consider seriously the idea of a constitutional right to be tried by an integrated jury (much less an all-black jury, as the Black Panthers demanded!).

There have been a few small breakthroughs in which the Court has been willing to recognize that the Fourteenth Amendment should provide blacks with not only negative protections but also positive entitlements. In the 1960s, for instance, the Supreme Court ruled that it was not enough for public school systems that had formerly segregated blacks as a matter of official policy to simply end segregation; what the Fourteenth Amendment required, the Justices concluded, were affirmative steps to insure integration. These openings, however, have been decisively limited, if not repudiated. And now the Court is hostile to any suggestion that the Fourteenth Amendment entitles blacks to some degree of substantive equality—proportional representation, for instance—in employment, education, or political position. It can plausibly be argued that in order for blacks to truly enjoy "the equal protection of the laws," they must be guaranteed at least some minimal degree of public power. Yet it is unlikely that in the forseeable future the Supreme Court will choose to develop that line of interpretation. Instead, the majority of the Justices will probably continue to view sameness of treatment as the chosen ideal of constitutional equality.

The ideal of sameness of treatment has been marked by the creation of exceptions that further underline the importance of judicial choice. The Court stated in *Strauder* that persons must be treated the same before the law, regardless of color. But during World War II, military authorities in the western United States imposed a curfew applicable only to Japanese-Americans, and then removed them from their homes and detained them in camps. In a series of decisions, the Court upheld the constitutionality of these measures. "All legal restrictions which curtail the civil rights of a single racial group are immediately suspect," Justice Hugo Black declared in *Korematsu* v. *United States*,[5] but "that is not to say that all such restrictions are unconstitutional." Restrictions may be justified by "pressing public necessity."[6]

The pressing necessity that was deemed to justify the government's action was the presence of an unascertainable number of disloyal Japanese-Americans who, according to the military authorities, could not be satisfactorily neutralized except by rounding up all Japanese-Americans. But the government knew even then that there was no substantial evidence of Japanese-American subversion. No adequate reason was ever given for the failure to treat Japanese-Americans on the same basis as the government treated citizens of German and Italian ancestry; nor was any adequate reason offered to explain why, in the face of the asserted emergency, the government never sought a general declaration of martial law. Nor did the opinion of the Court take into account the documented evidence that economic opportunism played an important role in mobilizing the government's internment program. And although the report on which the army based its action stated that Japanese-Americans belonged to "an enemy race," the Court resolutely declined even to acknowledge that racism played *any* part in the government's decision-making process.

Although Justice Black fancied himself a civil liberties absolutist(!), *Korematsu* is a graphic illustration of the general proposition that *no* constitutional right is absolute no matter what the framers' intent or the wording of the constitutional text. What we generally think of as an absolute right is in fact something far more provisional: a claim to legal support that will be honored by judges unless they perceive a compelling reason for not doing so. Deciding what counts as a "compelling" reason involves judicial choice. In *Korematsu*, Justice Black and five other Justices chose to side with the military's definition. Three Justices, however, chose differently. The military authorities, Justice Murphy concluded in the most powerful of the dissents, went beyond the limits of constitutional power and fell "into the ugly abyss of racism."[7]

2

At the same time that Japanese-Americans were being targeted by the government on account of their ancestry, the southern states were requiring the rigid segregation of blacks and whites in virtually every aspect of public life. Segregation statutes commanded blacks and whites to attend separate schools, board separate elevators, swear oaths on separate bibles, and be buried in separate cemeteries. These laws were justified on the grounds that they served the reasonable aim of decreasing racial friction and preserving racial custom, and imposed the burden of regulation with racial neutrality. After all, so the argument went, segregation applied to whites and blacks alike and therefore neither were denied the equal protection of the laws.

The idea that segregation is compatible with the Fourteenth Amendment was first articulated by the Supreme Court in 1896 in *Plessy* v. *Ferguson*.[8] In this case, the Court upheld the conviction of a black man in Louisiana who defiantly boarded a railway car reserved for whites only. The defendant conceded, for the sake of argument, that there was no discernible difference in quality between the cars reserved for whites and those reserved for blacks. His claim was that the very act of separating blacks from whites branded the minority race as inferior. The Court disagreed:

> The object of the [Fourteenth] amendment was undoubtedly to enforce the absolute equality of the races before the law [but] it could not have been intended to abolish distinctions based upon color. . . . Laws permitting, and even requiring [racial] separation . . . do not necessarily imply the inferiority of either race to the other.[9]

Homer Plessy's attorney charged that if the Justices themselves were black they would clearly see that, in the context of U.S. society, segregation both reflected and enforced the perpetuation of racial hierarchy. They would *feel* the stigma attached to isolation and understand that segregation was something being done *by* whites *to* blacks:

> Suppose a member of this Court, nay, suppose every member of it, by some mysterious dispensation of providence should wake tomorrow with a black skin and curly hair . . . and in travelling through that portion of the country where the "Jim Crow" car abounds, should be ordered into it by the conductor. It is easy to imagine what would be the result. . . . What humiliation, what rage would then fill the judicial mind![10]

This claim had some effect. "Everyone knows," observed Justice John Marshall Harlan in a lone dissent, "that the statute in question had its origins in the purpose, not so much to exclude white persons from railroad cars occupied by blacks as to exclude colored people from coaches occupied by or assigned to white persons."[11] The majority, however, chose to reject Plessy's plea:

> We consider the underlying fallacy of [his] argument to consist in the assumption that the enforced separation of the two races stamps the colored race with a badge of inferiority. If this be so, it is not by reason of anything found in the act, but solely because the colored race chooses to put that construction upon it.[12]

Plessy has rightly been condemned as one of the most socially destructive decisions in our constitutional history. It was, however, neither anomalous nor stupid. For nearly half a century, *Plessy's* "separate but equal" formula served well the complex political needs of dominant sectors of U.S. society. On the one hand, it satisfied demands for a clear acknowledgment of white supremacy—the "separate" side of the equation. On the other hand, it paid deference, at least formally, to equality before the law—the "equal" side of the equation. Although *Plessy* deserves no applause, it should be recognized that the thin and ultimately corrupt conception of equality that it embodied represented a better alternative than what many whites of the period had in mind. After all, during the two or three decades following *Plessy,* threats of racial extermination and calls for the repeal of the Fourteenth Amendment were significant aspects of southern political life. *Plessy* rested, moreover, on a developed set of precedents: by 1896 many state and federal judges had come to believe, as one of them put it, that "equality of rights does not necessarily imply identity of rights."[13]

In fact, of course, segregation in practice confined blacks to facilities that were both separate and unequal. For many years, the federal judiciary chose largely to ignore these inequalities. Although segregation frequently forced black children, for instance, to travel far greater distances to school than their white counterparts, accept far older facilities, and utilize far less public funding, judges initially held that such disparities did not amount to violations of the separate but equal doctrine. Segregation, they maintained, did not require complete or exact equality, but merely "substantial" or "practical" equality.

Under relentless prodding, much of it initiated and directed by the National Association for the Advancement of Colored People (NAACP), the courts eventually began to make segregation live up to its promises. Judges ruled that if white schools were given certain facilities, black schools must be provided with them as well; that if the state offered professional school education to whites, it must provide a similar opportunity to blacks; that if white teachers were paid a given salary, black teachers must be paid the same amount.

The NAACP simultaneously attacked segregation itself, arguing that apart from differences in the facilities or services provided, the very practice of government-enforced separation stigmatized blacks and thereby denied them due process and the equal protection of the laws. Winning public opinion and the Supreme Court over to this position proved difficult. Some observers viewed the NAACP's demand as akin to a plea for special treatment; after all, whites were also subject to the rules of segregation. Others suggested that by attacking segregation blacks demonstrated a lack of racial pride. If blacks possessed a healthy pride of race, so the argument went, they would not be obsessed with "mingling" with whites. Still others argued that Congress was the only agency of the federal government competent to order a change in social relations as radical as that demanded by the NAACP. And still others, surely the great majority of those favoring segregation, believed that blacks and whites should be separated because the two racial groups were essentially different, with whites superior in intelligence and common morals.

In 1954 the Supreme Court chose to reconsider the constitutionality of segregation in public schooling and held it to be inconsistent with the requirements of the Fourteenth Amendment. Writing for a unanimous Court in *Brown* v. *Board of Education,* Chief Justice Earl

Warren declared that "in the field of public education the doctrine of 'separate but equal' has no place. Separate facilities are inherently unequal."[14] The Court reached this conclusion by a route that even its supporters concede was rather awkward. First, the Court stated that referring to the original intent of the framers of the Fourteenth Amendment was "inconclusive" because of the variety of competing views expressed at the time. Chief Justice Warren also stated that referring to the origins of the amendment was inadequate because the social significance of public education had changed radically in the interim: "We cannot turn the clock back to 1868," he maintained, but must instead "consider public education in the light of its . . . present place in American life," as "the most important function of state and local governments," "the very foundation of good citizenship," and the "principal instrument in awakening the child to cultural values."[15] Having rejected any dependence on the way that the framers of the Fourteenth Amendment understood the legal status of segregated schooling, Chief Justice Warren looked to contemporary sources of authority and found it in common-sense observation and liberal social science. Explaining why segregation on the basis of race deprived black schoolchildren of the equal protection of the laws, he concluded that "to separate them from others . . . solely because of their race generates a feeling of inferiority as to their status in the community that may effect their hearts and minds in a way unlikely ever to be undone."[16] Affirmatively quoting the factual finding of a lower court judge, Warren maintained that "segregation with the sanction of law . . . has a tendency to [retard] the educational and mental development of negro children and to deprive them of the benefits they would receive in a racial[ly] integrated school system."[17] The basis of these factual assertions were studies by such liberal social scientists as Kenneth and Mamie Clark, E. Franklin Frazier, and Gunnar Myrdal. These studies were by no means uncontested. Segregationists argued, with good reason, that at least some of these studies were flawed methodologically and that all ratified the policy preferences of their authors. Such arguments fell on deaf ears, however. By 1954, the social science relied upon by segregationists had largely been discredited in the dominant elite spheres of U.S. culture. The unspeakable brutishness of Nazism's racial laws had cast a dark shadow over ideas that supported the South's peculiar ways. Moreover, in the Cold War struggle for international ideological dominance, important policymakers perceived that continued acquiescence to the codification of southern white bigotry would pose an acute embarassment to a nation that purported to be the "leader of the Free World." Although the reasoning set forth in Chief Justice Warren's opinion in *Brown* no doubt indicates part of what animated the decision, it is hard to believe that these other, unstated, considerations did not also play an important role in the Justices' decision to rid the nation of *de jure* segregation.

3

As we have seen, the history of the Fourteenth Amendment consists in large part of a record of choices in which judges have determined the acceptable parameters of U.S. race relations policy. The most consistent of these policies has been disapproval of laws, or other governmental actions, that burden a group explicitly on the basis of race. But what about harmful racist actions taken by private citizens, as opposed to government officials? The Fourteenth Amendment says that *no state* shall deprive any person of the equal protection of the law. Early on, the Court decided to interpret the Fourteenth Amendment's reference to states as a broad limitation on the amendment's reach. In 1883, in *The Civil Rights Cases,* still the leading decisions on the scope of the Fourteenth Amendment, the Supreme Court invalidated sections of the Civil Rights Act of 1875.[18] The act had been passed pursuant to the Fourteenth Amendment and provided that all persons were "entitled to the full and equal enjoyment" of places of public accommodation regardless of race, color, or previous condition of servitude.[19] This provision was unconstitutional, according to the Court, because it sought to regulate private rather than state action. Private action—activities such as marriage, torts, and contracts—had always been considered a domain that was only regulatable (if at all) by the states. In *The Civil Rights Cases,* the Court announced that in its view the Fourteenth Amendment had not changed this traditional arrangement. Ruling that the decision of an owner of a bar or restaurant or hotel to exclude or segregate a person on the basis of race is simply and essentially a matter of contract, the Court concluded that this type of action is "private" and therefore subject only to state regulation. Because the Civil Rights Act of 1875 reached into an area of activity outside the ambit of the Fourteenth Amendment's power, the offending provisions were nullified.

Dissenting once again, Justice Harlan indicated avenues down which the Court could have traveled to reach a different conclusion, had it chosen to do so. He maintained that the statutory sections under challenge could have been upheld by reference to constitutional provisions that had not been deemed to include state action requirements. Private racial discrimination could be viewed as a badge of servitude that provides a predicate for invoking the power of the Thirteenth Amendment: "Neither slavery nor involuntary servitude . . . shall exist within the United States." He also suggested that authorization for the public accommodations sections of the act might be grounded on the commerce clause of the Constitution, which provides that "Congress shall have Power . . . to regulate Commerce . . . among the several States." Although Justice Harlan did not flesh out his argument on this point, he might well have noted that humiliating treatment in places of public accommodation disuaded many blacks from traveling; or he might have noted that many businesses "affect" interstate commerce inasmuch as they order and sell out-of-state goods. Underscoring brilliantly the power of judicial choice, Justice Harlan pointed out the discrepancy between the Court's hostility to the Civil Rights Act and its protectiveness toward the antebellum Fugitive Slave Law: while the Court struck down the former as an unconstitutional intrusion on states' rights, it had upheld the latter as necessary to protect the human property of the southern slaveholders. Commenting on this difference in judicial response, Frederick Douglass called "for a Supreme Court which shall be as true, as vigilant, as active, and exacting in maintaining laws enacted for the protection of human rights, as in other days was that Court for the destruction of human rights!"[20]

Justice Harlan also argued, moreover, that it was possible to construe the Civil Rights Act as having satisfied the Court's state action requirement. Whites expected that they would be served by businesses without undergoing humiliating treatment. This expectation was so powerful, so accepted, so much a part of the social fabric that it did not need to be codified by statute. Yet this same expectation was withheld from blacks by businesses licensed by the state. This licensing could be considered state action, as could the decision by the state to permit humiliating "private" distinctions to be made between citizens on the basis of race. What is most impressive about Harlan's opinion, however, is not its mastery of legalistic exercises but its commitment to a choice that has yet to be fully realized. Positing as description what is actually aspiration, Justice Harlan insisted that "it is fundamental in American citizenship that . . . there shall be no discrimination by the State, or its officers, or by individuals or corporations exercising public functions or authority, against any citizen because of his race or previous condition of servitude."

Ever since *The Civil Rights Cases,* there have been continual battles over the state action doctrine. The reason is clear: protection against racial abuse by the state is significantly diminished if the same results can be accomplished by private parties. For instance, early in this century, in *Buchanan* v. *Warley* (1917), the Supreme Court held that the Fourteenth Amendment prohibits states from segregating blacks residentially by statute.[21] This ruling, however, did little to stem racial polarization in housing. Although the explicit use of state power to exclude blacks from white areas was no longer available after *Buchanan,* there were all sorts of private actions that whites could resort to in order to effect the same result. One popular expedient was for white residents in a community to enter into contracts with one another in which they promised never to sell their property to blacks and also to attach such restrictive covenants to the property itself, so that future owners would be similarly bound. In the event that a white person did try to sell property to a black, in contravention of the restrictive covenant, many judges chose to enforce the covenant and prevent the sale. These judges saw restrictive covenants as private actions beyond the jurisdiction of the Fourteenth Amendment. In 1948, however, in *Shelley* v. *Kraemer,* the Court interpreted the judicial enforcement of restrictive covenants in a new light.[22] In one of its most controversial and potentially far-reaching decisions, the Court invalidated judicial enforcement of racially restrictive covenants on the ground that such enforcement made the state complicit in private racism.

During the Second Reconstruction (1954–68), the Court continued to broaden the category of conduct deemed to be subject to the Fourteenth Amendment. A striking example of this tendency was

Griffin v. *Maryland* (1964), a case that involved the conviction of a black civil rights demonstrator arrested for trespassing on the property of a private amusement park open only to whites.[23] The Supreme Court invalidated the conviction on the grounds that the circumstances of the demonstrator's arrest improperly implicated the state in supporting "private" discrimination. The person who arrested the demonstrator was both an employee of the amusement park and a deputy sheriff. Even though the deputy was off-duty at the time he made the arrest, the fact that he was a state employee who was wearing his uniform at the time of the incident was enough to convince a majority of the Justices that they should interpret his conduct as a species of state action.

Yet even at the height of Warren Court activism, the Court's majority stayed within the doctrine it had inherited from the nineteenth century. The Court, for instance, declined to hold that the amendment prohibited owners of public accommodations—e.g., stores, gas stations, and restaurants—from segregating or excluding blacks. Continuing to respect the conclusion reached in *The Civil Rights Cases,* the majority construed these actions as private. Racism of this sort was only extinguished on a national basis by the public accommodations section of the Civil Rights Act of 1964, which was based primarily on the commerce clause of the Constitution—the source of authority to which Justice Harlan had referred over eighty years earlier.

In the wake of the Second Reconstruction, the Court's conception of state action has predictably narrowed. In *Moose Lodge No. 107* v. *Irvis* (1972), in an opinion authored by William Rehnquist, the Court held that a lower court had erred when it ordered a state agency to revoke the liquor license of a fraternal lodge that excluded blacks.[24] The black claimant argued that when the lodge obtained its liquor license, the state became an active participant in its discriminatory conduct. But the Court rejected that argument and concluded instead that the state's provision of a liquor license did not implicate it in the lodge's discriminatory actions enough to bring it within the reach of the Fourteenth Amendment.

There is nothing compelling about the Court's logic. It merely constitutes one of a number of indications that by the early 1970s a majority of the Justices had come to the end of their willingness to encourage continued struggle against racial hierarchy. The jurisprudence of "state action," in other words, is no different from the jurisprudence of "pressing public necessity" or "separate but equal" or "desegregation"; it is animated by the political values of its interpreters and subject to a wide variety of choices.

4

A major problem in developing the reach of the Fourteenth Amendment has been the difficulty of applying it to cases involving allegations of discriminatory administration of facially neutral laws. As we have seen, since the 1880s the Court has demonstrated a willingness to invalidate state laws that burden blacks explicitly on the basis of race. But how has the Court responded to allegations that complain not about the formal nature of a law but about its application in fact? It has responded in ways that have repeatedly failed to grapple realistically with the protean nature of racial domination.

After the collapse of Reconstruction in the 1870s, the southern states, where most blacks resided, expressly declared their intention to entrench white supremacy by keeping blacks "in their place"—which meant, among other things, keeping them *outside* of juries or voting booths. This purpose was accomplished by a variety of legal and extra-legal means. Whippings, lynchings, and arson effectively "persuaded" many blacks to forgo even the attempt to vote or serve on a jury. A favorite "legal" means of exclusion was for white officials to declare blacks unqualified as electors or jurors. Such discriminatory acts were facilitated—indeed, expressly invited—by laws characterized by two features: facial neutrality and vagueness. Facial neutrality was needed in order to satisfy the requirement of *Strauder* that laws be the same for blacks and whites. Vagueness was needed in order to give local white officials sufficient discretion to bar blacks on ostensibly nonracial grounds. Hence states conditioned voting on an applicant's ability to "understand" or "interpret" the state or federal constitutions. Similarly, states conditioned service on a jury on "good character" or "good judgment." Since these essentially subjective judgments were made by racially prejudiced local officials, they served as an informal, as distinct from a formal, system of exclusion.

In some of the Supreme Court's earliest encounters with informal discrimination, minority claimants prevailed. In *Neal* v. *Delaware* (1881), for example, a black defendant convinced the Court to overturn his conviction because state officials excluded blacks, because of their race, from the jury that had indicted him.[25] The Delaware attorney general conceded that no black had ever served on a grand jury in the state, yet he maintained that the mere absence of *all* blacks provided no basis for an inference that the state had purposefully excluded them on the basis of race. The Delaware supreme court accepted this argument:

> That none but white men were selected is in nowise remarkable in view of the fact—too notorious to be ignored—that the great body of black men residing in this State are utterly unqualified by want of intelligence, experience or moral integrity to sit on juries.[26]

Chief Justice Waite and Justice Field of the Supreme Court also accepted the state's rationale. The majority, however, decided that the state's reasoning constituted "a violent presumption" too improbable to be credited.[27] The Court concluded that the complete absence of blacks, along with the state's failure to offer any specific evidence supportive of a nonracial explanation, gave rise to the inescapable conclusions that officials had discriminated against blacks in violation of the equal protection clause.

Similarly, in *Yick Wo* v. *Hopkins* (1886), a Chinese petitioner successfully argued that his conviction for violating a municipal ordinance in San Francisco should be reversed because officials had violated the Fourteenth Amendment by purposefully discriminating against those of Chinese ancestry.[28] While the officials almost invariably granted permits to whites who sought to operate laundries, they consistently denied permits to similarly situated Chinese applicants. According to the Court:

> The facts shown establish an administration directed so exclusively against a particular class of persons as to warrant and require the conclusion, that . . . [the ordinances] are applied with a mind so unequal and oppressive as to amount to a practical denial by the State of the equal protection of the laws. Though the law itself be fair on its face and impartial in appearance . . . if it is applied and administered by public authority with an evil eye and an unequal hand . . . the denial of equal justice is still within the prohibition of the Constitution.[29]

These rulings, however, did little to redress the practice of widespread discrimination. *Neal* and *Yick Wo* presented extreme cases in which local officials brazenly displayed the discriminatory character of their decision-making. In cases less clear cut, however, the Court displayed extraordinary deference both to local officials who denied discriminating against blacks on the basis of race and to state court judges who routinely credited official testimony. In *Murray* v. *Louisiana* (1896), for instance, the Court affirmed the conviction of a black man even in the face of evidence that blacks comprised at the most only two of the thousand people selected for the county's jury wheel.[30] While the Justices were willing to redress *complete* exclusion of blacks, they were unwilling to redress anything less drastic. This complaisant response led to exclusion through token inclusion. In *Akins* v. *Texas* (1945), the Court affirmed the conviction of a black man who challenged the constitutionality of his trial on the ground that state officials had purposefully limited black participation on grand juries to one black per panel.[31] No one disputed that such a limitation constituted a violation of the Fourteenth Amendment; the only issue was whether, in fact, such a limitation had been intentionally imposed. The evidence demonstrated overwhelmingly that the local jury commissioners had conducted their selections with such a limitation in mind. As one jury commissioner candidly put it, "We had no intention of placing more than one negro on the panel. When we did we had finished with the negro."[32] Yet even in the teeth of this statement and corroborating evidence, the Court affirmed the conviction, once again emphasizing the presumption of legitimacy and fair-mindedness that it attached to the conduct of state officials.

The systematic exclusion of blacks from virtually every aspect of the administration of criminal justice in the South did not receive consistent judicial challenge until the 1960s. Educated by the open recalcitrance of die-hard white supremacists, the Court finally began to follow the path implicit in *Neal:* a challenged conviction should be invalidated unless the state could provide an adequate nonracial explanation for substantial statistical disparities between the numbers of blacks in the general population and the numbers selected for jury service. But even at the height of Warren Court protectiveness, the Justices' jurisprudence was riddled with misguided choices. In 1965, in the notorious case of *Swain* v. *Alabama,* the Supreme Court held that no violation of the equal protection clause would arise even if a state prosecutor used peremptory challenges to remove, because of their race, potential black jurors from a particular jury.[33] The Court justified its decision on two main grounds. First, peremptory challenges—a device that allows attorneys to strike jurors without having to state a reason—are rooted in a long tradition that would have had to be modified if prosecutors were told that they could not use race as a factor for excluding a particular juror. Second, the Court presumed that even if a prosecutor struck all potential black jurors in any one case, such action referred only to the particularities of that case and was not evidence of an intent to purposefully exclude blacks from *all* juries. In *Swain* itself the record indicated that, largely because of racially selective peremptory challenges, there had *never* been a black person who had actually sat on a jury in a criminal case in Talledega County, Alabama. Yet the Court found this fact an insufficient predicate for a finding of purposeful discrimination since the defendant had not demonstrated that the prosecutors were exclusively responsible for this long record of exclusion.

The use of peremptory challenges to bar blacks from juries, particularly in cases involving interracial violence or a potential death sentence, became so embarrassing that in the 1970s state courts, using state constitutions, began to ban the practice. The Supreme Court eventually followed suit when it overruled *Swain* in *Batson* v. *Kentucky* (1986).[34] Yet the attitudes that led to *Swain*—deference to local authorities, naive blindness to the realities of racism, and commitment to traditional practices—led to an even more appalling decision in 1987: *McCleskey* v. *Kemp*.[35]

This case involved a young black man, Warren McCleskey, who was convicted and condemned to death in Georgia for murdering a white police officer. McCleskey did not challenge the facial neutrality of the system under which he was sentenced but claimed that, as applied, the system was racially discriminatory in that it condemned the murderers of whites to death far more frequently than it did the murderers of blacks, and condemned *black* murderers of whites with the greatest frequency of all. Buttressing McCleskey's claim was an extraordinary study that reviewed over two thousand murder cases in Georgia during the 1970s and used sophisticated models to determine the variables that might account for the striking racial disparities uncovered. Justice William Brennan aptly described the study's conclusions:

[The study indicates] that, after taking into account some 230 nonracial factors that might legitimately influence a sentencer, the jury *more likely than not* would have spared McCleskey's life had his victim been black. . . . Race accounts for a six percentage point difference in the rate at which capital punishment is imposed. Since death is imposed in 11% of all white-victim cases, the rate in comparable aggravated black-victim cases in 5%. The rate of capital sentencing in a white-victim case is thus 120% greater than the rate in a black-victim case. Put another way, over half—55%—of defendants in white-victim cases in Georgia would not have been sentenced to die if their victims had been black. Of the more than 200 variables potentially relevant to a sentencing decision, race of the victim is a powerful explanation for variation in death sentencing rates—as powerful as nonracial aggravating factors such as a prior murder conviction. . . . These adjusted figures are only the most conservative indications of the risk that race will influence the death sentences of defendants in Georgia. Data unadjusted for the mitigating or aggravating effect of other factors show an even more pronounced disparity by race. The capital sentencing rate for all white-victim cases was *11 times* greater than the rate for black-victim cases. Furthermore, blacks who kill whites are sentenced to death at nearly 22 *times* the rate of blacks who kill blacks, and more than 7 *times* the rate of whites who kill blacks. In addition, prosecutors seek the death penalty for 70% of black defendants with white victims, but only for 15% of black defendants with black victims, and only 19% of white defendants with black victims.[36]

For those made anxious by the fact that McCleskey killed not an ordinary white person, but a white person who happened to be a *police officer,* a fact noted by Justice Harry Blackmun may be of interest:

Of the 17 defendants, including McCleskey, who were arrested and charged with homicide in Fulton County [Georgia, during 1973–1979], McCleskey alone was sentenced to death. The only other defendant whose case even preceded to [the special penalty phase of a trial reserved only to those deemed eligible for capital punishment] received a sentence of life imprisonment. That defendant had been convicted of killing a *black* police officer.[37]

A majority of the Supreme Court chose, however, to regard McCleskey's statistical presentation as "at most" a study that "indicates a discrepancy that appears to correlate with race."[38] While the dissenters believed that McCleskey's evidence constituted at least a *prima facie* case of discrimination that should require some sort of explanation from the state, the majority concluded that the evidentiary showing did not implicate the risk of a wrong sufficiently to trigger further inquiry. Behind that choice lay a host of others. The dissenters believed that McCleskey's evidence could only be fairly interpreted in the light of Georgia's long history of racial discrimination in the administration of justice. They pointed out, for instance, that during slavery Georgia criminal law expressly demanded the imposition of different punishments depending on the racial identity of the perpetrator or victim. The punishment for rape combined all of the features that, according to McCleskey's statistics, still characterize the actual operation of criminal "justice" in Georgia. The Georgia Penal Code of 1861 provided that the rape of a white woman by a black man compelled mandatory execution, while the rape of a white woman by a white man was punishable only by a prison term. The rape of a black woman by anyone was punishable by either a prison term or a mere fine. Yet this example, and others closer to the present, were peremptorily dismissed in a mere footnote: "Although the history of racial discrimination in this country is undeniable," Justice Powell acknowledged grudgingly for the majority, "we cannot accept official actions taken long ago as evidence of current intent."[39]

Perhaps the most important area of choice in *McCleskey*, however, had to do with determining the standard by which to judge whether sentencing in capital cases was infected by racial prejudice. Since 1976, in a case entitled *Washington* v. *Davis*,[40] the Burger-Rehnquist Court has been ruthlessly reducing the complicated question of racial oppression to one narrow inquiry: Did discriminatory purpose animate the action being challenged? Many strong supporters of the rights of racial minorities believe that while inquiry into purpose may usefully serve in some instances to help determine whether a given action or policy should be declared a violation of the equal protection clause, motive-centered inquiry should never have been made into the indispensable element of such a case. If blacks as a group are being disproportionately harmed without strong justification, why should the nature of the motivation matter? But putting that question aside and assuming that discriminatory purpose must be shown, new questions arise, questions that call for new choices: What is the nature of "discriminatory purpose"? What sorts of evidence will signal its presence? We could choose to infer the presence of discriminatory purpose from decisions that burden blacks disproportionately and that are not justified by any substantial nonracial explanation. Or we could choose to infer the presence of discriminatory purpose from actions taken by a decision-maker who knows that his or her actions will burden blacks disproportionately but who nonetheless fails to seek other, less burdensome, alternatives. Or we could choose, as the Court's majority has done, to infer discriminatory intent only from evidence that indicates positively that the decision-maker "selected or reaffirmed a particular course of action at least in part 'because of' and not merely 'in spite of,' " its adverse effects upon an identifiable group. In other words, because of the doctrinal choices made by a majority of the current Supreme Court, Warren McCleskey could succeed in invoking the equal protection clause of the Fourteenth Amendment only if he could show that a prosecutor or judge or juror was, at least in part, out to get him because of his race. Although there are some people so evil that they self-consciously and malevolently design to hurt black people, that is not the way in which most racism expresses itself nowadays. In our present stage of race relations, most racism expresses itself as what Paul Brest has described as "racially selective sympathy and indifference . . . the unconscious failure to extend to a minority the same recognition of humanity, and hence the same sympathy and care, given as a matter of course to one's own group."[41]

It is hard to imagine a decision more susceptible to "racially selective sympathy and indifference" than the inescapably intuitive judgment as to whether a person deserves to live or die. A gut-level response to both the defendant and the victim will determine this murky calculation. Such responses are like particles invisible to the naked eye but perceptible through cumulation. Yet the Supreme Court has ruled that statistical cumulations are not enough to show the "purpose" it seeks to prohibit. When blacks were hurt by purpose of this sort, and evidence was all too clear and available—the days, for instance, when politicians unashamedly proclaimed that their purpose was "to keep the nigger down"—the Supreme Court found a way to avert its gaze. Now, when the advance of decency has made the task of delineating racism a bit more complicated, the Court has chosen to pursue an avenue of constitutional interpretation that is of distressingly little relevance to modern forms of racial oppression.

5

The area of judicial choice that has given rise to the greatest degree of controversy during the past decade is the struggle over the constitutionality of classifications that prefer designated minority groups explicitly on the basis of race—affirmative action. As a question of policy, opponents of affirmative action deny that it is "affirmative." One argument is that it harms blacks by exacerbating existing racial animosities and thereby undercutting the possibility of constructing the sort of interracial coalitions necessary for truly significant social reform. Another is that preferential treatment stigmatizes blacks by implying that they cannot compete with whites without special support. Another is that affirmative action saps the internal morale of the black community and causes blacks to lower their own expectations—the "get over" mentality. Still another argument is that affirmative action tends to aid precisely those blacks least in need of assistance while it does little for those in the "underclass" who do not even possess the minimal qualifications needed to take advantage of preferential treatment.

Proponents of affirmative action, on the other hand, maintain that it enables racial minorities to advance in arenas previously barred to them at a modest pace but one that would otherwise be intolerably slow. Breakthroughs propelled by affirmative action then create self-perpetuating benefits: the accumulation of valued experience, the eradication of debilitating stereotypes, the inclusion of black partici- pants in the making of decisions that affect minority interests, the enlargement of a black professional class able to nourish the black community as a whole with its material advantages and elevated aspirations. Many proponents of affirmative action do not deny that it exacts costs; they simply conclude that the costs are outweighed by the benefits.

As a matter of constitutional principle, opponents of affirmative action contend that it represents a reversion to the very racialism that, in their view, *Brown* v. *Board of Education* had sought to destroy. They maintain that the Fourteenth Amendment requires that the government be color blind. Proponents of affirmative action maintain, by contrast, that all the Fourteenth Amendment prohibits is *harmful* discrimination. In their eyes, discrimination in favor of minorities does not deny the equal protection of the laws but creates a means by which to enable historically oppressed groups—and the nation as a whole—to attain the goal of equal citizenship for all regardless of race.

The Justices evaded a head-on adjudication of an affirmative case for over a decade, allowing the issue to be ventilated in the court of public opinion. This suggests another aspect of judicial choice, at least as practiced by the Supreme Court: the Justices can choose not only *how* to decide an issue, but *when* to decide it. Finally, in *Regents of University of California* v. *Bakke* (1978), the Court issued its first ruling on the constitutionality of an affirmative action program.[42] At the medical school of the University of California at Davis, a designated number of places had been set aside for minority group applicants. Since charges of incompetence often becloud the discussion of affirmative action, it is important to note that *all* of those admitted, including the beneficiaries of the affirmative action program, were deemed by the medical school to possess at least the minimal qualifications for pursuing training to become a physician. Further, to keep in mind the stakes at issue, it is worth noting that without an affirmative action program, only one minority applicant would have been admitted at Davis between 1970 and 1974; twenty-six were admitted under the program.

Although the Court's decision in *Bakke* is widely viewed as a defeat for affirmative action, in actuality the decision is more ambiguous than that. On the one hand, the Court invalidated the plan that was in place at the Davis medical school. On the other hand, the Court maintained that, within certain bounds, race can be taken into account in an affirmative way by agencies of government.

Elaborating views that proved decisive to the outcome of the case, Justice Lewis Powell maintained that the Davis program's "fatal flaw" was "disregard of individual rights."[43] "It tells applicants who are not Negro, Asian, or Chicano that they are totally excluded from a specific percentage of the seats in an entering class."[44] Justice Powell acknowledged, à la *Korematsu,* that racial classifications are constitutionally justifiable if they are necessary to promote a compelling state interest, but concluded that none of the explanations offered by the medical school sufficed as an adequate justification. The medical school suggested that affirmative action could appropriately be used to redress general societal discrimination rooted in the nation's history of racial oppression. Justice Powell rejected this argument, however, because "societal discrimination" is "an amorphous concept of injury that may be ageless in its reach into the past."[45] He indicated that, for him, the only time that reference to historical oppression takes on real meaning is when that reference is buttressed by specific judicial, legislative, or administrative findings that the institution in question has purposefully discriminated against minorities in the past. No such finding had been made with respect to the medical school at Davis.

The school also sought to justify its program on the grounds that black doctors were urgently needed in order to improve health care services in minority communities. This argument was rejected because in Powell's view there existed no proof that the minority beneficiaries of the program would indeed practice in disadvantaged communities in need of additional medical resources. The Justice suggested that race served as a poor proxy for identifying candidates committed to serving the underserved; the medical school could have directly inquired into the past actions or future plans of candidates to derive this information.

Finally, the medical school argued that its program was justified by a commitment to creating a diversified student body, a goal based on the belief that the sort of education the school sought to impart could best be nurtured in a racially pluralistic student community. This justification struck a chord with Powell, who assimilated it to the cause of academic freedom:

> [Attaining a diverse student body] is a constitutionally permissable goal for an institution of higher education. . . . The freedom of a university to make its own judgments as to education includes the selection of its student body. . . . The atmosphere of "speculation, experiment and creation"—so essential to the quality of higher education—is widely believed to be promoted by a diverse student body.

For Powell, the problem with the program at Davis was that its reservation of a specified number of places for racial minorities focused solely on ethnic diversity and not on the attainment of "genuine diversity" along various dimensions—geographical, sexual, class—including race.[46] He concluded that race could be considered as a "plus" in a broad examination of each individual candidate, but that it could not serve as a rigid, definitive criterion for selection.

Bakke allowed affirmative action to exist in public higher education as long as it sufficiently camouflaged itself. Eight years later the Court, again speaking principally through Justice Powell, gave notice that although affirmative action in employment might be acceptable in certain circumstances, it would definitely be unacceptable if the cost to "innocent" white workers was perceived to be too great. In *Wygant* v. *Jackson Board of Education* (1986), the Court invalidated a collective bargaining agreement between the municipality of Jackson, Michigan, and a union of primary and secondary school teachers.[47] The agreement provided that, in the event of layoffs, the percentage of black teachers in the school system would not be allowed to sink below a certain level, even if that meant retaining black teachers with less seniority than white teachers who would have to be laid off. This policy stemmed from a history of racial strife in Jackson, and was an attempt to redress past discrimination, facilitate interracial cooperation, and maintain a black presence within the community of teachers for the benefit of students.

White teachers who were laid off but who had more seniority than the black teachers who were retained sued the local schoolboard. They claimed that their rights under the equal protection clause had been violated. The Supreme Court agreed, mainly on the ground that the means used to achieve the municipality's stated goals imposed too heavy a burden on white teachers. Placing the seniority interests of white workers on a pedestal, Justice Powell concluded that "layoffs impose the entire burden of achieving racial equality on particular individuals, often resulting in serious disruptions of their lives. That burden is too great."[48] There is no constitutional principle that clearly identifies that cost as "too great"; it is simply where Justice Powell and a majority of his colleagues chose to draw the line.

At the moment, affirmative action continues to survive as a constitutionally legitimate device—if it is sufficiently disguised, portrayed as a short-term expedient, and justified on grounds other than those which in fact most animate the demands for such programs. In the last case in which an affirmative action plan was tested on constitutional grounds, *United States* v. *Paradise* (1987), the Court upheld the program against determined opposition from the Reagan administration Justice Department.[49] That outcome, however, was decided by a single vote. With the retirement of Justice Powell, it is now conceivable—even probable—that the small space in which government-sponsored affirmative action has been allowed to operate will be shrunk still further, perhaps to nothing.

Conclusion

As we embark upon a third century of constitutional development, progressives should keep two points in particular in mind. The first has to do with the political economy of concern: the delicate task of allocating attention, empathy, and power to various historically victimized groups—here I think in particular of Native Americans, Hispanic- and Asian-Americans, gay and lesbian persons, women, and blacks. On the one hand, progressives must be careful to recognize the particularity with which these and other groups have been denied "the equal protection of the laws," a recognition made both more easy and more difficult by the overlapping nature of these categories of personal identification. Coalitions of victims find it difficult to avoid being splintered by parochialism, envy, repressed animosities, and, of course, the age-old stratagems of ruling elites: cooptation and divide and conquer. Nothing illustrates this better than the tragic splintering that divorced the early feminist movement and the black rights movement in the aftermath of Reconstruction. At the very moment that blacks as a group attained formal rights of citizenship, women as a group became more formally stigmatized than ever before. Prior to the Fourteenth Amendment, gender had never been noted in the words of the Constitution. But in a section on voting that is now of virtually no practical significance, the Fourteenth Amendment specifically limited its reach to "male citizens."[50] Unable to prevent Reconstruction from being limited to what some called "the Negro's hour," important elements of the women's movement and the black liberation struggle split apart with considerable bitterness and did not come together again until the Second Reconstruction of the 1960s. To forestall a repetition of such self-defeating conflict, progressives of all stripes and persuasions will have to demonstrate a remarkable degree of self-control and generosity of empathy.

On the other hand, there must be limits imposed on the impulse to universalize the idea of victimhood. Otherwise the concept of historically disadvantaged groups will lose its capacity to inform public policy. This has already happened to some degree in the Supreme Court. One of the arguments *against* affirmative action for racial minorities is that every group in the United States—including WASP men—is a minority group that has suffered oppression in the past. Justice Powell expressed this view in his pivotal opinion in *Bakke* when he asserted that the national majority "is composed of various minority groups, most of which can lay claim to a history of prior discrimination at the hands of the State and private individuals."[51] In other words, when every group jealously claims victimhood status, the claim itself suffers powerful dilution.

My second and final point is that given the power of the Supreme Court to conceptualize the Fourteenth Amendment in any number of different ways, progressives should never identify constitutional virtue with the institutional voice of the Justices. We should recognize that the Supreme Court's interpretation of the Constitution is always one of many possible interpretations. We should recognize this when the Court rules in our favor as well as when it rules against our interests. We should be clear that the Supreme Court is an organ of political power that is no more immune from wrongful prejudice or harmful ignorance than any other organ of power. The reason for emphasizing this point lies in two important recent events. One was a speech given by Attorney General Meese in October 1986. In this speech, entitled "The Law of the Constitution," Meese cautioned against confusing the Constitution itself with judicial pronouncements about the Constitution made in the settlement of concrete cases.[52] More specifically, he criticized the Supreme Court's own declaration that its decisions represent the supreme law of the land. That notion is objectionable, Meese suggested, because it makes the Constitution subordinate to the Justices who interpret it.

The attorney general's remarks caused a tremendous uproar from a wide spectrum of people, including progressives. To a certain extent, the anti-Meese clamor responded to a realistic perception of the political agenda behind his speech—the desire to intimidate, weaken, and further domesticate the federal judiciary, the branch of the federal government that, for half a century, has been considered a bulwark of liberalism. Significantly, the Supreme Court dictum that bore the brunt of Meese's attack on judicial supremacy was the language in *Cooper* v. *Aaron* (1958), a crucial and dramatic case in

which the Court affirmed the reinstatement of a school desegregation plan even in the teeth of militant opposition from the governor of
Arkansas.[53] Many of those who attacked Meese rightly saw his
critique of *Cooper*'s language as yet another instance of the Reagan
administration's reaction against hard-fought victories that blacks
have won. On the other hand, if one cleanses from Meese's speech
the covert political purpose it sought to achieve, there is considerable
merit to the position he espoused. Sanford Levinson put it well when
he wrote that "just as a stopped clock is right twice a day, so Attorney
General Meese can be a source of insight."[54] The point is that
distinguishing between the Constitution on the one hand and Supreme Court interpretations of the Constitution on the other does
provide a basis for resisting judicial tyranny. As Meese rightly
contends, "To confuse the Constitution with judicial pronouncements allows no standard by which to criticize and to seek the
overruling of . . . the 'derelicts of constitutional law'—cases such as
Dred Scott[55] and *Plessy* v. *Ferguson*,"[56] or, one might add, the
atrocities that are certain to come from the Reagan-Meese federal
judges.

The point of my analysis has been to show that the political
coloration of the Constitution is essentially that of its judicial interpreters. At the present moment, the Supreme Court has chosen to
interpret the equal protection clause of the Fourteenth Amendment
in a way that protects blacks and other racial minorities against the
most blatant form of state-sponsored racism. It has also interpreted it
to allow voluntary affirmative action efforts by governmental agencies under extremely limited circumstances. The Court has not,
however, interpreted the Fourteenth Amendment as a positive charter for substantive equality that either authorizes or commands that
power be redistributed for the purpose of creating an authentically
democratic society that recognizes that need for a conception of
group rights that can enrich the nation's existing commitment to
individualism. That large goal lies ahead. The obstacle to its attainment exists not in the words of the Constitution itself, but rather in
"We, the People."

Notes

This essay is dedicated to Billy Riordan and his commitment to social justice.

1. The Fourteenth Amendment was ratified in 1868 and is now probably the single most important amendment in the Constitution. As interpreted by the Supreme Court, the Fourteenth Amendment is what subjects the states to most aspects of the Bill of Rights, the first ten amendments, which were all ratified in 1791. The Fourteenth is also one of the longest and most complicated amendments. The part of the amendment with which I shall be principally concerned in this essay is the "equal protection clause." That clause is embodied in Section 1 of the amendment, which reads as follows: "All persons born or naturalized in the United States and subject to the jurisdiction thereof, are citizens of the United States and of the state wherein they reside. No State shall make or enforce any law which shall abridge the privileges or immunities of citizens of the United States; nor shall any State deprive any person of life, liberty, or property, without due process of law; nor deny to any person within its jurisdiction the equal protection of the laws."
2. 100 U.S. 303 (1879).
3. Ibid., at 307.
4. Ibid., at 308.
5. 323 U.S. 214 (1944).
6. Ibid., at 216.
7. Ibid., at 233.
8. 163 U.S. 537 (1896).
9. Ibid., at 544.
10. Quoted in *Civil Rights and the American Negro: A Documentary History,* ed. A Blaustein and R. Zangrando (New York, 1968), pp. 303–4.
11. Ibid., at 557.
12. Ibid., at 551.
13. Bertonneau v. Board of Directors of City Schools [New Orleans], 3. F. Cas. 294 (C.C.D.La. 1878).
14. 347 U.S. 483, 495 (1954).
15. Ibid., at 493.
16. Ibid., at 494.
17. Ibid.
18. 109 U.S. 3 (1883).
19. Ibid., at 9.
20. *Reconstruction, the Negro, and the New South,* ed. L. Cox and J. Cox (New York, 1973), p. 150.
21. 245 U.S. 60 (1917). It is strikingly incongruous that the Court invalidated state-enforced residential segregation during the acme of segregationist thought and practice in U.S. society. Some have suggested that the decision principally reflected the Court's hostility to government regulation of property. Under that interpretation, blacks were simply inadvertent beneficiaries of the Court's laissez-faire economics.
22. 334 U.S. 1 (1948).
23. 378 U.S. 130 (1964).
24. 407 U.S. 163 (1972).
25. 103 U.S. 370 (1881).
26. Ibid., at 393–94 (quoting the Chief Justice of the State Supreme Court).
27. Ibid., at 347.

28. 118 U.S. 356 (1886).
29. Ibid., at 373–74.
30. 163 U.S. 101 (1896).
31. 325 U.S. 398 (1945).
32. Ibid., at 406.
33. 380 U.S. 202 (1965).
34. 106 S.Ct. 1712 (1986).
35. 55 U.S.L.W. 4537 (1987).
36. Ibid., at 4549–50.
37. Ibid., at 4558; emphasis added.
38. Ibid., at 4546.
39. Ibid., at 4542, n.20.
40. 426 U.S. 229 (1976).
41. "Foreword: In Defense of the Antidiscrimination Principle," 90 *Harv.L.Rev.* 1, 7 (1976).
42. 438 U.S. 265 (1978).
43. Ibid., at 320.
44. Ibid., at 319.
45. Ibid., at 307.
46. Ibid., at 315.
47. 106 S.Ct. 1842 (1986).
48. Ibid., at 1851–52.
49. 55 U.S.L.W. 4211 (1987).
50. Section 2 of the Fourteenth Amendment reads, in the relevant part, that "when the right to vote at any election . . . is denied to any of the *male* inhabitants of [a] State . . . the basis of representation therein shall be reduced in the proportion which the number of such *male* citizens shall bear to the whole number of *male* citizens . . . in such State." (Emphasis added.)
51. 438 U.S. at 295.
52. "The Law of the Constitution," 61 *Tulane L.Rev.* 977 (1987).
53. 358 U.S. 1 (1958).
54. "Could Meese Be Right This Time?" 61 *Tulane L.Rev.* 1071, 1078. Levinson's characteristically brilliant article was first published in *The Nation.*
55. In Dred Scott v. Sandford, 60 U.S. (19 How.) 393 (1856) the Supreme Court ruled, among other things, that even free blacks were not citizens within the meaning of the federal Constitution.
56. "The Law of the Constitution," p. 989.

UNPACKING PATRIARCHY:
Reproduction, Sexuality, Originalism, and Constitutional Change

Rhonda Copelon

In 1970, a collective of feminist lawyers and activists in the burgeoning abortion rights movement filed the first women's rights challenge to the criminal abortion laws.[1] Rather than envisioning abortion as a doctor's professional prerogative, as earlier cases and the major reform bills in the state legislatures had done, this case put women's right to control their bodies and lives at center stage. In the legislatures women had to break into an ongoing dialogue between male legislators and experts, but in court women could determine the agenda and focus on their experience, need, and entitlement to control reproduction.

This coalescence of the second wave of the feminist movement in the late 1960s around the demand for legal abortion and the effort to win constitutional protection for women's decisions about reproduction transformed a social reform movement for legal abortion led by doctors, family planners, and population controllers into a human rights struggle. As Ellen Willis wrote later, "It was the feminist demand for the *unconditional right to abortion* that galvanized women and *created effective pressure for legislation.*"[2] The conceptualization of abortion as a woman's right, and its acceptance by the court as such in *Roe* v. *Wade,* has contributed to both the virulence of the opposition and the empowerment of women.

Now, barely fifteen years after the qualified articulation of a woman's right to abortion in *Roe* v. *Wade,*[3] that right is in mortal jeopardy. Absent a broad and successful movement against confirmation of a conservative Reagan nominee, *Roe* v. *Wade* is likely to be reversed by a new majority or so severely curtailed as to make legal abortion accessible only to the most privileged.[4]

It is a cruel irony that this pivotal change in the personnel of the Court comes after the political effort to reverse *Roe* v. *Wade* has peaked. The campaign against abortion, spearheaded by the Roman Catholic church and joined by Protestant fundamentalists, has had its terrible successes, particularly the Court's decisions permitting legislatures to deny abortion funding to poor women and to predicate a teenage girl's right on parental approval or a judicial shaming ceremony. On the question of the legality of abortion, however, the majority of five has stood firm despite two efforts in Congress to enact constitutional amendments, as well as a spate of academic criticism attacking the Court's power to recognize a right to abortion.

In 1986, a bare majority in *Thornburgh* v. *American College of Obstetricians and Gynecologists* rejected Solicitor General Charles Fried's plea on behalf of the Reagan administration that *Roe* be overruled. Fried argued that neither the original Constitution nor the Fourteenth Amendment provides any warrant for a right to abortion, characterizing it as the product of roaming judicial imagination rather than historical intention or permissible interpretation.[5] In a powerful decision by Justice Blackmun, the majority responded that if abortion were not within the realm of constitutionally protected privacy, women would be denied equality in matters of the utmost significance to individual liberty, dignity, and autonomy. Justices White and Rehnquist, in dissent, agreed with the solicitor general and emphasized the need for fidelity to the constitutional text and the principles discernible from it.

By contrast, on the question of sexual self-determination, a majority of the Court has rejected, indeed denounced, a right to homosexual intimacy. Several weeks after *Thornburgh*, a different bare majority, in *Bowers* v. *Hardwick*, rejected the challenge of a gay man arrested in his bedroom, upholding a Georgia statute that punishes heterosexual and homosexual sodomy by a term of 1 to 20 years.[6] Justice White's majority opinion echoed his dissent in *Thornburgh* and disdained a right of sexual intimacy for homosexuals. In reasoning that as easily could have been applied to sustain miscegenation laws twenty years ago, White adopted uncritically the history of criminal sodomy laws (originally designed to enforce the injunction to procreate) and the fact of a long tradition of moralistic disapproval. Justice Blackmun wrote a beautiful, indeed landmark, dissent recognizing that the right to choose one's intimate relationships is central to the authenticity of personal life and equally protected for lesbians and gay men as it is for those who conform to the heterosexual norm:

> Only the most willful blindness could obscure the fact that sexual intimacy is a "sensitive, key relationship of human existence, central to family life, community welfare, and the development of the personality" . . . The fact that individuals define themselves in a significant way through their intimate sexual relationships with others suggests, in a Nation as diverse as ours, that there may be many "right" ways of conducting those relationships, and that much of the richness of a relationship will come from the freedom an individual has to choose the form and nature of these intensely personal bonds.[7]

Thus at the very point when one part of the Court is moving toward articulating the rights of reproductive and sexual autonomy in feminist terms—as an aspect of equality and not simply privacy—the other part is calling for the rejection of most or all constitutional protection. The eight current members of the Court are evenly divided on this fundamental question. Justice Powell cast the deciding vote to make *Thornburgh* a victory and *Hardwick* a travesty. The division highlights, and his resignation underscores, the fragile state of constitutional protection for reproductive autonomy and the depth of antagonism to sexual freedom.

In the rest of this essay I will examine the progress in, as well as the inadequacy of development toward, a right of reproductive and sexual autonomy. First, it is essential, particularly in light of the current threat to the Court, to refute the originalist critique of *Roe* v. *Wade* and its progeny. By understanding the gendered nature of the rights chosen by the framers for inclusion in the Bill of Rights, the infirmity of the originalist position, and the necessity of judicial interpretation to include rights of significance to women, become apparent.

Second, I will look at the influence of the original understanding on the Court's choice and elaboration of the right of privacy as the vehicle for protection of intimate matters. The creation of a right of privacy was a significant, albeit cautious, innovation that has been evolving toward recognition of the affirmative importance of personal autonomy with regard to reproduction. At the same time, the original gendered understanding has shaped and limited the development of the right of privacy. In particular, the right of privacy tends to embody, and has in the prevailing opinions of the Court been interpreted as, a qualified negative right, reinforcing the public/private distinction and producing a highly truncated concept of autonomy.

Finally, I will look at the relationship of privacy to a broader vision more consonant with a feminist understanding of rights and the social transformation feminism requires. I suggest that the principle of equality—equality of result rather than simple equality of opportunity—provides a more encompassing framework for feminist goals. Rather than trash privacy or be constrained by it, however, it is essential to appreciate the dialectical relationship between privacy and equality that is part of the broader dialectic between social agitation, transformation, and legal change.

Patriarchy and the Original Understanding

The opposition to abortion and sexual freedom parades as a seemingly neutral issue—that of the role of the Court in our system of government. If a new majority overrules or retreats from *Roe* v. *Wade,* it will be explicitly predicated not on the fetal rights claim that has fueled the popular movement, nor on an avowed refusal to accede full personhood to women, but on the claim that, in recognizing a right of privacy encompassing abortion or procreative autonomy, the Court overstepped the limits of its power under the original Constitution. In view of the Bicentennial and the threat of a dramatic rollback in the Court, it is important to expose the premises as well as the implications of this effort to delegitimate the recognition of sexual and reproductive self-determination as a constitutionally protected interest.

Since its inception, the Reagan administration has excoriated the civil rights decisions of the Supreme Court. It was not, however, until the spring of 1985 that Attorney General Edwin Meese unveiled a theory to advance his social goals.[8] Adapted from conservative judges and constitutional scholars into a political program,[9] the banner of this campaign is originalism: the notion that the text of the Constitution and the particular historical meaning the framers would give to that text define the outer limits of the judicial function.[10]

Originalism obscures the critical value choices at issue, cloaking the kind of society it would produce in a spurious debate about the usurpation of majoritarian preferences by a nonelected judiciary—as if legislative majorities invariably reflect either the people's preferences or democratic principles. Originalism creates a popular mythology that casts the "Founding Fathers" as the font of wisdom, the bearers of the true word, the secular gods. It sets up the patriarchs against the pretenders in much the same way as religious fundamentalism attacks the legitimacy of secular humanism. The fact that the founders wrote slavery into the Constitution while excluding women and the unpropertied from citizenship is not often discussed in the new quasireligious invocation of original authority.

The goal of the originalist campaign is less to establish a consistent principle for decision-making than to create the appearance of unassailable authority and value-neutrality. Within the judicial process, neither the solicitor general nor the Justices who share his view contend that a strict originalist position is tenable. Rather, originalism is invoked to justify a heightened emphasis on traditional views and uncritical deference, as in *Hardwick,* to history when that serves the conservative position. Originalism is applied, in fact, with great selectivity.

The administration's version of originalism is extreme and its implications sweeping. Ignoring the radical restructuring of federal power intended by the framers of the Fourteenth Amendment, Meese would have the courts vitiate the process of incorporating the basic guarantees of the Bill of Rights into the Fourteenth Amendment in order to restrict state power. The right to due process, to criticize governmental action, or to worship or not as one pleases would then rest not on the Constitution but on the grace of state and local officials. Originalism is invoked to restrict the meaning of the Fourteenth Amendment to eliminate constitutional protection for all but racial groups. The idea of originalism is being trained upon the judicial power to expand the scope of rights and to fashion such critical equitable remedies as Miranda warnings, suppression of illegal evidence, busing, and affirmative action.

A centerpiece of the originalist assault on the Constitution has been the Court's decision in *Roe* v. *Wade* and its power to recognize unenumerated rights, i.e., rights that are not explicitly articulated in the Constitution. The originalist underscores the absence of an explicit textual guarantee of a right to privacy embracing abortion or sexuality. Yet even this aspect of the originalist attack is highly selective since there are a number of unenumerated rights, not all of them under attack. The right to travel interstate, or to send one's children to private school, for example, occasioned little consternation when identified by the Court and are rarely alluded to in the tirades against judicial usurpation today. Neither the solicitor general nor Justice White question the validity of recognizing contraception in the context of marital sexual intimacy. Not surprisingly, it is those unenumerated rights that concern the sphere of personal life and that challenge traditional views of sexuality, the role of women, and the hegemony of the heterosexual nuclear family that draw the fire.

Examination of the ideology and social organization that shaped the Constitution is essential to exposing the values that underlie the originalist pretension to neutral denunciation of these rights. The patriarchal structure of society and the family in the eighteenth and nineteenth centuries illuminates the deeply gendered nature of the rights that emerged from this social ordering and explains the silence of the Constitution on matters affecting reproduction and sexuality. It helps to expose the illegitimacy of the originalist insistence on textual specificity, as well as the resistance to making the connections between the original freedoms and the new claims. It also provides insight into the current choice and limitations of privacy as the doctrinal shelter for sexuality and reproduction.

The Gendered Matrix of the Constitution

Consider the legal and ideological norms affecting women, reproduction, and sexuality that animated the framers of the original Constitution.[11] It is not insignificant that the framers accepted slavery and with it the objectification of slaves as property, the denial to human beings of possession of themselves. Nonslave women, though privileged by comparison, were also treated in law as a species of property. They were destined to marry and, under the common law (which prevailed until the mid-nineteenth century) a married woman had no will or identity in law separate from her husband. She was deemed to be in a state of coverture that suspended her legal existence and thereby her ability to own property, to contract, to do business, or to participate in political life.[12]

Woman was also the sexual and reproductive property of her husband. He was entitled to beat her with a rod no wider than his thumb (the dubious origin of the "rule of thumb"). He could not in law rape her because she owed him sexual service—an exemption from the rape laws that persists in twenty-four states today. A husband could sue his wife's sexual partners for damages (a legal claim called "criminal conversation"), and the crime of adultery was defined as sexual relations with a married woman. In a society that needed people, sex was for reproduction, although there is ample evidence of women's strategies for limiting or spacing childbearing. Interestingly, abortion was legal at least until quickening. It was, however, mainly the resort of the single woman, thereby functioning, together with the panoply of laws and customs, to restrict legitimate propagation to marriage—and inheritance to the husband's bloodline.

Deviations from legitimate procreative sex, including adultery, sodomy (heterosexual as well as homosexual), and bestiality, were closely monitored by the community and subject to severe sanctions as the common law took over the functions of the canon law. Departures from procreative sex were viewed as errant episodes, not a way of life. Because the household was, until the Industrial Revolution, the unit for both production and reproduction, a homosexual identity or subculture—a different sexuality as a lifestyle—was impossible. It did not emerge until the nineteenth century when the growth of wage-labor gave people, primarily men, the possibility of anonymity in the city and material independence from their biological families. The legally sanctioned organization of private life was thus patriarchal and heterosexual, leavened only by the power of the equity courts to recognize property or commercial rights in women, the discretion of religious and civil authorities to mitigate the severe punishments dictated for moral offenses, and the needs of husbands for the cooperation of a "helpmeet."

This public ordering of personal life depended on maintaining the gender hierarchy, and thus a gender dichotomy, in all aspects of life. In the tenets of coverture as well as the predominant heritage of the Enlightenment, women were denied any role in public life. The education of women was not for intellectual pursuit but interpersonal nurture. Though women and men worked interdependently in the household, the notion of men and women as having distinct roles was essential to justifying the system. Articulate or independent women, who were forced by, or took the opportunity of, the Revolutionary War to transcend dependency and the domestic sphere, were commonly reviled as "masculine." At the same time, the keepers of republican virtue denounced bourgeois consumption as "effeminacy" in men. Abigail Adams' private plea to her husband to "Remember the Ladies" by eliminating from law the tyranny of husbands in the private realm and the exclusion of women from the public realm drew a revealing retort from him:

> As to your extraordinary code of laws, I cannot but laugh! . . . [W]e know better than to repeal our masculine systems. Although they are in full force, you know they are little more than theory. . . . We have only the name of masters, and rather than give up this which would completely subject us to the despotism of the petticoat, I hope General Washington and all our brave heroes would fight.[13]

A Gendered Set of Rights

The assumed ineligibility of women to vote and thereby to participate in the polity created by the Constitution is only the most obvious problem of gender discrimination. Equally important is the fact that the rights chosen to be included in the Bill of Rights protected what was then exclusively male activity and male authority.

The predominant concern of the Bill of Rights was with protecting activity in the public sphere. Freedom of speech and the press, the right to bear arms, freedom from self-incrimination, cruel, and unusual punishment, and the protections of due process emerged from the political processes of a revolution in which men, not women, were the recognized actors. Men were likewise the intended beneficiaries of the protection of private property since women acquired control over property only as an exception (largely through widowhood) to the rule of coverture.

The Constitution protected the private realm by guarding the threshold of the home (through the rules against search and seizure and the quartering of soldiers), and thereby the sphere in which culture and law gave authoritative predominance to men.[14] The recognition in recent court cases that woman is a separate autonomous adult in the household would have been completely inconsistent with the premise of coverture, as well as with the procreative imperative. Only the right of religious conscience—obedience to a higher patriarch—was permitted to women.

My argument is not that the rights articulated in the Bill of Rights are quintessentially male or that they have no meaning to women, but rather that they reflected what was important to men—in particular, white, propertied men—and to the maintenance of both their freedom and power. Conversely, the silence of the Constitution on a right to bear children, or a right of bodily integrity explicit enough to embrace abortion or sexual self-determination, cannot be disconnected from the devalued status of women, the preeminence awarded to the public sphere of male activity, or the unquestioned hegemony of the heterosexual family and the prerogatives of the *pater familias* in the private sphere. The original Constitution's silence—or its failure to enumerate rights affecting woman in her person or activities—thus reflected and reinforced the largely unquestioned gender hierarchy and heterosexual norm in both the public and private spheres.[15]

The Fourteenth Amendment is likewise silent on reproduction[16] and sexuality because the basic patriarchal organization survived the first wave of the feminist movement.[17] While the Married Women's Property Acts of the mid-nineteenth century gave women limited rights to hold and exchange property in their own name, the suffragist demand for political equality was defeated.[18] Industrialization led to the development—to which feminists contributed—of a bourgeois ideology of separate spheres that celebrated women's domesticity. While this elevated the status and authority of middle-class women within the home, it also heightened women's essential differentness. Paradoxically, then, the cult of domesticity provided a basis for women to go out of the home to seek education and engage in social welfare agitation in the political sphere at the same time that it heightened the ideological split between male and female natures as well as between the public (male) and the private (female) spheres.

In the late nineteenth century, the Court seized upon this dichotomy to retard change in women's status. In response to feminist efforts to use the privileges and immunities clause of the Fourteenth Amendment as a vehicle to acquire rights of citizenship and participation in the public realm for women, Supreme Court decisions began to inscribe the notion of women's difference into law. Justice Bradley's now infamous concurring opinion justified Myra Bradwell's exclusion from the bar in the following terms:

> The civil law as well as nature itself, has always recognized a wide difference in the respective spheres and destinies of man and woman. Man is, or should be women's protector and defender. The natural and proper timidity and delicacy which belongs to the female sex evidently unfits it for many of the occupations of civil life. . . . The constitution of the family organization, which is founded in the divine ordinance, as well as in the nature of things, indicated the domestic sphere as that which properly belongs to the domain and functions of womanhood. The harmony, not to say identity, of interests and views which belong, or should belong, to the family institution is repugnant to the idea of a woman adopting a distinct and independent career from that of her husband.[19]

Judicial approval of protective labor laws for women only emphasized the special role and special weakness of women.[20] Indeed, the separate sphere ideology was so powerful that even after the Nineteenth Amendment had given women the vote, they were excluded from jury service (notwithstanding that juries were selected from qualified voters) because the Nineteenth Amendment "conferred the suffrage on an entirely new class of human beings."[21] Though references to divinity diminished in later decisions, the notion of woman as properly subject to different treatment and legal disabilities because she is by nature the center of home and family life survived until 1971.[22]

Thus the originalist adherence to the particular meaning of a Constitution structured by and for the nineteenth century is hardly value-free. Yet this reverence for the original understanding denies the personhood, if not the existence, of women by privileging a very limited set of rights drawn from and tailored to male experience. That the revolutionaries who designed the Constitution or the republicans who led the fight for the Fourteenth Amendment intended to bind future generations by the literal limits of their own understanding of oppression is a dubious proposition at best.[23] Indeed, the originalists' contention that the particular historical meaning must govern constitutional interpretation for all time is only one interpretation of the framers' intent. There is ample evidence that in using such sweeping and indeterminate concepts as liberty and equality, the framers envisioned constitutional interpretation as a process of evolving the concrete meaning of these values rather than freezing them.[24] Even if the framers were so crabbed and unimaginative as the originalists contend, it would still be encumbent on succeeding generations to make a choice—political and ethical—whether to obey the letter as opposed to the spirit of the Constitution. The Court made a choice to uphold slavery in the Dred Scott case while wrapping itself in the flag of originalism.[25] The resurrection of the originalist position today likewise flows from a political choice, not a constitutional mandate.

The originalist counters that the scope of protectible rights can be modified, but only by the supermajoritarian process of amending the Constitution. To so constrain the ability of the Constitution to evolve would, however, turn the Bill of Rights on its head—from a protection, however imperfect, of minoritarian rights into a protection of only those rights that majoritarian legislatures are unlikely to challenge. This would preserve virtually in perpetuity the original hierarchies of privilege based on race, gender, and class that underlay the original Constitution and Civil War amendments and that continue to affect contemporary laws and attitudes. If the Bill of Rights is to protect minoritarian rights, it is more appropriate to permit judicially recognized rights to stand unless a supermajority coalesces to eliminate them through amending the Constitution.

To give constitutional protection to reproductive and sexual autonomy is thus not an excess of the interpretive power of the Court but the necessary exercise of such a power in a society where gender equality has emerged as a fundamental tenet. Recognition of rights not enumerated or contemplated by the original framers is part of the process of making visible the previously invisible, of including the excluded, of filling in gaps that are irreconcilable with equal justice.[26] The power to recognize rights must be grounded in a sense of justice derived from the interplay among original values, changed historical conditions, and evolving insights about liberty and equality. The women's and lesbian/gay movements have, like the abortionist and civil rights movements before them, made new connections between old promises and current oppressions. They have elucidated the connection between the new rights of sexual and reproductive autonomy and the textual guarantees of expression, association, bodily integrity, the privacy of the home, gender equality, and the rule against involuntary servitude.[27] The logic of these connections becomes accessible to those who, through experience, empathy, or ethical insight, understand the deep and systemic significance of their nonrecognition. The originalists would short-circuit the very effort to embrace new understandings.

Privacy and the Original Understanding: Wedge and Residue

The original understanding and the social matrix that created it shed important light on the resistance to, and limitations of, current doctrinal developments. The fundamental paradox of constitutional change is that evolving conceptions of equality must be fit into a structure whose original premises have generated powerful institutional and ideological constraints. The feminist project for the revision of the Constitution and society requires challenging a deeply ingrained ideology in which gender difference, heterosexism,[28] and the separation of the public and the private spheres are inextricably intertwined. Reproductive and sexual autonomy are a critical aspect of this challenge. But the articulation by the Court of a right of privacy as the vehicle for their protection is double-edged. On the one hand, it has constrained the ability of legislatures to maintain— through both intervention and nonintervention—the patriarchical order. On the other hand, it has reinforced the original distinction between public and private that has been essential to the patriarchal differentiation of male from female, the family from the state and market, the superior from the inferior, the measure from the other.

From the beginning, feminist attorneys, echoing the movement's insistence on the right of women to control childbearing, sought abortion rights not simply as a matter of privacy but more importantly as fundamental to women's liberty.[29] The movement made the analogy between forced pregnancy and slavery, and some feminist attorneys have sought to elucidate the Thirteenth Amendment implications of criminal abortion laws.[30] Feminists elaborated the early idea that abortion is essential to women's equality in terms both of full personhood and the capacity to participate in society,[31] and emphasized the disproportionate toll of criminalization on the poor. Feminist activists have also linked the right to terminate an unwanted pregnancy with the right of women to be sexual, free of either the patriarchal constraints of uncontrolled pregnancy or the mandate to be heterosexual.

With a few exceptions,[32] however, abortion rights advocates have been wary of the sexuality argument, even though antagonism to women's sexual freedom is the leitmotif of the attack on abortion. Thus it has been left principally to the lesbian/gay movement to confront the volatile issue of sexual autonomy. The right of privacy has figured prominently in gay rights litigation, in part because the doctrine of privacy was well established when this work began and in part because the lesbian/gay movement, like the mainstream women's and abortion rights movement,[33] has given privacy center stage in its own advocacy. Lesbian/gay advocates have also sought, largely unsuccessfully, to apply the constitutional guarantee of equal protection to discrimination based on sexual orientation. There has, however, been very little attention to gender equality as an argument against this discrimination (and the few cases that have tried it have failed).[34] Privacy, in part because of its success and in part because of its broad appeal, has emerged as the predominant argument for reproductive and sexual rights advocates.

Against this array of available theories, however, it is significant that the Court chose privacy as the vehicle for protecting contraception and abortion. The selection of privacy over the more affirmative notion of liberty can be explained in part as a way for the Court to distinguish protections for personal liberty from the repudiated use of the concept of liberty of contract under the due process clause to defend economic privilege against social welfare legislation.[35] The effort to navigate the shoals of economic liberty does not fully explain the choice of privacy, however, since the Court ultimately treated privacy as an aspect of substantive liberty protected by due process.

Rather, the choice of privacy is the progeny of the original patriarchal dichotomy between public and private that has survived in liberal thought. Privacy was compatible with the common law tradition of noninterference in the marital home, a tradition that denied legal relief to women from economic and physical abuse by their husband and thereby assured the dominance of men in the home. Privacy reinforces the idea that the personal is separate from the political, implying that the individual freedom to differ has no significant impact on the larger social structure and that the larger social structure has no impact on the realm of private choice. Privacy calls for toleration of otherness, thereby perpetuating the original hierarchy of norms rather than embracing and celebrating diversity, and privacy assumes that the individual is isolated and self-sufficient, not one to whom society bears affirmative responsibility.[36] This notion of privacy appealed to a broad constituency favoring contraception and abortion: the doctors who urged decriminalization on the basis of the privacy of physician/patient relationship; the family planners who sought, among other things, to rationalize marriage; the population controllers who wanted only to discourage childbearing; and the libertarians who insist that in exchange for being left alone a person should ask nothing from society by the way of support.

In the twenty-three years since the right of privacy was first suggested by the Court, there has emerged a sharp tension between the liberal idea of privacy as the negative and qualified right to be let alone as long as nothing too significant is at stake and the more radical idea of privacy as an affirmative liberty of self-determination and an aspect of equal personhood. Before turning to the constraining application and implications of privacy doctrine, it is crucial to examine, both practically and theoretically, its progressive role, as well as the role of feminist understanding in shaping the Court's formulation of the meaning of privacy in this sphere.

Privacy as Wedge

Pragmatically, there is probably no decision that has had as a profound an impact on women's lives as *Roe* v. *Wade*. Legalization of abortion transformed unwanted pregnancy from a potentially life-shattering event into one over which a women could take rightful control. Abortion was no longer a life-endangering, desperate, criminal, and stigmatizing experience but rather a safe, legitimate health-care option. The right to abortion recognized women as decision-makers, as agents of their destiny.

Abortion is also a necessary, through insufficient, precondition for liberating female sexuality. By removing for many heterosexual women the duty or terror of unwanted pregnancy, legal abortion has alleviated the repression and shame of female sexual desire.[37] By permitting the separation of sexuality and reproduction, abortion indirectly affirmed the right of lesbians to be sexually self-determining.

On the theoretical level, privacy has evolved into a doctrine that has undermined patriarchal control by men, and to a lesser extent by the state, over women's reproduction. And despite the rejection of sexual autonomy in *Hardwick*, Justice Blackmun's dissent for four members of the Court, which recognized the positive value of sexual self-definition, is a powerful challenge to the heterosexual norm.

The notion of an independent right of privacy was first suggested in *Griswold* v. *Connecticut* to protect marital intimacy and the use of contraceptives.[38] Although a significant innovation in constitutional law, particularly at a time when Comstockery ran deep, marital privacy has operated historically to reinforce patriarchal power.

The subsequent recognition that the married couple consists of two independent persons was far more radical.[39] It began the transformation of the family in constitutional law from a corporate body or unit, with privacy protecting the male-controlled entity, into an association of separate individuals, each of whom has a separate claim to constitutional protection.[40] The journey from familial privacy to individual autonomy was further advanced with the Court's rejection of the power of a husband/father to veto an abortion.[41] That a married woman has an independent right to decide significant questions affecting her life sounded the deathknell for the concept of merger at the heart of coverture.

A similar evolution occurred in relation to woman's role in the abortion decision. Just as the caution or conservatism of the Court was expressed in the first contraception case by emphasizing the sacredness of marital intimacy, so when the Court first recognized the right to abortion (in *Roe* v. *Wade*), it described the decision as the physician's.[42] However, women (and many of the doctors who assisted them) believe that the decision whether to bear a child is in the first instance a conscientious and not a medical decision. Feminist attorneys have insisted, and the Court has clarified, that the woman is the source of the abortion decision. Although doctors still exercise considerable control over the conditions under which abortion is performed,[43] the need for medical legitimation of the decision has diminished.

Interestingly, the Court's most forceful articulation of the right to abortion came in response to the most serious challenge to its legitimacy: the Reagan administration's request in *Thornburgh* that the Court overrule *Roe* v. *Wade*. In response, Justice Blackmun wrote:

> Few decisions are more personal and intimate, more properly private, or more basic to individual dignity and autonomy, than a woman's decision—with the guidance of her physician and with the limits specific in *Roe*—whether to end her pregnancy. A woman's right to make that choice freely is fundamental. Any other result, in our view, would protect inadequately a central part of the sphere of liberty that our law guarantees to all.[44]

This formulation of the abortion right is doubly significant because it situates the right to make autonomous decisions about childbearing in the context of equality. That women should have the right to abortion is not an instance of special treatment; it is instead an extension of the basic principle of liberty and possession of the self to women. The opinion reflects, for the first time, a deeply feminist understanding of the necessity of the abortion right to women's full personhood.[45] It is significant that when the challenge to abortion rights intensifies, it is the feminist argument for self-determination rather than the liberal idea of being left alone that comes to the fore.

The doctrine of privacy has thus evolved in important ways toward recognizing the autonomy of woman as the foundation of the abortion right.[46] The right to abortion has the potential to emerge not simply as the right to be left alone, but as a right to be self-determining. This is a critical distinction for the feminist critique of privacy. A mere right to be let alone reinforces the traditional liberal dichotomy between the public and private, between the state and family. It is invoked against state intervention that is necessary to protect autonomy and well-being.[47] By contrast, privacy as the protector of self-determination is a radical and deeply important idea for women. It enables women to envision themselves as rightfully sovereign over themselves, as agents of their own lives.[48]

The idea of women as decision-makers about reproduction, as subjects of their own destinies, also has important implications for social policy. It contrasts sharply with the traditional view of women as objects of male need or state imperative. Slave women were at the mercy of the masters' desire for sex and the production of new slaves. The "free" women of colonial and postrevolutionary America were expected (by laws prohibiting nonprocreative sex), encouraged (by custom and dependency), and sometimes coerced (by chastisement) to serve the sexual and reproductive needs of their husbands and the developing society.

In the nineteenth century, the states began to formulate explicit class-differentiated policies to control reproduction and population. Criminal abortion laws, effective by the end of the century, were addressed to white Anglo-Saxon middle-class women who had begun to assert a right to limit motherhood.[49] Conversely, a movement for the eugenic sterilization of the "unfit," directed at immigrants, minorities, and the disabled, took hold.[50] By contrast, the recognition of a right to abortion requires, for the first time, that reproductive policies and laws take account of the right of women to self-determination. As shall be seen in the next part, however, reproductive self-determination remains a sharply qualified principle.

Unfortunately, only four justices are willing to extend the right of privacy to embrace sexual autonomy.[51] Apart from marital sexual intercourse, the Court has refused even to recognize *heterosexual* sexual expression as a positive right. Legalization of contraception was based, not on a right to be sexual, but on the impermissibility of "prescrib[ing] pregnancy and the birth of an unwanted child as punishment for fornication, a misdemeanor."[52] By consistently refusing to question the validity of fornication and adultery statutes, the Court laid the foundation for upholding the criminalization of consensual sodomy between people of the same sex.[53]

Nonetheless, Justice Blackmun's dissent in *Hardwick,* perhaps the most far-reaching of his career, elaborated further the positive meaning of privacy. Privacy, he suggested, means not simply that the state should not interfere with cloistered sexuality, but that the

Constitution should protect sexual intimacy affirmatively and respect difference because the process of sexual and familial self-definition is central to authenticity and self-realization.[54]

Despite the efforts of opponents of abortion and sexual freedom to trivialize these rights,[55] Justice Blackmun's decision in *Thornburgh* and his dissent in *Hardwick,* have, for the first time, ranked self-determination in intimate matters as an equality concern and as equivalent in importance to the intellectual.[56] In so elevating the personal to constitutional *importance,* as opposed to mere constitutional *tolerance,* Blackmun challenged the original understanding by integrating the interpersonal, traditionally associated with the female sphere, into a Constitution designed exclusively to protect the male sphere.

Privacy as Residue of the Original Understanding

Notwithstanding the potential for transforming privacy into positive liberty, prevailing opinions have implemented privacy as no more than a very circumscribed right to be let alone. As a means of eliminating criminal sanctions, a negative right of privacy, when successful, provides a foothold from which to seek broader legitimacy. It is thus no small matter that the Court both legalized abortion and refused to invalidate the criminalization of homosexual sodomy. But the fact that the traditional idea of privacy is negative and defensive reinforces rather than undermines the power of the original patriarchal order in at least two ways: (1) it renders privacy a weak vehicle for challenging the hegemony of traditional norms of behavior, and (2) it denies the relationship of social conditions and public responsibility to the ability of the individual to exercise autonomy.

Privacy and the Hegemony of Traditional Norms

The traditional theory of privacy protects the right to differ from majoritarian norms where there is no deleterious impact on others.

Private choices are tolerable because they are of little consequence to society or, as Justice White recently said of abortion, "the evil does not justify the evils of forbidding it."[57] Moreover, while society must tolerate difference, it need not either encourage it or desist from discouraging it.[58]

The negativity of privacy has consequences both for the development of constitutional protection and for the progress of a movement that relies too heavily on this. The privacy argument is appealing at first blush because of its lowest common denominator character. Theoretically, to accept that an activity is protected by privacy, a court need not renounce society's prejudices and a little breathing space is gained. But the position that "Even though homosexuality is disgusting or abortion is murder, we must allow it," or "It's okay to be homosexual as long as it doesn't show in public," carries prejudice and shame. The notion of privacy as the protection of sexual difference reinforces the exclusion of sexual minorities from the mainstream and thus reinforces the traditional hierarchy, as well as the fear of exclusion. Privacy as it was argued before the Court in *Hardwick* was the right to be an exception as long as this was within the home or duly cloistered. Thus the concept of privacy does not, at least in common parlance, allow for the expression of difference in everyday life.[59] It carves out an exception to the norm; it preserves deviance at the same time that it permits it.

Privacy, like originalism, erroneously purports to be a value-free basis for decision. The result in *Hardwick* demonstrates, however, that the agnosticism of privacy as to the value of the protected activity does not survive where prejudice is deep. Justice Burger made clear his hostility by quoting Blackstone's description of sodomy as " 'the infamous crime against nature,' as an offense of 'deeper malignity' than rape . . ."[60] Justice White's opinion for the majority was more sanitized but equally barbed. He compared sodomy to the possession of "drugs, firearms, or stolen goods," and dismissed the claim that there is a relationship between homosexuality and the protected realm of family, marriage, and procreation as "facetious."[61] Even Justice Powell, though disinclined to imprison gay people, was content to maintain the stigma of criminality.[62]

These opinions indicate indirectly that *Hardwick* lost because of the perception that same sex intimacy is dangerous to the public order. Homosexuality threatens gender identity, the expectation of heterosexuality, and the power relations it embodies. A heterosexist culture will go to elaborate lengths to construct distinct gender identities as well as the propensity toward heterosexuality.[63] It may be that the very fragility of the channeled sexual self heightens the danger presented by crossing the line, that precisely because sexual identity and heterosexuality are not ordained but choosable,[64] those who deviate from the heterosexual norm must be stigmatized and excluded.[65]

Same-sex relationships also threaten the traditional hegemony of men in the sexual pecking order. Just as Justice Burger thinks homosexual sodomy worse than rape, the possibility of homosexual solicitation is treated more harshly than the sexual harrassment of women.[66] Moreover, the potential for women to have sexual pleasure and to construct relationships and communities without men changes the balance of sexual power.[67]

The sense in which the *Hardwick* majority is right highlights the shortsightedness of relying on a negative right of privacy. Sexual self-determination must cross the bounds of privacy, for autonomy cannot be realized apart from social interaction. While privacy implies secrecy and shame, the choice of sexual partners of the same sex is no more intrinsically private than the identity of a person's spouse. Nor is this choice easily confined to the private realm of the bed or the closet. It involves not only sexual but also familial and social identity—who one is in public as well as in private, and what the legal norms are. To accept mere tolerance of sexual difference is not only degrading; it is ultimately self-defeating.

Privacy and the Legitimation of Social Irresponsibility

Privacy is also deficient as a theory for reproduction and sexual self-determination because it presumes that the right to choose is inherent in the individual rather than shaped, and potentially denied, by social conditions. As Rosalind Petchesky reminds us, women exercise reproductive choice under the constraint of *material conditions* that set limits on "natural" reproductive processes—for example, existing birth control methods and technology and access to them; class divisions and the distribution of financing of health care; nutrition and employment, particularly of women; and the state of the economy generally. And she does so within a specific network of social relations and social arrangements involving herself, her sexual partners, her children and kin, neighbors, doctors, family planners, birth control providers, manufacturers, employers, the church and the state.[68]

The right of privacy not only disassociates the individual from this broader context; it also exempts the state from the responsibility for fostering material conditions and social relations that facilitate autonomous decision-making.

Nowhere is this negative aspect of privacy theory more clearly or cruelly demonstrated than in the Court's decisions permitting the state to deny Medicaid funding for abortion. The decisions recognize that by funding childbirth and not abortion the state is seeking to influence private choice. They also recognize that the absence of funding will make it "difficult, if not impossible," for some poor women to implement their choice. But the Court treats both the intent and effect of this policy as constitutionally irrelevant because the inability to obtain an abortion flows not from an obstacle created by the state but rather from the fact of the woman's "indigency . . . [which] is neither created nor in any way affected by the . . . [Medicaid] regulation."[69] Not only does the negative right of privacy carry no corresponding state obligation to facilitate choice, but the integrity of the decision-making process is not protected even against purposeful manipulation.[70]

To treat a woman's poverty and her inability to exercise choice as a consequence not of public policy but of private fault is an erroneous and dangerous fiction built upon the traditional separation of the public and private spheres. It rests on the idea, central to capitalist patriarchy, that the family unit has the responsibility of being economically self-sufficient. Not only does privatization permit the state to escape responsibility for the tragic conditions of people's lives. The ideology of private responsibility also makes it possible to blame the poor, who are overwhelmingly women, for their inability to be self-sufficient.

It is a small step, as the Medicaid cases indicate, from blame to control. The Court is explicit that where exercise of the right of privacy depends on public resources, moralistic disapproval or demographic considerations will justify its destruction.[71] Moreover, by attributing dependency to individual failure, the need to examine the feasibility and fairness of the original functions assigned to the family, and to remedy them, is avoided.

The gap between a private right of choice and autonomy widens when we consider the broad range of factors that influence (and in many cases determine) women's choices about reproduction. The prevalence of economically influenced abortions and the sterilization campaigns against poor, minority, and disabled women illustrate that autonomy is impossible without the eradication of discrimination and poverty. Autonomy presupposes a society in which both the workforce and the family are restructured to encourage gender-neutral, same-sex, and communal childrearing. Autonomy also requires a society that guarantees to all the preconditions for self-realization, including shelter, food, day care, health care, education, and the possibility of meaningful work, relationships, and participation in political and social life.

Autonomy with regard to sexual self-determination is likewise inseparable from material and ideological conditions. It depends on redistributing power between the sexes, as well as on dismantling heterosexism. The continuing economic and social reality of male power and female dependency, as well as their translation into male aggression and female passivity in the sexual realm, complicate the ability of women to make autonomous choices about their intimate sexual and familial relations. The possibility of choosing to live one's life as gay or lesbian did not emerge until social conditions permitted independence from the traditional family, and this choice will not be fully guaranteed until the right to express sexual identity is recognized and materially supported.

Thus to protect a "right to choose" without assuring the social conditions necessary to foster autonomous choice creates an appearance of autonomy where it cannot exist. The full capacity for autonomy may not be magically achieved, even with the eradication of gender, sexual, race, and class discrimination; but autonomy cannot be assured short of major social transformation. The idea of privacy obscures the necessity of public responsibility to bring this transformation about.

Conclusion: The Potential of Equality

The extensive social transformation needed if autonomy is to be guaranteed cannot be accomplished through the mechanism of judicial recognition or enforcement of rights. Rather, it requires a multifaceted strategy to eradicate discrimination and change the nature of the family and the market, and the relationship between them. Nonetheless, the ability, which the originalists deny, of our Constitution to embrace new insights about human rights is a critical component of the process of undoing oppression and empowering the excluded. Constitutionalization is important because it reflects not simply desirable social policy, but an ethical bottom line.

Just as the original Constitution arose from a particular social matrix, so does the evolving one. Material and ideological conditions lay the foundation for the demand for, and acceptability of, new rights.[72] And liberation movements, their activists and legal advocates, are an essential part of the forces that ultimately move the Court to take another tiny step forward.

It thus matters to constitutional development, as well as to the broader process of social change, how a movement and its advocates articulate its demands and its vision. While the notion of a right of privacy has substantively advanced reproductive and even sexual autonomy, it has also permitted their disconnection from the broader vision of equality that women's and lesbian/gay liberation requires. The danger is that the Court's mediated version of rights will become the measure of the movement's goals. The antidote is to recognize the dialectical character of the interaction between limited doctrine and broader visions, as well as between social activism and legal reform.[73]

In both legal and political advocacy for reproductive and sexual rights, privacy need not be jettisoned but it must be transformed into an affirmative right to self-determination and grounded in the broader principle of equality and in the concrete conditions of people's lives. Equality is important because it refutes the hierarchy of importance between the personal and the political and demands examination of the gendered assumptions that underlie this dichotomy. With regard to abortion, the equality principle would require recognition that forced pregnancy is involuntary servitude and that abortion is essential to women's full personhood and participation in all spheres of life. Moreover, equality attends to rather than ignores the social and material preconditions for the exercise of liberty. With regard to sexuality, equality does not simply carve out an exception to the heterosexual model; it challenges the hegemony of the model itself. Rather than a society in which heterosexuality is programmed and presumed, equality counsels genuine acceptance of sexual diversity to protect the expression of sexual difference as well as the possibility of authentic self-definition and intimacy for everyone.

Although equality is a more capacious theory for the protection of autonomy and intimate association, equality doctrine is currently (like that of privacy) negative and truncated.[74] Equality should not be judged by its doctrinal condition, but rather by its potential as an encompassing and ever evolving vision for advancing social as well as constitutional change.

The originalists, of course, would have cut off constitutional evolution long ago and would preclude the Court from the task of trying to hear the cries of pain and new stirrings for liberation. It is critical to defend the Court's ability to do that. The fact that the Court will invariably be inadequate to the task argues not against rights advocacy but against acceding to the adequacy or legitimacy of its limited formulations.

Notes

This article is a revision of a presentation delivered as part of the Rothstein Dickenson Memorial Lectures of the Chicago chapter of the National Lawyers' Guild. I am immensely grateful for the insightful comments of Susan Bryant, Howard Lesnick, Jules Lobel, Maureen McCafferty, Dorothy McCarrick, Rosalind Petchesky, Elizabeth Schneider, Nadine Taub, Sharon Thompson, Marilyn Young, and Patricia Williams.

1. The case, Abramowicz v. Lefkowitz, filed by three hundred women plaintiffs in January 1970 in federal district court, was withdrawn after the New York State legislature, by a margin of one, voted on April 3, 1970, to repeal restrictions on

abortion within the first twenty-four weeks of pregnancy. The work in this case provided the foundation for other feminist challenges to criminal abortion laws. The testimony, which provides fascinating reading, is excerpted in D. Schulder and F. Kennedy, *Abortion Rap* (New York, 1971).

2. Ellen Willis, *Village Voice*, 3 March 1980, p. 8; see also R. Petchesky, *Abortion and Women's Choice: The State, Sexuality, and Reproductive Freedom* (Boston, 1984), pp. 125–29.

3. 410 U.S. 113 (1973).

4. Justices White and Rehnquist have already called for the overruling of Roe v. Wade in their dissent in Thornburgh v. American College of Obstetricians and Gynecologists, 106 S. Ct. 2169 (1986). It is fully expected that Justice Scalia and Reagan's current nominee, Judge Robert Bork, if approved, would join them. Justice O'Conner thus becomes the critical fifth vote. Because she refused on procedural grounds to join Justices White and Rehnquist in Thornburgh, her position on that ultimate question is unknown. But the practical consequence of her current position is indistinguishable from theirs. She considers the potential of human life from the moment of conception to be a compelling reason for the state to restrict abortion and has voted to sustain every restriction on access to abortion that has come before the Court. Thus at best she might insist on an exception to criminal statutes in therapeutic cases. As to those states where the legislature cannot garner a majority for recriminalization, she would sustain a broad range of regulation that would make legal abortion as inaccessible as it was before Roe v. Wade to young, poor, and working-class women. (See City of Akron v. Akron Center for Reproductive Health, 462 U.S. 416, 452 [1983].)

Moreover, while some states will undoubtedly maintain abortion as legal, Congress, rid of the constitutional constraint of a fundamental right, may try to enact antiabortion legislation to override permissive state laws. In those states where abortion remains legal, it is predictable that unrestricted teen access and medical reimbursement will be jeopardized in the bargaining for legal abortion.

5. Brief for the United States as Amicus Curiae in Thornburgh v. ACOG.

6. Bowers v. Hardwick, 106 S. Ct. 2841 (1986).

7. Ibid., at 2841.

8. Address of Attorney General Edwin Meese, III, before the American Bar Association, 9 July 1985; see also Meese before the American Enterprise Institute, 6 September 1986.

9. See, e.g., Bork, "Neutral Principles and Some First Amendment Problems," 47 *Ind. L. J.* (1971); Rehnquist, "The Notion of a Living Constitution," 54 *Tex. L. Rev.* 693 (1976); R. Berger, *Government by Judiciary: The Transformation of the Fourteenth Amendment* (Boston, 1977).

10. Proponents of originalism differ, of course, on how to discern the framers' intent. None would or could confine the Court to the literal text because the text was purposely written in broad generalities that, for the most part, demand interpretation. Nor do originalists agree about how to interpret the "intention" or "understanding" of the framers because it is fundamentally indeterminate. Indeed, to focus on particular historical meaning, rather than the broad purposes of the framers, would lead to untenable and absurd results. For example, the debates on the Fourteenth Amendment could support an argument that the Court intended to invalidate the black codes but not school segregation. (See Bickel, "The Original Understanding and the Segregation Decision," 69 *Harv. L. Rev.* 1 [1955].)

11. The history that follows has drawn from the following ground breaking work: N.

Cott and E. Pleck, eds., *A Heritage of Her Own* (New York, 1979); N. Cott, *The Bonds of Womanhood: "Women's Sphere" in New England, 1780–1835* (New Haven, 1979); C. Degler, *At Odds: Women and the Family from the Revolution to the Present* (New York, 1970); J. D'Emilio, "Capitalism and Gay Identity," in *Powers of Desire: The Politics of Sexuality,* ed. A. Snitow, C. Stansell, and S. Thompson (New York, 1983); Freedman and D'Emilio, "Intimate Matters: A History of Sexuality in America," unpub. ms.; L. Gordon, *Woman's Body, Woman's Right* (New York, 1976), J. Katz, *Gay American History* (New York, 1976); J. Katz, *Almanac* (New York, 1983); L. Kerber, *Women of the Republic: Intellect and Ideology in Revolutionary America* (Chapel Hill, 1980); J. Mohr, *Abortion in America* (New York, 1978); M. Norton, *Liberty's Daughters: The Revolutionary Experience of American Women* (Boston, 1980); S. Okun, *Women in Western Political Thought* (Princeton, 1979); M. Ryan, *Womanhood in America: From Colonial Times to the Present* (3rd ed., New York, 1983); N. Taub and E. Schneider, "Perspectives on Women's Subordination and the Role of Law," in *The Politics of Law,* ed. D. Kairys (New York, 1982).

12. Blackstone's *Commentaries on the Laws of England* (Chicago, 1884), pp. 441–44.
13. M. Friedleander and M. Kline, *The Book of Abigail and John: Selected Letters of the Adams Family, 1762–1784* (1975), p. 123.
14. Taub and Schneider, "Perspectives on Women's Subordination and the Role of Law."
15. Feminists use the public/private dichotomy to describe the distinction between the home or the personal sphere and both the market and politics which comprise the public sphere. See Z. Eisenstein, *Feminism and Sexual Equality* (New York, 1984), p. 97; Olsen, "The Family and the Market: A Study of Ideology and Legal Reform," 96 *Harv. L. Rev.* 1497 (1983); Polan, "Towards a Theory of Law and Patriarchy," in *The Politics of Law,* p. 301.
16. The Fourteenth Amendment was not silent on the question of the exclusions of women from the vote, however. The amendment provided a remedy for denial of the franchise only to men and thereby wrote gender discrimination into the Constitution for the first time.
17. It should be noted that there was no need for constitutional protection of abortion because until the end of the nineteenth century, women had access to early abortion. A campaign, led by doctors, to restrict abortion began in the mid-nineteenth century. The new medical profession seized on the criminalization of abortion as a means to establish itself. But social factors clearly influenced this choice. The significant rise of abortion, as well as feminist aspirations among white Protestant middle- and upper-class women were a major factor fueling restriction. (See Gordon, *Women's Body, Women's Right;* Mohr, *Abortion in America.*)
18. On the women's struggle in this period see E. DuBois, *Feminism and Suffrage: The Emergence of an Independent Women's Movement in America, 1848–1869* (Ithaca, 1978), and her article in this volume.
19. Bradwell v. Illinois, 83 U.S. (Wall.) 130 (1873).
20. Muller v. Oregon, 208 U.S. 412 (1908).
21. Commonwealth v. Welosky, 276 Mass. 398 (1931).
22. Hoyt v. Florida, 368 U.S. 57 (1961); Reed v. Reed, 404 U.S. 71 (1971), was the first case to reject this classic sex-role stereotype.
23. Thomas Jefferson, for example, criticized "those who look at constitutions with sanctimonious reverence and deem them like the ark of the covenant, too sacred to be touched. Let us not weakly believe that our generation is not as capable as another of taking care of itself and of ordering its own affairs." (Letter to Samuel

Kercagval, 12 July 1761, in *The Portable Jefferson,* ed. M. Peterson [New York, 1973], pp. 552, 559–60).

24. See, e.g., Powell, "The Original Understanding of Intent," 98 *Harvard L. Rev.* 885 (1985); Brest, "The Misconceived Quest for the Original Understanding," 60 *B. U. L.* 204 (1980); Bickel, "The Original Understanding and the Segregation Decision," 69 *Harv. L. Rev.* 1 (1955). As Justice Hughes said, in Home Building & Loan v. Blaisdell:

> If by the statement that what the Constitution meant at the time of its adoption it means today, it is intended to say that the great clauses of the Constitution must be confined to the interpretation which the framers, with the conditions and outlook of their time, would have placed upon them, the statement carries its own refutation. It was to guard against such a narrow conception that Chief Justice Marshall uttered the memorable warning— "we must never forget that it is a *constitution* we are expounding." (McCulloch v. Maryland, 4 Wheat 316, 407). (290 U.S. 398, 442-43 [1934].)

Likewise, Chief Justice Warren wrote, in Brown v. Board of Education, 347 U.S. 483, 492 (1954): "In approaching this problem [of the constitutionality of school segregation] we cannot turn the clock back to 1868 when the Amendment was adopted, or even to 1896 when *Plessy v. Ferguson* was written." More recently, Justices Marshall, Brennan, and Stevens have responded to the Reagan administration's attack on the Court in public addresses explaining the necessity of a living constitution.

25. "No one, we presume, supposes that any change in public opinion or feeling in relation to this unfortunate race, in the civilized nation of Europe or in this country, should induce the court to give to the words of the Constitution a more liberal construction in their favor than they were intended to bear when the instrument was framed and adopted. Such an argument would be altogether inadmissible in any tribunal called upon to interpret it. If any of its provisions are deemed unjust, there is a mode prescribed in the instrument itself by which it may be amended; but while it remains unaltered, it must be construed now as it was understood at the time of its adoption. . . . Any other rule of construction would abrogate the judicial character of this court, and make it the mere reflex of the popular opinion or passion of the day." (Dred Scott v. Sandford, 60 U.S. [19 How.] 1393, 1426 [1856].)

26. Understood in its historical context, the enumeration of rights in the Bill of Rights was also animated by an equality principle. Thus, for example, the First Amendment envisioned free speech for the pamphleteer as well as the powerful; the due process clause protected the property of anyone who could get it and not just those born into the landed class; and the establishment clause precluded unequal treatment of different religions.

27. For example, the due process clause was intended to protect one's body and liberty against unfair arrest and incarceration. More recently, the Court held that pumping a suspect's stomach "shocks the conscience" (Rochir v. California 342 U.S. 165 [1952]). But being dragged off to jail, or having one's stomach pumped, are not the only ways one can be seized. If women or gay people have an equal right to the possession of themselves, is not the state's seizure of control over the womb or the expression of sexual intimacy a comparable deprivation?

28. Heterosexism is the systematization of the ideology that treats the heterosexual organization and its concomitant gender differentiation of intimacy, family, and social life as "natural" and superior. It is distinct from, although fed by, homophobia, the fear or loathing of gay men or lesbians.

29. This was the primary argument in the Amicus Curiae Brief on behalf of New Women Lawyers (CCR Amicus) filed in Roe v. Wade. Nancy Stearns from the Center for Constitutional Rights, author of the brief and one of the architects of the constitutional theory of women's right to abortion, explained the difference between privacy and liberty:

> The right to privacy is a passive right. The right to privacy says that the state can't interfere. The right to liberty . . . would seem to imply that the state has some kind of affirmative obligation to ensure that a women exercise that right to liberty. Other aspects of the feminist understanding of abortion have been minor, although now growingly important themes in the legal advocacy. (Goodman, Schoenbrod, and Stearns, "Doe and Roe: Where Do We Go From Here?" 1 *WRLR* 20, 27 [1973].)

30. The Amici Curiae Brief on Behalf of Organizations and Named Women written by Joan Bradford in Roe v. Wade developed the Thirteenth Amendment analogy. The argument has particular power against the claim that fetal life should qualify a women's autonomy, since the Thirteenth Amendment forbids the forced labor or subordination of one person to the needs or desires of another. The Thirteenth Amendment implications have also been suggested in Tribe, "The Abortion Funding Cunundrum: Inalienable Rights, Affirmative Duties and the Dilemma of Dependence," 99 *Harv. L. Rev.* 330 (1985); Regan, "Rethinking Roe v. Wade," 77 *Mich. L. Rev.* 1569 (1977); U.S., House, Committee on the Judiciary, Subcommittee on Civil and Constitutional Rights, Hearings on Abortion Clinic Violence, testimony of Rhonda Copelon, 3 April 1985, pp. 173, 188–95. See also Thomson, "A Defense of Abortion," 1 *Phil. & Pub. Affairs* 1 (1971), reprinted in J. Feinberg, ed., *The Problem of Abortion* (Belmont, Calif., 1973).

31. In the Roe v. Wade amicus, Stearns also argued the centrality of abortion to women's equality. This was explicit in her contention that the law, not nature, punished women but not men for "illicit" sex, and implicit in her cataloguing of the manifold ways that pregnancy operated to exclude women from public life. The equal protection argument has been developed more recently by Nadine Taub and the Rutger's Litigation Clinic in the Brief for Amici Curiae on behalf of New Jersey Coalition for Battered Women et al. in Right to Choose v. Byrne, reprinted in 7 *WRLR* 286–90, 296–99 (1982) (Right to Choose Brief), in Appellees' Brief, in Harris v. McRae, 448 U.S. 297 (1980); and in Law, "Rethinking Sex and the Constitution," 132 *U. Penn. L. Rev.* 955 (1984).

32. CCR Amicus; Right to Choose Amicus; "Introduction" to *Powers of Desire;* E. Willis, "Abortion: Is a Woman a Person?" in *Powers of Desire,* p. 471; and Petchesky, *Abortion and Women's Choice.*

33. The National Organization for Women (NOW) has deliberately and shortsightedly excluded abortion and lesbian/gay rights from the ERA, out of concern that these issues would be responsible for its defeat. Conversely, the mainstream abortion rights movements have tended to situate abortion in a libertarian, as opposed to feminist, context. While the approach of the latter groups appears to be changing, NOW continues to separate reproduction and sexuality from its equality agenda.

34. But see S. Law, "Homosexuality and the Social Meaning of Gender," unpub. ms., 1987. Litigative efforts include Singer v. Hara Co., 11 Wash. App. 247 (1974); DeSantis v. Pacific Telephone and Telegraph Co. 608 F.2d. 327 (9th Cir. 1979).

35. See, e.g., Lochner v. New York, 198 U.S. 45 (1905).

36. See Taub and Schneider, "Perspectives on Women's Subordination and the Role

of Law"; C. MacKinnon, *Feminism Unmodified* (Cambridge, Mass., 1987), pp. 93–102.

37. One strand of late-twentieth-century feminism rejects the contribution of contraception and abortion to a more liberated female sexuality, holding that heterosexual sexual relations, in a gender unequal society, are by definition oppressive (see, e.g., MacKinnon, *Feminism Unmodified*, pp. 93–102). This view is a flat and dangerous stereotype, for it precludes exploration and appreciation of women's capacity for sexual agency, power, and desire. Even accepting, as I do, that many women are vulnerable to sexual coercion as a product of inequality, abortion does not increase their abuse. At the very least, abortion enables them to relieve the further degrading and potentially life-destroying consequences thereof. For many, it is an act of self-affirmation, even in the face of victimization and despair.

38. 381 U.S. 479 (1965).

39. In Eisenstadt v. Baird, the Court struck down a prohibition on the distribution of contraceptives to single people, stating:

> The marital couple is not an independent entity with a mind and heart of its own, but an association of two individuals, each with a separate intellectual and emotional make-up. If the right of privacy means anything, it is the right of the *individual,* married or single, to be free from unwanted government intrusion into matters so fundamentally affecting a person as the decision whether to bear or beget a child. (405 U.S. 438, 453 [1972].)

40. The recognition that the family is comprised of separate right-holders has played a critical role in averting, on a doctrinal level, one of the major feminist concerns about privacy doctrine—that it would be used offensively to shield familial abuse from state intervention (see Powers, "Sex Segregation and the Ambivalent Directions of Sex Discrimination Law," 1979 *Wisc. L. Rev.* 55, 88). While the right of marital or personal privacy has been advanced by state authorities to justify the nonenforcement of the criminal laws against battering and marital rape, these arguments have been largely rejected on the basis that intervention is necessary to safeguard the woman's privacy and autonomy. Despite the doctrinal rejection of privacy as a shield for familial abuse, the ideology dies more slowly and women continue to face multiple hurdles in obtaining effective state intervention.

41. Planned Parenthood of Central Missouri v. Danforth, 420 U.S. 918 (1975). One lower court decision has extended the concept of bodily autonomy dispositive in Danforth to decisional autonomy in rejecting statutes requiring notification of a husband as a precondition of abortion. But the notion of the wife as property dies hard, for the court held in Scheinberg that if it could be shown that an abortion would have more than a *de minimis* impact on her reproductive capacity, the husband's procreative interest in consultation would be given preeminence. (659 F. 2d 476 (5th Cir. 1981), rehearing denied 677 F. 2d 931 (1982) on remand 550 F. Supp 1112 [S.D. Fla. 1982].)

42. Roe v. Wade 410 U.S. at 164. See also K. Glen, "Abortion in the Courts: A Lay Woman's Guide to the New Disaster Area," *Feminist Studies* 4, no. 1 (1978).

43. Although prevailing medical views now support limited regulation, for example, the Court's deference to the expertise of the medical establishment on the need for regulation is troubling. A medical establishment less supportive of the abortion option could endorse burdensome restriction. See City of Akron v. Akron Center for Reproductive Health.

44. Thornburgh v. ACOG, 106 S. Ct. at 2185.

45. In response to the attack on Roe v. Wade in Thornburgh, Lynn Paltrow wrote an

amicus brief on behalf of the National Abortion Rights Action League (NARAL) that placed the experience and meaning of abortion in women's lives movingly before the Court. The brief is also a reflection of the increasing focus by mainstream abortion rights groups on the feminist arguments for abortion. The brief is reprinted in 9 *Women's Rights L. Reptr.* 3 (1987).

46. However, the Court's recognition of viable fetal life as a constraint upon a woman's decision has grave implications for women's autonomy. Notwithstanding the fetus's potential for independent life after birth, to so qualify a woman's autonomy during gestation authorizes the subordination of a woman's body and will—essentials of her very personhood—to the needs of another. (See n. 30 above) This dilution of her integrity threatens not only to preclude abortion, since technological developments for saving fetuses or even embryos render viability a shifting and meaningless demarcation. (See Fost, Chudwin, and Wikler, "The Limited Moral Significance of Fetal Viability," *Hastings Center Report* [December 1980]; City of Akron, 462 U.S. at 452 [O'Connor, J., dissenting].) It has already opened the door to coerced prenatal interventions in wanted pregnancies, further depriving women of the control over their bodies accorded all other persons. (See Gallagher, "Prenatal Invasions and Interventions: What's Wrong with Fetal Rights," 10 *Harvard Women's L. J.* 9 [1987].) Fetal protection has also been invoked as a justification for restricting women's employment opportunities. (See Williams, "Firing the Woman to Protect the Fetus: The Reconciliation of Fetal Protection with Employment Opportunity Under Title VII," 69 *Geo. L. J.* 641 [1981].)

47. See MacKinnon, *Feminism Unmodified.*

48. Carol Gilligan's study of abortion decision-making highlights the critical transition in thinking from a traditional maternal morality that equates goodness with self-abnegation to a morality that encompasses the responsibility to care for both self and others. See *In a Different Voice* (Cambridge, Mass., 1982), pp. 64–105.

49. See Gordon, *Women's Body, Women's Right;* Mohr, *Abortion in America;* Petchesky, *Abortion and Women's Choice.*

50. A. Davis, *Women, Race, and Class* (New York, 1983); Gordon, *Women's Body, Women's Rights.* Women were also disproportionately affected by eugenic sterilization laws: two-thirds of those sterilized as feebleminded were women. Being sexually active was a key sign of feeblemindedness. My research assistant Betsy Kane (CUNY '86) discovered a striking disparity in judicial response to surgical invasion depending on whether the candidate was male or female: it was dismissed as inconsequential as to women and likened to torture or castration as to men. Compare, e.g., Buck v. Bell, 274 U.S. 200 (1927) and Davis v. Berry, 216 F. Supp. 413 (D. Iowa 1917).

51. In a provocative essay, Tom Grey suggests that the fear of uncabined sexuality underlies the Court's resistance to recognizing a right to be sexual, while abortion is acceptable because it serves family stability. (See Grey, "Eros, Civilization, and the Burger Court," 43 *L. & Contemp. Prob.* 83 [1980].) While there is truth to this, it is critical to recognize that the only effective legal or social sanctions are directed to women's and lesbian/gay sexuality, not to that of heterosexual men. In addition, the continued instability of the abortion right and the particular focus on limiting teen women's access attest to the sharp tension in regard to abortion between controlling women's sexuality and providing a safety valve for family stability in terms of preserving both the boundaries of nuclear heterosexuality and the ability of women to contribute wages to the family. (See Petchesky, *Abortion and Women's Choice,* pp. 205–33, 302–19.)

52. Eisenstadt v. Baird, 405 U.S. (1972)

53. In Hardwick, the Court avoided the question of the validity of Georgia's criminal sodomy statute with respect to heterosexual sodomy by treating the case as involving the issue of homosexual sodomy only. In fact, the reasoning of Hardwick is largely applicable to heterosexual sodomy, but the Court has refused to face that question and is unlikely to follow its own logic, at least as relates to married couples. See Post v. Oklahoma, 107 S. Ct. 290 (1987), where the Court refused to review an Oklahoma decision invalidating the state's sodomy law as applied to heterosexuals.

54. Bowers v. Hardwick, 106 S. Ct. 2841 (1986).

55. For example, Justice Stewart's dissent in Griswold trivialized the impact of the prohibition on contraception by describing it as an "uncommonly silly law," and Robert Bork denounced that decision as constitutionalizing "gratification." ("Neutral Principles and Some First Amendment Problems.") In the same vein, Justice White characterized abortion as a matter of "convenience, whim or caprice" (Roe v. Wade, 410 U.S. at 221).

56. Karst, "The Right of Intimate Association," 89 *Yale L. J.* 624 (1980).

57. Dissenting in Thornburgh, 106 S. Ct. at 2196.

58. In the medicaid abortion cases, the majority capitalized on the negative aspect of privacy by permitting the state to implement its hostility to abortion by denying funding because "the right [to abortion] . . . implies no limitation on the authority of a state to make a value judgement favoring childbirth over abortion, and to implement that judgement by the allocation of public funds." (Maher v. Roe, 432 U.S. 472, 474 [1977].) If abortion were a matter of affirmative liberty rather than privacy, it would be impermissible for the state to manipulate how one exercises the right through selective funding. Under the First Amendment, for example, the state cannot rent buses to take Republican but not Democratic voters to the polls. The theory of privacy thus maintains the original hierarchy between personal rights and the more traditionally political ones.

59. People have a lot less trouble with the idea of noninterference with a person's choice of sexual partners than they do with the idea of gay or lesbian marriage. Similarly, lesbian and gays are frequently accused of "flaunting it" simply because they are expressing affection in public in a way that would be considered cute or sweet or heartwarming if they were heterosexual. The very choice of the descriptor "flaunting it" captures the degree to which the expression of gay or lesbian identity is felt as an attack.

60. 106 S. Ct. at 2847 (Burger, J., concurring).

61. Ibid., at 2846

62. Ibid., at 2847 (Powell, L., concurring).

63. See J. Money and A. Ehrhardt, *Man and Woman, Boy and Girl: The Differentiation and Dimorphism of Gender Identity from Conception to Maturity* (Baltimore, 1972); A. Rich, "Compulsory Heterosexuality and Lesbian Existence," in Snitow, Stansell, and Thompson, *Powers of Desire;* and G. Rubin, "The Traffic in Women: Notes on the 'Political Economy' of Sex," in *Toward an Anthropology of Women,* ed. R. Reiter (New York, 1975), p. 157.

64. While some lesbians and gay men experience their sexual orientation as determined and immutable, others are very clear that it is a matter of choice. To reduce self-definition to biological, psychological, or cultural determinism, as the medical model does, argues for tolerance of the pathetic, not respect for the courageous. Nor does it help people who do not identify as gay to examine sexual hypocrisy or desire in their own lives.

65. Adrienne Asch, in speaking of disability-based discrimination, noted that one of

the reasons people have so much trouble treating disabled people as equal is that people fear crossing the line into disability.

66. Dronenburg v. Zech, 741 F. 2d 1388, rehearing denied 746 F. 2d 1579 (D.C. Cir. 1984), where Judge Bork wrote that the disruption from potential sexual solicitation justified total the exclusion of homosexuals from the military.

67. "Even women who had not the slightest inclination to cross the threshold of taboo reaped some benefits in their heterosexual negotiations from the general acknowledgment that lesbianism was not within the realm of the imaginable." Introduction, *Powers of Desire*, p. 34.

68. Petchesky, *Abortion and Women's Choice*, p. 9.

69. Harris v. McRae, 448 U.S. at 315, citing Maher v. Roe, 432 U.S. 464, 474 (1977).

70. It should be noted, however, that several state courts have invalidated the cut-off of abortion funds as an invasion of privacy protected under their state constitution, and have thus rejected the wholly negative view of privacy adopted by the Supreme Court. See, e.g., Moe v. Secretary of Admin. and Fin., 382 Mass 629 (1981); Committee to Defend Reproductive Rights v. Myers, 29 Cal. 3d 252 (1981); Right to Choose v. Byrne, 91 M.J. 287 (1982).

71. Maher v. Roe, 432 U.S. at 478, n. 11.

72. Both Brown v. Board of Education and Roe v. Wade, perhaps the most significant and controversial civil rights decisions of the current period, were preceded by significant economic and social changes, the exposure of inequities, and the coalescence of widespread acceptance of the need for change. The narrow margin in Hardwick, the breadth of the Blackmun dissent, and state court decisions favorable to lesbian/gay rights indicate that social change in regard to sexual self-determination is already underway.

73. For a provocative examination of this dialectic in feminist legal work, see Schneider, "The Dialectic of Rights and Politics: Perspectives from the Women's Movement," 61 *N.Y.U. L. Rev.* 589 (1986).

74. With regard to reproductive and sexual autonomy, for example, the Court has refused to recognize that pregnancy-based discrimination is within the constitutional prohibition on sex discrimination. (See Geduldig v. Aiello, 477 U.S. 484 [1974].) The medicaid abortion cases rejected the claims that the state was required to treat abortion and childbirth equally and ignored the argument that the exclusion of abortion is sex-discriminatory. And the Hardwick majority made clear that moralistic disapproval is an acceptable basis for unequal treatment.

REFLECTIONS ON THE CIVIL RIGHTS MOVEMENT AND THE FIRST AMENDMENT

Margaret Burnham

In the full summer months leading up to the 1964 Democratic Convention in Atlantic City, I—then a teenager—joined scores of other Student Nonviolent Coordinating Committee (SNCC) workers in a door-to-door campaign to enlist members in the Mississippi movement's alternative, the Freedom Democratic Party. The days had run into weeks and the August convention deadline was pressing in on us when, one day, a simple and short encounter brought home to me the core contradiction in this line of work.

I knew the awful oppression of summer heat, for I had double-dutched through childhood on Bed-Stuy streets; but July in Jackson was something else altogether. So heavy and still was the air on this particular evening that it took ever so great an effort to bring voice and mind together in the friendly but earnest presentations we had so carefully prepared for the strangers behind those doors: "Hi. I'm here on behalf of the Mississippi Freedom Democratic Party . . . right to participate in our government . . . right to vote (are you registered?) . . . mass meeting tonight (will you come?) . . . join MFDP? . . . name, address?"

Perhaps, then, it was the heat, and not my conscious feet that carried me, having finished one block, both sides, across a street to the Other Side of Town. I had knocked on the door and was straightening the leaflets on my clipboard and readying my pen and my little speech when a white man, a veritable giant (it seemed), appeared. The terrycloth robe he wore against the summer heat and the toddler scampering about his slippered feet made it all the more apparent that that misguided knock-knock had invaded white private space.

Oh, how I would have liked to have withdrawn right then, excuse me, sir, and good evening. I did drop my eyes, but, true to my training (courage, at all costs) and to the MFDP philosophy that the party we were building was to be made up of *all* Mississippians, black and white, I persevered. The words about voting, justice, and fairness were valiantly rolling off my startled tongue even as I came to feel the shock, reproach, and fury of the giant's gaze searing through my body, pushing the blood up into my face, and starting up a tremble within that reverberated from my heart to my head.

I was almost grateful to hear the scratchy, violent voice with which he broke the rhythm of my speech: "Gal, git on away from hyear; git on back over those tracks; git, now, git, before I give it te yah!" And then that door, which had moments before represented not fear but just the possibilities of a place unknown, slammed hard on my clipboard, my trembling, my stammered little speech. Tumbling back down the few porch steps, I face the heat and the street I had so wrecklessly crossed. Looking closely now, I could see that, yes, there were tracks in that street, cleverly obscured by weeds grown up high all around them and trash (black and white, given the Janus-like nature of the tracks).

Back at the office, I found someone to tell about my misadventure, and the story quickly melted into a day's post mortem, which included dozens of incidents of far greater danger and political consequence. And although I was shaken, the matter promptly faded as I put it in the perspective of my own year's experience with violence and conflict as a Mississippi SNCC worker. But I remember to this day what Hattie Palmer, my confidante that evening and a senior leader of the Jackson MFDP, said to soothe the razor edges of my nerves: "You have the Constitution behind what we're doing. It's our right to organize this party, to show how rotten the regular democrats are, and it's our right to try to get all people, black and white, into the MFDP. Don't worry, child; you did nothing wrong."

Set up against Hattie Palmer's simple civics homily was a confusing and contradictory legal landscape in which the Constitution represented at once a promise and a curse to the movement. The Constitution anchored our demands and our public rhetoric, but we knew it provided no sanctuary against Mississippi police and politicians. If we continued, as did Hattie Palmer, to promote the Constitution as the fountain of the rights we claimed, it was a strategic choice rather than a genuine ideological commitment to a document whose eyes were still half-closed to our blood and pain.

So fundamental was the moral reordering sought by the civil rights movement's manifesto that a document born out of—and yet still wedded to—the U.S. racial caste system could not be the principle agent of change. The very qualities of the Constitution which placed it on history's pedestal—its standing as a statement of First Principles, its longevity—rendered it problematic for those urging a political rebirth and seeking to bury the burden of a racist history. But at the same time, the concrete expression of the revolutionary aspirations of the Founders provided a set of ideals more revered than any we could fashion. The Constitution thus represented an ideological trap, as it were, that made it as much part of our arsenal as it was our target.

Preceding movements for radical social change had also confronted this problematic duality of the Constitution. But, in contrast to the legacy of these previous movements, the civil rights movement of 1954–1966 effected a deep and distinctive transformation of the document as well as of the people's consciousness of the rights it afforded them. It is neither hyperbolic nor trite to say that no other historical event has so shifted the turf upon which constitutional issues are played out as did the Afro-American civil rights movement. It is thus all the more disturbing that the Bicentennial commemorations have virtually ignored the place of this movement in constitutional history. So misrepresenting this rich and grand inheritance effectively erases much of what was accomplished by the civil rights movement and distorts our understanding of the route that the Constitution has taken to arrive at its present place.

When Harriet Palmer and I spoke in 1964, much had already transpired to shape the relationship between the protest movement and the Constitution as a tool of struggle. Blazoning a hitherto unexplored legal trail in the 1950s, the NAACP had marshalled all of its resources to literally take its case to court. In choosing to fight in the courts, the organization was pursuing a line of attack that it had initiated in the 1940s, but the legal campaign really moved into high gear in the 1950s, reaching its historic and climactic victory in 1954.

It was against the ambiguous and grudging backdrop of *Brown* v.

Board of Education II (1955) that the movement was to proceed. *Brown* represented both a momentous theoretical victory and a practical quagmire. For better and for worse, the decision firmly reinforced the commitment of a certain sector of the movement to the courtroom battle, for it clearly situated the rights that Afro-Americans were claiming in the text of the legal system's bible. Only hindsight would reveal the quicksand character of the Supreme Court's enjoinder to grant these long-denied rights with "all deliberate speed." And thus the NAACP rushed back to court quickly to secure *Brown's* promise, unaware of the tortuous and costly path it would have to travel, and unmindful, too, of the price to an infant movement that might have put its few and fragile eggs in a different basket.

In the process, however, the NAACP perfected a wholly new political *modus operandi*. Drawing on the lessons of the Brandeis school of advocacy, the NAACP took to the courts the grievances of an entire constituency, carefully crafting litigation strategies that would yield universally applicable legal principles. Upon these principles, other constitutional claims would be based, thus pushing the courts and the political system they were a part of to untangle, piece by piece, the web of racial oppression.

Several features of the NAACP's courtroom strategy were new. In the first place, these early antidiscrimination cases signalled the inception of class-action litigation. Second, the strategic employment of the judicial forum by a political organization, with careful attention to timing, deliberate selection of plaintiffs, and the commitment to the building-block approach, represented a novel means of forcing the resolution of a political controversy. Third, these early cases forced the Supreme Court to put flesh on the First and Fourteenth amendments, thereby fundamentally altering the federal-state relationship in constitutional jurisprudence. And finally, the new law that this process generated created the opportunity for attention to these issues in legislative and other forums.

But after *Brown* v. *Board* was decided, the NAACP did not have the luxury of remaining on the offensive in the courts for very long. The southern states were pursuing an aggressive, multifaceted campaign to outlaw the organization and the movement it was part of. Legislatures made it illegal for NAACP members to, variously, hold public employment, teach school, or take out loans. State and local authorities sought court injunctions to bar NAACP meetings and to seize membership lists. In Alabama, the NAACP was virtually outlawed from 1958 to 1964, creating a vacuum that was partially filled by the Southern Christian Leadership Conference (SCLC). In defending its right to exist, the NAACP appealed again and again to the protections of the First Amendment. The ensuing litigation kept the organization on a conveyer belt from state to federal court, thereby tying its hands on other political fronts, but the rules of law that emerged once again constituted the starting line for virtually the entire body of First Amendment law that is operative today.

Where it had only just compromised the First Amendment in the case of the victims of McCarthyism, the Supreme Court ultimately shielded the NAACP from attack by the Right. These cases gradually (some would argue much too gradually) decriminalized the organization and established rights that were to become central protections for the movement: the right to employ litigation as an organizing tool; the right to maintain the privacy of one's membership lists; and the right to organize openly against segregation.

As it happened, this expansion of the First Amendment to embrace the conduct of antiracist activists was to take on special significance when, in the late 1950s and early 1960s, the protest movement took to the streets. The NAACP was still on the defensive in the courts, but it was also continuing to pursue desegregation litigation all over the South. At the same time, it was becoming ever clearer that the federal courts were not keeping pace with the movement's demands, and that true justice did not reside in the hallowed halls of the Supreme Court. The movement could not be held hostage to "all deliberate speed," especially in the face of massive southern resistance. New actors were on the scene—young people like the Freedom Riders, anxious to confront southern intransigence; new organizations like SNCC, SCLC, and CORE, seeking a place for themselves in an increasingly militant climate; and brilliant new spokesmen like Fannie Lou Hamer, Medgar Evers, and the Rev. Martin Luther King, Jr.

Thus the NAACP confronted a dilemma: it could pursue the Constitution's promise full-throttle in the courts, or it could commit its resources to the struggle in the streets. Limited resources dictated a choice. Of course, the two battlegrounds were organically connected—the pronouncements of the courts on issues like segregation in public accommodations influenced the tempo of the protest movement, and street actions like lunch-counter sit-ins resulted in arrests, injunctions, and other grist for the courts. It cannot be gainsaid that civil rights lawyers performed an essential defensive role, clearing the protest road of the myriad obstructions thrown up by the local authorities. But there was nevertheless a certain element of strategic choice about the question of whether, for example, to chase the elusive goal of school desegregation in the courts or to mobilize a mass movement against voting restrictions.

The problem was exemplified by an incident in Mississippi in June 1963. A lunch-counter sit-in in Jackson, initiated by Medgar Evers, field secretary for the NAACP, had prompted a vicious attack on the demonstrators by local thugs. Mayor Thompson stubbornly resisted efforts to reach an accord with the town's black leadership and tensions began building. Some days after the sit-in, a march protesting the brutality took place downtown, to which the police responded by throwing hundreds of demonstrators into the state fairgrounds, which had been turned into a makeshift prison.

Medgar Evers wanted to protest the treatment of the demonstrators, but the NAACP headquarters did not want to allocate money it had reserved for its court cases to the bail fund that would have been necessary to take the street demonstrations to the next stage. Evers cancelled the plans for the demonstration, and instead sought himself, independent of the national office, to raise the funds required by the movement that was quickly gathering momentum in the streets.

Notwithstanding the seeming ambivalence of the NAACP, by 1963 the movement had so grown in numbers and in scope that there was no real way to contain its expression in the streets. And indeed, as the movement took its case directly to the people, it successfully escalated the pace of change, expressing a vitality, creativity, and political muscularity that would win it international attention and respect.

Again, this period yielded a new corpus of First Amendment law. It was left for the higher federal courts to determine the boundary between public and private in the context of the picket line and the sit-in; to reshape the doctrine of state action to reach assertedly private actors offering segregated public services; to review the injunctions against boycotts so readily entered by the southern state and federal courts; and to define what official conduct constituted a prior restraint on political expression. In some instances, these rulings won for the movement breathing space and legitimacy, but just as often they enhanced the control of racist local officials.

Considered in its entirety, the resulting body of law gave shape and specificity to the principle that a political movement could utilize nontraditional modes of communication to get its message across costly media barriers more effectively. The civil rights movement hardly invented the picket line, the mass meeting, or even the sit-in, but it did constitutionally legitimate and institutionalize these forms as the protest mode of choice for poor organizations.

Nevertheless, despite these landmark achievements, the First Amendment legacy of the civil rights movement speaks also to the inadequacy of the Constitution and its principle voice box, the Supreme Court, as the country's fundamental guarantor of equality. Here was a period of vibrant and enriching political engagement that provided both contour and context for the Constitution's ambitious democratic message. But the Supreme Court weaved its way through the large and complex thicket of litigation that came up from the protest in the streets with more ambivalence and reluctance than clarity and consistency.

The sit-in cases exemplify the pattern. Between 1961 and 1965, the Court addressed the rights of sit-in demonstrators on not less than thirty different occasions. It is a testament to the political strength of the movement that in the great majority of these cases the Court reversed the criminal convictions of the demonstrators. But this relief came so late and in so compromised a fashion as to have very little prophylactic impact on the movement. Wherever possible, the Court avoided a wholehearted embrace of the constitutional claim of the protesters that they had a right to eat at those lunch counters, reaching instead for less sweeping legal ground. In some cases, the Court struck down the sit-in convictions because it found that the evidence of criminal violation adduced at the trial court level was insufficient, while in others it deemed the trespass laws, upon which the convictions were based, to be unconstitutional. In other words, the Court looked for legal technicalities on which to hang its sit-in reversals, intentionally bypassing the opportunity to draw a national consensus around the moral ground that the protesters had carved out. Finally, the Civil Rights Act of 1964, which mandated the desegregation of public accommodations, took the Court off the constitutional hook, and in the end it never directly passed on the question of whether sit-ins against illegal exclusion were protected speech.

As, in the mid-1960s, the movement's demands were pressed with increasing militancy, the Court responded with less and less grace. It began to refuse to review state court convictions and injunctions, leaving protesters to seek their remedies in the segregationist state and lower federal courts. Even when state court collusion with racist political authorities was manifest, the Supreme Court increasingly closed the gate to federal relief on the ground that principles of federalism required such deference. And where before it had stretched the First Amendment to cover protest activity that was inherently challenging and upsetting, it now weighed the First Amendment scales in favor of those who might be affected by the protest activity, like the targets of selective boycotts and the white patrons of segregated public facilities.

In refusing to hear the claims of the civil rights appellants, the Court was retreating behind the very same doctrine of federalism that had spelled defeat for black rights after the first Reconstruction. This disgraceful abdication of responsibility for constitutional enforcement, under the guise of respect for federalist principles, was also the hallmark of the Justice Department's approach to the crisis of racist violence. The full import of the pervasive violence visited upon the civil rights forces is only now being widely acknowledged, due in part to the work of today's historians and documentarians of the civil rights era, like those who produced *Eyes on the Prize*. That the movement persevered in the face of the scores of bombings, beatings, and even murder—that the Mississippi Summer proceeded even after Chaney, Goodman, and Schwerner were brutalized and buried in a pit—is in itself a remarkable story. But the most bitter lesson is to be drawn not from the horrific story of southern violence, but from the obdurate refusal of the federal authorities to enforce the law. Deferring to state authorities who had already and repeatedly demonstrated their commitment to segregationist terror, federal authorities routinely failed to police the demonstrations of civil rights workers, to prosecute those who assaulted them, and in general to set the law enforcement standard for local police agencies. There were some well-publicized and notable exceptions, like the use of federal marshals during the Alabama Freedom Rider crisis, but by and large the Justice Department spurned the several legal tools at its disposal to shield civil rights workers from violence and harassing local arrests. Indeed, in one instance, in Albany, Georgia, Robert Kennedy's department lined up on the side of the local authorities and indicted six civil rights workers for spurious offenses. In sum, as in the first Reconstruction, federal prosecutorial authorities and courts were never the haven for a besieged movement that they should and could have been.

But the measure of the significance of the First Amendment for the movement did not entirely lie in the record of the Supreme Court, or even in the bloody trail left by those hundreds of courts that collaborated with racist violence. For even though the Court was at best only a reluctant partner in the effort to breath the life of contemporary reality into the amendment, the movement resulted in a critical new consciousness that the right to organize was the linchpin of the right to free speech.

The movement interpreted the First Amendment as protecting its thrust toward a different order, the idea that "movement," fluidity, and dynamism are political necessities and political rights. The First Amendment was akin to natural law; it represented a higher order, a court of last resort. In this sense, it arched over the nominally illegal acts of civil disobedience which were the movement's stock-in-trade. It offered sanction to the central tenet of the philosophy of creative nonviolent confrontation: the right—nay, the necessity—to disobey racist laws.

It perhaps represents one of the supreme victories of the civil rights movement that this revolutionary reading of the First Amendment won wide public consensus. When the movement was at its height, each day's headlines reiterated the message of the Montgomery boycott, that resistance was the answer to unconstitutional laws. Transforming the Constitution into a self-executing document, the movement envisioned the First Amendment as providing the constitutional security for this resistance. What is remarkable about the Supreme Court's approach to the civil disobedience cases it addressed is not that it often ducked the underlying constitutional questions—which it did—but that it usually reached the right result. This "bottom line" communicated the justice of the cause to the troops and to the public, reinforcing an expansive consciousness of the First Amendment that clearly was not justified by the evolving doctrinal line of the cases. Because the Court had to pass on the movement's controversial tactics, the perception of what was constitutionally permissible changed, even if the law's doctrinal trail did not justify the more expansive view.

This altered perception of the permissible—the sense that the movement had not only justice, but, ultimately, law on its side—was to transform the nature of political protest. The deepened First Amendment well was one that would water the political expression of the peace movement, the women's movement, and the welfare rights movement. From the civil rights movement, these later efforts took the mass protest form, the boycott tool, and the connection between mass media and protest as theater. These were undeniably critical contributions to the U.S. tradition of radical activism.

But because of its investment in righting legal wrongs, the civil rights movement passed to its successor causes a more ambiguous legacy as well. The movement sought to capture and resolve in its favor the legal contradiction represented by the promises of the Constitution itself. The lawsuit became a political petition and litigation an act of free speech. Robust court action moved hand in hand with, and in some cases took the place of, more direct forms of political expression. What emerged was a litigation explosion, a whole new generation of rights-minded advocates and a perhaps misplaced confidence that the legal tools were at hand to work the necessary social transformations. Other movements established legal offices spinning off from the model of the NAACP Legal Defense Fund, relying on the precedents and the legal methods employed by the civil rights struggle.

It is appropriate to ask at this point whether these movements would more profitably have taken off in other directions but for the legalistic tone set by some sectors of the civil rights movement. For while this intensive labor in the litigation vineyards has borne sweet fruit, it has also thrown up some thorns and weeds. In the case of welfare reform, for example, a massive legal attack on the inequities of the welfare system has resulted in almost no material change in the lives of the recipients. In fact, the available federal dollars were shrinking at the very moment that welfare reformers were attempting to get a fair hearing. And while the NAACP Legal Defense Fund was pursuing recalcitrant southern school districts, the right to quality public education in the urban setting was rapidly disintegrating for everyone, black and white.

Sojourner Truth is said to have remarked about the Constitution: "Now I hear talk about the Constitution and the rights of man. I comes up and I takes hold of this Constitution. It looks mighty big, and I feels for my rights, but there aren't any there. Then I say 'God, what ails this Constitution?' And you know what He says to me? God says, 'Sojourner, there is a little weasel in it.' "[1]

That the weasel is still there thirty-four years after the glorious promise of *Brown* v. *Board of Education,* and after thousands of lawsuits addressing all the myriad permutations of race, sex, and economic inequity, speaks volumes about the much-touted elasticity of the document. We would at our peril let the weasel continue to bore away at the Constitution, but the lesson of the civil rights movement is that it would be equally foolhardy to chase the Constitution's weasel at the expense of a more promising search for extra-constitutional definitions of twentieth-century equality.

Note

1. Victoria Ortiz, *Sojourner Truth: A Self-Made Woman* (Philadelphia, 1974), pp. 67–68.

FREE SPEECH AND SOCIAL STRUCTURE

Owen M. Fiss

Freedom of speech is one of the most remarkable and celebrated aspects of American constitutional law. It helps define who we are as a nation. The principle is rooted in the text of the Constitution itself, but it has been the decisions of the Supreme Court over the last half century or so that have, in my view, nurtured that principle, given it much of its present shape, and account for much of its energy and sweep. These decisions have given rise to what Harry Kalven has called a "Free Speech Tradition."[1]

In speaking of a Tradition, Kalven, and before him Llewellyn[2] and T. S. Eliot[3] (talking about the shoulders of giants), aspire to an all-embracing perspective. Everything is included—nothing is left out, not the dissents, not even the decisions overruled. Every encounter between the Court and the First Amendment is included. There is, however, a shape or direction or point to the Tradition. It is not an encyclopedia or dictionary, but more in the nature of a shared understanding. Those who speak of a Free Speech Tradition try to see all the decisions and to abstract from them an understanding of what free speech means—what lies at the core and what at the periphery, what lies beyond the protection of the First Amendment and what is included, where the law is headed, etc. The whole has a shape. The shape is not fixed for all time, since each new decision or opinion is included within the Tradition and thus contributes to refiguring the meaning of the whole, but the Tradition also acts as a constraining force on present and future decisions. The Tradition is the background against which every judge writes. It defines the issues; provides the resources by which the judge can confront those issues; and also creates the obstacles that must be surmounted. It orients the judge.

I believe it is useful to view the free speech decisions of the Supreme Court as a Tradition, and I am also tempted to celebrate that Tradition in much the way that Kalven does. But for me that is only half the story. It also seems to me that the Tradition is flawed in some important respects—so much so that it might be necessary to begin again (if that is even possible).

My concerns first arose in the 1970s—one of the few periods when America wondered out loud whether capitalism and democracy were compatible. In the political world these doubts were linked to Watergate and the eventual resignation of President Richard Nixon. The precipitating event was the break-in at the Democratic National Headquarters, but by the time the impeachment process had run its course, we realized how thoroughly economic power had begun to corrupt our politics. Congress responded with the Campaign Reform Act of 1974,[4] imposing limits on contributions and expenditures and establishing a scheme for the public funding of elections. The tension between capitalism and democracy was also a special subject of concern to the academy, as evidenced by the excitement and controversy generated by the publication in 1977 of Charles Edward Lindblom's book *Politics and Markets*.[5] Lindblom tried to show that, contrary to classical democratic theory, politics was not an autonomous sphere of activity, but was indeed shaped and controlled by the dominant economic interests. As a consequence of this "circularity," the most important issues of economic and social structure—what Lindblom called the "grand issues"—remained at the margins of politics. Voters were not actually considering the continued viability of capitalism, the justness of market distributions, or the structure within which organized labor was allowed to act, because, Lindblom hypothesized, of the control exercised by corporate interests over the political agenda.[6]

While academics were reading and debating Lindblom's book, and while politicians were trying to make sense of Watergate, the Supreme Court was faced with a number of cases that required it to examine the relationship of political and economic power. The Court was asked whether it was permissible for a state to extend the fairness doctrine to the print media,[7] and whether the FCC was obliged to provide critics of our efforts in Vietnam access to the TV networks.[8] In another case the Campaign Reform Act of 1974 was attacked;[9] and in still another a challenge was raised to a Massachusetts statute limiting corporate expenditures in a referendum on the income tax.[10] Political activists, lacking funds to purchase space or time in the media, sought access to the shopping centers to get their message across to the public, and they also turned to the courts for this purpose.[11] Admittedly, issues of this character had been presented to the Court before, but in the 1970s they arose with greater frequency and urgency, and they seemed to dominate the Court's First Amendment docket.

These cases presented the Court with extremely difficult issues, perhaps the most difficult of all First Amendment issues, and thus one would fairly predict divisions. One could also predict some false turns. What startled me, however, was the pattern of decisions: capitalism almost always won. The Court decided that a statute that granted access to the print media to those who wished to present differing views was invalid; that the FCC did not have to grant access to the electronic media for editorial advertisements; that the political expenditures of the wealthy could not be curbed; and that the owners of the large shopping centers of suburban America need not provide access to pamphleteers. Democracy promises collective self-determination—a freedom to the people to decide their own fate—and presupposes a debate on public issues that is (to use Justice Brennan's now classic formula) "uninhibited, robust, and wide-open."[12] The free speech decisions of the 1970s, however, seemed to impoverish, rather than enrich, public debate and thus threatened one of the essential preconditions for an effective democracy. And they seemed to do so in a rather systematic way.

My first inclination was to see these decisions as embodying a conflict between liberty and equality—as another phase in the struggle between the Warren and Burger courts. I saw the decisions of the 1970s as part of the program of the Court largely (and now, it seems, ironically) constituted by Nixon to establish a new priority for liberty and to bring an end to the egalitarian crusade of the Warren Court. The idea was that in these free speech cases, as in *Rodriguez*,[13] the Burger Court was not willing to empower the poor or less advantaged if that meant sacrificing the liberty of anyone. On reflection, however, the problem seemed deeper and more complicated. I saw that at issue was not simply a conflict between equality and liberty, but also, and more importantly, a conflict between two conceptions of liberty. The battle being fought was not just Liberty v. Equality, but Liberty v. Liberty, or, to put the point another way, not just between the First Amendment and the Equal Protection Clause, but a battle *within* the First Amendment itself. I also came to understand that the Court was not advancing an idiosyncratic or perverted conception of liberty, but was in fact working well within the Free Speech Tradition. The Court was not crudely substituting entrepreneurial liberty (or property) for political liberty;[14] the rich or owners of capital in fact won, but only because they had advanced claims of political liberty that easily fit within the received Tradition. Money is speech—just as much as picketing is.

In time I became convinced that the difficulties the Court encountered in the free speech cases of the 1970s could ultimately be traced to inadequacies in the Free Speech Tradition itself. The problem was the Tradition, not the Court. The Tradition did not *compel* the results—as though any body of precedent could. Arguably, there was room for a nimble and determined craftsman working within the Tradition to come out differently in one or two of these cases, or maybe in all of them. But, on balance, it seemed that the Tradition oriented the justices in the wrong direction and provided ample basis for those who formed the majority to claim, quite genuinely, that they were protecting free speech when, in fact, they were doing something of a different, far more ambiguous, character. This meant that criticism would have to be directed not simply at the Burger Court but at something larger: at a powerfully entrenched, but finally inadequate, body of doctrine.

1

For the most part, the Free Speech Tradition can be understood as a protection of the streetcorner speaker. An individual mounts a soapbox on a corner in some large city, starts to criticize government policy, and then is arrested for breach of the peace. In this setting the First Amendment is conceived of as a shield, as a means of protecting the individual speaker from being silenced by the state.

First Amendment litigation first began to occupy the Supreme

Court's attention during World War I, a time when the constitutional shield was rather weak. The streetcorner speaker could be arrested on the slightest provocation. Those early decisions were openly criticized, most notably in the dissents of Brandeis and Holmes, but that criticism—eloquent and at times heroic—stayed within the established framework and sought only to expand the frontiers of freedom incrementally; it sought to place more restrictions on the policeman and to give more and more protection to the streetcorner speaker. In this incremental quality, the criticism took on the character of the progressive movement in general, and also shared its fate. The progressive critique achieved its first successes during the 1930s, at the hand of the Hughes Court, but its final vindication awaited the Warren Court: It was only then that the shield around the speaker became worthy of a democracy.

What largely emerged from this historical process is a rule against content regulation—it now stands as the cornerstone of the Free Speech Tradition. The policeman cannot arrest the speaker just because he does not like what is being said. Time, place, and manner regulations are permitted—the speaker must not stand in the middle of the roadway—but the intervention must not be based on the content of the speech, or a desire to favor one set of ideas over another. To be sure, the Court has allowed the policeman to intervene in certain circumstances on the basis of content, as when the speaker is about to incite a mob. But even then the Court has sought to make certain that the policeman intervenes only at the last possible moment, that is, before the mob is unleashed. In fact, for most of this century First Amendment scholarship has largely consisted of a debate over the clear and present danger test, and the so-called incitement test, in an effort to find a verbal formula that best identifies the last possible moment.[15] The common assumption of all those who participated in that debate—finally made explicit in the 1969 decision of *Brandenburg* v. *Ohio*,[16] perhaps the culmination of these debates and in many respects the final utterance of the Warren Court on this subject—is that the policeman should not step in when the speaker is only engaged in the general expression of ideas, however unpopular those ideas may be.[17]

I would be the first to acknowledge that there has been something noble and inspiring about the fifty-year journey from *Schenck*[18] in 1919 to *Brandenburg* in 1969. A body of doctrine that fully protects the streetcorner speaker is of course an accomplishment of some note; the battles to secure that protection were hard fought and their outcome was far from certain. *Brandenburg* is one of the blessings of our liberty. The problem, however, is that today there are no streetcorners, and the doctrinal edifice that seems to someone like Kalven so glorious when we have the streetcorner speaker in mind is largely unresponsive to the conditions of modern society.

Under the Tradition extolled by Kalven, the freedom of speech guaranteed by the First Amendment amounts to a protection of autonomy—it is the shield around the speaker. The theory that animates this protection, and that inspired Kalven,[19] and before him Meiklejohn,[20] and that now dominates the field,[21] casts the underlying purpose of the First Amendment in social or political terms: The purpose of free speech is not individual self-actualization, but rather the preservation of democracy, and the right of a people, as a people, to decide what kind of life it wishes to live. Autonomy is protected not because of its intrinsic value, as a Kantian might insist, but rather as a means or instrument of collective self-determination. We allow people to speak so others can vote. Speech allows people to vote intelligently and freely, aware of all the options and in possession of all the relevant information.

The crucial assumption in this theory is that the protection of autonomy will produce a public debate that will be, to use the talismanic phrase once again, "uninhibited, robust, and wide-open." The Tradition assumes that by leaving individuals alone, free from the menacing arm of the policeman, a full and fair consideration of all the issues will emerge. The premise is that autonomy will lead to rich public debate. From the perspective of the streetcorner, that assumption might seem plausible enough. But when our perspective shifts, as I insist it must, from the streetcorner to, say, CBS, this assumption becomes highly problematic. Autonomy and rich public debate—the two free speech values—might diverge and become antagonistic.[22] Under CBS, autonomy may be *insufficient* to insure a rich public debate. Oddly enough, it might even become *destructive* of that goal.

Some acknowledge the shift of paradigms, and the obsolescence of the streetcorner, but would nonetheless view CBS as a forum—an electronic streetcorner.[23] They would demand access to the network as though it were but another forum and insist that the right of access should not follow the incidence of ownership. This view moves us closer to a true understanding of the problem of free speech in modern society, for it reveals how the freedom to speak depends on the resources at one's disposal, and it reminds us that more is required these days than a soapbox, a good voice, and the talent to hold an audience. On the other hand, this view is incomplete: It ignores the fact that CBS is not only a forum, but also a speaker, and thus understates the challenge that is posed to the received Tradition by the shift in paradigms. For me CBS is a speaker and in that capacity renders the Tradition most problematic. As speaker, CBS can claim the protection of autonomy held out by the Tradition, and yet the exercise of that autonomy might not enrich, but rather impoverish, public debate and thus frustrate the democratic aspirations of the Tradition.

In thinking of CBS as a speaker, and claiming for it the benefit of the Tradition, I assume that the autonomy protected by the Tradition need not be confined to individuals. It can extend to institutions. Autonomy is not valued by Meiklejohn and his followers because of what it does for a person's development (self-actualization), but rather because of the contribution it makes to our political life, and that contribution can be made either by individuals or organizations. The NAACP, the Nazi Party, CBS, and the First National Bank of Boston are as entitled to the autonomy guaranteed by the Tradition as is an individual, and no useful purpose would be served by reducing this idea of institutional autonomy to the autonomy of the various individuals who (at any one point of time) manage or work within the organization.

Implicit in this commitment to protecting institutional autonomy is the understanding that organizations have viewpoints and that these viewpoints are no less worthy of First Amendment protection than those of individuals. An organization's viewpoint is not reducible to the views of any single individual, but is instead the product of a complex interaction between individual personalities, internal organizational structures, the environment in which the organization operates, etc. The viewpoint of an organization such as CBS or the First National Bank of Boston might not have as sharp a profile as that of the NAACP or the Nazi Party (that is probably one reason why we think of a network as a forum), but that viewpoint is nonetheless real, pervasive, and communicated almost endlessly. It is not confined to the announced "Editorial Message," but extends to the broadcast of *Love Boat* as well. In the ordinary show or commercial a view of the world is projected, which in turn tends to define and order our options and choices.

From this perspective, the protection of CBS's autonomy through the no-content-regulation rule appears as a good. The freedom of CBS to say what it wishes can enrich public debate (understood generously) and thus contribute to the fulfillment of the democratic aspirations of the First Amendment. The trouble, however, is that it can work out the other way too, for when CBS adds something to public debate, something is also taken away. What is said determines what is not said. The decision to fill a prime hour of television with *Love Boat* necessarily entails a decision not to broadcast a critique of Reagan's foreign policy or a documentary on one of Lindblom's "grand issues" during the same hour. We can thus see that the key to fulfilling the ultimate purposes of the First Amendment is not autonomy, which has a most uncertain or double-edged relationship to public debate, but rather the actual effect of a broadcast: On the whole does it enrich public debate? Speech is protected when (and only when) it does, and precisely because it does, not because it is an exercise of autonomy. In fact, autonomy adds nothing and if need be, might have to be sacrificed, to make certain that public debate is sufficiently rich to permit true collective self-determination. What the phrase "the freedom of speech" in the First Amendment refers to is a social state of affairs, not the action of an individual or institution.

The risk posed to freedom of speech by autonomy is not confined to situations when it is exercised by CBS, or by the other media, but occurs whenever speech takes place under conditions of scarcity, that is, whenever the opportunity for communication is limited. In such situations one utterance will necessarily displace another. With the streetcorner, the element of scarcity tends to be masked; when we think of the streetcorner we ordinarily assume that every speaker will have his or her turn, and that the attention of the audience is virtually unlimited. Indeed, that is why it is such an appealing story. But in politics, scarcity is the rule rather than the exception. The opportunities for speech tend to be limited, either by the time or space available for communicating or by our capacity to digest or process information. This is clear and obvious in the case of the mass media, which play a decisive role in determining which issues are debated, and how, but it is true in other contexts as well. In a referendum or election, for example, there is every reason to be concerned with the advertising campaign mounted by the rich or powerful, because the resources at their disposal enable them to fill all the available space for public discourse with their message. Playing Muzak on the public address system of a shopping mall fills the minds of those who congregate there. Or consider the purchase of books by a library, or the design of a school curriculum. The decision to acquire one book or to include one course necessarily entails the exclusion of another.

Of course, if one has some clear view of what should be included in the public debate, as does a Marcuse,[24] one has a basis for determining whether the public debate that will result from the exercise of autonomy will permit true collective self-determination. Such a substantive baseline makes life easier but it is not essential. Even without it there is every reason to be concerned with the quality of public discourse under a regime of autonomy. For the protection of autonomy will result in a debate that bears the imprint of those forces that dominate the social structure. In the world of Thomas Jefferson, made up of individuals who stand equal to one another, this might not be a matter of great concern, for it can be said that the social structure, as well as the formal political process, is itself democratic. But today we have every reason to be concerned, for we live in a world farther removed from the democracy Jefferson contemplated than it is from the world of the streetcorner speaker.

The fear I have about the distortion of public debate under a regime of autonomy is not in any way tied to capitalism. It arises whenever social power is distributed unequally: Capitalism just happens to be one among many social systems that distribute power unequally. I also think it wrong, even in a capitalist context, to reduce social power to economic power, and to attribute the skew of public debate wholly to economic factors; bureaucratic structure, personalities, social cleavages, and cultural norms all have a role to play in shaping the character of public debate. But I think it fair to say that in a capitalist society, the protection of autonomy will on the whole produce a public debate that is dominated by those who are economically powerful. The market—even one that operates smoothly and efficiently—does not assure that all relevant views will be heard, but only those that are advocated by the rich, by those who can borrow from others, or by those who can put together a product that will attract sufficient advertisers or subscribers to sustain the enterprise.

CBS is not a monopoly, and competes with a few other networks (and less powerful media) for the public's attention. The fact that CBS's managers are (to some indeterminate degree) governed by market considerations does not in any way lessen the risk that the protection of autonomy—staying the hand of the policeman—will not produce the kind of debate presupposed by democratic theory. The market is itself a structure of constraint that tends to channel, guide, and shape how that autonomy will be exercised. From the perspective of a free and open debate, the choice between *Love Boat* and *Fantasy Island* is trivial. In this respect, CBS and the rest of the broadcast media illustrate, by example, not exception, the condition of all media in a capitalist society. True, CBS and the other networks operate under a license from the government or under conditions of spectrum scarcity. But the dangers I speak of are not confined to such cases, for distortions of public debate arise from social, rather than legal or technical, factors.

Individuals might be "free" to start a newspaper in a way that they are not "free" to start a TV station, because in the latter case they need both capital and government approval, while for the newspaper they need only capital. But that fact will not close the gap between autonomy and public debate; it will not guarantee that under autonomy principles the public will hear all that it must. Licensing may distort the market in some special way, but even the market dreamed of by economists will leave its imprint on public debate, not only on issues that directly affect the continued existence of the market, but on a much wider range of issues (though with such issues it is often difficult to predict the shape and direction of the skew). No wonder we tend to identify the Free Speech Tradition with the protection of "the marketplace of ideas."[25]

2

Classical liberalism presupposes a sharp dichotomy between state and citizen. It teaches us to be wary of the state and equates liberty with limited government. The Free Speech Tradition builds on this view of the world when it reduces free speech to autonomy and defines autonomy to mean the absence of government interference. Liberalism's distrust of the state is represented by the antagonism between the policeman and soapbox orator and by the assumption that the policeman is the enemy of speech. Under the received Tradition, free speech becomes one strand—perhaps the only one left[26]—of a more general plea for limited government. Its appeal has been greatly enhanced by our historical commitment to liberalism.

Nothing I have said is meant to destroy the distinction presupposed by classical liberalism between state and citizen, or between the public and private. Rather, in asking that we shift our focus from the streetcorner to CBS, I mean to suggest that we are not dealing with hermetically sealed spheres. CBS is neither a state actor nor a private citizen but something of both. CBS is privately owned and its employees do not receive their checks directly from the state treasury. It is also true, however, that CBS's central property—the license—has been created and conferred by the government. It gives CBS the right to exclude others from its segment of the airwaves. In addition, CBS draws upon advantages conferred by the state in a more general way, through, for example, the laws of incorporation and taxation. CBS can also be said to perform a public function: education. CBS is thus a composite of the public and private. The same is true of the print media, as it is of all corporations, unions, universities, and political organizations. Today the social world is largely constituted by entities that partake of both the public and private.

A shift from the streetcorner to CBS compels us to recognize the hybrid character of major social institutions; it begins to break down some of the dichotomies between public and private presupposed by classical liberalism. It also renders pointless the classificatory game of deciding whether CBS is "really" private or "really" public, for the shift invites a reevaluation of the stereotypical roles portrayed in the Tradition's little drama. No longer can we identify the policeman with evil and the citizen with good. The state of affairs protected by the First Amendment can just as easily be threatened by a private citizen as by an agency of the state. A corporation operating on private capital can be as much a threat to the richness of public debate as a government agency, for each is subject to constraints that limit what it says or what it will allow others to say. The state has a monopoly on the legitimate use of violence, but this peculiar kind of power is not needed to curb and restrict public debate. A program manager need not arrest someone (lawfully or otherwise) to have this effect, but only choose one program over another, and although that choice is not wholly free but constrained by the market, that does not limit the threat that it poses to the integrity of public debate. Rather, it is the source of the problem. All the so-called private media operate within the same structure of constraint, the market, which tends to restrict and confine the issues that are publicly aired.

Just as it is no longer possible to assume that the private sector is all freedom, we can no longer assume that the state is all censorship. That too is one of the lessons of the shift from the streetcorner orator to CBS. It reminds us that in the modern world the state can enrich as much as it constricts public debate: The state can do this, in part, through the provision of subsidies and other benefits. Here I am thinking not just of the government's role in licensing CBS, but also and more significantly of government appropriations to public television and radio, public and private universities, public libraries, and public educational systems. These institutions bring before the public issues and perspectives otherwise likely to be ignored or slighted by institutions that are privately owned and constrained by the market. They make an enormous contribution to public discourse, and should enjoy the very same privileges that we afford those institutions that rest on private capital (and, of course, should be subject to the same limitations).

We can also look beyond the provision of subsidies, and consider whether the state might enrich public debate by regulating in a manner similar to the policeman. CBS teaches that this kind of government action—once again based on content—might be needed to protect our freedom. The power of the media to decide what it broadcasts must be regulated because, as we saw through an understanding of the dynamic of displacement, this power always has a double edge: It subtracts from public debate at the very moment that it adds to it. Similarly, expenditures of political actors might have to be curbed to make certain all views are heard. To date we have ambivalently recognized the value of state regulation of this character on behalf of speech—we have a fairness doctrine for the broadcast media and limited campaign-financing laws. But these regulatory measures are today embattled, and in any event, more, not less, is needed. There should also be laws requiring the owners of the new public arenas—the shopping centers—to allow access for political pamphleteers. A commitment to rich public debate will allow, and sometimes even require, the state to act in these ways, however elemental and repressive they might at first seem. Autonomy will be sacrificed, and content regulation sometimes allowed, but only on the assumption that public debate might be enriched and our capacity for collective self-determination enhanced. The risks of this approach cannot be ignored, and at moments they seem alarming, but we can only begin to evaluate them when we weigh in the balance the hidden costs of an unrestricted regime of autonomy.

At the core of my approach is a belief that contemporary social structure is as much an enemy of free speech as is the policeman. Some might move from this premise to an attack upon the social structure itself—concentrations of power should be smashed into atoms and scattered in a way that would have pleased Jefferson. Such an approach proposes a remedy that goes directly to the source of the problem, but surely is beyond our reach, as a social or legal matter, and maybe even as an ethical matter. The First Amendment does not require a revolution. It may require, however, a change in our attitude about the state. We should learn to recognize the state not only as an enemy, but also as a friend of speech; like any social actor, it has the potential to act in both capacities, and, using the enrichment of public debate as the touchstone, we must begin to discriminate between them. When the state acts to enhance the quality of public debate, we should recognize its actions as consistent with the First Amendment. What is more, when on occasion it fails to, we can with confidence demand that the state so act. The duty of the state is to preserve the integrity of public debate—in much the same way as a great teacher—not to indoctrinate, not to advance the "Truth," but to safeguard the conditions for true and free collective self-determination. It should constantly act to correct the skew of social structure, if only to make certain that the status quo is embraced because we believe it the best, not because it is the only thing we know or are allowed to know.

Notes

This is a shortened version of an article that appeared in 71 *Iowa Law Review* 1405 (1986), and is reprinted with the permission of the author.

1. H. Kalven, *A Worthy Tradition* (New York, 1988).
2. K. Llewellyn, *The Common Law Tradition: Deciding Appeals* (Boston, 1960).
3. T.S. Eliot, "Tradition and the Individual Talent," in *Selected Prose of T.S. Eliot* (1919; rept. ed., New York, 1975), p. 37.
4. Federal Election Campaign Act Amendments of 1974, Pub. L. No. 93-443, 88 Stat. 1263 (codified at 2 U.S.C. 431–434, 437–439, 453, 455, 5 U.S.C. 1501–1503, 26 U.S.C. 2766, 6012, 9001–9012, 9031–9042 [1982]).
5. C. E. Lindblom, *Politics and Markets: The World's Political-Economic Systems* (New York, 1977).
6. Ibid., pp. 201–21.
7. Miami Herald Publishing Co. v. Tornillo, 418 U.S. 241 (1974).
8. Columbia Broadcasting Sys. v. Democratic Nat'l Comm., 412 U.S. 94 (1973).
9. Buckley v. Valeo, 424 U.S. 1 (1976).
10. First National Bank of Boston v. Bellotti, 435 U.S. 765 (1978).
11. Lloyd Corp. v. Tanner, 407 U.S. 551 (1972).
12. New York Times Co. v. Sullivan, 376 U.S. 254, 270 (1964).
13. San Antonio Indep. School Dist. v. Rodriguez, 411 U.S. 1 (1973).
14. But see Dorsen and Gora, "Free Speech, Property, and the Burger Court: Old Values, New Balances," 1982 *Sup. Ct. Rev.* 195.
15. See, e.g., Gunther, "Learned Hand and the Origins of Modern First Amendment Doctrine: Some Fragments of History," 27 *Stan. L. Rev.* 719 (1975); Kalven, "Professor Ernst Freund and Debs v. United States," 40 *U. Chi. L. Rev.* 235 (1973).
16. 395 U.S. 444 (1969).
17. Ibid., at 447–49.
18. Schenck v. United States, 249 U.S. 47 (1919).
19. Kalven, "The New York Times Case: A Note on 'The Central Meaning of the First Amendment,' " 79 *Harv. L. Rev.* 1 (1965).
20. See Meiklejohn, "The First Amendment Is an Absolute," 1961 *Sup. Ct. Rev.* 245; see also Brennan, "The Supreme Court and the Meiklejohn Interpretation of the First Amendment," 79 *Harv. L. Rev.* 1 (1965).
21. See, e.g., Bollinger, "Free Speech and Intellectual Values," 92 *Yale L.J.* 438 (1983). The breadth of the support is indicated by adherents as diverse as Kalven and Bork. See Bork, "Neutral Principles and Some First Amendment Problems," 47 *Ind. L.J.* 1 (1971).
22. On the two free speech values, see Justice Brennan's remarks in "Address," 32 *Rutgers L. Rev.* 173 (1979). For an opinion informed by this perspective, see Richmond Newspapers v. Virginia, 448 U.S. 555, 584–89 (1980) (Brennan, J., concurring in judgment). See also Blum, "The Divisible First Amendment: A Critical Functionalist Approach to Freedom of Speech and Electoral Campaign Spending," 58 *N.Y.U. L. Rev.* 1273 (1983).
23. See, e.g., J. Barron, *Freedom of the Press for Whom? The Right of Access to Mass Media* (Bloomington, Ind., 1973).
24. H. Marcuse, "Repressive Tolerance," in R. P. Wolff et al., *A Critique of Pure Tolerance* (Boston, 1969), p. 81.
25. The metaphor stems from Holmes's famous dissent in Abrams v. United States,

250 U.S. 616, 630 (1919) (Holmes, J., dissenting) ("But when men have realized that time has upset many fighting faiths, they may come to believe even more than they believe the very foundations of their own conduct that the ultimate good desired is better reached by free trade in ideas—that the best test of truth is the power of the thought to get itself accepted in the competition of the market."). The actual phrase "marketplace of ideas" is, oddly enough, Brennan's. See Lamont v. Postmaster General, 381 U.S. 301, about the 308 (1965) (Brennan, J., concurring). The deliberative element in Brennan's thinking about the First Amendment can ultimately be traced to Brandeis, who is often linked to Holmes in his use of the clear and present danger test, but who in fact had no taste for the market metaphor. On the poetics of the tradition, see the inspired essay by David Cole, "Agon at Agora: Creative Misreading in the First Amendment Tradition," 95 *Yale L.J.* 857 (1986).

26. See Coase, "The Market for Goods and the Market for Ideas," 64 *Am. Econ. Rev. Proc.* 384 (1974); Director, "The Parity of the Economic Market Place," 7 *J. Law & Econ.* 1 (1964).

CRIME, LAW ENFORCEMENT, AND CONSTITUTIONAL RIGHTS

David Rudovsky

1

The public controversy that surrounds the issue of the constitutional rights of those accused or convicted of crimes has recently taken a new and ominous turn. As part of a program to weaken or eliminate a number of basic democratic rights, the Justice Department and its conservative allies have attempted to make the Constitution a scapegoat for a variety of social and political problems. In particular, they assert that adherence to constitutional principles is incompatible with effective law enforcement. Doctrines and rulings that promote fairness and equality in the criminal justice system are now blamed for aggravating crime and violence.

It is not of course unusual for government officials, law enforcement officers, and others to exploit the public's legitimate fear of crime for partisan political purposes. Ethnic and minority groups are often blamed for crime, regressive and harshly punitive legislation is passed in the name of crime control, the courts are attacked for being too soft, and the police are encouraged to use extra-legal methods to control crime and criminals. Rarely do these measures actually reduce levels of crime or increase public safety, however; instead they enable their proponents to demonstrate their "toughness" and "concern" on this issue.

In the past twenty-five years we have seen dramatic changes in the direction and scope of this debate. The Warren Court, in a series of cases, established a set of basic procedural protections that limited governmental investigative powers and created a modest level of fairness and equality in the criminal justice system.[1] In reaction, first the Nixon administration and now the Reagan administration have sought to denigrate the principles of due process, the right to counsel, privacy, and the privilege against self-incrimination. This attack is part of a larger program that seeks to subordinate democratic rights to claims of order, efficiency, and executive power; its target is the judiciary's role in defining fundamental liberties.

The interplay of constitutional protections and law enforcement is the principal focus of this article. This issue, however, is part of a larger public debate that is marked by deep philosophical and political divisions, the characteristics of which can be sketched as follows:

First, conservatives tend to believe that crime is essentially unrelated to property, discrimination, or status. People rob, steal, or are assaultive not because of deprivation, hunger, or discrimination but out of a conscious choice of a criminal lifestyle, or in some cases because of genetic factors. According to this view, people are poor *and* commit crimes because of similar character faults and deficiencies.

Second, the Right tends not to be concerned with the question of whether the criminal process affords due process or equal justice. The crime-control model emphasizes arrest, prosecution, and punishment as effective means of incapacitation and deterrence, and views any obstacles to such a course of action as ill-conceived.

Third, operating on the assumption that crime is the result of free personal choice, strict and harsh punishment is put forward as the best and perhaps only effective form of crime control and deterrence. The greater the disincentive, the more likely the criminal will be deterred. Incentives for productive social behavior are largely ignored.

Fourth, under this theory crime is linked to what is considered to be the general breakdown of the institutions of law, order, and moral authority—the church, the family, and the schools. Thus the social agenda of the conservative movement is presented as an antidote to the crime problem.

Fifth, since principles of punishment are paramount, it is asserted that constitutional protections that are unrelated to guilt or innocence or that impede the police and prosecutors are unacceptable obstacles to effective law enforcement. Where state power and individual liberties conflict, the state should prevail and the courts should not interfere with the political processes that determine the balance of law, order, and constitutional rights.

There is no difficulty in demonstrating the flaws in this approach. Twice as many people are now incarcerated in the United States as only ten years ago (there are over 800,000 men and women in our prisons, jails, and juvenile facilities). And even in the face of the death penalty, preventive detention, and mandatory sentencing, there has been no decrease in crime.

It should be understood that while incarceration may incapacitate some offenders and may satisfy our need for punishment and retribution, as the social and economic conditions of significant parts of our society become increasingly ruinous, even the most extreme punishment can provide only marginal protection. For every thief we send to prison, scores of others are being nurtured in the dangerous and often hopeless conditions of a permanent underclass. Our society simply lacks the elementary social and economic fairness to make possible a solution to the problem of crime without the radical restructuring of our entire social system.

It has recently become fashionable to make light of the social and economic reasons for crime. New York City's Mayor Edward Koch says that "hungry people" do not commit violent crimes. But few suggest that immediate hunger or starvation lead to crime, or even that there is a single root cause of criminal conduct; rather, history and common sense teach that years of hunger, discrimination, despair, and exposure to violence, particular in childhood, lead a disproportionate number of people in that social setting to criminal conduct.

This is not to excuse or justify violent crime; nor is it to ignore the fact that most people, even in desperate circumstances, do not turn to crime. But can anyone seriously deny that crime is increased by social forces that relegate minority youth to unemployment or meaningless work, that promote inequality in educational opportunity and in private and public benefits, and that deprive communities of a decent level of housing, nutrition, and support? As Kenneth B. Clark aptly put it, if we continue to mug our schools, communities, and neighborhoods, we should not be surprised if those who turn to crime increase "in number, defiance, and venom."[2] Nor should we expect a drop in recidivism if we continue to lock people up in inhumane conditions and release them into communities with overwhelming unemployment rates. Those who ignore the widening economic cleavage in this country and who advocate a program of cells instead of classrooms and jobs should at least be honest enough to recognize that this policy promises no safer a society, today or in the future.

But criticism of the repressive approach is not sufficient. The task is to develop a program that credibly protects essential guarantees of fairness and equality, treats the accused, the convicted, and the victim with dignity, *and* controls and deters crime and violence. While sharply conflicting attitudes toward crime and violence are understandable, an inability to analyze and confront extremely difficult issues, including some that challenge deeply held beliefs, has left progressives without a credible voice in this discussion.

Different strands of analysis have marked a progressive approach. At times crime has been considered a form of social and political protest. Some have asserted that in a society with gross disparities in opportunity, material benefits, race and sex discrimination, and unpunished corporate and political corruption, the "criminal" is hardly blameworthy. Some have focused on the unequal impact of criminal law or on the brutalizing effects of overcrowded prisons. For others, differential treatment of white collar and street crime, the racial considerations that infect police prosecutorial and court processes, and overall neglect of police crimes, renders the crime-control apparatus illegitimate.

Furthermore, many find it difficult to support the police, and the use of police and prosecutorial powers, when these same institutions enforce the economic and social status quo, protect management against labor, disrupt and punish legitimate political protest and dissent, and at times brutalize citizens. How do you cooperate with or rely upon those whose vision is so fundamentally antagonistic to your own?

But such concerns, while extremely important, are not sufficient to provide a coherent theory of crime, violence, and punishment. What should the response be when inexplicable violence and serious crime disrupt and damage the lives of so many, including those who are often without power or influence—poor people, minorities, workers, and women. That corporate and political criminals are not punished for their acts is not an excuse for condoning violent crime; that the police brutalize as well as protect is not an insurmountable barrier to demanding adequate police protection; that discrimination, lack of opportunities, abusive relationships, and inequality may lead to the creation of an underclass from which a disproportionate amount of crime is committed may not be sufficient reason for not incapacitating or otherwise deterring those convicted of serious crimes.

In short, the failure to effect significant changes in our political/ economic system is not an excuse for not dealing with the current problems of crime. The difficult problem is to differentiate between legitimate and illegitimate uses of police power. If institutions are too frequently corrupt and repressive, do we therefore disregard their legitimate functions? A fairer, more equitable society may well reduce the incidence of rage, violence, and crime. In the meantime, is there no validity to the call for protection against the current destructive impact of crime?

I do not underestimate the complexity of this issue. It is far too easy to be drawn into an "us" vs. "them" approach, in which protection from crime is a code for racist attitudes and where "just deserts" masks a mean-spirited system of retribution. Surely the Goetz verdict should make us seriously consider the underlying stereotyping and invidious assumptions that are often part of the "war on crime." Because these questions pose important challenges, it is important that a coherent critique be developed. In this essay I will address one aspect of this very large and complicated problem: how should the tension between the constitutional safeguards for the accused and the proper enforcement of criminal laws be resolved? As I will show in the next section, the notion that law enforcement and police obedience to law are mutually exclusive goals has led to excesses that violate constitutional norms, with very little gain in law enforcement. Moreover, because our political democratic rights are inextricably linked to the rights of the accused, to allow community prejudice and fear to override the Constitution will inevitably weaken the fabric of rights and protections that are essential to progressive change in all societies.

2

It is not surprising that the debate over the impact of constitutional rights on the incidence of crime is of relatively recent vintage. Before the Warren Court articulated basic constitutional protections for the accused, there was no right to appointed counsel, limited remedies for illegal police arrest, search, or interrogation practices, no protection against unfair identification procedures, and the prosecutor did not even have an obligation to divulge exculpatory evidence. Under these circumstances crime could hardly be blamed on the Constitution.

The Warren Court made substantial changes in criminal procedure, but it did not always side with the accused and it often deferred to law enforcement interests. For example, the Court limited the defense of entrapment by adopting a rule that focuses on the intent of the defendant to commit a crime, thus permitting broad overreaching by agents—even the creation of a crime—if the defendant had some "predisposition" toward criminal activity.[3] Similarly, the Court declined to restrict police use of agents and stoolpigeons to manipulate personal, political, and business relationships, and to intrude into homes and offices.[4]

In addition, the Court framed several of its significant rulings in a manner that allowed the police, prosecutors, and lower courts to ignore or undermine constitutional protections. A notable example was the Court's failure to require disclosure and identification of police informers who allegedly provided information in support of search warrants.[5] Many warrants are issued on the assertion of a police officer that an "informant" observed criminal activity. By crediting this assertion without determining whether the informant exists, the Court, in the words of one observer, winked its eye at the police "perjury routine."[6] Similarly, the refusal in the *Miranda* case to require counsel's presence before the questioning of a suspect has led to "swearing contests" between police and defendants as to whether the proper warnings of the right to remain silent were given. Since trial judges invariably believe police testimony, the *Miranda* protections are often illusory. If the Court had intended fully to protect the accused from police overreaching, it would not have permitted waiver of *Miranda* protections without counsel.

By the same token, while the Burger-Rehnquist Court has not rejected every claim made on behalf of the accused, it has made serious inroads on the Warren Court precedents and has in many instances rationalized the denial of constitutional protections on the basis of the asserted needs of public safety and law enforcement. Most recently, for instance, the Court has permitted pre-trial preventive detention of "dangerous" defendants. Not only has the debate on this issue focused almost exclusively on those who are released and arrested for new crimes (as opposed to those who spend months in jail, only to be found not guilty at trial), but the danger to the public has been greatly exaggerated. In a study in Washington, D.C., it was determined that only 2 percent of those charged with violent crimes were arrested for a violent or property crime while on bail.[7] Indeed, given the difficulty of predicting dangerousness with any accuracy, to be confident of preventing one person from committing a violent crime while on bail we would have to incarcerate up to ten who would not.

Justice Marshall pointed to the real dangers or preventive detention:

> Such statutes, consistent with the usages of tyranny and the excesses of what bitter experience teaches us to call the police state, have long been thought incompatible with the fundamental human rights protected by our Constitution. Today a majority of this Court holds otherwise. Its decision disregards basic principles of justice established centuries ago and enshrined beyond the reach of governmental interference in the Bill of Rights. . . .
>
> Throughout the world today there are men, women and children interned indefinitely, awaiting trials which may never come or which may be a mockery of the word, because their governments believe them to be "dangerous." Our Constitution, whose construction began two centuries ago, can shelter us forever from the evils of such unchecked power. Over two hundred years it has slowly, through our efforts, grown more durable, more expansive, and more just. But it cannot protect us if we lack the courage, and the self-restraint, to protect ourselves.[8]

Moreover, those who believe that only "dangerous" criminals will be confined should understand the significant precedent that incarceration without conviction can have for people who vigorously oppose governmental policies, particularly in time of war. The Court's opinion contains this ominous reference:

> We have repeatedly held that the government's regulatory interest in community safety can, in appropriate circumstances, outweigh an individual's liberty interest. For example, in times of war or insurrection . . . the government may detain individuals whom the government deems to be dangerous.[9]

This decision thus provides an important lesson on the integral relationship between the rights of the accused and other democratic rights, such as freedom of speech, that are more generally regarded as essential by progressive movements. The liberties provided to criminal suspects are part of a broader scheme of political rights and their significance extends beyond the issue of the proper balance of powers and rights between the state and criminal defendants. Conservative forces in this country certainly recognize this distinct relationship. Consider the recent statements by Attorney General Edwin Meese, in a 1986 report calling for the overturning of the *Miranda* decision. Notwithstanding abundant evidence that *Miranda* does not hamper law enforcement and is if anything too deferential to the police, the attorney general states that *Miranda* should be discarded:

> An abrogation of Miranda would be of broader import because of its symbolic status as the epitome of Warren Court activism in the criminal law area. We accordingly regard a challenge to *Miranda* as essential, not only in overcoming the detrimental impact caused directly by this decision, but also as a critical step in moving to repudiate a discredited criminal jurisprudence. Overturning *Miranda* would, accordingly, be among the most important achievements of this administration—in restoring the power of self-government to the people of the United States in the suppression of crime.[10]

Plainly, the struggle over preventive detention and the privilege against self-incrimination have consequences that range beyond the limits of the Fifth and Eighth amendments. This is also true for other constitutional criminal procedural issues. To further demonstrate the connection between these rights and the broader scheme of democratic protections, and to further analyze the relationship between "rights" and crime, it is instructive to focus on two areas: the privacy protections against police power to arrest and seize evidence, and the due process limitations on how identification evidence is secured.

Initially, it is important to note that the history of Fourth Amendment interpretation is hardly one of acute sensitivity to personal rights. Indeed, it was only for the ten-year period that started with *Mapp* v. *Ohio* and ended with the onset of the full Burger Court that there was any consistent development of Fourth Amendment doctrine. *Mapp* v. *Ohio* decided that where the police violate the Fourth Amendment by improperly seizing evidence, that evidence must be excluded from any criminal prosecutions. For the better part of 175 years prior to *Mapp*, most states provided no remedy for unlawful police arrests or searches.

The Court's Fourth Amendment decisions of the 1960s, although hardly of one piece and hardly without important limitations grounded in deference to law enforcement needs, established several basic propositions.

First, the Court ruled that all searches conducted without a warrant are per se unreasonable, subject to only a few "jealously and carefully drawn exceptions," and the Court in fact required government officials to demonstrate a compelling need for an exception to the search warrant requirement.[11]

Second, the Court required that searches, arrests, and seizures be undertaken only where probable cause existed to believe that criminal activity was afoot, and defined probable cause in a manner that required the police to have an articulable and reliable basis for their actions. A limited exception to the probable cause standard was the "stop and frisk" doctrine which originally, at any rate, permitted a very limited intrusion into personal privacy where reasonable grounds existed to believe that the person was involved in criminal activity and was armed and dangerous.[12]

Third, in a watershed opinion, *Katz* v. *United States,* the Court broadened the scope of the Fourth Amendment by ruling that electronic surveillance constituted a search even where no physical trespass had occurred.[13] Placing an electronic amplifier on a telephone booth "violated the privacy upon which [the user of the booth] . . . justifiably relied." Personal privacy, not narrow property notions, was now the touchstone of the Fourth Amendment.

Fourth, government violation of the Fourth Amendment was remediable by exclusionary rules in criminal trials and by civil rights actions in federal court.[14]

The Burger Court undercut all of these premises. One of the most remarkable developments has been the transformation of the principles of *Katz,* a case that broadened and deepened our notions of privacy, into rules that have been manipulated to reduce Fourth Amendment protections. It will be recalled that the Court's emphasis on personal privacy provided the basis for its conclusion in *Katz* that "what one seeks to preserve as private may be constitutionally protected." *Katz* expanded the scope of the Fourth Amendment by making explicit the notion that it was intended to protect our privacy from unreasonable government intrusion.

Quite rapidly, however, the doctrine underwent a subtle but

significant change: now the Court required the individual to show both a subjective expectation of privacy and a claim that society is prepared to say is reasonable. Put aside for the moment the difficulties with the subjective prong—that is to say, whether given the government misconduct that has been disclosed over the past fifteen years, including spying, disruption of political dissidents, government-approved burglaries,surveillance, and the increasing use of technology to trace our steps and activities—leaves anyone able to claim with a straight face a reasonable expectation of privacy in any aspect of everyday life. That is troublesome enough. Let us focus instead on the issue of how we determine whether the public is prepared to say that *your* expectation of privacy is legitimate. Who is to define when you have a "legitimate" expectation of privacy? Can the government defeat privacy interests by simply stating that it will search all persons in particular areas (e.g., airports or "high-crime areas")? How do we decide whether our private conversations with friends or associates are protected from governmental overhearing, bugging, or the use of informers? Must we draw curtains around our lives to assert an expectation of privacy for personal matters in our homes and offices?

We are told by the Court that we have no legitimate expectation of privacy in personal bank accounts, that we should not be surprised if the telephone company makes our records available to the police, that as passengers in cars or guests in homes we may not have a sufficient interest to object to unlawful police intrusions, and that a fenced-in backyard is not protected against aerial searches.[15] Further, the Court has ruled that society is not prepared to recognize the right of a prisoner to even limited privacy with respect to items kept in his cell—a Bible, photos of his family, personal letters or books. On what empirical or other basis was that conclusion drawn?[16]

One of the most troublesome anomalies in Fourth Amendment jurisprudence—and its most serious weakness with respect to the rights of the political opposition—is the distinction the Court has drawn between intrusions into our homes, offices, and political and personal relationships by a police officer, which is fully subject to the Fourth Amendment, and the use of agents and informers, which remains virtually unregulated. By affording law enforcement free reign to use informers and agents, the Court has told us not to expect privacy in our relationships, including our political associations. The distortion of Fourth Amendment doctrine that results is succinctly described by Anthony G. Amsterdam: "I can conceive of no rational system of concerns and values that restrict the government's power to rifle my drawers or tap my telephone but not its power to infiltrate my home or my life with a legion of spies."[17]

The Court has justified this practice by saying that you "assume the risk" that the people you deal with may be agents of the police. But is that the kind of society we want to build? Is there not a crucial difference, grounded in notions of liberty, between the normal risk we all take that a friend today may be a turncoat tomorrow, and the risk of faithlessness that is incurred when the police bribe, threaten, or otherwise convince our associates to become informers and enter our lives and premises as police agents? Is there any difference between the injury to privacy caused by bugging or wiretapping and that achieved by police spies who record everything we say? Again, is the price of privacy the total shutdown of communication? And, as Justice Harlan has pointed out, the issue is not simply whether *criminals* place unjustified reliance on so-called friends:

> By casting its "risk analysis" solely in terms of the expectations and risks that a "wrongdoer" or "one contemplating illegal activities" ought to bear, the plurality opinion, I think, misses the mark entirely. . . . The interest [to be protected] is the expectation of the ordinary citizen, who has never engaged in illegal conduct in his life, that he may carry on his private discourse freely, openly, and spontaneously without measuring his every word against the connotations it might carry when instantaneously heard by others unknown to him.[18]

Not satisfied with its erosion of the substantive protections of the Fourth Amendment, the Court has also restricted the remedial mechanisms that are necessary for effective vindication of Fourth Amendment rights. Like the *Miranda* rule requiring warnings to suspects of their rights to silence and a lawyer, the exclusionary rule has become an issue as significant for its symbolic status as for its actual affects on criminal prosecutions. It is clear that the exclusionary rule—which in effect says that evidence the state should never have obtained cannot be used against a defendant in a trial—does not lead to the release of many defendants. Studies show that evidence was excluded in only 1.3 percent of all federal cases, and that in state prosecutions only 0.8 percent of all arrests were declined for prosecution because of unlawful arrests or searches.[19] Nevertheless, attacks on the exclusionary rule continue, on the theory that crime control will be significantly enhanced if the rule is abolished.

At the same time that the Court has limited remedies in criminal cases, it has also created doctrines that reduce the efficacy of civil remedies for Fourth Amendment violations. One such doctrine is the immunity defense, which has been construed by the Supreme Court to deny civil damages to persons arrested or searched without probable cause if the officer in "good faith" believed cause to exist.[20] Compensation for the victim of a constitutional violation is thereby given a subordinate position in our hierarchy of values.

The Court has also made it practically impossible to obtain injunctive relief from proven unconstitutional police actions. For example, in *Los Angeles* v. *Lyons*, a plaintiff had been rendered unconscious as a result of a police "choke hold," after the police stopped his car for a motor vehicle violation.[21] The plaintiff had offered no threats or resistance. Accordingly, he sued for an injunction against the use of this police practice in similar situations and supported his claim with evidence of fifteen deaths (mostly of blacks) that had occurred as a result. The Court refused to issue an injunction since Lyons could not prove that he would be subject to such a hold in the future. If he was, the Court assured him, he could sue for damages (or, if he was so unfortunate to die, his family could sue). Showing little concern for the existence of an unconstitutional police practice, the Court blithely reasoned:

> Of course, it may be that among the countless encounters between the police and the citizens of a great city such as Los Angeles, there will be certain instances in which strangleholds will be illegally applied and injury and death unconstitutionally inflicted on the victim. . . . it is no more than conjecture to suggest that in every . . . encounter between the police and a citizen, the police will act unconstitutionally and inflict injury without provocation or legal excuse. And it is surely no more than speculation to assert either that *Lyons* himself will again be involved in one of those unfortunate instances, or that he will be arrested in the future and provoke the use of a choke hold by resisting arrest, attempting to escape, or threatening deadly force or serious bodily injury.[22]

The debate over the proper interpretation of the Fourth Amendment holds serious implications for important issues that are just now appearing. What limits, if any, should be placed on drug and AIDS testing? As technology advances, how do we balance the increased capabilities of law enforcement to invade and monitor our lives with the privacy rights of individuals? Can the government continue to infiltrate and monitor political organizations through the use of agents and informers? Can they, as one court has authorized, place a secret video camera in an apartment to record every movement of the occupants for months on end? Are the interests protected by notions of autonomy and privacy the kind of fundamental democratic rights that are critical to any fair society? It is important to note that each incursion on civil liberties discussed above was justified by the government or courts as a necessary crime-control measure, yet the incremental impact of this trend will be a substantial lessening of political liberties for all.

Because the exclusionary rule may result in the release of a guilty person, the Court has at times found this remedy to be too high a price to pay. But the Burger Court has not only changed the rules where probative evidence might otherwise be excluded; it has subverted another important constitutional principle—the requirement that pre-trial identification procedures be conducted fairly, with a lawyer present at a lineup, and without unnecessarily suggestive conditions—a principle that is designed to make the identification process more reliable and thus enhance the truth-finding aspect of the criminal justice system. Since so many cases turn on the issue of identification and since mistaken identification is probably the single greatest cause of conviction of the innocent, it might have been thought that a Court that stressed reliability of the trial process in weakening the exclusionary rule would embrace procedures designed to make the trial verdict more accurate. But the Court has ruled that only post-indictment lineups require a lawyer (most lineups are pre-indictment), and has further held that even unnecessarily suggestive identifications can be used at trial.[23] These decisions not only strike a serious blow at fairness but they demonstrate that "reliability of the fact-finding process," which has been used as a justification for denying certain rights, will itself be subordinated to state claims of efficiency, police control, and finality.

Plainly, the attack on protections provided by the Constitution is fundamentally flawed. The work of the Warren Court was not a function of radical political or legal theory. Rather, that Court's insistence on fair procedure, equal rights for the indigent, elimination of racial bias, and limits on overbearing police procedures were based on conventional liberal notions of due process, equality, and fairness. The Court never questioned the legitimacy of police authority or of most penal sanctions.

Even with the obvious limitations, the Left supported the decisions of the Warren Court and has generally been critical of any retrenchment. That support was more than philosophical. Political dissenters, radicals, social critics, and others who struggle for economic and political change in this country have often found themselves the subject of serious criminal prosecutions. In many cases, the existence of criminal procedural rights has been critical to their defense.

Of course, their support has not been without serious reservations and critical analysis. It is widely recognized that the rights granted at one time can be limited or withdrawn by a Court with differing views at a later date. Thus many of the Warren Court precedents have been severely restricted by cases decided by the Burger Court. To some degree, the "rights" approach has provided the government with a legitimacy that is ill-deserved: an appearance of fairness, rather than actual protections.

Nevertheless, the struggle to establish and strengthen the rights of the accused and those who are involved in incidents with the police is an important one for progressives, not only in this society but in others as well. This is not to suggest that a proper litmus test is whether a criminal justice system has an exclusionary rule or whether it has juries of six or twelve people. Rather, the issue is whether the core protections are enforced in a way that protects against arbitrary and discriminatory police actions. Why is this so?

First, to the extent that these rights provide a *fairer* determination of guilt or innocence, interests of individual autonomy and liberty are served. Thus, requiring that all defendants be provided counsel, limiting police interrogation practices, mandating fair identification procedures, and requiring prosecutors to turn over exculpatory evidence all make the adversary system fairer and more reliable.

Second, because those who are most frequently the subjects of police investigation or prosecution are generally those without real power, status, or influence, it is important that they be treated fairly. Providing a guarantee of basic protections helps to ensure against unnecessary overreaching by government and gives some measure of protection against unfair politically or racially inspired prosecution.

Third, the values that are the basis of these guarantees—privacy, autonomy, and personal dignity—are values that are significant not only in liberal/bourgeois societies, but under socialism as well. Where government is forced to respect those rights, even for individuals who are deemed unworthy of such treatment, the values and norms are better protected for the society as a whole.

Fourth, a critical aspect of the legal development in this area is the doctrine of equality. Several of the decisions specifying limitations on governmental power or of granting protections have rested on the concept of equal treatment of suspects and defendants, particularly with regard to ensuring that race, sex, and wealth play no role in the way people are treated. Equality is a fundamental goal, and where courts and other institutions must shape their policies with the equality principle as a significant factor, the progressive cause is furthered.

Finally, certain rights are so basic to a fair and equitable allocation of power between the state and the individual that no matter what political or economic system is in power, these rights provide an indispensable check on arbitrary state power. Even if the society is fundamentally fair, it is unwise to trust to government the power to decide what issue or ideas are worthy of debate. It is also wrong to allow the state to use arbitrary procedures to control crime, even if the criminal conduct is apparently undermining progressive principles. Unless we are ready to deny the lessons of history and to assume (erroneously) that "progressive" governments have a monopoly on wisdom, we should insist on the provision of fundamental democratic rights in all societies.

Notes

1. See, e.g., Mapp v. Ohio, 367 U.S. 643 (1961); Gideon v. Wainwright, 372 U.S. 335 (1963); Brady v. Maryland, 373 U.S. 83 (1963); and Miranda v. Arizona, 384 U.S. 436 (1966).
2. *New York Times*, 14 January 1985, Op-Ed page.
3. Sherman v. United States, 356 U.S. 369 (1958).
4. E.g., Hoffa v. United States, 385 U.S. 293 (1966).

5. McCray v. Illinois, 386 U.S. 300 (1967).
6. Younger, "The Perjury Routine," *The Nation*, 8 May 1967.
7. "Pretrial Release: An Evaluation of Defendant Outcomes and Program Impact" (1981), cited in Bazelon, "The Crime Controversy: Avoiding Realities," 35 *Vanderbilt L. Rev.* 487, 494 (1982).
8. United States v. Salerno, ____U.S.____, ____(1987) (Marshall, J., dissenting).
9. United States v. Salerno, ____U.S.____, ____(1987).
10. *Report to the Attorney General on the Law of Pre-Trial Interrogation*, Office of Legal Policy, February 12, 1986, p. 115.
11. United States v. United States District Court, 407 U.S. 297 (1972); Chimel v. California, 395 U.S. 752 (1969).
12. Terry v. Ohio, 392 U.S. 1 (1968).
13. 389 U.S. 347 (1967).
14. Mapp v. Ohio, 367 U.S. 643 (1961); Monroe v. Pape, 365 U.S. 167 (1961).
15. United States v. Miller, 425 U.S. 435 (1976); Smith v. Maryland, 422 U.S. 735 (1976); Rakas v. Illinois, 439 U.S. 128 (1978); California v. Ciraolo, 106 S. Ct. 1809 (1986).
16. Hudson v. Palmer, 468 U.S. 517 (1984).
17. Amsterdam, "Perspectives on the Fourth Amendment," 58 *Univ. of Minn. L. Rev.* 349, 365 (1974).
18. United States v. White, 401 U.S. 745, 789 (1971) (dissenting opinion).
19. U.S. General Accounting Office, "Impact of Exclusionary Rule on Federal Criminal Prosecutions" (1979); Brosi, *A Cross-City Comparison of Felony Case Processing* (1979).
20. Anderson v. Creighton, ____U.S.____ (1987).
21. 461 U.S. 95 (1983).
22. Ibid., at 110.
23. Kirby v. Illinois, 406 U.S. 682 (1972); Manson v. Brathwaite, 432 U.S. 98 (1977).

PART 5

The Constitution in an International Context

The Constitution has been called our most valuable export. Its basic principles—separation of powers, representative government, individual rights—are seen by Americans as both universally applicable and the test of a "democratic" government. Yet despite this belief, the principles embedded in the Constitution are far from universal. Many constitutions, both in capitalist countries, such as Great Britain or Israel, as well as in socialist states, do not contain such separation-of-powers concepts as judicial review of legislative acts. International human rights treaties, as well as many national constitutions, develop different views of rights than does ours. Indeed, even our government has not applied these principles universally, as can be seen in the trampling of First Amendment rights during World War I or in the suspension of the right to habeas corpus by President Lincoln during the Civil War. Yet we demand compliance with these principles by governments we oppose, such as Nicaragua, even though they are at war. In a sense, then, this section looks at our Constitution as an imperialist document, one that has been used as a club against divergent cultural and ideological views. Understanding other constitutional frameworks helps us grapple with the problems of our own.

Three key areas in which the U.S. Constitution is portrayed as reflecting the best that democratic government has to offer are human rights, freedom of speech, and representative, electoral government. Debra Evenson's essay shows how narrow are our views of human rights. Reflecting capitalist ideology, we reject concepts of economic rights, affirmative state obligation, the right to economic and social equality. Her essay should be read in conjunction with some of those in Part 4, such as Burnham, Kennedy, Copelon, and Fiss.

David Kairys addresses the use of the First Amendment as a club to justify U.S. intervention in Central America. The Reagan administration sought to justify aid to the contras by pointing to the Nicaraguan government's closing a newspaper and radio station which were supporting the contras, ignoring our own (and other countries) restrictions on freedom of speech during wartime. Kairys analyzes whether the First Amendment is universally applicable, including to socialist societies. Finally, my essay ends the section with a discussion of the role of representative democracy in revolutionary and socialist societies. I contrast the American concept of representative democracy with the socialist concept of participatory or direct democracy, and use the Nicaraguan example to explore the possibility of combining the two conceptions.

COMPETING VIEWS OF HUMAN RIGHTS:
The U.S. Constitution from an International Perspective

Debra Evenson

Almost forty years after the United Nations adopted the Universal Declaration of Human Rights, the issue of human rights has become a significant focus of U.S. foreign policy, although not in a way that the drafters and original signers of the declaration might have expected. Holding the U.S. Constitution out as a model of respect for such rights, the United States uses human rights concerns to justify any number of government actions that violate international law, from economic embargo to military intervention. Yet far from providing broad protection for human rights, U.S. constitutional doctrine embodies a very narrow view of the principles embraced by the Universal Declaration of Human Rights, its supporting covenants, and other human rights instruments recognized under international law. In fact, the United States has not ratified most of the international human rights agreements, including the International Covenant on Civil and Political Rights, the International Covenant on Economic, Social, and Cultural Rights, and the U.N. Convention on the Elimination of All Forms of Racial Discrimination.

It may come as a surprise to many Americans that the scope of rights enumerated in the U.S. Constitution is, by international standards, not only extremely limited but ignores some of the major premises of international human rights doctrine. United Nations documents recognize two categories of rights: (1) political and civil rights and (2) economic, social, and cultural rights. The two categories are considered under the international human rights instruments to be equal in significance and indivisible. Thus the right to such basic necessities as employment, food, shelter, health, and education is essential to the exercise of political and civil rights. The U.S. Constitution, however, while it protects individual autonomy in the sphere of political and civil rights, excludes rights to economic, social, and cultural well-being.

At the core of the divergence of these two concepts of rights are conflicting views of the role of the state in postindustrial society and of the nature of individual rights vs. groups rights; more simply put, the debate is over which should predominate, capitalist or socialist ideology.

Capitalist ideology reveres individual over group rights. The common good is the sum of the freedom of autonomous individuals to pursue their interests, within the bounds of generally accepted rules. One of the paramount rules is that it is individuals, not society at large, who have the right to control the means of production, free from interference. Individuals are granted no affirmative rights by the state, except the right to have the law enforced and the right to protection from external threats to their nation's security. Since the state's primary role is to resolve disputes among individuals, pursuant to rules collectively adopted, it must refrain from intruding on those individual rights that are believed necessary to the enjoyment of autonomy. Thus liberty is defined as "freedom from" government intrusion on individual conduct, from the government's taking of property, or from inequitable treatment under the law. For example, citizens are "free from" government interference in the exercise of religion and "free from" government establishment of religion. Individuals may express ideas "free from" government censorship or restraint. Individuals may enjoy the use and ownership of private property "free from" government interference or uncompensated taking. In every instance, the right is individual and is to be enforced by the individual through the judicial system.

According to the prevailing contemporary interpretation of the U.S. Constitution, however, none of these rights is absolute and all are subject to restraint in certain circumstances. For example, private property may be taken for legitimate public use, with fair compensation, and freedom of speech may be curtailed when it poses a risk to national security or the public safety.

In protecting the individual from interference in the exercise of such rights, the Constitution defines the space within which individuals must seek self-development. Thus with respect to the issue of economic well-being the state is neutral, and in maintaining this neutrality provides the broadest range for the exercise of individual autonomy. The sole responsibility of the state is to apply the law equally and in a nonarbitrary way.

But this capitalist notion of a "neutral" state is palpably false. Under capitalism, distribution of resources is not a public but a private matter, and the "neutrality" principle prevents state interference in the private control and distribution of resources. By playing its role as enforcer of the law, however, the state acts primarily to protect private property interests against incursions by the nonpropertied, while it leaves the nonpropertied unprotected from the ravages of the market system.

Equality under such a regime means neither equality of opportunity nor of result. If self-development and economic well-being are dependent on access to resources, then those who control property are the primary benefactors of capitalist individual rights doctrine because they enjoy a broad range of possibilities, while the nonpropertieds' choices are restricted in proportion to their financial resources. For example, public education is not constitutionally required, and to the extent that individual states provide free primary and secondary education they need not do so evenhandedly. Thus, as the Supreme Court ruled in *Rodriguez,* children in a poor school district in Texas who are provided with public primary and secondary education are not entitled to the same educational resources available to children in wealthier districts.

The biased nature of this "neutrality" is also clear in race discrimination cases under the Fourteenth Amendment. Recent constitutional jurisprudence requires a complainant to prove intentional discrimination before supposedly neutral legislation that has a negative impact on racial and ethnic minorities can be remedied. Thus discriminatory consequences of neutral legislation are considered benign.[1] The result, however, is neither neutral nor benign as it erects a formidable barrier against eradication of the perpetuation of racial inequality.

Neutrality is not only a false concept with respect to equality, but it has been discarded by the Supreme Court when applied to so-called moral issues, such as gay rights and reproductive rights for poor women. Nor is the system neutral with respect to political expression. For one thing, control over mass communication belongs to those who represent property interests, while individuals or groups that attempt to organize to promote an opposing view are frequently the target of state interference. National security rationales often shield the disruption of legitimate political activity, and even where the right to organize dissent is ultimately upheld in the courts, the damage done by government investigation, harassment, and disruption is often irreparable. And in almost all cases, the "national security interest" relates not to any imminent threat of foreign military intrusion, but rather to preventing legitimate challenges to the capitalist ideology or to particular political policies of the governing bodies. Many examples can be drawn from the actions of the House Un-American Activities Committee in the 1950s, the illegal surveillance and disruption of civil rights and antiwar activists in the 1960s and 1970s, and current harassment of opponents to U.S. policy in Central America, as well as the denial of visas to persons expressing views critical of U.S. government policies.

While the Constitution recognizes extensive private property rights and a more limited sphere of protection to individuals from interference in the exercise of political rights, the Universal Declaration of Human Rights and its supportive covenants express a completely different approach to the issue of what are inalienable "human rights." International standards implicitly reject the notion of neutrality and presume that the role of the state is to provide for the welfare of *all* its citizens, while at the same time ensuring individual political and civil rights (such as the right to due process, to free expression and association, and to privacy). Economic, social, and cultural rights are declared co-equal in importance to, and interdependent with, political and civil rights. The interdependence of these rights is underscored in the preambles to the various covenants. For instance, the preamble to the International Covenant on Civil and Political Rights states that "the ideal of free human beings enjoying civil and political freedom and freedom from fear and want can only be achieved if conditions are created whereby everyone may enjoy his civil and political rights as well as his economic, social, and cultural rights." Similar language appears in the preambles to the International Covenant on Economic, Social, and Cultural Rights and to the American Convention on Human Rights.

Articles 22–27 of the Universal Declaration set out the economic, social, and cultural rights that are characterized as indispensable for human dignity and the free development of personality. These rights are to be realized not by individual autonomous action but "through national effort and international cooperation." Because of its recognition of collective responsibility for social welfare, socialist ideology is far more hospitable to the full recognition of these rights than is capitalist ideology. Indeed, by making society responsible for providing basic necessities to all, these covenants reject the conservative capitalist ideology of individualism and the preeminence of private property rights. International human rights instruments give only limited recognition to private property rights. For example, the American Declaration of the Rights and Duties of Man, adopted by the OAS in 1950, simply provides that "Every person has a right to own such private property as meets the essential needs of decent living and helps to maintain the dignity of the individual and of the home." Socialist constitutions, such as the Swedish and Cuban constitutions, generally protect these property rights but also make the universal entitlement to employment, education, food, and health a part of fundamental public policy.

Clearly, human rights instruments cannot mandate universal well-being since many countries, particularly developing nations, do not have the economic capacity to provide even minimal nutrition and shelter to their populations. The Universal Declaration recognizes that the material limitations of developing nations may impede the full provision of economic rights. It therefore qualifies the entitlement to such rights with the proviso "to the maximum of its available resources." However, full enjoyment of economic rights remains a universal ideal, achievement of which demands national and international commitment. There is hardly a credible excuse for the world's wealthiest nation to fail to provide full economic, social, and cultural rights to its entire population.

Furthermore, under the human rights covenants and resolutions governments have an affirmative obligation to promote social and economic equality and a duty to take affirmative steps to assure its achievement in fact. For instance, one of the centerpieces of international human rights concerns is the eradication of racial discrimination, as well as of the inequality between women and men. Thus the U.N. Conventions on the Elimination of All Forms of Racial Discrimination and on the Elimination of All Forms of Discrimination against Women make it the duty of governments to take *positive* measures to eradicate racial and gender discrimination and to provide the means of achieving equality for those who have suffered the debilitating effects of such discrimination.

Further, racism and racial discrimination are not simply civil wrongs but are crimes against society. While some socialist constitutions, and even those of some other capitalist nations (notably Great Britain), expressly embrace this concept, in this area, as in the area of economic rights, the U.S. Constitution falls far short of international standards. The Fourteenth Amendment provides merely for equal protection of the laws, and, as previously noted, has been interpreted to uphold legislation that appears neutral but has a negative impact on racial minorities unless there is proof of intentional discrimination. Further, the civil rights acts, while prohibiting discrimination on the basis of race, focus on redressing individual cases of discrimination as civil wrongs and on providing injunctive and remedial relief for individuals. Although affirmative remedial measures are sometimes available, they are at the discretion of the courts and are generally limited to situations where a specific showing of past discrimination has been made. Broad remedial measures to correct the inequalities of historic racism and sexism fall outside prevailing U.S. constitutional interpretation.

Moreover, under international human rights doctrine not only are racial discrimination and its effects to be eliminated, but racist propaganda is also proscribed. Article 20 of the Covenant on Civil and Political Rights calls for the prohibition, by law, of any propaganda for war and of any advocacy of national, racial, or religious hatred that constitutes an incitement to discrimination, hostility, or violence. Similarly, the International Convention on the Elimination of All Forms of Racial Discrimination exhorts all states to "condemn all propaganda and all organizations which are based on ideas or theories of superiority of one race or group . . . or which . . . promote racial hatred and discrimination in any form" and to "adopt immediate and positive measures . . . to eradicate all incitement to . . . discrimination." Thus freedom of individual expression must be limited by society's right to live free of racial hostility and discrimination.

Precisely because of the limitation on freedom of expression imposed by these instruments, President Jimmy Carter expressed reservations about the provisions that ban racist propaganda. Such reservations highlight the biased nature of a state that asserts a societal interest in prohibiting the entry of foreign speakers critical of U.S. policy but fails to recognize the compelling societal interest in prohibiting racist propaganda. Were the United States within the tradition of international human rights, the Skokie case, upholding the right of Nazis to march through a largely Jewish community in Illinois, and others like it would have been resolved differently.

With its emphasis on individual autonomy and the preeminence of private property rights to the exclusion of group rights, capitalist democracies are in opposition to international human rights doctrine and to the ideal of human beings living free from fear and want. The capitalist argument is that individual economic autonomy (translated as private control of resources) is essential to liberty and is the bedrock of political democracy. The autonomous individual, however, exists, if at all, only in part of the capitalist class; without social and economic rights being guaranteed, the human rights of the nonpropertied classes have little substance. Economic opportunity is a fiction without guarantees of quality education, health care, shelter, and cultural development. Further, adherence to capitalist ideology neither enhances protection of political and civil rights nor strengthens democracy, but rather narrows the opportunities for effective political participation. The danger to political democracy posed by the concentration of wealth influenced many early (and now discarded) Supreme Court opinions protecting small businesses under the federal antitrust laws. Moreover, without the financial means of gaining access to the electronic and mass print media, the vast majority of the nonpropertied cannot effectively influence the political agenda, and without an expansion of economic, social, and cultural rights these same people can enjoy little participation in the daily workplace decisions that affect their lives.

Thus the contradiction is not between *social* control of property and liberty, as the capitalists argue, but rather between *private* control of property and liberty. In fact, there is in principle no contradiction between the full enjoyment of human rights and socialist democracy. Social ownership of the means of production devoted to social welfare enhances the opportunity for all to participate in economic activity and in decisionmaking that affects quality of work, working conditions, and daily life. With political rights guaranteed, a more equitable distribution of resources also provides a more equitable access to political participation, thereby broadening democracy and safeguarding human rights.

Note

1. See Washington v. Davis, 426 U.S. 229 (1976); Village of Arlington Heights v. Metropolitan Housing Corporation, 429 U.S. 252 (1977).

EXPORTING FREEDOM OF SPEECH

David Kairys

In April 1986, the National Conference on the Nicaraguan Constitutional Process was held at the New York University School of Law. The conference was attended by North American lawyers and scholars and by a delegation of Nicaraguans involved in drafting Nicaragua's new constitution. One of the key issues that the conference addressed was the role of freedom of expression in the Nicaraguan constitutional scheme. This theme had a duality, particularly for the North American civil liberties lawyers, who in the present context in the United States advocate increased forms of expression and considerable limits on the government. First, it was critical to analyze and respond to the Reagan administration's use of the issue of freedom of speech—or the supposed lack of it—in seeking to justify military aid to the contras attacking Nicaragua. At the same time, and recognizing that context, it was important for both the Nicaraguan and North American participants to understand the role and nature of freedom of expression in the construction of a new society in Nicaragua. What follows is an edited version of a presentation that David Kairys made at the conference reporting and commenting on a day-long workshop on freedom of expression.

Our government is attacking Nicaragua, attempting to crush the revolution; and much of the rationale for that attack is expressed in very typical North American terms—in terms of the lack of freedom of speech in Nicaragua. This is a rallying cry used to justify

387

U.S. intervention. It is a kind of ideological club. There is an ironic twist to it: the people who use freedom of speech as an excuse for intervention are often the ones who really respect it the least in our domestic context. They are against us when civil libertarians, like the group of North Americans in our workshop, go into court or other forums to advocate increased free speech. Nor are they bothered by the state of emergency or death squads in places like pro-U.S. El Salvador.

We are not here to do anything like that, but I think we feel uneasy because our own government is attempting to destroy the victory of the Nicaraguan people over a long-standing tyranny (installed and imposed by our government); because we are domestic advocates of free speech, which is a major rationale for U.S. intervention; and because we are used to piercing through and dismissing rationales for limiting speech, but in this instance must face a situation where a nation is being militarily attacked without legitimate cause or provocation by a neighbor of overwhelmingly superior might. It is not unusual or necessarily important to see a group of educated North Americans having what looks like an identity crisis, but I think something more significant than that was going on: We therefore approached our role in this conference with an appropriate sense of humility and political reality.

We should start a discussion of freedom of speech in someone else's country by being very realistic about our own history and contemporary system of free speech.[1] Free speech is not only used ideologically vis-à-vis the rest of the world, but our own people are taken up with the ideological myths, which have a very depressing effect on political movements for progressive change in the United States.

We have this deep-seated belief in a set of free speech values and traditions that are depicted as universal, timeless, and derived from the Constitution, natural law, or, for some, directly from God or science. Well, they are not universal or timeless, and they developed historically and culturally in a way that is very specific to this country.

Our country was not founded on free speech. The framers of the Constitution largely had the pre-existing English conception of free speech, which disfavored prior censorship of the press but embraced criminalization of seditious libel (criticism of the government or government officials) and control of speech in public places by local authorities.

There were various political movements—principally the early labor and women's movements and the Abolitionists—that organized and fought for free speech. However, the courts regularly rejected all legal challenges to repressive practices. For example, in the first major decision on free speech by the Supreme Court, which did not come until 1897, the conviction of a preacher for handing out tracts from the Bible on Boston Common was unanimously affirmed. The Court ruled that city officials could "absolutely or conditionally forbid public speaking in a highway or public park" and that such an action is "no more an infringement of the rights of a member of the public than for the owner of a private house to forbid it in his house."[2]

The system of free speech we celebrate today was sought and won by the labor movement in the 1930s, which wanted to organize workers and saw the right of free speech as a necessary component of the right to organize. They needed to leaflet, to picket, to canvass door-to-door, to demonstrate and meet on the streets, sidewalks, and parks.

Those were the relevant means of communication in the 1930s. However, our rights have stayed essentially frozen at the 1930s level, although other means of communication—television, radio, newspapers, and magazines—are more relevant today. The rights won in the 1930s provide, in the current context, only the ability to display displeasure, rather than the ability to engage meaningfully in a discourse on the issues of the day.

There has been almost no coverage of this conference in the mass media, even though our media purports to be interested in democracy and civil liberties in Nicaragua and even though the conference has included addresses by a justice of the Nicaraguan Supreme Court and members of the Nicaraguan National Assembly from a variety of parties.[3] We have an obsession with limiting the government while there are these large corporate entities—often as powerful and every bit as impenetrable as any government—that decide what our society hears and thinks about. These media businesses monopolize the marketplace of ideas, and they have commandeered the empowering and liberatory history and content of free speech by claiming absolute protection from popular access as well as from government censorship. The courts have accommodated them;[4] the result is a public discourse from which people of ordinary means are effectively excluded.

This is the appropriate context in which North Americans should discuss free expression in Nicaragua. The first conclusion that I reached in our discussions, and I think was unanimous among the North Americans, was that it is very clear from both the draft of the Nicaraguan constitution,[5] and from the discussions and positions and attitudes of our Nicaraguan guests, that Nicaragua is committed to free expression and pluralism.

The draft constitution is an inspiring statement of values and aspirations.[6] There are numerous provisions which, although their language is different in some ways from ours, embody the basic rights we hold fundamental. It is considerably more libertarian and more cognizant of the basic needs of the people in many aspects than is our own Constitution.[7]

An example of the kind of discussions we had will best illustrate the approach of the Nicaraguans toward open debate and pluralism. We talked about the question of permits for certain types of speech, which are used in the United States as well, and there was a dispute between a Nicaraguan member of the National Assembly from the Conservative Democratic Party and a Nicaraguan from the Sandinista party. The Conservative Democrat thought that permits should only be issued on the authority of the National Assembly. The Sandinista thought that, more like the United States, it should be done by the executive authority or the police.

In justifying that position, the Sandinista representative referred to the state of emergency and to the war that is being waged on Nicaragua now. The Conservative Democratic delegate called that argument a subterfuge and a pretext, saying that no, that's not really what's going on. Eventually, agreement was reached that to the extent possible, it might make sense to draft the constitution as if the war and the state of emergency did not exist, and then to provide explicitly for mechanisms to deal with such situations, which are very real problems and call for very different solutions. All of the people present wound up in agreement with that and with each other. There was clearly no lack, or fear, of vigorous disagreement; open debate was welcome and expected.

There were two areas where some of the North Americans disagreed with what seemed to be the position of the draft constitution.

One concerned the freedom of the press, a cherished issue in North American history—for very good reason. There is a general provision in the draft constitution that guarantees freedom of expression. Many of us on the North American side assumed that this included freedom of the press, but there was some doubt as to exactly how it would be interpreted. The suggestion was therefore made to include freedom of the press explicitly. In response to that we were drawn to the particular context in Nicaragua. Many of the North Americans thought that allowing the possibility of any limit on the press was unnecessary or even counterproductive for the revolution itself.

As we talked about this at length, some lessons from our own history and policies became clear. First of all, the United States regularly backs regimes in Central America and throughout the world that are not noted for honoring freedom of the press. The Nicaraguan newspaper *La Prensa* is being censored, but its editors are alive. And its reporters are alive and functioning, unlike dissident journalists in similar situations in, for instance, Chile, Guatemala, Colombia, and El Salvador.

In our own history, moreover, we have censored the press during almost every war we have engaged in. We have never established absolute protection of freedom of speech or the press; censorship and punishment of speech have always been allowed in certain circumstances.[8] It would be inappropriate for those of us who have unsuccessfully advocated broader protections in the United States to urge a government under attack by our government to adopt these defeated views.

When we censor or punish speech, we leave it to a court. We can bring a lawsuit about such things. The court decides, in the usual familiar phrase, whether there is a clear and present danger.[9] We are very used to someone dressed in robes making such decisions. The result, of course, is not very different from a declaration of a state of emergency—particularly to, for example, the Japanese who were put in internment camps during World War II, or to the many people with progressive politics who were imprisoned or lost jobs during the Cold War era.

The Nicaraguans also pointed to the example of the newspaper *El Mercurio* in Chile. That newspaper was funded by the CIA as part of our government's efforts to overthrow the freely elected progressive government of Salvador Allende. *El Mercurio* was in the habit of making very destabilizing and upsetting reports that were usually totally false or at least distorted to arouse the population against the government. The Nicaraguans said that *La Prensa* has done a very similar thing. Over three-quarters of the editors and the staff quit after the revolution when the editorial position changed drastically, and it is now peopled by a different crew. They are supported by foundations that are CIA-backed and have other connections to the CIA and the U.S. government[10]—which is conducting a war against their country—and they are putting out false stories that tend to make people upset with the government. One story that was discussed concerned the deaths of a group of women that were maliciously and without foundation blamed on the government.[11]

The question is, should the Nicaraguans be in a position where a newspaper such as that cannot be limited, cannot be censored? Certainly, in a state of war and with the survival of the nation at risk, the sentiment was no, the revolution and the sovereignty of Nicaragua should not be risked for such an abstract ideal, one realized nowhere else in the world. Nor can I imagine any court in the United States ruling otherwise if we were faced with an analogous situation.[12] Various formulations could hopefully put the minimum necessary limit on freedom of speech, and everybody, North American and Nicaraguan, agreed that it might be a better idea to put freedom of the press explicitly in the constitution.

The final issue, and probably the most difficult, was the suspension of rights. The draft constitution has a section of articles that relate to the suspension of rights, which constitutes a kind of a declaration of marshal law, but in a much lesser form. The setting out of rights and then the provision for their possible suspension is a format that is found in Western European and Latin American constitutions and international human rights covenants.[13] But to the North American civil libertarian, this is viewed very negatively. And given our history, of course, for very good reason. So we had a long discussion as to whether this provision should be there at all, whether there should be limits on it, whether particular limits, such as suspension only to the extent necessary, might be added. But again, keep in mind that in our own history, we have limited our speech rights in emergencies, we have just left it to judges. What the constitution does is to put the issue before the National Assembly, a more public, political forum where it can be debated more easily and directly than if it were given only to a judge.[14]

Overall, I think the North Americans learned more than the Nicaraguans at the free expression workshop and throughout the entire conference. I saw many provisions in their constitution that I would love to have in ours. Let me give one example.[15] We can go outside and picket anything we want, but how do our workers participate in questions of work conditions or toxic chemicals in the workplace? Nicaraguan workers have that right under the draft constitution. I also got a glimpse of what it is like to be part of a society's collective commitment to improving the lives of its people.

Every society and political system that values democracy and the basic needs and dignity of its people must have some mechanism for guaranteeing that the people have the ability to express themselves freely without prior censorship or punishment. Much can be learned from the history of free speech in the United States, but it is first and foremost a history of political struggle by progressive movements to empower the people. Our forms and traditions of expression, of which we can rightly be proud, are very specific to our particular historical development and culture, and the contemporary reality of free expression in the United States falls far short of the rhetoric.

Extreme arrogance, hypocrisy, and a malicious blindness to the democratic institutions being developed in Nicaragua, as well as to the repressive side of our own history, now characterize our government's ideological use of free speech to further its reactionary aims. Our fundamental principles of freedom and democracy are being cynically manipulated to gain support for the Reagan administration's unpopular military intervention in Nicaragua.

Notes

1. This history is traced in considerable detail in D. Kairys, "Freedom of Speech," in D. Kairys, ed., *The Politics of Law* (1982); E. Levy, *The Emergence of a Free Press* (1986); L. Whipple, *The Story of Civil Liberty in the United States* (1927); J. Roche, *The Quest for the Dream* (1963); J. Auerbach, *Labor and Liberty* (1966); P. Murphy, *World War I and the Origins of Civil Liberty in the United States* (1979).
2. Davis v. Massachusetts, 167 U.S. 43 (1897).
3. Eduardo Molina, a member of the National Assembly from the Conservative Democratic Party, spoke at a plenary session and had some harsh criticisms: he

thought the Sandinistas were too tightly in control of the army, that abortion should be banned, that the name of God should be invoked in the preamble to the constitution, and that the United States should mind its own business.

4. See, e.g., Miami Herald Pub. Co. v. Tornillo, 418 U.S. 241 (1974), invalidating as a violation of free speech a state statute providing political candidates a right to reply in newspapers. The Court has also recently enlarged the free speech rights of corporations and very wealthy people, and restricted and retrenched the rights of people of ordinary means. See Buckley v. Valeo, 424 U.S. 1 (1976) (invalidating limits on the amount of money an individual can spend in support of an electoral candidate); First National Bank of Boston v. Bellotti, 435 U.S. 765 (1978) (protecting corporate speech even if unrelated to corporate purposes); Hudgens v. NLRB, 424 U.S. 507 (1976) (overruling earlier decisions that had granted a right to leaflet in privately owned shopping centers).

5. The final draft was adopted in November 1986, and it included modifications of the draft that had been discussed at the conference.

6. The extent to which these values and aspirations will be realized is, as with all constitutions, a matter only time will tell. It is encouraging that the government has widely publicized the promises of the new constitution, which it would not do if the intention were not to abide by them. When I visited Nicaragua in January 1987, after the constitution was adopted, there was widespread publicity and prominent billboards extolling its importance and promises. For example, a frequently seen billboard celebrated the constitution's guarantee of freedom of religion.

7. Various provisions require that the needs of the people for housing, medical services, and education be met and that the people actively participate in workplace, neighborhood, and societal decisions that affect their lives. Also, certain civil liberties can never be suspended or limited, even in emergencies. For example, the provisions that deal with suspension of rights in a state of emergency specifically exclude suspension of freedom of religion, making that right essentially absolute (unlike the decidedly nonabsolute protection of our rights).

8. This was very recently reconfirmed by Chief Justice Rehnquist in his majority opinion upholding preventive detention of people charged with crime:

> We have repeatedly held that the government's regulatory interest in community safety can, in appropriate circumstances, outweigh an individual's liberty interest. For example, in times of war or insurrection, when society's interest is at its peak, the government may detain individuals whom the government believes to be dangerous. Even outside the exigencies of war, we have found that sufficiently compelling governmental interests can justify detention of dangerous persons. (United States v. Salerno, 55 U.S.L.W. 4663, 4666 [January 26, 1987]; citations omitted.)

9. This formulation, while we are used to viewing it as very protective of speech, is vague and particularly open to subjective considerations, and it has sometimes been used in our history to legitimate suppression. See Kairys, "Freedom of Speech," pp. 165–66.

10. Some of these connections have been openly admitted. For example, La Prensa acknowledges receiving substantial funding from the National Endowment for Democracy, which is a corporation established and funded by the U.S. Congress.

11. In January 1987, after the conference, I visited Nicaragua and was provided with another example of the censorship of La Prensa by Horacio Ruiz, its managing editor. Ruiz told of a story that he had wanted to run the day before the Nicaraguan elections. He claimed, and the story would have reported, that Sergio Ramírez,

vice-president of Nicaragua and a prominent Sandinista (and well-known poet), had suggested in a speech broadcast on radio that people who do not vote might be killed by the Sandinistas. No one else I spoke to, including contra sympathizers who heard the speech, recalls Ramírez saying anything like that; nor can it be imagined as part of any plausible Sandinista strategy. The effects of such a story, particularly in a country where it cannot be rebutted effectively or quickly, would likely be disastrous—substantially worse, it would seem, than the effects of someone falsely yelling fire in a crowded theater.

12. See, e.g., United States v. Salerno, quoted in n. 8 above. I have suggested an analogy elsewhere, although this is difficult, given the extreme differences in military power, stability, and context between Nicaragua and the United States:

> It is roughly as if the Soviets mined our harbors and organized and funded a band of malcontent Americans to amass in Canada and attempt to overthrow our government with military and terroristic incursions into the United States, while funding a newspaper in the United States that supports the deadly incursions and publishes destabilizing stories. I do not believe we would allow this to happen, and nothing in our constitutional history suggests that the courts would protect such a newspaper. (D. Kairys, "Nicaragua Isn't the First Government to Censor," *Washington Post*, 7 June 1986, p. A21.)

13. See, for example, the Spanish constitution, Art. 55, discussed in Glas, "The New Spanish Constitution, Comments and Full Text," 7 *Hast. Const. L.Q.* 47, 61–62, n.70–71 (1979); the Irish constitution, Art. 28, discussed in Clarke, "Emergency Legislation, Fundamental Rights, and Article 28.3.3⁰ of the Irish Constitution," 12 *Irish Jur.* 217 (1977); the Mexican constitution, Art. 29, reprinted in A. Peaslee, *Constitutions of Nations*, vol. 4 (rev. 3rd ed., 1970), p. 907. See also the European Convention for the Protection of Human Rights and Fundamental Freedoms, U.N.T.S., vol. 213, p. 221 (Art. 15), and the International Covenant on Civil and Political Rights, U.N. Doc. A/6316 (1966), p. 52, Art. 4.

14. It is possible that a state of emergency could then also be challenged in court.

15. For other examples, see n. 7.

THE MEANING OF DEMOCRACY:

Madison, Lenin, and the New Nicaraguan Constitution

Jules Lobel

In 1987 we in the United States celebrated the two hundredth anniversary of our Constitution; at the same time the Nicaraguan people were celebrating the enactment of their new revolutionary constitution. The challenge presented by Nicaragua and its new constitution to the United States in Latin America is fundamentally an ideological one, for Nicaragua seeks to develop a system of government that combines social justice with a new vision of democracy. If left alone, it may very well be successful, pointing the way for other third world nations.

For the past two centuries, the United States has defined democracy as representative government. On the bicentennial anniversary of the Constitution's drafting, the United States extols the stability and virtues of a representative government which, despite wars, depressions, and scandals, has never missed or postponed a national election. Internationally, the U.S. government views holding a national election as the litmus test for democracy, at least where it approves of the results.

Revolutionary socialist governments have generally rejected this United States and Western notion of democracy for two reasons. First, representative democracy is viewed as fundamentally flawed in that it is based on the separation of the state structure from the masses of people. The cure for this separation is participatory democracy, where all take part in the everyday administration of the state. Secondly, socialist revolutions have all faced military intervention and economic retaliation by the Western capitalist governments, leading them to conclude that the toleration of an organized opposition would merely aid the counterrevolution.

Two hundred years after the enactment of our Constitution and seventy years after the Bolshevik revolution, the Nicaraguan government has drafted a new constitution for Nicaragua. That constitution seeks to unify and transform these opposing views of democracy. The Sandinista Liberation Front (FSLN) has attempted over the last eight years to integrate elements of Western notions of pluralistic representative democracy with a Marxist-Leninist view of participatory democracy. Whether the Nicaraguan experiment in combining political pluralism with radical social and economic change is ultimately successful in the midst of U.S. aggression remains to be seen; the mere effort, however, represents a new departure in the concept of democracy in postrevolutionary society. This article will analyze that effort in order to understand if, and under what conditions, representative pluralistic democracy can be used to aid the radical transformation of society and be a part of socialist democracy.

Representative v. Participatory Democracy: Madison v. Lenin

The framers of the U.S. Constitution confronted a central ideological and political task in its drafting and ratification. Americans in 1776 thought of democracy as government by and of the people, government that directly expressed the will of the majority. In the classical tradition, democracy was believed to be best effectuated in a small assemblage of the people, such as a town meeting.[1] While such "pure" or "direct" democracy was viewed as impractical in eighteenth-century America, the state governments, and the directly elected houses of representatives in particular, were institutions that in certain respects resembled direct democracy. The election districts were small, elections were held frequently, and the representatives elected were often men of humble and rural origins.[2]

As Gordon Wood and others have persuasively argued, the central problem in the 1780s, which led the country to go beyond reforming the Articles of Confederation to creating a new Constitution, was not the weaknesses of the Articles but the "excesses of democracy" in the state governments. James Madison and Edmund Randolph complained of "the turbulence and follies of democracy," Elbridge Gerry spoke of democracy as "the worst of all political evils," and Roger Sherman hoped that "the people . . . have as little as possible to do as may be about the government." Madison complained that the state representatives were imbued with "a spirit of locality," which was "unseparable" from elections by small districts; each legislator spent too much time thinking about how a bill would "affect his constituency."

The Madisonian and Federalist solution to the vices of democracy was to expand the sphere of representation. In *Federalist No. 10* Madison wrote that the "various and unequal distribution of property . . . forming distinct interests in society" was the source of what he termed factionalized disputes.[3] The problem was not primarily with a minority faction graining dictatorial control but with a majority interest controlling government and passing "unjust" legislation (such as legislation repudiating debts or interfering with property rights). The smaller the society, "the more frequently will a majority be formed of the same party":

> Extend the sphere and you take in a greater variety of parties and interests; you make it less probable that a majority of the whole will have a common motive to invade the rights of other citizens; or if such a common motive exists, it will be more difficult for all who feel it to discover their own strength and to act in unison with each other.[4]

For Madison, the advantage of representative government over direct democracy was that it would "refine and enlarge the public views, by passing them through the medium of a chosen body of citizens."[5] Electing representatives from a large district would further "refine the public view" by producing representatives "whose enlightened and virtuous sentiments render them superior to local prejudice, and to schemes of injustice."

The Madisonian theory was therefore designed to produce "a spirit of moderation," to ensure that factions—or, as Marx would put it, classes—whose "distinct interest" favored such "schemes of injustice" as renunciation of debts or violation of property rights would be unable to form a majority. Representation was one path to that goal; separation of powers and checks and balances was the other. And as Madison noted in *Federalist No. 51,* separation of powers performed the same function as the extended sphere of representation, making it more difficult for the majority to unite to oppress a minority. The "Madisonian accommodation," as it has been called,[6] was therefore a means to reconcile extended suffrage and widespread inequality in property holding.

Yet the framers' political wisdom lay not only in the system of representation they devised, but in their portrayal of the new constitutional government as "a perfectly democratic form of government." Democracy was thereby conflated with representative government. By 1787–88, democracy had come to mean not government by and of the people, but simply representative government.[7] This transformation stemmed both from the Federalists' tactical need to appropriate the democratic discourse as their own, as well as from a fundamental change in the political theory of constitutions that developed throughout the 1780s. By 1787, a constitution was no longer seen as a compact between ruler and ruled, but as a document whereby the sovereign people delegated their power to representatives. A constitution represented the most fundamental democratic expression of the people's will; the exercise of constitutionally delegated power thus became democratic, irrespective of popular will—indeed, even if undertaken by unelected officials such as judges.[8] Democracy had become unhinged from its classical moorings in popular participation in government to mean popular delegation to others to run their affairs.

Over a century later, Lenin grappled with this same issue of the relationship between representative government and democracy. And while Lenin urged a strong central government in order to suppress the bourgeoisie, his seminal work on the nature of the state harkens back to the direct democracy of the classical tradition. In *State and Revolution,* he uses Marx's analysis in *The Civil War in France* to address the "specific" form of a proletarian socialist republic: A standing army would be supplanted by an armed people, salaries of all officials would be reduced to those of the workers. Parliamentarianism—the division of tasks between executive, legislative, and judicial branches encapsulated in the principle of the separation of powers—would be abolished. The new forms of state power would be soviets or councils, which would be working bodies that would both enact and enforce the law. The salient feature of this new form of democracy would not be representative democracy but participatory democracy, to be based on the actual involvement of the population in state affairs.

While Lenin believed that a strong central state structure was needed during the transition to socialism to suppress class enemies, he also felt that the "transition from capitalism to socialism is *impossible* without a certain 'reversion' to 'primitive' democracy."[9] It was not merely the transfer of power from one class to another that concerned Lenin; it was also "the passage from one type of power to another."[10] The problem with bourgeois democracy is not simply the inequality of wealth or power; its fundamental structure is flawed—because it is based precisely on the separation of the state structure—legislature, bureaucracy, judiciary—from the masses of people. This separation of the state from the population corresponds to the relative independence of the state from the relations of production under capitalism, which is in turn ultimately derived from the separation of the producer from ownership of the means of production.[11] Lenin's cure for this separation was the revival of "much of primitive democracy," where "the *mass* of the population will rise to taking an *independent* part, not only in voting and elections, but also in the *everyday administration of the state*. Under socialism *all* will govern in turn."[12]

It was precisely the tendency to "primitive" democracy in the states, the closeness of the representatives to the population, that made Madison favor broader representative government. Marxist-Leninist governments thus see democracy in a completely different light from "representative" democracies. They see it as resting on actual participation of the population in state affairs. Thus mass organizations, such as trade unions—or, as in Cuba, women's organizations and block associations—are assigned a direct role in the administration of the state. To use Cuba as an example, the constitution (and sometimes major legislation) is subject to discussion and ratification by the mass organizations. Principles embedded in the separation of powers, such as judicial review of legislative acts, are rejected. Power is unified under the leadership of the Communist Party and the principle of democratic centralism.

The second reason for the Marxist-Leninist governments' rejection of the Western model of pluralistic representative democracy is the hostile environment faced by many victorious socialist revolutions. The capitalist states have either directly intervened to overturn these revolutions, as was the case in the Soviet Union and Vietnam, or have used surrogate forces to do so, as in Cuba, Mozambique, and Angola. The new revolutionary governments have faced the imposition of economic embargos designed to severely hinder construction of a socialist society. Moreover, every Latin American government that has sought to introduce radical change has faced military intervention inspired by the United States—Guatemala in 1954, Cuba in 1961–62, the Dominican Republic in 1965, Chile in 1973, Grenada in 1983, and of course Nicaragua.

It is therefore not merely overreaction or paranoia that has led Communist parties to believe that an organized domestic opposition will aid international military intervention. The Soviet example under Lenin is instructive. In the period immediately after the October Revolution, the Bolsheviks sought to negotiate a coalition government and work with the various democratic parties, such as the Mensheviks and the Socialist Revolutionaries. Indeed, for a period a coalition government was formed, made up of 11 Bolsheviks and 7 left Socialist Revolutionaries. Until the end of 1921, opposition parties were represented in local soviets, an opposition press was allowed, Menshevik and left Socialist Revolutionary Party congresses were held.[13] Despite these efforts, the opposition parties vacillated between the revolution and counterrevolution, engaging in armed counterrevolutionary plots, including attempts to assassinate Lenin and other high Bolshevik officials. While the Bolsheviks took repressive action, it is clear that none of the opposition parties were willing to work within the new revolutionary order, seeking instead to overthrow the new government.[14]

In the last few years both views of democracy have been increasingly questioned. In the United States, the central position of large corporations, wealthy financiers, and the media in financing and determining the outcome of elections is such that even segments of the political elite have called for election reform. Representative democracy and separation of powers have provided a certain space for public debate, as well as checks on arbitrary government action, but their role in resisting demands for structural change is increasingly clear. As even pluralist political scientists like Robert Dahl now recognize, "Our constitutional and political institutions operate, in no small measure by design, to weaken majority rule and heighten the effectiveness of minorities in resisting political changes, particularly, of course, minorities well endowed with political resources."[15]

While the tension between representative constitutional government and popular democracy is increasing in the United States, the 1980s have seen a number of socialist governments experimenting with extending representative democracy and elections. Mikhail Gorbachev has argued that in the Soviet Union "vigorous debate and creative ideas disappeared from theory and from the social sciences, while authoritarian evaluations and opinions became unquestioned truths that could only be commented on."[16] In response to this problem, the Politburo has called for "the perfection of the Soviet election system to be one of the main avenues in democratizing our life. . ."[17] In Cuba, Hungary, Poland, and now China and the Soviet Union, electoral systems that offer voters a choice of two candidates for various local and national positions have been or are being developed.[18] In Hungary, the new system of competitive elections led to between 25 and 33 independent candidates winning election to the Hungarian parliament, in at least five cases defeating members of the Central Committee of the Communist Party.[19]

While these new changes do not introduce Western-style representative democracy, they do point out a deeply felt need for experimentation with traditional Leninist notions of socialist democracy. Indeed, some on the left have criticized Lenin's attack on representative democracy as being at the heart of the problem. They quote Rosa Luxemburg, who argued that Lenin's emphasis on the soviets as the only true representatives of the laboring masses "in place of representative bodies created by general popular elections" would lead to the "dictatorship of a handful of politicians." "Without general elections, without unrestricted freedom of press and assembly, without a free struggle of opinion, life dies out in every public institution, becomes a mere semblance of life, in which only the bureaucracy remains as the active life. Public life gradually falls asleep."[20]

The leadership of the Nicaraguan revolution has, for the past eight years, been struggling with the issues raised by Madison and Lenin in their discussion of the nature of democracy. In their newly drafted constitution, as well as their political practice, the Nicaraguans have sought to combine, and thereby transform, aspects of participatory and representative democracy in order to attain a new democratic vision. This vision presents a challenge both to the conceptions of democratic government held by the United States and socialist governments.

The Nicaraguan Revolutionary Model

The Nicaraguan attempt to combine representative and participatory democracy stems from the FSLN's strategy for the social, economic, and political transformation of their society. The Sandinista revolution has been called "anti-oligarchic" but not socialist.[21] It is a nationalist revolution, uniting various sectors of the society, including the anti-Somoza middle classes. While the FSLN has sought to ensure that the needs and interests of workers, peasants, and the poor and marginalized are dominant in all aspects of Nicaraguan life, it has at the same time attempted to preserve political, economic, and cultural space for capitalist relations. In economic life this has meant that the state has taken over the commanding heights of the economy—the financial system, foreign trade, mining, strategic industrial sectors—in order to secure economic development designed to serve popular needs, but has allowed those private landowners and factory owners who use their land or invest in their companies to continue and develop.

Just as this model of a mixed economy seeks to mediate aspects of capitalist development in an economic structure oriented toward the interests of the majority, the political structure seeks to combine aspects of representative Western democracy under popular hegemony. The relationship between these two key aspects of the revolutionary project is seen clearly by the FSLN leadership. As Carlos Chamorro, director of the FSLN newspaper *Barricada*, has noted, "If we have a mixed economy, we must have a political system that corresponds to that; we want to constitutionalize dissent and opposition."[22]

In a sense, the Nicaraguans have understood one of the lessons of the Soviet experience with the New Economic Policy (NEP) in the 1920s. The NEP attempted to develop a class alliance with the peasantry through voluntary compromise, as opposed to coercion. The Soviet government saw the NEP as a retreat from the process of developing socialism and it was eventually replaced by Stalin's revolution from above. But Bukharin, and at times Lenin, had a different interpretation of the NEP, viewing it not as a retreat but as a long-term mechanism for transforming society along more voluntary and cooperative lines. As some writers now recognize, the NEP, if allowed to continue, would have led toward the development of relative cultural and political pluralism, and possibly even toward representative democracy.[23]

The Nicaraguan leadership seems to have recognized precisely that connection. Both conceptions—mixed economy and political pluralism—represent an attempt to organize the nation as a whole, including the middle classes, for national development. Both seek to gain allies both internally and internationally. Both contain internal tensions that require flexibility if they are to be resolved. Finally, both contain the key notion of popular hegemony.

The FSLN has been faced with several key questions in its attempt to implement political pluralism. First, is it possible to reverse the assumption made by Madison and the framers of the U.S. Constitution that representative elections and separation of powers favor rule by the elite, separate the majority of the people from direct involvement in state power, and prevent radical interference with existing property and social relations? Second, are representative elections and separation of powers consistent with the need to combat U.S. aggression?

The FSLN has thus far assumed that both questions can be answered in the affirmative, but only if the working class and peasantry maintain a hegemonic position in the political, economic, ideological, and cultural apparatus of society. Politically, what this popular hegemony requires is the construction of a new form of democracy that will represent the needs and interests of the poor and working population and at the same time provide a framework within which representative democracy can operate. That new democracy is based on two pillars: first, mass participation, and particularly the development of mass organizations that allow the population to become involved in state affairs; and second, explicit revolutionary control of the key ideological and military state apparatus—the educational system and the army. If these mechanisms function, the Nicaraguan elections will be the mirror image of elections in capitalist countries. They will relegate the former elite to the role that the progressive movement has played in the United States—that of a tolerated opposition that presents competing ideas and at times influences government policy without fundamentally threatening the overall direction of the society.

Popular hegemony and participatory democracy

Central to the development of a form of democracy that seeks to insure that the workers and peasantry maintain hegemony in the Nicaraguan political system is the role of the mass organizations and of popular participation in state affairs. The FSLN believes that "democracy is not measured solely in the political sphere, and cannot be reduced only to the participation of the people in elections . . . it means *participation* by the people in political, economic, social, and cultural affairs. The more the people participate in such matters, the more democratic they will be . . . democracy neither begins nor ends with elections."[24] Immediately after the revolution, therefore, key social and economic projects, such as the national literacy campaign and the popular health campaign, were undertaken through mass mobilization, consultation, and participation. In 1980, the legislative branch of government, the Council of State, was reorganized to include representatives of the mass organizations (women's organizations, trade unions, neighborhood associations [CDS], the Union of Farmers and Cattle Ranchers). These groups also played a key role in important ministries, in many cases influencing or changing government policy. For example, when the Rural Workers' Union (ATC) sought to legalize the land seizures that had taken place immediately following the July 1979 triumph, the FSLN and the government were at first opposed but later agreed to support the union.

Similarly, the FSLN's response to the military threat from the U.S.-backed contras has been to rely upon popular participation in the armed struggle. Providing arms to the people and building a substantial militia has been a key mechanism in combatting the contras. The regular army has been encouraged to have the greatest possible interaction with the civilian population.

Both the substance of, and procedures by which, the new Nicaraguan constitution was adopted reflect the FSLN view of democracy as popular participation. Article 2 states that "the people exercise democracy by freely deciding on and participating in the construction of the economic, political, and social system," while Article 48 obligates the state to remove obstacles "that impede effective participation of Nicaraguans in the political, economic, and social life of the country." These general principles are further developed by providing the right of social and economic groups to organize associations of their own choosing (Art. 49); the right of citizens to participate under equal conditions in public affairs and in state management (Art. 50); the right of workers "to participate in the management of their enterprises" (Art. 81); the right of the people to arm themselves in defense of their sovereignty (Art. 93); the right of the peasantry and other productive sectors "to participate, through their own organizations, in establishing the policies of agrarian transformation" (Art. 111); the right to a "participatory" educational system that "links theory with practice and manual with intellectual labor" (Art. 117); the obligation of all officials to "answer to the people for the correct fulfillment of their functions" and to inform them of their work and official activities (Art. 131); and the right to popular participation in the judiciary below the Supreme Court level (Art. 166).

The Sandinista conception of democracy as participatory and direct can also be seen in the process by which the constitution was enacted. The original draft, developed by a committee of the National Assembly, was submitted to Nicaraguan citizens in a series of town hall forums, called *cabildos abiertos*. The *cabildos* raised a number of important concerns, some of which were included in the second draft of the constitution. For instance, the demands of Miskito and other Indian groups on the Atlantic Coast were generally incorporated. Their languages were officially recognized, alongside Spanish, in their respective regions, and communal landholding rights and the right to the free use of waters and forests on their land was constitutionally protected. Despite opposition from the Conservative Party, Article 72 of the final draft incorporated a demand made in the women's *cabildo* that divorce be liberalized to allow for a marriage to be dissolved "by the will of one of the parties." A new Article 50 established "absolute equality of rights, duties, and responsibilities between men and women." As many FSLN supporters requested, the second draft also provided that various acts against the homeland could lead to loss of citizenship, a provision later removed during the debate the preceded the final ratification by the Assembly. While none of these and other modifications were radical, they nevertheless reflected important contributions made by the participatory process. They also constituted an important recognition by the FSLN that participatory democracy is not merely an educational tool but is a mechanism of popular power. As one FSLN representative noted,

> We had thought of the *cabildos* as a great campaign to help the people understand the constitutional issues, but now we see them differently. They have been a practical school to help the representatives learn how to legislate according to the people's interests.[25]

In addition to mass participation, a second crucial aspect of the new state apparatus is the abandonment of the notion of state neutrality. In Western societies, the state is portrayed as a neutral instrument. The hegemony of the ruling classes thus appears to be exercised not by affirmative state action, but by state inaction. It is civil society that reproduces capitalist social relations and ideology, making any alternative seem quixotic, hopeless, or totalitarian. Madisonian democracy, replete with representative elections and separation of powers, does not act primarily to construct new social relations but to constrain the radical disruption of the old. Constitutional rules are perceived to be procedural rules, not creating substantive policy but merely setting the ground rules for competition.

The construction of popular hegemony, however, requires affirmative, openly substantive, state action. As in the economic arena, what is particularly necessary is more direct and affirmative political involvement in certain critical arenas, in particular education and the army. The educational system of any stable Western capitalist society is political; the U.S. educational system teaches respect for private property, for the American form of government, for entrepreneurial initiative. Because of the population's acceptance of existing social relations, however, this political education is accepted by most Americans as the natural order of things—as neutral, objective, and apolitical.

The relations of production in any postrevolutionary society are still in flux. Neither workers, peasants, or the middle classes experience the new educational system as reflecting the only order of things. Therefore a "distinctive feature of the Nicaraguan New Education is its political *explicitness,* in contrast to bourgeois education that sells its product without advertising it."[26] As Sergio Ramírez has noted, the explicit task of the Nicaraguan educational system is to ensure "that education will no longer be a vehicle for transmitting the ideology of imperialism. Instead, a set of revolutionary values will form the new woman, the new man, for the new society."[27]

Similarly, the U.S. army is portrayed as politically neutral, although clearly it is a mechanism for maintaining the hegemony of the ruling elite both abroad, and if all else fails, at home. In Nicaragua, however, the political nature of the army in defending the gains of the revolution has been made explicit. As Rafael Solis, secretary of the National Assembly and an FSLN leader, explained, "There is no question in this project of a classical conception of an army that is supposedly apolitical."[28]

Representative, pluralistic democracy

While Nicaragua has incorporated elements of the Marxist-Leninist perspective on participatory democracy into its constitution and society, it has also included aspects of pluralistic representative democracy found in capitalist countries. The strategic commitment made by the FSLN to political pluralism and elections in the course of the revolution has both deepened and been transformed as the postrevolutionary process has unfolded.

Initially, some in the FSLN argued for political pluralism and elections along the model of some countries in Eastern Europe, such as the GDR, Czechoslovakia, and Bulgaria. While these countries have various parties and national elections, the elections are not competitive but are designed to transmit a program jointly adopted under the leadership of the Communist Party, whose leadership is accepted by the other political parties; their function is to help administer the state and to articulate the specific needs of the class interests they represent, not to contest for basic political power.

The first draft of the Political Parties Law put forward by the FSLN contained conceptions similar to this East European model. While recognizing the right of a party to have its "own political platform" (unlike some of the East European models), the draft suggested that a party's role was merely to participate in administration and not to struggle for political power.

This view was criticized by virtually all of the other political parties, which declared their goal to be the assumption of power in order to put into practice a government program that accorded with their respective ideologies. It became clear that in order to attain the participation of the different strata of Nicaraguan society, competitive and not merely cooperative parties would have to be allowed. The FSLN agreed to an amendment to the Political Parties Law that adopted the opposition viewpoint.

The agreement on the role of political parties, as well as the need to maintain international support in the face of U.S. aggression, led to the 1984 elections. Those elections deepened the FSLN's commitment to competitive elections as an important part of the political process. According to independent observers, the electoral process was, by Latin American standards, "a model of probity and fairness."[29] Seven parties ran candidates for the presidency and National Assembly. Americas Watch, a human rights group often critical of the Nicaraguan government, noted that "the parties that chose to participate in the 1984 national elections—from which no party was banned—were free to be as strident as they chose in attacking the Sandinista Party and its leaders, and frequently exercised this right on television and radio time provided to them without cost to conduct this campaign."[30]

Each party that ran was provided access to 22 hours (15 minutes per day) of free, uninterrupted television time, in prime early evening hours, on both state-run channels; and to 44 hours (30 minutes per day) of free radio time on all the state-run radio stations. Each party was given substantial campaign funds. While there was some censorship of *La Prensa* (an opposition newspaper), this was far from complete, and each day's edition during the last week of the campaign was full of anti-FSLN material. There was no censorship of the country's thirty-nine radio stations, including two run by the church hierarchy and others in neighboring countries run by the contras. As the U.S. Latin American Studies Association (LASA) reported, "While all the opposition parties had some valid complaints about the government's management of the 1984 election, no party was prevented from carrying out an active campaign."[31]

In addition, a proportional representation model was used in order to encourage the participation of various political parties and to ensure them some representation in the National Assembly. The opposition received approximately 33 percent of the popular vote and 36.5 percent of the seats in the Assembly.

The process of organizing the state in order to include the various strata was reflected in the recent struggles over the constitution. Forty-five percent of the members of the commission that drafted the constitution were from the opposition parties, a greater percentage than their 36.5 percent in the National Assembly. There were extensive and heated discussions in the Assembly itself. The various parties put forward different perspectives on the constitution which were debated on national television and printed in the newspapers. On a number of critical issues the opposition parties' position was adopted in the final draft. Examples include requiring legislative approval of the national budget in nonemergency periods; granting any citizen the right to judicial review over legislative or executive actions in violation of the constitution; providing for the nonretroactivity of any law, not just penal laws; and deleting the provision that would have given the president the right to appoint the mayor of Managua. The opposition also lost some particularly heated debates, such as the debate over limiting the president to one term of office.

The constitutional provisions reflect the reality of Nicaragua as both a "participatory and representative democratic republic" (Art. 7). Constitutionalizing the Political Parties Law, citizens have "the right to organize or affiliate with political parties with the objective of participating in, exercising, or vying for power." No one political party is declared to represent the vanguard or leadership of the revolution. Moreover, the constitution incorporates a number of separation of powers concepts. The president can veto legislation, either totally or *partially;* the National Assembly can override the veto by majority vote. While the president prepares the budget, negotiates treaties, and declares states of emergency, the Assembly must ratify each of these executive acts. The Assembly elects judges to the Supreme Court and members of the Supreme Electoral Council from slates of three candidates proposed by the president. Finally, the Supreme Court has the power to review and hold unconstitutional executive and legislative actions. The new constitution incorporates the experiences of the past eight years, during which there has been considerable "friction" between the different branches of government: the legislature has rejected or modified acts proposed by the executive, while the Supreme Court (three of whose seven members are from opposition parties) has declared executive actions to be unlawful, although until now it has not had the power to review legislative action.

The development of political pluralism has been an outgrowth of the FSLN's basic strategy for reconstructing Nicaraguan society as a broad multiclass effort under popular hegemony. Representative elections and separation of powers have been incorporated into that strategy as an outgrowth of the class struggle. To say that either the elections or the particular form of the constitution were agreed to by the FSLN simply to gain domestic support and international legitimacy is to miss the point. For part of the FSLN's fundamental strategy for social transformation has from the beginning been to win that support by means of a pluralistic economy and polity. While the particular forms such pluralism have taken were indeed influenced by the positions put forward by the domestic middle classes and international community, the FSLN has consistently sought to recognize pluralism in national reconstruction as long as fidelity to majority interests—what is termed the "logic of the majority"—is maintained. In the United States, First Amendment rights were won through class struggle—yet they are not seen as being cynically granted but as part of the logic of incorporating trade unions or minority groups into U.S. society. The difference between the United States and Nicaragua is not the form of participation but that instead of a class compromise allowing the working classes and the poor peasantry to participate in a state apparatus dominated by a ruling elite, representative democracy in Nicaragua allows the middle classes to participate in a system in which the working and peasant classes have hegemony.

Tensions and Contradictions in Unifying Participatory and Representative Democracy

The attempt to unite various strata of Nicaraguan society in a project of revolutionary transformation involves a number of serious tensions and contradictions: the tension between developing a mixed economy in which land and industry are largely in private hands and transforming the economy so as to serve majority interests and the contradiction between political pluralism and participatory democracy reflect this basic dilemma.[32] In the political arena, these contradictions have two key manifestations: first, in the opposition of the conservative parties to mass participation and to an explicitly revolutionary army and educational system; second, in the refusal by elements of the middle classes to accept popular hegemony and their consequent joining the counterrevolution.

One of the demands of the more conservative parties has been to decrease the role of mass organizations and mass participation in Nicaraguan life. Indeed, it is precisely the promotion of the mass organizations that the opposition groups, such as the church hierarchy, view as a step toward totalitarianism. These parties were able to remove direct participation by the mass organizations in the National Assembly elected in 1984, thus ending the organizations' strong participation in the legislative branch which had existed since 1980. The FSLN responded creatively, including in its 1984 electoral slate representatives of the mass organizations who were not FSLN members as a way to include those groups in the Assembly.

In the constitutional process, the middle-class parties also opposed mass participation. Several of the opposition parties, including the traditionalist Democratic Conservative Party (PCD) and the Independent Liberal Party (PLI), refused to participate in the open forums. The PCD argued that since the population had already elected representatives to draft a constitution, there was no need for further popular participation. While this opposition did not prevent the open forums, the creative proposal that came out of several of the cabildos for a permanent parliamentary chamber for popular organizations did not prevail in the voting in the National Assembly.

Similarly, the non-neutrality of the state in such key areas as the educational system and army has been the focus of intense struggle by the centrist parties. The Popular Social Christian Party early on argued for an apolitical educational system. The opposition parties to the right of the FSLN fought for provisions designed to insure a nonpartisan army, including prohibiting political instruction and dropping the name Sandinista People's Army.

The FSLN's response to these contradictions between popular participatory democracy and the demands of the middle-class parties has been to compromise on many issues but to maintain the essential basis for popular hegemony. Thus the FSLN has compromised on the nature of the educational system, agreed to clarify that the army is a national not an FSLN army (while keeping the name), and agreed to deny mass organizations a direct role in the National Assembly. It has not been willing to renounce the generally political nature of the educational system or the army, however, or to stray from its basic conception of participatory democracy.

The extension of the mass organizations, the development of mass participation, revolutionary control over key institutions such as the educational system and the army, combined with economic and social change, serve to make it extremely difficult for the middle-class parties to win national elections. They, unlike the FSLN, do not organize popular organizations, they tend to oppose popular participation, and they have not sought to widen their base to include women. This has led to a second and potentially more dangerous set of contradictions. While the first set involve compromising popular democracy for the sake of maintaining pluralism, the second involve the inability of many of the middle class to accept popular hegemony *at all,* irrespective of whatever compromises the FSLN is prepared to make.

The reaction of both the United States and substantial segments of the domestic Nicaraguan opposition has been to use the political space of the revolution to organize to overthrow the FSLN. Instead of accepting the class struggle as internal, they externalize it. Over the past six years, a number of industrialists have simply let their capital run down and left for Miami; in the political arena, many opposition leaders, such as Arturo Cruz, have thrown in their lot with the contras. The Reagan administration has sought to dissuade opposition participation within the system, as was evidenced by the U.S. attempt to pressure the Independent Liberal and Democratic Conservative party candidates to withdraw at the last moment from the 1984 elections.

The contra war makes it inevitable that certain distortions of political pluralism, such as those occasioned by the declaration of a state of emergency, will occur. Some, but not most, of the rights and procedures guaranteed by the constitution are now suspended under the state of emergency. The war has also made it difficult if not impossible for the FSLN to tolerate those who directly act as U.S. agents inside Nicaragua. In opting for political pluralism, the Sandinistas have taken a large risk: they have gambled that, given the proper incentives and sufficient FSLN compromise, the middle classes will not opt out of the system. Yet at the same time they are aware of the risks of this path and have taken what are seen as necessary measures against those who cross the line between legitimate, constitutional opposition and supporting the military counterrevolution.

In the past, socialist governments have sought to transform society and defend against foreign and domestic reaction by developing a unity that excluded an organized opposition representing the former dominant classes. Contradictions between the worker-peasant alliance and the middle classes were externalized, in large part by the opposition groups themselves. The FSLN has sought to *internalize* these contradictions, thus seeking the support of other strata and at the same time risking more space for counterrevolutionary forces to work within the society. As the constitutional process demonstrates, the FSLN has in general sought to rely heavily on persuasion and compromise rather than coercion in order to transform society. For eight years it has been able to maintain and develop this strategy—a remarkable accomplishment in the face of U.S. aggression and a regional economic crises.

Socialism and Representative Democracy

The Nicaraguan constitution, while not socialist, clearly enshrines the interests of the popular classes—workers, peasants, and marginalized and excluded strata so typical of third world societies—as the guiding principles of the new Nicaragua. It provides that the aim of the Nicaraguan state is "to eliminate all forms of exploitation and submission of human beings" and "to ensure that the interest and rights of the popular majority prevail" (Art. 4). To that end it guarantees not merely the civil and political rights found in the U.S. Bill of Rights, but also social, economic, and cultural rights not guaranteed by the U.S. Constitution. It recognizes rights to education, health care, social security, equitable distribution of food, decent, comfortable and safe housing, an eight-hour work day, and land reform (Arts. 57–69, 80–84, 106–7). As even U.S. officials will sometimes admit, the FSLN has sought to implement these rights for the poor people of Nicaragua. Any Nicaraguan government, to be in accord with the constitution, will have to take whatever measures are feasible under prevailing economic and political conditions to realize these guarantees.

In setting forth these goals the constitution commits the nation to move in the direction of socialism. The key ingredients for a transformation toward socialism are not particular forms of state ownership of property, nor particular juridical relations, or defining a country as socialist, but a state apparatus that in practice and by constitutional mandate is affirmatively committed to promoting the interests of the popular majority and ensuring that they participate in all aspects of political and social life. In particular, it requires ensuring both popular power over the state apparatus and that the economic, social, and cultural interests of the majority prevail. The inclusion of this guiding principle in the Nicaraguan constitution implies the institutionalization of a continuing process of revolution.

The thrust of the Nicaraguan constitution will, if not thwarted by counterrevolution, involve a series of changes in the relations of production and class structure, leading to further amendments and changes in the constitution itself. It will also lead to a gradual shrinking of the bourgeoisie and a strengthening of the popular majority. For example, as the Nicaraguans recognize, "Participatory democracy, when combined with the new economic orientation of the state, will lead in time to a logical shift of managers of private capital into administrators of state enterprises, and to a more social orientation of the profits from production."[33]

These changes will further undercut the economic and social base of the middle-class parties to the right of the FSLN, raising the question of the future role of representative electoral democracy. The FSLN's experience with representative democracy has led many to recognize its usefulness to a socialist society, independent of the strategy of sustaining broad class support. In the process of implementing political pluralism, many in the FSLN have recognized the advantage of elections in legitimating and aiding open public debate and dissent, not merely to incorporate the middle classes into the national project but also as part of their vision of a future Nicaraguan society.

As the class structure changes, there still will be different political and ideological points of view. To take only one example: three of the seven parties now represented in the National Assembly, albeit small parties, consider themselves to be to the left of the FSLN and clearly do not represent the middle classes. All have different views as to socialist and working-class policies than those of the FSLN.

The Nicaraguan experience has demonstrated several important advantages of representative democracy that are important for socialist democracy in general and are independent of the strategy of sustaining broad class support. Representative government and separation of powers developed alongside of capitalism and were well suited to the needs of the rising bourgeois class. Yet while ideological elements or institutions may have been produced, or may function, in relation to particular class interests in particular historical situations, they can sometimes be disarticulated from this connection and attached to other class interests in other situations. The Nicaraguan experience suggests that representative democracy can be a helpful adjunct to socialist democracy where the masses of the population have a mechanism for participation which breaks down the separation engendered by representative democracy and separation of powers.

Providing for an organized opposition in the form of various political parties has had several effects that go beyond the strategy of merely winning middle-class support:

(1) FSLN leaders have come to view the opposition as being a "correcting force." It is seen as "healthy, because mistakes sometimes come from being isolated, from not having another point of view."[34] One aspect of the 1984 elections provided a graphic example of this "correcting force": in those rural municipalities where less than 10 percent of the population had received land under the agrarian reform, the opposition fared better than it did nationally.[35] This was the first hard evidence that peasants with little or no land had felt let down by the FSLN and led to a change in government policies.

(2) The toleration of autonomous and opposition parties that compete for power institutionalizes and legitimates public debate and dissent and the notion of autonomous organization, not merely among parties but in all sectors of society. For example, in discussing the constitution, the mass organizations did so with a recognition that there were competing views. To publicly put forward opposing positions in the mass organizations on important national issues is

legitimated in a society that permits opposition parties to publicly criticize the governing party.

While political parties struggling for power are not an absolute necessity for such debate, the acceptance of different platforms raising different and *contradictory* interests or points of view clearly facilitates that debate. It does so in a different way than simply having different cooperating parties. It legitimizes strong opposing or contradictory views, which are not cooperative but competing. While it could be argued that such competition is based on bourgeois notions of capitalist competition and the corollary "marketplace of ideas" notion of First Amendment law, Marxist philosophical analysis emphasizes truth as arising from contradiction. Recognition that the essence of dialectics is the "unity of opposites" and the "splitting of a single whole and the cognition of its contradictory parts" requires legitimizing, not suppressing, social, class, political, and ideological conflict. That conflict will continue even in socialist society as long as different political and ideological points of view continue.

(3) Probably most important is the connection between inter- and intraparty debate. The existence of opposition parties means that the revolutionary party must publicly debate and express its views on a wide variety of proposals, requiring considerable flexibility and intraparty dialogue. For example, in Nicaragua the multiparty debate has developed alongside an FSLN view of its own structure that has provided for considerable flexibility in the notion of democratic centralism. First, many important policy issues are not resolved by the FSLN, allowing individual members to develop their own positions. Second, even after the FSLN takes a clear position, the practice has developed of tolerating individual members' public dissent. For example, at a conference on the Nicaraguan constitution held in New York City, a leader of the Nicaraguan delegation (a FSLN member who served on the Supreme Court) stated his opposition to the principle of judicial review of legislative acts. Another FSLN member who was working with the National Assembly's constitutional commission disagreed, as did the text of the draft constitution. Several U.S. law professors were somewhat perplexed and did not understand how such differences could arise until it was explained that the FSLN did not have a unified position on this issue. In addition, there are numerous cases of FSLN members publicly disagreeing with positions the party and the government have al-

ready agreed to. This looser interpretation of the notion that democratic centralism requires public unity on the central questions of the revolution but allows public divergence on a host of lesser, but nonetheless important, policy issues (sometimes even after a decision has been made) is related to a policy of legitimizing public political criticism by maintaining opposition parties.

(4) Finally, political pluralism allows persons with differing ideological views to have alternative space for participating in politics, instead of seeking to join the revolutionary party. By providing an alternative political space, those who may not agree with the FSLN ideologically but want to participate in national politics have an alternative organizational mechanism for doing so. (The alternative would be the opportunistic one of joining the FSLN, if that were the only political party.) This will probably help the FSLN to maintain a clearer revolutionary perspective and organization committed to the interests of the working classes.

Conclusion

Liberal theory postulates that elections are the key mechanism for determining political power. The Nicaraguan experience suggests that elections between competitive parties struggling for power can be an important device for institutionalizing public dissent, both in a long transition stage and in socialist society. The inherent contradiction between having parties which seek power in order to control the direction of society and having elections in order to institutionalize disagreements within a given social and economic framework is always present. That contradiction can only be resolved by means of the social, political, economic, and ideological hegemony of the dominant classes, both in capitalist and in socialist societies.

The Nicaraguan revolution has raised many new ideas and possibilities: of integrating Christian and Marxist perspectives, of utilizing a mixed economy for social transformation, of uniting participatory with representative multiparty democracy. In the political sphere, it offers a new vision of the nature of democracy, one that seeks to combine but ultimately transform the perspectives of Madison and

Lenin. It is precisely this new vision that the progressive movement needs to understand and explore, and which the United States government seeks to ignore, deny, harass, and ultimately destroy.

Notes

I would like to thank Michael Ratner, Carlin Meyer, Art McDonald, Rhonda Wasserman, John Beverley, Barbara Wolvovitz, and Debra Evenson for their invaluable comments on earlier drafts of this article.

1. R. Hofstadter, *The American Political Tradition and the Men Who Made It* (New York, 1967), p. 12.
2. G. Wood, "Democracy and the Constitution" in *How Democratic Is the Constitution?*, ed. R. A. Goldwin and W. A. Schambra (Washington, 1980).
3. *The Federalist No. 10* (J. Madison), *The Federalist Papers*, ed. J. Cooke (Middletown, Conn., 1961), p. 39.
4. Ibid., p. 64.
5. Ibid., p. 62.
6. S. Bowles and H. Gintis, *Democracy and Capitalism* (New York, 1986), p. 52.
7. Wood, "Democracy and the Constitution," p. 15.
8. *The Federalist No. 78* (A. Hamilton), *The Federalist Papers*, pp. 524–25.
9. V. Lenin, *State and Revolution*, vol. 25: Collected Works (Moscow, n.d.), p. 425.
10. L. Colletti, *From Rousseau to Lenin* (London and New York, 1972), p. 221.
11. N. Poulantzas, *State, Power, Socialism* (London, 1978), pp. 49–51.
12. Lenin, *State and Revolution*, pp. 492–93.
13. C. Bettelheim, *Class Struggles in the USSR, First Period: 1917–1923* (New York, 1976), pp. 257–70; E. H. Carr, *The Bolshevik Revolution 1917–1923*, vol. I (London, 1950), pp. 171–74.
14. Ibid, pp. 269–70, 183.
15. R. Dahl, *Dilemmas of Pluralist Democracy: Autonomy v. Control* (New Haven, 1982).
16. Speech to Central Committee, reprinted in *New York Times*, 28 January 1987, p. A8.
17. Ibid.
18. See, i.e., *Bodies of Peoples' Power* (Cuba, 1981), p. 12; *New York Times*, 28 December 1986, p. 1 (Peking requires more than one candidate in municipal elections); *New York Times*, 9 June 1985, p. 5, col. 3 (Hungarian and Polish systems).
19. *New York Times*, 23 June 1985.
20. Rosa Luxemberg, *The Russian Revolution*, reprinted in *Rose Luxemberg Speaks* (New York, 1970), p. 391; Poulantzas, *State, Power, Socialism*, p. 253.
21. Carlos Vilas, *The Sandinista Revolution* (New York, 1986).
22. J. Nichols, *The Issue of Censorship*, reprinted in *Nicaragua: The Unfinished Revolution*, ed. P. Rosset and J. Vandermeer (New York, 1986), p. 115. See also Bayardo Arce's recent interview, "What Is Sandinismo?" published in *Barricada International*, 19 July 1987, p. 10.

23. M. Lewin, *Political Undercurrents in Soviet Economic Debates* (London, 1975), pp. 97–98; A. J. Polan, *Lenin and the End of Politics* (Los Angeles, 1984), pp. 75–76.
24. FSLN statement on the electoral process, 23 August 1980, reprinted in *Central American Crises Reader*, ed. R. Leiken and B. Rubin (New York, 1986), p. 227.
25. *Envio*, no. 62 (August 1986): 27. For an excellent overview of the constitutional process, see A. Redding, "By the People: Constitution-Making in Nicaragua," *Christianity & Crisis*, 8 December 1986, p. 434.
26. See Vilas, *Sandinista Revolution*, p. 225.
27. *Barricada International*, 21 May 1987, p. 5.
28. *Envio*, no. 65 (November 1986): 36.
29. *Report of the Latin American Studies Association Delegation to the Nicaraguan General Election of November 4, 1984*, p. 32.
30. Americas Watch, *Human Rights in Nicaragua: Reagan, Rhetoric, and Reality*, reprinted in *Nicaragua: The Unfinished Revolution*, p. 125.
31. *Report of the Latin American Studies Association*; see also Americas Watch report.
32. For an understanding of these tensions, see X. Gorostiaga, "Dilemmas of the Nicaraguan Revolution," in *The Future of Central America*, ed. R. Fagen and O. Llicer (Stanford, 1983), p. 47.
33. *Envio*, no. 53 (November 1985): 96.
34. Arce, "What Is Sandinismo?"
35. I. Luciak, "Popular Hegemony and National Unity: The Dialectics of Sandinista Agrarian Reform Policies, 1979–1986," *LASA Forum* 71, no. 4 (1987): 17.

Notes on Contributors

Anne Braden has been active for forty years in southern movements for civil rights, civil liberties, peace, and labor rights. She is now co-chair of the Southern Organizing Committee for Economic and Social Justice (SOC), an interracial, multi-issue network of grass-roots activists, as well as regional organizer for the National Rainbow Coalition. She is the author of numerous articles and pamphlets, as well as one book, *The Wall Between*.

Margaret Burnham practices, teaches, and writes on family and civil rights law in Boston. She is a fellow at the W.E.B. DuBois Institute for Afro-American Research at Harvard University, and is working on a book entitled *Law and the Construction of the Afro-American Family*. She is a former judge and former director of the National Conference of Black Lawyers.

Rhonda Copelon is associate professor of law at the City University of New York Law School at Queens College, and a vice-president and volunteer staff attorney at the Center for Constitutional Rights. She has litigated major constitutional cases involving reproductive and sexual rights, and is a co-author of the second edition of Barbara Babcock et al., *Sex Discrimination and the Law*.

Robert M. Cover was Chancellor Kent Professor of Law at Yale Law School until his death in 1986. He was an activist during the civil rights movement in the South, as well as a legal scholar. He is the author (with Owen Fiss) of *The Structure of Procedure*, and his book *Justice Accused* won the Ames Award, given by Harvard University to the best piece of legal scholarship published each five years.

Vine Deloria, Jr., is professor of political science at the University of Arizona. He is former executive director of the National Congress of American Indians, and the author of many articles and books, including *Custer Died for Your Sins, God Is Red,* and *Behind the Trail of Broken Treaties.* He is a member of the Standing Rock Sioux Tribe.

Ellen Carol DuBois is a professor of history and American studies at the State University of New York, Buffalo. She is the author of *Feminism and Suffrage: The Emergence of an Independent Women's Movement in America, 1848–1869, Elizabeth Cady Stanton, Susan B. Anthony: Correspondence, Writings, Speeches,* and, with others, *Feminist Scholarship: Kindling in the Groves of Academe.* She will complete her reinterpretation of the women suffrage movement with *Generation of Power: Harriot Stanton Blatch and the Achievement of Votes for Women,* to be published in 1989.

Debra Evenson is associate professor of law at DePaul University College of Law, and has written extensively on the Cuban revolution. She is a vice-president of the National Lawyers Guild.

Owen M. Fiss is Alexander M. Bickel Professor of Public Law at Yale University. He was law clerk to Thurgood Marshall, then a circuit judge, and to William J. Brennan, Associate Justice of the U.S. Supreme Court, and an attorney of the civil rights division of the Department of Justice in the 1960s.

Edward Greer maintains a civil litigation practice in Cambridge, Massachusetts. He is the author of *Big Steel: Black Politics and Corporate Power in Gary, Indiana* (Monthly Review Press, 1979), and co-author of *Toxic Torts: A Litigator's Guide.*

David Kairys practices constitutional law and is adjunct professor of sociology at the University of Pennsylvania. He is the editor of *The Politics of Law: A Progressive Critique,* and the author of numerous articles on the Constitution.

Lawrence Kaplan is professor of history at City College of the City University of New York. He is the author of *Politics and Religion During the English Revolution,* the editor of *Revolutions: A Comparative Study,* and co-editor of *Conflict in Indochina.* He has also written many articles and reviews on topics as diverse as revolution, Scottish seventeen h-century politics, and psychohistory.

Randall L. Kennedy is an assistant professor at the Harvard Law School. He has contributed articles on race relations law to a variety of publications, including the *Harvard Law Review* and the *Columbia Law Review,* and has a long-standing association with the NAACP Legal Defense Fund.

Arthur Kinoy is Distinguished Professor of Law at Rutgers University School of Law in Newark, New Jersey, vice-president of the Center for Constitutional Rights, and national co-chair of the National Committee for Independent Political Action.

Walter LaFeber is Noll Professor of History at Cornell University and the author of a number of books, including *America, Russia, and the Cold War, 1945–1985* and *Inevitable Revolutions: The United States in Central America.*

Jules Lobel teaches constitutional and international law at the University of Pittsburgh School of Law. His articles on constitutional and international law have appeared in *Harvard International Law Journal, University of Pennsylvania Law Review,* and *Virginia Law Review.* He is a cooperating attorney with, and member of the board of, the Center for Constitutional Rights and is a member of the National Lawyers Guild.

Staughton Lynd practices labor law for the Legal Services Corporation in Youngstown, Ohio. He was previously an historian, as well as chairperson of the first march on Washington against the Vietnam war and director of Freedom Schools in the Mississippi Summer Project of 1964. His books include *Labor Law for the Rank and Filer, The Fight Against Shutdowns: Youngstown's Steel Mill Closings,* and, with Alice Lynd, *Rank and File: Personal Histories by Working-Class Organizers,* which will be reissued by Monthly Review Press in early 1988.

Paul Mishler has been an activist for many years, particularly in the antiracist movement and the movements in solidarity with Latin America. He is currently teaching U.S. history at Vassar College and completing a study of Communist activities for children from the 1920s through the 1950s.

Neil Mullin is a civil rights lawyer. He has had articles on law and politics published in various newspapers and journals, including the *New York Times* and *Monthly Review*. He was a founder of the Theoretical Studies Committee of the National Lawyers Guild.

Victor Rabinowitz is a long-time constitutional and labor lawyer in New York City. He had written extensively, and litigated a number of important constitutional cases before the U.S. Supreme Court. He is also former president and founding member of the National Lawyers Guild.

David Rudovsky practices law in Philadelphia, where he specializes in criminal justice and civil rights litigation. He is also visiting associate professor of law at the University of Pennsylvania Law School. In 1986 he was granted a MacArthur Foundation Award for his work in public interest law.

Mark Tushnet is professor of law at Georgetown University Law Center and the author of numerous articles on constitutional law and history. His books include *The American Law of Slavery, 1810–1860: Considerations of Humanity and Interest, The NAACP's Legal Strategy Against Segregated Education, 1925–1950,* and the forthcoming *Red, White, and Blue: A Critical Analysis of Constitutional Law.*

Patricia J. Williams is associate professor of law at the City University of New York Law School at Queens College. She has worked for the Los Angeles City Attorney's Office in the areas of consumer and health litigation, with the Western Center on Law and Poverty, and has taught legal writing for the Council on Legal Educational Opportunity. She has written and lectured widely on consumer protection law.